INCORPORATING

INCORPORATING

A Guide for Small-Business Owners

Carolyn M. Vella
John J. McGonagle, Jr.

amacom

AMERICAN MANAGEMENT ASSOCIATIONS

This book is available at a special
discount when ordered in bulk quantities.
For information, contact Special Sales Department,
AMACOM, a division of American Management Associations,
135 West 50th Street, New York, NY 10020.

Library of Congress Cataloging in Publication Data

Vella, Carolyn M.
    Incorporating : a guide for small-business owners.

    Bibliography: p.
    Includes index.
        1. Incorporation—United States. 2. Small business—
Law and legislation—United States. I. McGonagle, John J.
II. Title.
KF1420.V44 1984   346.73'06622   83-45206
ISBN 0-8144-7608-2   347.3066626

Printing number

10 9 8 7 6 5 4 3 2 1

To John, to Prissi, and to Kali

Carolyn M. Vella

To Hashi, Gaiety, and Sascha

John J. McGonagle, Jr.

Preface

This book is an introductory guide to incorporation for the small-business owner. It can be used whether or not your business has already been incorporated. The book has several aims: to help you decide whether to incorporate or not, to help you choose the type of corporation that is right for you, and to introduce you to the basics of how a corporation is set up, managed, and controlled.

The various chapters in this book will address the why, what, who, where, and how of incorporation:

1. Why should you incorporate?
2. What kind of corporation do you want?
3. Who can and cannot incorporate?
4. Where should you incorporate?
5. How do you incorporate?
6. How do you finance, control, and update your corporation?

Although this book contains a lot of information about the pros, cons, and "how-to's" of incorporating, it is not a substitute for the advice of an accountant or lawyer. But it will make small-business owners better clients by preparing them for the questions they will have to answer and the decisions they will have to make. Many of the technical terms we use are not defined in the text but appear in the Glossary at the back of the book instead. If a word is unfamiliar, check there for a definition. In the back you will also find a list of reference materials that give additional technical information on many of the subjects covered here.

The guidance contained in this book is aimed at helping set up and control a corporation that is small—*at the start*. However, we do not presume that your business will necessarily stay small. With proper long-range planning, your business can expand and be as big as you want it to be. So don't let people tell you that you are dreaming. If they do, let them know you are planning, not dreaming, and then stick with your plan and make it work.

We *do* presume that you already own a business or have made the decision to go into business. For those of you still in the deciding stage, let us briefly mention a few of the important questions you should address before starting a business:

Are you a self-starter, and do you finish what you begin?
Do you assume responsibility, and can you lead others?
Are you good at organizing and decision making?
Do other people respect you?
Are you in good health, and do you have lots of energy?
Do you have previous business or managerial experience?
Do you have experience in your chosen line of business?
Do you have enough money to adequately finance your business and to provide for your living expenses if the business is not successful immediately?
Can you show that your product or service will sell?

If you answered yes to these questions, you can probably run a business successfully. If not, find a partner who is strong on the points where you are weak. Before you open for business, you will also have to decide on everything from the building and equipment to your customer credit policy. A useful reference in this regard is *Checklist for Going into Business* (SMA-71), available from the Small Business Administration.

A final word: What happens in Washington, D.C., is a critical element of this book. Since we started work on the manuscript, Congress has passed two major tax bills affecting how small corporations conduct their business: the Economic Recovery Tax Act

(ERTA) and the Subchapter S Revision Act of 1982. (The latter renamed the Subchapter S corporation the "S corporation.") In addition, the Securities and Exchange Commission changed the way that private placements of securities are handled, and portions of the federal bankruptcy laws (enacted in 1978) were held unconstitutional by the U.S. Supreme Court. What you read in this book reflects all these changes. Where appropriate, we have noted that other changes may be around the corner. Keep this rapid pace in mind. One of the responsibilities of having your own corporation is keeping up with changes in the laws that affect your business.

Carolyn M. Vella
John J. McGonagle, Jr.

Acknowledgments

The authors would like to thank the following people for their assistance in writing this book:

Ayn Decker, for her expertise in the field of human dynamics and career choices;

Ronald Kita, for talents too vast to list here;

Carl Steinman, for his special contributions in the field of insurance;

Ron Watson, for his story concerning the Small Business Administration.

These individuals have contributed much to this book in terms of their special knowledge, and much to us in their enthusiasm and interest in this project. We hope this book serves them well. Our even greater hope is that this book serves you, our readers, well, and that you will enjoy success in your present and future business ventures.

Contents

xiii

xvi

A Word About New Legislation

Even as this book is going to press, the U.S. Congress is considering changes in the tax laws that may have an impact on small businesses. If the Tax Reform Act of 1983 (H.R. 4170, 98th Congress) is enacted, its major changes will take effect retroactively to January 1, 1984. The sections of most importance to small businesses fall into two groups:

- Technical changes in the laws governing Subchapter S corporations. These changes would involve accounting treatment, inactive subsidiaries, and corporate liquidations. None of the changes would be critical as they are now proposed.
- A major overhaul of the rules governing fringe benefits. Under the proposed act, there would be a set of statutory rules making certain fringe benefits tax-free for both income tax and payroll tax purposes. All other fringe benefits would be taxable. Various proposals to establish permanent rules on tax-free fringe benefits have been before Congress and the IRS since 1975, and Congress has neither resolved them nor permitted the IRS to resolve them.

It is not useful to summarize here the specifics of H.R. 4170, because it is likely to be modified before it is finally passed—if indeed it is passed. However, you should be aware that these kinds of changes in the law are possible, because they might affect some of the information presented in this book.

PART I

Choosing to Incorporate

CHAPTER 1

Why Incorporate?

Incorporating your business involves much more than simply filing some papers with the state authorities. It requires making some serious decisions about the way your business will be run, about its managerial and financial structure, and about the future of the business and the fate of your investment in it.

Incorporating a new or existing business can provide advantages in five basic areas, and these are the areas you will want to look closely at in deciding whether or not to incorporate. They are:

1. Managerial flexibility
2. Limited liability
3. Financial advantages
4. Tax advantages
5. Estate planning

We will look at each of these in turn below, but first a word about what incorporating will *not* do for you. By incorporating, you create a legal entity separate from the persons of the owners. The creation of this separate entity is the foundation on which many of the financial, tax, liability, and estate planning benefits rest. However, the new entity, the corporation, is required to obey laws and pay taxes; it can be sued, audited by the IRS, and held accountable for its deeds in court. Incorporating will *not* provide you with tax-free income or lucrative, untaxable benefits, nor will it permit you to do business on the fringes of legality and then, when exposed, protect you behind the corporate name. Although the stockholders are not personally liable for damages caused by the corporation's actions, the officers of a corporation are legally responsible for the actions of the corporation.

Now let's look at five good reasons to incorporate.

Managerial Flexibility

One benefit of operating through a corporation, rather than in a partnership or sole proprietorship, is the possibility of improving the management of the business. Having stockholders (investors) separate from officers (managers) permits responsibilities to be assigned as suits the needs of the business and the talents of the people involved. Just because someone has invested most of the money in the business does not mean that that person must or should run it.

On the other hand, many owners do not want to give up the management of the business to a board of directors. They would prefer to maintain direct control and structure the business, as in a partnership. The Internal Revenue Code recognizes the usefulness of this type of management structure and as a result has created the Subchapter S corporation, which is a cross between a corporation and a partnership. This is an attractive option for many small businesses and is discussed in more detail in Chapter 4.

Note that we talk about stockholders, employees, officers, and directors of a corporation as if they were all separate. In a small business, of course, one person can be several or all of these. But if your corporation is to function properly, you must always keep in mind which role you are playing. This is important because if the roles become confused, you may lose the benefits of incorporating. (See Chapter 18 for more about this.)

6

Why Incorporate?

Limited Liability

Protection from personal liability in the event of a suit for damages against the business or default on a loan by the business is one of the things that makes incorporation attractive to business owners. The separate legal entity that is created through incorporation is legally responsible for actions taken in its name. For the owners of the business, this means that if the corporation borrows money, the corporation is liable to repay it, and that if someone is hurt by the business, the corporation is liable for damages. Incorporation limits the personal exposure of the owners to risks such as business lawsuits and defaults on business loans. Therefore, owners of a corporation (the shareholders) are said to have limited liability.

There are some situations, however, where the boundaries of liability are not so clearly drawn. If a corporation is new, lenders will often ask the stockholders to cosign loans to the corporation, in which case the stockholders cannot separate themselves from liability for the corporation's actions. Furthermore, if there is not enough money to adequately finance and operate the corporation, that is, if it is inadequately capitalized, persons hurt by what the business does may be able to collect damages from the stockholders as well as from the corporation. (See "Piercing the Corporate Veil" in Chapter 18.)

Financial Advantages

Financially, incorporating has many attractive features. Other types of businesses depend on loans or credit as a source of capital, but corporations can also issue stock to finance their operations. Using a mix of both stocks and loans provides a wide variety of capitalization options not otherwise available. Incorporation also provides a way to build up goodwill in a business, which is an asset that can later be sold at a favorable tax rate. This cannot be done with a partnership or a sole proprietorship.

In addition, since the corporation is a "person" separate from the stockholders, ownership of business assets can be arranged to the benefit of both the stockholders and the corporation. For example, a

7

stockholder might be able to lease business property to the corporation and receive tax and cash-flow benefits even when the corporation is barely breaking even.

Some of the most significant benefits of incorporating are in the area of salaries and fringe benefits. Tax laws permit corporations to offer pension plans, profit sharing, group insurance, and other employee benefits that are more diverse and generous than those available through other forms of business. These benefits can be designed to accommodate business growth and provide for employee ownership (if that is desired) without control of the business being lost.

Some of the more popular benefits areas are described below.

Salaries and Fringe Benefits

In determining salaries for your employees, including family members, it is best to pay salaries that are competitive with those generally paid in your field and in your locale. If the salaries paid to owner/employees are too low, the IRS may suspect you of trying to avoid personal income taxes; if they are too high, they may be suspected of being disguised dividends.

Fringe benefits such as deferred profit-sharing plans, pension plans, insurance programs, and stock purchase programs are other excellent ways to help compensate your employees and divide profits equitably among them.

Salary Continuation Agreements

A salary continuation agreement, or deferred compensation plan, provides regular annual payments for a specified period of time to a selected employee or his family in the event of retirement, disability, or death. Because of tax benefits that are available, the corporate employer in a high tax bracket can provide the benefits inexpensively and receive full recovery of the entire cost. An option that may be attractive to an employee in a high tax bracket is to defer receipt of a part of his salary until retirement years, when he will presumably be in a lower tax bracket.

The most common way to fund salary continuations is through purchase of cash-value life insurance. Upon an employee's death, the corporation receives the benefits tax-free and begins paying a stated beneficiary a certain sum for a specified period of time. If disability occurs, benefits will be paid directly by the insurance company; this frees up corporate money for other purposes. In the case of retirement, the policy can be cashed in. The cash value of the policy as well as corporate funds will be available to provide retirement benefits.

Medical Expense Plans

A corporation can agree in writing to reimburse its owners and employees for all or part of the medical and dental expenses they incur. Expenses are deductible by the corporation, and the reimbursement is tax-free to the owners and employees since it is not considered a part of personal income. Commonly, funding can be facilitated by insurance; the premiums are tax-deductible and the benefits are received tax-free. In contrast, in an unincorporated business the premiums paid on behalf of employees can be deducted by the business, but the individual partner or sole proprietor cannot take a tax deduction for such a plan. Any such reimbursement to the partner or proprietor is considered part of personal income and is taxable.

Wage Continuation Plans

Along with the medical expense plan, a corporation may set up, in writing, a wage continuation (or disability income) plan for employees. The premiums are tax-deductible. However, the Internal Revenue Code limits how generous such a plan paid for by the corporation can be and still be tax-free to the employee.

Tax Advantages

The key to understanding some of the tax advantages of incorporating is to remember that the corporation and its owners are, for tax purposes, separate "persons." Because you own stock in a corporation does not make you and the corporation one taxpayer. This means the corporation can make money, lose money, pay dividends, or be sold independently of your personal financial status.

One of the main tax advantages of incorporating has to do with the tax-free transfer of property to the corporation. Usually, in creating a corporation, the transfer of any property to the corporation does not result in taxes being paid by the stockholders. If the property they transfer to the corporation has increased in value since they bought it, they do not pay a tax on the "profit." In this way, taxpayers can put valuable property to work without having to sell it. If they sold it and then put the money into the corporation, they would have to pay taxes on the profit from the sale first, reducing what the corporation would get. Of course, this means that if the corporation sells this transferred property, then the corporation will have to pay taxes on its profit.

There are occasions when the organizers might wish to make the transfer of property to the corporation a taxable transaction. The key here is whether they are willing to pay a capital gains tax on the sale (assuming the property has increased in value) in order to increase the basis of the property. The higher property value can enable the corporation to get higher depreciation allowances or improve the initial financial strength of the corporation on paper. In either case, the organizers can manage the creation of the corporation to benefit either themselves or the corporation at tax time.

Using a corporation, since it is a separate tax-paying entity, permits the stockholders to accumulate earnings in the business without paying personal income taxes on them, to distribute the profits in a wide variety of ways (salaries, dividends, interest on loans made by the owners to the business, etc.), and to deduct the initial operating losses of the corporation from its future profits. Furthermore, in a family corporation, family member employees will get money out of the corporation as salary, which is a deduction for the corporation.

Estate Planning

Incorporating a business can offer several advantages in the way of estate planning. Using stock makes it easier to transfer an interest in a business without having to get all the other owners to agree. In other words, it is easier to sell a part of the business, and this makes incorporating a device for easing estate problems. Not only is there the possibility of creating a public market for the stock, but the corporation can accumulate earnings to enable it to buy out deceased stockholders. In addition, the corporation may be able to buy insurance on the lives of the stockholders, permitting their stock to be purchased from their estates with the proceeds of the insurance. This assures that the estate of the deceased stockholder will be liquid and there will be no need for a forced sale of the stock of the corporation upon the death of an owner.

The Drawback—Double Taxation

Although forming a corporation can provide a number of tax and financial advantages to the new stockholders, the separation of the corporation from its stockholders has an important drawback. This is the problem of double taxation.

As the corporation earns money, it pays taxes on its earnings to the extent they are profits. If the earnings are paid to the stockholders as salary, the stockholders pay income tax on the salary, and the corporation deducts the salary as an expense. That means salaries come from the pre-tax funds of the corporation, thereby reducing the taxes paid by the corporation. However, dividends to the stockholders come out of the after-tax funds of the corporation and are also taxed in the hands of the stockholders. Thus, the Internal Revenue Service collects a double tax on these profits.

The different tax status of salaries and dividends has led to a continuing battle between the Internal Revenue Service and the owners of corporations on how the profits of the business are paid out. The IRS prefers to see them paid as dividends; the owners as salaries. This has led the IRS to take the position that a corporation, particularly a small, closely held one, can pay only "reasonable" compensation to its officers and employees, and that any payments above a reasonable level are really disguised dividends.

In the Subchapter S corporation, profits (and losses) are passed on to the stockholders of the corporation, so there is no question about whether profits are dividends or salary. However, the Subchapter S corporation is not always appropriate, in part because it is

11

very costly to accumulate income in the business because the income is taxed as personal income whether it is kept in the corporation or not.

Should You Incorporate?

The decision to incorporate can be made only after a careful analysis of the pros and cons of incorporating and how they apply in your particular case. It is possible that incorporating is not to your advantage and that you would be better off sticking with another business form. (The next chapter offers a brief comparison of the sole proprietorship, the partnership, and the corporation.)

Consider incorporating if:

1. You want limited liability for the investors in the business.
2. You want or need relatively free transferability of ownership of the business, either while the owners are alive or when they die.
3. You want the business to continue even if one or more of the owners die.
4. You want a business with centralized management and control. Every partner can act for the partnership, but only the duly elected officer(s) can act for the corporation.
5. You need financial flexibility to attract outside investments in the business. Corporations are more attractive to investors than partnerships or unincorporated businesses because of limited liability, the corporate assets and liabilities are on record, the interest in the business can be sold, and the corporation does not collapse upon the death of a major stockholder.
6. You expect that the business will be large and complex. Large businesses can often achieve greater operational and managerial efficiency if they are incorporated.
7. You can minimize the impact of double taxation by paying the owners salaries and interest on their loans to the business. Salaries and interest are taxable to the individual recipients, not the corporation.
8. The owners' income tax rates are higher than that of the

corporation, so funds can be accumulated in the business more efficiently than if all earnings were taxed as personal income.

9. You want to take advantage of the tax benefits available under Subchapter S (see Chapter 4).

10. You anticipate selling the business and want to take out the growth of the business in the form of capital gains, or to deduct initial losses as ordinary income by using Section 1244 stock (see Chapter 12).

Consider using another business form if:

1. You plan to have a small or a temporary business and there is no great risk of personal liability in operating it.
2. You see that the costs and difficulty of starting a corporation are too high compared with the amount of business you expect to do at the beginning.
3. You find that the effect of double taxes on dividends means that you will pay more taxes on the expected profits of the business than you would if you did not incorporate.
4. You do not need to accumulate funds in the business for future growth.
5. Your income tax rate (and that of your associates) is higher than the rate of the corporation and you will not be accumulating funds in the business.
6. Because you have income from outside of the business, you can deduct any losses of the business from your own income.
7. You want to be able to move assets freely in and out of the business.

CHAPTER 2

Types of Corporations and Other Business Organizations

To understand how a corporation differs from other forms of businesses, you must first understand a little about the most basic form of business, the sole proprietorship.

The Sole Proprietorship versus the Corporation

The sole proprietorship is the oldest and most elementary form of business operation. It is one person, doing business. The business and personal lives of the owner are not separated, nor are the assets. Everything the person owns is in the business, and the person typically lives on what the business produces. If the business makes money, the person lives well. If the business is sued, all of the owner's assets, whether or not they are connected with the business, are available to satisfy any judgment against the business. The owner and the business cannot be separated. The tax laws recognize this by lumping what the sole proprietor earns under his or her income on the personal income tax return.

At the other extreme is the business operation in which the owners and the management of the business are strictly separate, and all that the owners have at risk is what they choose to invest. This extreme is the corporation. By law, a corporation is a "person," just as each individual is. It pays taxes, and it can sue and be sued. However, unlike the sole proprietorship, a corporation is quite distinct from its owners. The owners of the corporation are its stockholders. They invest a limited amount of money in the business and in return are issued stock. The stock represents that investment. If the corporation fails or has to pay a legal judgment, all the owners can lose is that investment; their personal assets cannot be sold to pay the debts of the corporation. In exchange for this protection, which is known as limited liability, the stockholders do not run the corporation. Instead, they elect directors to run it. The directors, representing the stockholders, select officers to handle the day-to-day business of the corporation and make most major decisions on behalf of the stockholders. The stockholders vote on only the biggest decisions, such as selling the corporation and electing new directors.

Another feature that distinguishes the corporation from the sole proprietorship is that all of the profits of the business do not automatically go to the owners (stockholders). Only dividends, voted by the board of directors, are paid to the stockholders. The directors may decide that the long-run interests of the corporation demand that some profits be kept in the corporation to fund future growth. In the case of the sole proprietorship, all profits are in his or her bank account.

If the corporation needs to expand, it can do so by selling more stock, and thus bringing in new owners. The sole proprietorship cannot bring in new owners. It can, however, become a partnership, which is an assemblage of proprietors.

Other Forms of Business

In between the sole proprietorship and the business corporation are a variety of other business forms that vary in terms of the number of owners, their liability for the losses of the business, their ability to share its profits and growth, the life span of the business, and the ability to bring in new owners or pass on the business after death. These forms are the general partnership (or the partnership), the limited partnership, the Subchapter S corporation, and the professional corporation. If you think of these forms as representing a spectrum of options between the sole proprietor and the business corporation, you can understand the variations in their characteristics.

For example, the partnership can be viewed as a group of sole proprietors. The limited partnership can be seen as a compromise between a partnership and a corporation in that the limited partners, like stockholders, invest money and have limited liability, but they do not run the business. In exchange for limited liability, however, their share of potential profits may also be limited. The general partner runs the business and bears unlimited liability. The Subchapter S corporation, covered in Chapter 4, can be viewed as a tax compromise between a partnership and a corporation. The professional corporation is one in which only licensed professionals such as doctors or lawyers can own stock. This makes it more like a partnership because outsiders who are not licensed professionals cannot join the corporation on the death or departure of a stockholder.

For your convenience, we have provided a table at the end of this chapter comparing the principal characteristics of the four most common forms of business operations: the sole proprietorship, the partnership, the Subchapter S corporation, and the ordinary business corporation (as distinct from the Subchapter S corporation). A few things should be kept in mind when reviewing this table. First, it simply summarizes the differences, touching on the most important ones. Do not let the concise nature of the descriptions deceive you—these are really very different forms of doing business.

Second, each form can be converted into one of the other forms, but this is complex and costly, particularly in terms of federal taxes. If you can, select the best form for your business and do not switch unless absolutely necessary. Third, many of the differences among the forms of business are due to federal income tax laws, not to the state laws that create and govern the way these businesses operate. Perhaps the most striking example of this is the Subchapter S corporation, covered in Chapter 4, whose characteristics are defined by tax law only.

Since this book is about incorporating the small business, we will not attempt to touch on every form of business enterprise. After reviewing the table, if you feel you need additional information about businesses other than the corporation and Subchapter S corporation, you can consult the following sources (additional resources will be found in the References at the back of this book):

Marc J. Lane, *Legal Handbook for Small Business* (New York: AMACOM, 1977), Chapters 1 and 2.

John J. McGonagle, Jr., *Business Agreements—A Complete Guide to Oral & Written Contracts* (Radnor, PA: Chilton Book Company, 1982), Chapter 5.

Edward N. Rausch, *Financial Management for Small Business* (New York: AMACOM, 1979), Chapter 1.

Internal Revenue Service Pub. 334, *Tax Guide for Small Business.*

Internal Revenue Service Pub. 533, *Self-Employment Tax.*

Internal Revenue Service Pub. 541, *Tax Information on Partnerships.*

Internal Revenue Service Pub. 587, *Business Use of Your Home.*

Internal Revenue Service Regulations, Sections 301.7701-1, 301.7701-3

Table 2-1. Comparison of forms of business operations.

Characteristic	Sole Proprietorship	Partnership	Subchapter S Corporation	Corporation
Limited liability for owner/employees	No	No	Available	Available
Ease of transfer of ownership	Moderately complex	Could be complex	Easier because of stock	Easier because of stock
Filing required with state/local government	Only if operated under an assumed name	Yes	Yes	Yes
Number of owners, partners, stockholders	1	2 or more	Up to 35; husband and wife count as one	1 or more
Directors, officers	None	None	Required	Required
Annual meetings, minutes	No	Advisable	Required	Required
Federal and state unemployment benefits	Not available for owner	Not available for partners	Owner/employees may be eligible	Owner/employees may be eligible
Worker's compensation	Not available for owner	Available	Required for officers (see state law)	Required for officers (see state law)

Health and accident insurance	Limited deduction available for medical insurance only on Schedule A, Form 1040	Nondeductible for partners on Form 1065, but deductible on Schedule A, Form 1040	For owners of more than 2% of stock, same as partners; otherwise, same as corporation	Deductible by corporation; not taxable for owner/employees
Medical reimbursement plans	Not available	Not available for partners	Same as health and accident insurance	Available if nondiscriminatory
Group term insurance	Nondeductible by owner	Nondeductible by partners	Same as health and accident insurance	Premiums for up to $50,000 in coverage are deductible by the corporation and not taxable to employees (see IRS regulations for coverage over $50,000)
Accounting period	When established, must use same year end as in past years for Form 1040 (no approval needed)	May use same year as partners use (no approval); if principal partners have different tax years, it can use calendar year without approval	Indicated by election filed by stockholders; may require use of calendar year	Established when first return filed; date is flexible

Characteristic	Sole Proprietorship	Partnership	Subchapter S Corporation	Corporation
Income splitting among family members	Only if family members work	Only if a family partnership	By gifts of stock to family members	By gifts of stock to family members
Tax effect of liquidation	Generally as ordinary income	May be capital gains or ordinary income, depending on nature of property	Generally as capital gains	Generally as capital gains
Selection of business form	Automatic	By partnership agreement in writing	Incorporation filing with state; file "Sub S" election with IRS	Incorporation filing with state
Federal income tax rates	Same as those applied to Form 1040, starting at 11% of $3,400 and up to 50% of $109,400+ (1983 rates)	Same as sole proprietorship; income passes through to partners, whether distributed or not	Same as sole proprietorship; income passes through to stockholders whether distributed or not	$0–25,000 @ 15%; $25–50,000 @ 18%; $50–75,000 @ 30%; $75–100,000 @ 40%; $100,000+ @ 46% (1983 rates)

	Sole Proprietorship	Partnership	Subchapter S Corporation	Regular Corporation
Social security taxes (FICA)	11.3% of first $37,800 (not deductible); under 1983 amendments, the self-employed rate is expected, over the course of several years, to equal the rate on employees	Same as sole proprietorship for each partner	Employees—effective rate of 6.70% on first $37,800; employer share is 7% in 1984 (deductible by corporation)	Same as Subchapter S corporation
Federal and state unemployment taxes	Not applicable to owner	Not applicable to partners unless partnership is employed by another entity	Corporation is liable, including owner/employees	Corporation is liable, including owner/employees
Stock available	No	No	Only one class	One or more classes
Federal tax forms filed	Form 1040—Schedule C	Form 1065—Information Return; Form 1040—Schedule E (partners)	Form 1120S; Form 1040—Schedule E (stockholders)	Form 1120

Characteristic	Sole Proprietorship	Partnership	Subchapter S Corporation	Corporation
Income (loss) to owners	Schedule C—net	Net on partnership return, divided among partners; partners must treat partnership items consistent with partnership return	Passed through to stockholders on 1040 returns	Stays with corporation
Investment credit benefits	Accrue to sole proprietor as credit against 1040 liability	Passes through to partners the same as to sole proprietor	Passes through to stockholders as individuals the same as to sole proprietor	For use by corporation only
Dividend exclusion	Maximum of $200 on joint return, $100 on single return	Not applicable to partnership; dividends pass through to partners as individuals	85% deductible if received from domestic corporations (see IRS regulations on foreign dividends)	Same as for Subchapter S corporation
Subject to accumulated earnings tax	Not applicable	Not applicable	No	Yes

	Sole proprietorship	Partnership	Subchapter S corporation	Corporation
Long-term capital gains	Form 1040—Schedule D 60% excluded; maximum tax rate is 20% (40% of 50%)	Passed through to partners as to sole proprietorship	Passed through to stockholders as individuals as to sole proprietorship; if gains exceed $25,000, the corporation could be liable at a tax rate of 15% or more	Corporation pays 15% or more on gains; no liability to stockholders
Carry-back and carry-forward of net operating losses	Carry-back for 3 years and forward for 5 years available	Available to partners (proportionately), but not to partnerships; loss to partners limited to the adjusted basis of their interest in the partnership.	Available to stockholders as individuals as to sole proprietor	Carry-back for 3 years and forward for 5 years available
Estate planning	At death, business dies with the owner; assets belong to estate and pass to heirs	Without prior agreement, partnership ends at death; assets are distributed and taxes on gains are paid	Death of stockholder does not dissolve the corporation; heirs receive the stock	Same as for Subchapter S corporation

CHAPTER 3

Closely Held Corporations

The closely held corporation (or close corporation) is a type of business organization that is particularly appropriate for many small-business owners. In fact, it is the most common form of incorporation that small businesses use. Forming a closely held corporation is an option under state law. In this type of corporation, the stock is held by a single stockholder or by a small group of stockholders. Sometimes only the voting stock is limited and nonvoting stock is widely held. In either case, the corporation is not publicly owned, and transfer of stock is strictly limited.

Most closely held corporations are small businesses without public investors, and the stockholders are actively involved in the management of the business. The close corporation is usually formed to obtain the advantages of incorporation—limited liability, tax minimization, and benefits flexibility—while retaining the more simplified, informal operational advantages of the sole proprietorship or partnership. However, in order to enjoy the benefits of incorporation, the stockholders must remember to operate as a corporation and not as a partnership (that is, they must conduct all business using the corporate name, not their own names or a short form of the corporate name).

The closely held corporation has several features that distinguish

24

it from the ordinary business corporation. First of all, the closely held corporation tends to be an intimate association of a few people pooling their talents and working together, as opposed to the ordinary business corporation whose stock may be widely held. As a result, managerial efficiency tends to be enhanced because management answers to a small number of shareholders, not to a large number of investors. There is also little chance for a stockholder who does not "do his part."

Another important difference is that, in the close corporation, the protection of limited liability is not as easily obtained because many lenders require the owners, instead of or in addition to the corporation, to incur the debt. Last, but not least, because of stock transfer restrictions, there is no outside market to purchase shares during the life or upon the death of a stockholder of a close corporation. In other words, liquidity is lost in favor of predictability.

Forming a Closely Held Corporation

There used to be no easy way to operate as a closely held corporation. The corporation laws of the various states were designed to control the operation and management of all corporations, and this resulted in definite disadvantages for very small businesses. Prior to revisions in the state corporation laws, close corporations were required to hold stockholder meetings, even if there were only one stockholder voting 100 percent of the stock. Also, corporations could take action only by simple majority vote, which shut out minority stockholders in the close corporation from any participation in the corporation's decisions. One or two major shareholders could badly damage the interests of minority shareholders; this is harder to do in an ordinary, more widely held corporation.

Today, most state incorporation laws recognize the special needs of the close corporation. Stringent voting requirements previously imposed on everything from quorums to issuing new stock have been relaxed. In addition, these laws often provide that the directors or stockholders can act without a meeting if there is a written consent by all those qualified to vote, that stock transfer restrictions are to be included in the articles of incorporation and/or bylaws of the corporation to assure control of ownership, and that the corporation can be operated by the stockholders themselves, without a board of directors.

In most states today, the key element in forming a closely held corporation is the declaration by a small number of stockholders that they have done so. In Pennsylvania, for example, if you are creating a closely held corporation, you can have no more than 30 stockholders. You must state in the articles of incorporation that it is a close corporation and select, from a pre-established list, the means by which the transfer of stock will be restricted. For example, you might specify that the corporation has the right to buy back the stock from departing owners. You must also agree that the corporation will make no public offering of its stock.

Once these requirements are met, the law permits a great deal of flexibility in how you structure the corporation. For example, the corporation can be run by the stockholders and does not need a board of directors. (Ordinary corporations are required to have a board of directors of at least three members, even if there are fewer than three stockholders.) If you have fewer than three stockholders and want a board of directors, your board need be only as large as the number of stockholders. The stockholders can also sign an agreement among themselves for managing the business of the corporation. This allows all stockholders to control the corporation without having to be on the board. The stockholders may also have the option to dissolve the corporation under a specified set of circumstances.

Most states permit existing corporations to convert to a close corporation merely by amending the articles of incorporation.

Managing the Business

The management of the close corporation can take a number of forms, depending on the extent to which the owner or owners want to be actively involved in the day-to-day management of the business. In establishing a management structure, the owners of the close corporation can consider the traditional management techniques (such as having a board of directors and separate officers, who are not stockholders), and then decide whether or not they wish to use these or be innovators of new techniques (such as having a large board of directors comprised of all the stockholders and only two officers, each a stockholder). In many close corporations, the management functions are directly controlled by the stockholders, rather than by a board of directors.

Number of Directors

Most ordinary corporations are required to have a minimum number of directors, usually three, even if there are fewer than three stockholders. However, some states have recognized the problems inherent in this requirement and have made concessions to the close corporation. Generally the laws of these states provide for a minimum number of directors, but if there are fewer than three stockholders, the board can have as many members as there are stockholders.

When organizing, most close corporations generally make use of a commercial "corporate kit" that includes the embosser, stock certificates, and canned bylaws. These bylaws typically are not aimed at taking advantage of the flexibility of state laws. To be safe, the one- and two-person corporation that wants to operate with a small board should consider adopting a special bylaw such as the following:

BYLAW ON NUMBER OF DIRECTORS: The business and affairs of the corporation shall be managed by a board of directors who shall all be natural persons of full age. The directors need not be residents of this State or stockholders in the corporation. The board of directors shall consist of three (3) directors, except that in cases when all the shares of stock of the corporation are owned beneficially and of record by either one (1) or two (2) stockholders, the number of directors shall be the same as the number of stockholders. The directors shall be elected by the stockholders at the annual meeting of stockholders of the corporation. Each director shall be elected for the term of at least one year, and until his or her successor shall be elected and shall qualify.

Unreasonable Compensation

Closely held corporations are a particular target for IRS scrutiny for "unreasonable" compensation—that is, high salaries (which are a deduction on corporate tax forms) that disguise dividends (which are not a deduction). If the IRS rules that the compensation paid to a stockholder/employee is "unreasonable" in part or in whole, the corporation will lose the deduction for that payment. Protecting your corporation against a claim of unreasonable compensation is dealt with in more detail in Chapter 4.

Section 1244 Stock

Section 1244 stock, named after Section 1244 of the Internal Revenue Code, is typically used by new corporations with a small number of stockholders. Its advantage is that it permits losses on a stockholder's investment to be deducted from the ordinary income of the stockholder to the extent of $50,000 per year (or $100,000 per year on a joint return). This applies whether the loss was incurred on the sale of the stock or on its becoming worthless. This benefit is available only to the original purchaser of the stock. Section 1244 stock is discussed in more detail in Chapter 12.

Piercing the Corporate Veil

Piercing the corporate veil refers to holding the individual stock-holders personally liable for damages caused by the corporation, contrary to the concept of limited liability. Close corporations usually have the most difficulty in protecting stockholders from lawsuits. Circumstances under which the courts may find the owners, not the corporation, liable are discussed in more detail in Chapter 18.

CHAPTER 4

Subchapter S Corporations

If your business is a small one, you may decide to form a close corporation under state corporation laws *and* elect to be a Subchapter S corporation under federal tax law.*

The Subchapter S corporation is sometimes referred to as an "incorporated partnership," but that is a misnomer. It is most certainly a corporation (operating under special sections of the Internal Revenue Code), not a partnership. Its name derives from the Internal Revenue Code's Subchapter S of Chapter 1 of Subtitle A. This subchapter of the Code allows corporations to enjoy some of the tax benefits of individuals and partnerships while still operating as a corporation. Recent amendments to Subchapter S moved the tax status of the Subchapter S corporation even closer to that of a partnership. Nevertheless, it is still a true corporation.

In the past several years, Congress has made major changes in the law dealing with the Subchapter S corporation. The first was the Economic Recovery Tax Act (ERTA) passed in 1981, and the second

*Following tax legislation in 1982, the IRS has begun to call this type of corporation the "S corporation." Since most people familiar with this concept will continue to use the old name for a while, we have used the term "Subchapter S corporation" throughout this book.

was the Subchapter S Revision Act of 1982. This text reflects these changes. When doing further research on this subject, be sure to check the date on the materials. If they are dated before 1981, then they will not reflect any of these important changes. To be doubly sure, use only sources dated 1983 or later.

Qualifying Under Subchapter S

Not all corporations can qualify under Subchapter S. Congress and the IRS have established basic standards designed to permit only small businesses to benefit from these special provisions of the tax law. For example, the corporation cannot have more than 35 stockholders. (A husband and wife are considered one owner, even if their stock is held separately.) The corporation cannot be a member of an affiliated group in which one corporation owns 80 percent or more of another corporation. Furthermore, if the corporation receives too much passive income (rents, royalties, bond coupons, etc.), it can automatically lose its status as a Subchapter S corporation. (There are other qualifications, many of them highly technical, which we will not go into here.)

Advantages of Subchapter S

The key advantage of operating under Subchapter S is that both profits and net operating losses of the corporation are passed directly on to the stockholders. This means that profits are taxed only once—to the owners of the business. In an ordinary corporation, the profits are subject to the corporate income tax. Then, as profits are paid to the stockholders in the form of dividends, they are taxed again, with the stockholders paying personal income taxes on them. In the Subchapter S corporation, all profits are distributed to stockholders as salary or dividends and are taxed as personal income only. Likewise, corporate net operating losses are deducted from ordinary income by the stockholders, although deducted losses cannot exceed their investment in the corporation.

Because all gains and losses are passed on directly to the stockholders, earnings are not generally accumulated in the corporation, and there is no regular corporate income tax. Any earnings that are left in the corporation are taxed as if they were personal income of the stockholders, but accumulated earnings, taxed in prior years, can be removed from the corporation in cash, without their being taxed as a dividend.

What do these benefits mean in dollars and cents for your corporation? In its early stages, a corporation might well operate in the red. With no profits to deduct losses from, the corporation will be paying out the losses and getting no tax benefits at the beginning. If the corporation is expected to run at a deficit for several years, it is even possible that it will not be able to completely offset its past losses against future profits. From a tax point of view, those losses are quite costly.

However, if the corporation has qualified under Subchapter S, the losses the corporation has at the beginning can be passed on to the stockholders. The stockholders can then deduct these losses from their other income and reduce their personal taxes.

On the other hand, if the business is expected to be profitable from the start and the stockholders expect to accumulate some of the profits in the business to fund future expansion, then a Subchapter S corporation is not a good idea. This is because all the profits of the corporation are assumed to be distributed to the stockholders, who pay taxes on them. This makes it almost impossible to accumulate profits in the corporation for future growth.

This leads us to the Subchapter S rule of thumb:

When the corporation is expected to produce over $30,000 in annual income for each stockholder, it is not beneficial to operate as a Subchapter S corporation.

Disadvantages of Subchapter S

The primary disadvantage of operating under Subchapter S is that the stockholders pay taxes on the full amount earned by the corporation, whether or not the corporation actually pays the profits out to them as dividends. This is a major problem if the stockholders plan to reinvest the profits of the business and not pay dividends.

Reinvesting the profits means that the stockholders pay a tax, with funds from other income, on money they did not receive.

Becoming a Subchapter S corporation also has major benefits consequences. In the past, stockholders of Subchapter S corporations who were also employees were eligible for the same fringe benefits that are available to employees of ordinary corporations, including health insurance and group life insurance plans. The 1982 amendments to Subchapter S changed this, so that anyone owning more than 2 percent of the stock of a Subchapter S corporation is treated as if he or she were in a partnership for purposes of tax-free benefits.

For example, in an ordinary corporation, amounts paid to cover the medical expenses of an employee/stockholder under a medical expense plan can be deducted by the corporation, and they are tax-free to the employee. However, under the same medical expense plan run by a Subchapter S corporation, the medical expenses of an employee who owns more than 2 percent of the stock are not deductible by the corporation. They are deductible by the employee only to the extent that he or she is itemizing medical deductions on an individual return. The upshot is that there are fewer tax-free benefits to employee/stockholders under Subchapter S.

There are other drawbacks to consider as well. One is that if the stockholders terminate their election to have the corporation taxed as a Subchapter S corporation, this eliminates the right to treat previously taxed accumulated earnings as if they were not dividends when paid to the stockholders. This means that paying past accumulated earnings out in the future can result in the stockholders' having to pay taxes on them again, because the payments will be considered to be dividends. Another point to consider is that stockholders cannot deduct any losses passed on to them that exceed their investment in the corporation.

Should You Have a Subchapter S Corporation?

Whether you should use Subchapter S or not depends on your particular circumstances. However, several types of businesses will generally benefit from operating as Subchapter S corporations:

1. Companies just starting up, particularly those with high research and development expenses. Expected losses can be passed on to the stockholders as tax deductions. After the new business is profitable, it can be sold, can be merged into another corporation, or can elect not to operate under Subchapter S in the future.
2. Established corporations that are profitable but do not need to accumulate earnings in the corporation because of low capital needs. When such corporations are owned by persons who would normally need to take out substantial dividends, the desirability of Subchapter S increases.
3. Businesses that do not have heavy capital expenses, predominately those in the service areas such as consulting. Here, the owners generally expect to realize the fruits of their labors in the form of dividends and other direct compensation. They are not planning to build up the value of the business in order to sell it.
4. Businesses producing less than $30,000 in annual income for each stockholder (see the Subchapter S rule of thumb on page 31).

Election and Termination

To become a Subchapter S corporation, the corporation files Form 2553 with the Internal Revenue Service. All of the stockholders must agree to the election, and all of them must sign the form. In addition, the corporation must be qualified, as previously outlined.

The election can be made as late as 75 days into the tax year of the corporation and still be effective as of the beginning of that tax year. If it is made later, it will take effect for the next tax year.

Sample minutes for Subchapter S election are shown below:

MINUTES OF A SPECIAL MEETING OF THE DIRECTORS OF
_____. A special meeting of the Board of Directors of the Corporation was held on _____, 19___ at _____, starting at _____M. All of the directors were present and the meeting was called to order by the Chairman of the Board of Directors. The Chairman advised the Board that all of the stockholders of the Corporation have

executed written consents to the election by the Corporation to be treated as a "small business corporation." On a motion duly made, seconded, and carried by a unanimous vote, it was RESOLVED that the appropriate officers of the Corporation are hereby authorized to take any and all actions necessary to comply with the requirements of the Internal Revenue Service for making an election pursuant to Subchapter S of the Internal Revenue Code of 1954, and it was further RESOLVED that the signing of these minutes by the Directors of the Corporation constitutes full ratification thereof and waiver of notice of the meetings by the signatories. There being no further business to come before the meeting, on motion duly made, seconded, and carried unanimously, the meeting was adjourned.

If something happens to make the corporation ineligible to continue as a Subchapter S corporation, such as having more than 35 stockholders, the corporation's status ends as of that date. If the termination was inadvertent, Congress now permits the IRS to waive the terminating event. This means the corporation can continue as a Subchapter S corporation, in spite of the event. This is a major change. In the past, Subchapter S corporations often found that they had accidently lost their special status, and suffered both because the change was retroactive and because they were unable to file as a Subchapter S corporation again for a stipulated number of years.

To end the status under Subchapter S, a majority of the stockholders can file a revocation. No longer does it need the consent of all stockholders to end the status. The revocation can be filed as late as 75 days into a corporation's tax year and take effect retroactively.

The ability to make retroactive decisions about creating and ending the Subchapter S status is very valuable. It permits the owners of the business to estimate how the business is doing with some precision and elect to be under or out of Subchapter S, depending on how beneficial it is to them. If the business has early-year losses, it may be a good idea to get under Subchapter S. If the business is going to be more profitable than expected and wants to start accumulating its earnings for future growth, it can get out.

If a corporation has been under Subchapter S and terminates its election, it cannot get back in for five years. Thus, don't expect to move in and out every year to adjust your taxes. It cannot be done that way.

Operating Under Subchapter S

Deducting Losses

When passing losses on to the stockholders of a Subchapter S corporation for them to deduct from their income, remember that there is a limit to what they can deduct. The stockholders can deduct their losses *only* to the extent of their investment in the corporation. This means the stockholders can deduct losses on their own income tax returns up to the amount of their contribution to the capital of the business, plus any loans they have made to the business.

In the past, losses could be taken only in one tax year. Now losses that exceed the stockholder's *present* investment in the corporation can be carried forward to the next tax year. To use that loss in a future year, however, the stockholder must increase his basis in the corporation by providing new loans or equity. The stockholder can still arrange to take the losses in the year they occur, even if his present investment in the corporation is too small, by increasing his investment during the current year.

A hint: If it seems that the losses of the corporation will exceed your current investment in the corporation (which means you cannot deduct it all in that tax year), plan to loan money to the corporation before the end of its tax year. Loan enough money so that your basis in the corporation (the total of the stock plus loans less losses already taken) is increased to cover the anticipated losses you will receive.

Loans

A stockholder's investment in the Subchapter S corporation includes any loans made to the business. The IRS takes the position that, in order for a loan to be considered part of a stockholder's contribution, the loan must be made by the stockholder to the business. Thus a bank or other loan that is simply guaranteed by the stockholders (so that if the corporation does not pay it, the stockholders will) does not qualify as a stockholder contribution.

When seeking bank financing, where guarantees are usually insisted on, consider having the loan made to you and to other stockholders, and then have the stockholders reloan the money to the corporation. This will increase your own investment in the business. As the loan is repaid to you and the other stockholders, the interest repaid will be taxed as ordinary income to you, and you can take a personal deduction for the interest you pay to the original lender.

Capital Gains

As of 1983, Subchapter S corporations handle taxable income very much like a partnership. This means that when the separate tax treatment of an income item could affect the way taxes would be paid, the income items will be kept separate. For example, if the corporation has a capital gain resulting from the sale of a capital asset, that gain will be passed through directly to the stockholders. The corporation will not offset these gains with other losses as was done in the past. This benefits stockholders since capital gains are taxed at a lower note than ordinary income. Each stockholder can then offset the gains with his or her *own* losses, if any.

In general, the easiest rule to remember is that each stockholder of a Subchapter S corporation will take into account *separately* his or her proportional share of all the elements of the corporation's income, deductions, credits, and so on.

Unreasonable Compensation

Stockholder/employees of a Subchapter S corporation are not usually subject to challenge on unreasonable compensation. This is because, for tax purposes, all earnings go directly to the owners. However, even in this situation, an attempt to create an unusual compensation structure can be open to attack. One such attack occured in 1980.

In this case, a stockholder owned 100 percent of a Subchapter S corporation. He entered into an employment contract with the corporation, giving him an increasing percentage of the corporation's gross receipts as salary. His salary almost equaled the corporation's income. The IRS disallowed most of the corporation's deductions and was upheld by the Tax Court. The court ruled that, since the owner's salary was only about one-third of the corporation's income before the contract was signed, the compensation after the contract should be in the same range. The court reasoned that, therefore, the payments to the stockholder above this range should be treated as dividends, and not be deductible as a salary expense to the corporation.

To defend against a claim of unreasonableness, you must establish that there is a reasonable relationship between performance and compensation. To do this, follow these guidelines:

1. Show that the compensation received by the stockholder/employee is comparable to compensation packages both inside and outside of the corporation given to those with similar responsibilities and assignments.

2. Do not link compensation and profitability. It is possible that this tie could be considered as evidence that equity in the corporation, and not performance on the job, is the real basis for compensation.

3. Pay some of the compensation as a fixed salary. This shows that the corporation intends to pay a regular salary rather than distribute all of its profits disguished as salary. Pay as much as you can in the form of salary, because a high ratio of bonus to salary could result in an IRS audit, with the IRS equating a bonus to a dividend.

4. Base any bonuses on performance, and measure performance by a formula established before the period in question. This will help show that the bonus is really earned, and not merely distributed at the end of the year on the basis of what is on hand. This will shift the burden of proof back to the IRS to show that the contingent compensation formula was not arrived at in good faith.

5. If possible, put outsiders on the board of directors. It is more difficult for the IRS to support a claim of unreasonable compensation when there are independent directors (hopefully with business experience) who voted for the compensation package for the stockholder/employee.

6. Pay dividends. Pay them on some reasonable basis, such as a return on investment, particularly in the case of a capital-intensive business.

7. Get a payback agreement from all stockholder/employees. They should agree, in writing, to refund to the corporation any part of their compensation ruled "unreasonable." Of course, the very

existence of such an agreement might lead the IRS to assert that the stockholder/employees and the corporation had prior knowledge that such compensation was unreasonable. One way around this double bind is to have agreements not only with stockholder/employees but also with nonstockholder officers, if any.

8. If the compensation is questioned, do not simply back off. Be prepared to defend it. If necessary, be prepared to pay the disputed amount of taxes under protest, and sue the IRS in Federal District Court where you can get a jury trial. You may have to wait quite a while, but a jury may be more understanding than a judge sitting alone.

CHAPTER 5

Who Can and Cannot Incorporate?

In previous chapters we have covered some of the advantages of incorporating and the features of various types of business organizations. It is time now for a word of caution. While incorporating might seem to be a very attractive option, not everyone can incorporate. Most states have restrictions as to age, competency, residency, and occupation of incorporators. In addition, the federal tax law tries to prevent "incorporating your pocketbook," that is, using a corporation as a tax shelter for personal income. These and other limitations are covered below.

Age and Competency

In some states, persons under the legal age (18 or 21) cannot incorporate a business, serve on the board of directors, or hold stock in a corporation. If a minor wishes to own and control a corporation, the stock might have to be held in trust until he or she reaches legal age. The same generally holds true for persons regarded as incompetent by the law. They can participate in the ownership and control of a corporation only through a trustee or legal guardian.

Residency

Some states require that the incorporators of the business be residents of the state. However, that requirement is vanishing rapidly from the books, and today it is usually found only in laws dealing with special kinds of corporations, such as banks and insurance companies, where the states have decided that some or all of the directors must be state residents in order to protect the public interest. On the other hand, many close corporation laws permit the organizers of the corporation to establish their own residency requirements for stockholders and/or directors. This provides greater selectivity in the ownership of the small corporation.

More on the question of residency will be found in Chapter 6.

Occupation

In the past, many types of occupations were not allowed to be practiced in corporate form. Chief among them were professions such as doctor, attorney, engineer, and accountant. The reason was that state legislatures felt that licensed professionals should always be personally liable for any injuries their clients suffered. It was thought that if such professionals operated through corporations, their clients could be injured by their malpractice or negligence but would be unable to collect adequate damages. In addition, many professional associations felt that it was improper, or unprofessional, for their members to incorporate—it seemed too commercial.

During the 1960s, however, many, but not all, states passed professional corporation laws designed to cover the activities of many licensed professionals. The result is that such professionals can incorporate, but only under special laws. They cannot incorporate themselves as an ordinary business corporation, which is the type discussed in this book.

Some states do not permit people in a number of other licensed occupations to incorporate. These might include a licensed physical therapist or the owner of a tavern. There are various reasons for this restriction. In some cases, it stems from the attitude that it is unprofessional to practice a licensed occupation as a corporation. In other cases, such as with taverns, it is aimed at preventing licenses from being sold by merely selling the stock of the corporation that holds the license.

Some states also require that persons holding certain licenses, such as a license as an insurance broker, must get the permission of the body regulating them *before* they can operate as a corporation. The rationale evidently is that since the licensed individual is subject to regulation by the licensing agency, the corporation for which he or she will work (and which itself may be licensed) should also be regulated by that agency. The best way to achieve this is by requiring the prior approval of the regulating agency before incorporation.

As a general rule, if the business you intend to operate requires you to have a license to conduct it, then you might not be able to incorporate it or you might have to get permission to operate as a corporation before you incorporate.

Multiple Corporations

In most states, a corporation cannot organize another corporation, but it can own the stock of another corporation. This means that the incorporators of a corporation must be people, but the stock of the new corporation can be acquired by an existing corporation as soon as the new corporation comes into existence. The new corporation is called a subsidiary.

Business Benefits

Operating a business by establishing several corporations can be a good idea. It can provide flexibility in financing as well as increased operating efficiency resulting from dividing the business into manageable parts, instead of simply creating one corporation with several divisions or departments (which are management labels without any separate legal existence). The decision to operate through several corporations should be based on an understanding of the business consequences as well as the benefits of such a decision. The main benefits (including a few words of caution) are these:

1. *Separate liabilities and exposure to risk.* The legal liabilities

41

and debts of one part of the current corporation might be jeopardizing the entire corporation's operation. For example, the credit available to a retailer could be impaired after a large lawsuit for injuries to a customer has been filed following an accident at one store in the chain. Incorporating each of the stores can help limit the liabilities of the entire system.

However, merely setting up multiple corporations to restrict liability is not going to offer any protection if each of the corporations is not adequately capitalized. If the subsidiaries are undercapitalized, a court will "pierce the corporate veil" and hold the parent corporation's assets hostage for any judgment. In addition, today you can expect to have the parent organization sued if the subsidiary is sued for a large sum of money.

2. *Reduced accumulated earnings.* Creating multiple corporations can help the entire corporate fleet reduce the risk of exceeding legal limits on accumulated earnings. Currently, the limit on accumulated earnings in one corporation is $250,000 ($150,000 for service corporations such as consulting firms). A firm with accumulated earnings greater than this can avoid an IRS challenge and resulting penalties by establishing two corporations, each with less than the maximum amount of accumulated earnings.

3. *Improved employee incentives.* Having several corporations can be beneficial if a business operates in several locations and wants to give its employees an equity interest in the business. With several corporations, it can arrange for employees to invest in the local operations of the business.

However, setting up separate corporations with local employees investing in each can result in a nightmare for the holding corporation. Any attempt to merge the subsidiary into the parent may result in complex buy-out arrangements. These can be even more complex if the corporations are in different states.

4. *Improved financing flexibility.* A corporation that operates several lines of business often has varying credit needs as well. One business might need accounts receivable financing, another a line of credit only at certain seasons. By establishing separate corporations, the credit rating and strength of each can be improved and the relationship between its needs and assets made clearer.

However, having separate corporations will not automatically improve credit availability. In fact, some banks limit the total amount of credit outstanding to a fleet of corporations, even when the law only requires them to put a ceiling on loans to a single corporation.

5. *Separate handling of labor issues.* If all of a firm's operations are under the same corporate umbrella, a major labor dispute at one facility can result in a strike or boycott impacting all facilities. Having separate corporations can help contain labor disputes in their home ground.

6. *Separate identities.* If your business is essentially wholesale, it might be more profitable if it sells directly to the public as well. A separately incorporated (and even separately managed) retail business, operating under a different name, will avoid direct competition with your own retailing customers.

7. *Resolving stockholder disputes.* If two major groups of stockholders in a business cannot agree on major policy decisions and there is no prior stockholder agreement among them to invoke to break the deadlock, the only solution might be to divide the business. Then each group will be in control of its own corporation.

8. *Increased flexibility of compensation arrangements.* By dividing a business into portions, whether both are incorporated or not, the owners can increase the flexibility of their compensation arrangements. For example, say a business is owned by three shareholders, and it operates in both the retail and manufacturing areas. One of the stockholders is drawing what might be considered unreasonable compensation. In addition, the corporation is facing problems with unreasonable earnings accumulations. Dividing the operations into two corporations, with different owners, might permit accumulations of earnings consistent with the needs of each business. In addition, the problem of potential unreasonable compensation might be solved by permitting the most highly compensated stockholder to set up an unincorporated business and draw compensation through it.

Tax Consequences

Dividing a corporation into several corporations can cut state and local taxes, but it will not necessarily reduce federal taxes. Before considering a breakup for this reason only, work through with your accountant or tax advisor the answers to the following questions:

1. What will it cost to separate the business into one or more corporations?
2. To whom will this cost be allocated? In general, if the parent pays it, most of it would be deducted as an expense; if the new corporation pays it, it would be handled like other organizational expenses—that is, capitalized and deducted over 60 months.
3. What will the resultant tax position of each corporation be? What are the annual state taxes on the stock of each corporation? What are the state income and sales taxes? It would help to divide up the businesses on paper first, and then make up state and local tax returns for the past two and next two years, both with and without the division.
4. How will intercompany transactions be handled? Will sales by one corporation to the other result in sales and use taxes being paid that are not paid now?

If there were no restrictions in the Internal Revenue Code, businesses would organize themselves into multiple corporations to limit their taxes, since the first $25,000 of each corporation's earnings is taxed at a lower rate than the rest. However, the Internal Revenue Code effectively prevents the accumulation of tax breaks in multiple corporations by treating them, for tax purposes, as if they were all one larger corporation. Even when there are good business reasons for operating by means of multiple corporations, the federal tax laws limit these tax benefits.

In spite of the limitations on tax benefits, a corporation still may desire to divide into two or more corporations after it has come into existence. However, the Internal Revenue Code prevents corporate transformations that are designed to distribute earnings of the corporation. This means that the decision to break up into several corporations should be made for nontax reasons.

Problem Corporations

Certain types of business operations, which might look to you like tempting candidates for incorporation, will actually lead to some costly confrontations with the IRS. Some people are inspired by the apparent tax benefits to incorporate solely to take advantage of these benefits, with no other business purpose in mind. One of the most attractive benefits is that the owners of a business can permit business assets to appreciate without paying personal income tax on the profits. For this reason, many have tried to use corporations as tax shelters.

There are two principal types of problem corporate tax shelters. One is the "incorporated pocketbook" and the other is the "collapsible corporation." In each case, the Internal Revenue Code has special provisions to prevent abuses of the corporate tax structure. While it is unlikely that you will be operating your business as one of these problem corporations, you should be aware of these two areas so that you do not do so accidentally. If your business falls into one of these categories, even accidentally, you will be in trouble with the IRS and face enormous tax penalties.

The "Incorporated Pocketbook"

Some people put their investments into a corporation and manage them through the corporation, avoiding taxes on the profits until they are ready to take them out. This is known as a personal holding company, or "incorporating your pocketbook." In the eyes of the IRS, a corporation in which five or fewer individuals own more than half of the stock during the last half of a taxable year could be a personal holding company. It *is* a personal holding company if 60 percent or more of the corporation's income comes from dividends, royalties, interest, and rent.

The tax law recognizes that there are corporations in the legitimate business of holding and managing real estate. However, the IRS imposes rigid standards on the sources and relative amounts of various types of income in order to qualify as a legitimate incorporation and not a personal holding company. A personal holding company is subject to a 70 percent penalty tax by the Internal Revenue Code.

Collapsible Corporations

Some people incorporate solely in order to sell the assets put in the business. By selling the stock of the corporation and not the assets, they assume that they will pay only a capital gains tax on the profits. That is known as "collapsing a corporation."

When this occurs, the IRS usually intervenes. The IRS "collapses" the corporation according to its own tax rules and prevents the owners of the corporation from removing their profits and appreciation in the form of capital gains. Section 341 of the Internal Revenue Code converts the capital gains available on liquidations and sale of corporate stock into ordinary income. If part of the gain is attributable to appreciated corporate property that has been held for less than three years, collapsibility rules may apply.

CHAPTER 6

Where to Incorporate? (Why Not Delaware?)

Where should you incorporate your business? Perhaps you have heard that Delaware is the holy land of incorporation. True, Delaware does have definite benefits in terms of cost of incorporation and flexibility in corporate structure and operations. But in the end, you can make a costly mistake by incorporating outside your home state.

In the past, the corporate laws of most states did not permit holding meetings by mail, did not recognize the special needs of small corporations, and required relatively high levels of capitalization to incorporate. Delaware was much more flexible in its corporate laws, so many new businesses incorporated there and existing businesses reincorporated there.

Virtually all states have now modernized their corporate laws, catching up with Delaware. In fact, many have special statutes aimed to help the smaller corporation operate efficiently and cheaply.

Domestic or Foreign?

Before deciding whether to incorporate in-state (domestic) or out-of-state (foreign), consider the following questions:

1. Where will the business be operated?
2. Is your business regulated by the state where you want to operate?
3. Where will the shareholders live?
4. Will the business operate in more than one state? Which states?
5. Do you plan to sell the corporation in the near future?

Like the majority of small and medium-size businesses, you will probably choose to incorporate in the state in which you reside. If you set up an out-of-state or "foreign" corporation, it must still obey the laws of the state in which it operates. Using a foreign corporation does not save fees, because you still have to pay a fee to the state in which you operate. In fact, some state laws favor the corporations that are in their state rather than the foreign corporations when it comes to things like getting state contracts or licenses.

However, if the laws of the state in which you are doing business restrict corporate powers or lines of business or have very high capital requirements, then you might be better off incorporating in a different state. If you do this, remember to follow the rules of your home state on getting a certificate from the secretary of state in order to conduct business in your home state. Without this certificate to do business, you might be surrendering some of the rights to which you are entitled, such as the right to sue in that state.

Qualifying to do business in a state is not inexpensive. In fact, most states set the fees for a foreign corporation (that is what you are to the state in which you will be doing business if you are incorporated elsewhere) as high as or higher than for a corporation starting in its own state.

State law could require you to incorporate locally for regulatory purposes. Some businesses can operate in a state only with a license from the state and, in some cases, only if the corporation is a domestic corporation. That means to operate in Illinois, you must be incorporated there. If you need a special license to operate in a state, make sure you can be a foreign corporation instead of a domestic corporation before you incorporate.

Comparing States of Incorporation

Corporation laws, fees, taxes, and statutes governing the conduct of business vary from state to state. When selecting a state of incorporation from among several possibilities, use the following checklist as a basis of comparison.

1. Compare the corporation laws of the possible states for their requirements for capitalization, powers of directors, and flexibility in operation and capitalization.
2. Compare organization fees and related taxes.
3. Compare the cost of qualifying a foreign corporation in states where the corporation will have to do business with the cost of incorporating there in the first place.
4. Compare statutes dealing with tender offers, if the stock of the corporation will be widely held.
5. Check on annual fees and taxes in each state.
6. Check on state stamp taxes applicable to the original issue of the stock and on any later transfers.

PART II

The Process of Incorporating

CHAPTER 7

Tax-Free and Taxable Incorporation

The first steps in incorporating involve transferring money or property to the new corporation. Before you do that, however, you have to decide whether you want a tax-free (not tax-exempt) or taxable incorporation.

Transferring property to a new corporation could end up costing the stockholder at tax time. For example, assume that in setting up your corporation, you decide to contribute some property that is now worth $25,000, but you paid $10,000 for it eight years ago. If you sold it now to someone else for $25,000, you would have a taxable gain of $15,000 on the sale. In a *taxable* incorporation, if you transferred the property to your new corporation for $12,500 in stock and a note for the remaining $12,500, you would incur the same taxable gain. As far as the IRS is concerned, you have "sold" the property and would be expected to pay taxes on the "profit" of $15,000.

To relieve new stockholders of this tax burden, the Internal Revenue Code permits the transfer of property to a new corporation to be tax-free. The Code requires that the ownership of the corporation be substantially the same as the ownership of the property being transferred, so that the transfer of the property does not disguise its movement from one owner to another.

The Tax-Free Incorporation

In general, it is useful to have a tax-free incorporation, both for the stockholder transferring the property and for the new corporation. Using the same situation described above, in a tax-free incorporation, the stockholder gives the property to the corporation for $25,000 in stock. The stockholder now has stock and the basis (tax cost) of that stock is what the basis of the property was—namely, $10,000. The corporation now has property worth $10,000, the same basis as the stockholder had. If the stockholder now sells that stock for $25,000, he will have a taxable profit of $15,000. Similarly, if the corporation sells the property for $25,000, it (but not the stockholder) will have a profit of $15,000. (For additional information on valuing property, see IRS Publications 534, 542, 544, and 551.)

Essentially, no one escapes a tax in a tax-free incorporation. Although no current tax is owed, the tax on the increased value of the property must ultimately be paid, but only when the property is sold by the corporation.

The Internal Revenue Code makes most incorporations tax-free. To make sure that it is tax-free, you have to meet two standards set by IRC 351:

1. The property that you give to the corporation must be given *only* in exchange for stock or securities of that corporation. Securities include debt to the corporation that is not short-term in nature. A demand note (a note paid upon the demand of the lender rather than at a specified time) would not be considered a security.
2. Immediately upon the exchange of property for stock, the person making the transfer of property to the corporation must be in control of the corporation.

The Taxable Incorporation

An incorporation can be set up to be taxable. That means the stockholder pays the tax on the increase in the value of the property given to the corporation at the time the stockholder gets stock in the corporation. The corporation, however, will never pay tax on that profit.

Using the same situation described above, in a taxable corporation, the transfer of the property to the corporation would result in a taxable gain to the stockholder of $15,000, and he or she pays taxes on that gain. However, the stock now held by the stockholder has a basis (tax cost) of $25,000, not $10,000 as under the tax-free incorporation. This is because taxes have been paid on that profit. To the corporation, the property has a basis of $25,000, not $10,000, as it did before under the tax-free incorporation. If the corporation later sells that property for $25,000, there is no taxable gain to the corporation on that sale.

In order to make the transaction taxable, you will have to navigate a series of complex rules, established by the Internal Revenue Code. Unlike almost any other situation, you will have to work to make the deal taxable. This should be done only with competent tax advice.

Choosing Between Tax-Free and Taxable Incorporation

Most people go through an incorporation without considering whether or not it should be tax-free or taxable. Given the standards set up by the Internal Revenue Code, most incorporations are automatically tax-free. But, as with any other decision involving taxes, do not assume that tax-free incorporation is necessarily better for you. The particular tax situation of one of the stockholders-to-be can make a taxable incorporation desirable.

For example, suppose that the stockholder-to-be wants to transfer to the corporation property that has a built-in loss, not a profit. That is, it was purchased for $15,000 but is now worth only $5,000. If the incorporation is tax-free, that potential loss stays with the corporation. But if the transfer is taxable, then the stockholder may be able to show a loss on the acquisition of the stock. How useful that loss is depends upon the personal tax situation of the stockholder. If that stockholder has a lot of long-term capital gains, the long-term capital loss resulting from the transfer may offset the gains dollar for dollar, resulting in major tax savings. If there are no long-term capital gains, the long-term loss will offset other income two to one, so each $1.00 of the loss on incorporating will save $.50 in taxable income that year for the stockholder.

In addition, it could be important for the corporation to have a higher basis in the property than the stockholder did, in order to take higher depreciation deductions, for instance. However, the Internal Revenue Code, through what are known as recapture provisions, prevents corporate taxpayers from taking depreciation on property that has already been depreciated by them as individuals.

CHAPTER 8

How to Incorporate

Most incorporations are handled by an attorney, and with more and more lawyers making their services available to the middle-income person, you would be wise to shop around for the best price. However, incorporating does not have to be handled by an attorney. You can use a commercial service to do it or you can do it yourself.

Some commercial services avail themselves only to lawyers, which means you have to hire a lawyer to use them. A commercial service generally costs about $150 in addition to the fees connected with the incorporation itself. The service will ask you to fill out a questionnaire with all the information needed to complete and file the articles of incorporation. Commercial services do not give advice about which incorporation option is preferable for you.

If you do it yourself, you will save the commercial service fee, but there are still other fixed costs that you have to pay in order to incorporate in any state. A list of typical costs is provided in the next chapter.

Checklist for Corporate Formation

The checklist below gives an overview of the steps involved in incorporating. These steps are discussed in more detail in the sections that follow.

- Select state of incorporation.
- Select and reserve the corporate name.
- Prepare and execute preincorporation agreements among the stockholders.
- Draft and file articles of incorporation.
- Draft bylaws.
- Obtain corporate minute book, corporate seal, and stock certificates.
- Hold organizational meetings of the directors and stockholders. Typically these meetings will include making a Subchapter S election, adopting bylaws, electing a permanent board of directors and officers, and selecting an accounting system and fiscal year.
- Apply for an IRS identification number.
- Accept stock subscriptions, that is, the agreements to purchase the stock of the corporation.
- Study and decide on employee benefits options, including pension and profit-sharing plans.

Select State of Incorporation

Selecting the state of incorporation is discussed in Chapter 6. You should weigh several factors before making this decision.

Reserve Corporate Name

To reserve a name for the corporation, a written request must be filed with the secretary of state, together with a filing fee. If you proceed with the incorporation without reserving a name, you run the risk that your incorporation papers will be rejected because the name you selected closely resembles that of an existing corporation or uses terms that might mislead the public, such as "insurance" if the corporation is not a licensed insurance company.

The secretary of state will return to you a certificate stating that the name you want has been reserved. For a period of time, usually 30 days, no one else can incorporate using that name. If you cannot complete your paperwork in the 30 days, you can often apply for a 30-day extension for an additional fee.

How to Incorporate

Prepare Preincorporation Agreements

Stockholders agreements are covered in Chapter 11.

File the Articles of Incorporation

After the corporate name is reserved, you can file the articles of incorporation. In the past, the articles of incorporation were elaborate documents, always prepared by lawyers, and looking very much like wills. Today, many states make available a standard incorporation form for businesses seeking to incorporate. The following information is typical of what is required on these forms. When completed, they are filed and become the articles of incorporation.

1. Corporate name of the business.
2. Purposes for which the corporation is formed. This is usually expressed in very broad language such as "for all legitimate purposes in the state." This allows you to expand or change the business without having to amend the articles of incorporation.
3. Length of time for which the corporation is being formed. This can, of course, be perpetual and usually is.
4. Names and addresses of the incorporators. In some states, at least one of the incorporators must be a resident of the state in which you are incorporating.
5. Location of the registered office of the corporation. In most states, the "office" can be a postal box. However, many states also require a street address for purposes such as mailing tax forms, so be prepared to give either or both. You will be required to have access to the office or have an agent receive mail there for you. This is so that the corporation can be served process in case of a lawsuit.
6. The maximum amount and kinds of stock that the corporation will be issuing. At this point you will have to decide the capital structure of the corporation, which is a very important part of the incorporating process. You will have to designate the number and classification of the shares of stock, as well as the rights, preferences, and limitations of each

class of stock. In some states, much of this can be left to be included in the bylaws. Issuing your stock is covered in Chapter 10.

7. Capital required at the time of incorporation. Some states require that a specific percentage of the par value of the capital stock be paid in cash either before the certificate of incorporation is submitted to the state for final approval or just after the business is incorporated and before it starts operations.

8. Provisions for preemptive rights, if any, to be granted to the stockholders and any restrictions on the transfer of shares of stock of the corporation. Preemptive rights give existing stockholders the right to buy any new stock before it is offered to any outsiders. Restrictions on the transfer of stock include, for example, provisions that all stock be offered to the corporation or to existing stockholders before it can be sold to an outsider.

9. Provisions for the regulation of the internal affairs of the corporation. Many of these, such as requirements for special majorities to amend the bylaws or to sell the business are now included in the bylaws, instead of in the articles of incorporation. Provisions such as setting the number of directors and the quorum for meetings of directors and stockholders can be included in the articles of incorporation in order to make it more difficult to amend them. The articles generally must be amended by the stockholders; the bylaws are usually amended by the directors.

10. Names and addresses of the persons who will serve as directors until the first meeting of stockholders or until their successors are elected and qualify.

11. Who has the right to amend, alter, or repeal any provisions contained in the certificate of incorporation. In some states, this right is statutory, being reserved to a majority or two-thirds of the stockholders. In other states, you can specify who has this power in the articles of incorporation.

Before you file the papers to create your corporation, review them carefully to be sure they are complete and accurate. The following questions can serve as a checklist and help you avoid some problems commonly encountered when filing documents with state corporation offices:

- Are you filing the right papers?
- Has every article of the document been completed, including complete addresses?
- Have all the documents been signed by the proper parties?
- Have the correct fees been included? Has the check been made payable to the correct office?
- Has the corporation's name been reserved and is a copy of the document certifying that reservation included?
- Does the corporation's name include one of the required terms, such as "corporation," "incorporated," "inc.," "corp.," "company," "co.," "limited," "ltd."?
- Have the documents that require notarization been notarized?

When complete, the papers are sent to the state along with a filing fee. The state will make certain that all the necessary information has been provided, that all the papers have been properly executed, and that there is nothing in the articles of incorporation that violates state law or public policy. At this point the certificate of incorporation will be issued. The corporation now exists.

Draft the Bylaws

The bylaws of the new corporation are among the most important items adopted at the organizational meeting of the directors. The bylaws of a corporation generally cover the following items:

1. Location of the corporation's principal office and other offices.
2. Time, place, and required notice of annual and special meetings of the stockholders, including the required quorum and voting privileges of the stockholders.
3. The number of directors, their compensation, their term of office, the method of electing them, and the method of creating or filling vacancies.
4. Time and place of regular and special directors' meetings, as well as notice and quorum requirements.

5. Method of selecting officers, their titles, duties, terms of office, and salaries.
6. Form of stock certificates (that is, what they actually look like and who signs them), how they are transferred (typically by returning them to the corporation to be recorded in the books and a new certificate issued), and any limits on their transfer (such as rights of first refusal to existing stockholders).
7. When and by whom dividends may be declared, including any limits on paying dividends.
8. The fiscal year of the corporation, the form of the corporate seal, and who has the authority to sign checks.

Corporate Kits

In most magazines for lawyers (such as the *American Bar Association Journal*), there are ads for "corporate kits." The kits contain materials which are used to incorporate a business. Some are general and are designed to be used in most states; others are geared to the requirements of states such as New York, Delaware, California, and Pennsylvania, which have substantial numbers of new corporations. The kits are of two kinds: one contains a binder for storing the corporate minutes and papers, a corporate seal, and preprinted stock certificates; the other also contains preprinted articles of incorporation, bylaws, and minutes for the meetings of directors.

The kits containing preprinted documents can be useful, as long as the parties incorporating the business, whether it be an attorney or a stockholder, use them intelligently. Merely because the document is worded a certain way does not mean you have to go along with it. Make any changes you want in the preprinted materials, but make them clearly because the originals of these documents have legal significance. Don't just scratch out a provision you don't want and write a new one in. Make the deletions in black ink and type in the changes.

As long as they are not followed blindly, these preprinted documents can be useful and cost-effective. In fact, if you are using an attorney to incorporate the business, ask whether he will be using a corporate kit. If not, make sure there is a reason and that you will not be paying for the preparation of bylaws by hand. If your lawyer does not use a kit, make sure that he has his own set of "canned" bylaws, probably on a word processor. You should not pay for a hand-made corporation if you do not need it.

Hold Organizational Meetings

After the articles of incorporation have been accepted by the state and the corporation has come into being, you must arrange for a first meeting of the board of directors and the stockholders. Among the items covered as a part of these meetings are the following:

Initial Board of Directors

- Adopt bylaws, if the articles or bylaws permit them to do that.
- Elect the officers of the corporation.
- Authorize Section 1244 stock, and/or make an election to be a Subchapter S corporation. These are covered in Chapters 4, 7, and 12.
- Ratify any contracts made by promoters. For more on this, see Chapter 13.
- Approve the forms of stock certificates, together with any legends on the certificates that indicate restrictions on their transfer.
- Authorize the acceptance of any stock subscriptions, and issue stock to new stockholders in exchange for money or assets. Put a value on these assets. Issue any debt securities.
- Elect officers and set their salaries. Approve the execution of employment contracts.
- Open a corporate bank account.
- Appoint any accountants for the corporation.
- Complete any other organizational steps, such as paying bills in connection with the incorporation.

Stockholders

- Elect directors of the corporation to replace the organizing board.
- Adopt the bylaws, if state law or the articles of incorporation require them to be adopted by the stockholders.

Application for Taxpayer's Number

The IRS Form SS-4, Application for Employer Identification Number, is one that you will encounter perhaps once in your business life. It is the way that the IRS assigns a tax number to your corporation, the number that you will use for all federal and most state tax purposes as long as the corporation exists. The form is simple and direct. Perhaps the most difficult item to answer is the "nature of principal business activity." For help on this, consult IRS Publications 334, 542, and 583. They will list the SIC (Standard Industrial Codes) from which you will choose.

Once you have completed this application, mail it as directed to the IRS office indicated in the directions. It will take 5 to 20 days for it to be returned to you. Make sure that the address on the form is that of the corporation and not of the lawyer or accountant who may be doing the paperwork. Official IRS papers will come to that address from then on.

To determine when you have to file the application, check all the papers you will be filing in connection with the organization of the corporation. If none of the papers you have to file with the state require that you show the employer identification number, then the filing of the SS-4 can wait until the corporation has been formally incorporated. However, some states have a Catch-22. To file their papers, you need the employer identification number. But to get that number, you need to have a corporation, or so it would seem. To solve this problem, file the SS-4 after you have reserved the corporate name, but before filing the articles of incorporation. When the SS-4 is returned, you can then file the state papers.

Accept Stock Subscriptions

Accepting stock subscriptions is one of the steps involved in issuing the stock of the corporation. In order to assure that the corporation will have capital before it is even in existence, many persons organizing corporations obtain agreements to buy the stock of the new corporation. These are called stock subscription agreements, since the signers agree to subscribe to, that is buy when issued, the stock of that corporation. After the corporation is organized, issue the stock as soon as possible.

Employee Benefits Options

While not required as part of the incorporation procedure, it is a good idea to use the occasion of forming the new corporation to consider employee benefits options, such as pension and profit-sharing plans. These options may have tax consequences and will require action by the board of directors and possibly by the stockholders. Thus, while all parties are together, both physically and emotionally, consider how you plan to compensate employees (whether or not they are stockholders), both now and in the future. It will be time well spent.

Pre- and Postincorporation Checklists

You now have a pretty good idea of whether incorporating is the right move for you and what decisions must be made before you incorporate. The two checklists below will take you through the steps you have to cover before the papers are prepared and filed. Study both lists, because when you do things can depend on state law. In some states, for example, you have to apply for your federal employer identification number (tax number) before you file the articles of incorporation because the forms require the tax number to be included on them. In other states, you apply for the tax number afterward.

If you cannot answer a particular question in the checklists, don't just skip it. Instead, review what this book covers on the subject and get professional advice if you need it. Skip the question only if it does not apply to your situation. For example, if your corporation will be run by the stockholders without a board of directors, you do not need to select a first board of directors.

Make sure that you can resolve all the items in the postincorporation checklist as well as those in the preincorporation list. They can have a significant impact on whether and when you can start your business. For example, if you need special permits to start operations, can you apply for them while you are still in the act of incorporating? If you can, that may move up the date you can start your business. If you cannot apply for the license until after you are incorporated, do not let the matter rest. Check the application you will have to file. Do you need extra copies of the certificate of incorporation with the application? Get them early. Do you have to adopt any special resolutions in order to file the application? If so, adopt them at the organizational meeting.

Preincorporation Checklist

1. Who serves as the incorporators? Where do they live?
2. In what state will the business be incorporated?
3. Will the corporation's existence be perpetual or limited in duration?
4. What name do you want the corporation to have? Has it been reserved?
5. Where will the principal place of business be? Will it be owned or leased? Who owns it or has the lease now? Will it be transferred to the corporation? In exchange for what?
6. Where else will the corporation operate? Will it own property or have operations in other states? When?
7. What is the nature of the business to be conducted? Is that likely to change?
8. Will the new corporation receive any patents or copyrights? From whom and for what?
9. Does the corporation need any state or local licenses? Are any licenses to be transferred to it? By whom? How long will this take? Can the corporation hold such a license or permit?
10. What will be the initial investment in the corporation? Will it be in cash or in some other form?
11. How many shares will be authorized by the corporation? How many will be issued? To whom? For what consideration?
12. Will there be more than one class of stock? For each class of stock, will there be preemptive rights? Restrictions on transfer? Cumulative voting?
13. Who will subscribe to the initial issue of stock? How many shares will they get? What will they pay in terms of cash or property?
14. When will the corporation begin business?
15. Who executes the articles of incorporation and files them?
16. Will the articles of incorporation provide for indemnification

of officers and directors? For the removal of directors by shareholders at any time, with or without cause?

17. How many directors will there be?
18. Who will serve on the first board of directors?
19. When will the directors hold their first meeting?
20. What will be done at the organizational meetings of the incorporators and the directors?
21. Who will be the initial officers?
22. When will the annual meeting of the shareholders be held? Where? On what notice?
23. How will special meetings of the shareholders be called?
24. What kind of quorum is needed for a meeting of shareholders?
25. How many days notice is needed to call a meeting of the directors? What is the quorum for a meeting of the directors?
26. What is the fiscal year of the corporation going to be?
27. How can the bylaws be amended: by the directors, the shareholders, or either?
28. Where will the corporation open its bank account?
29. Who will keep possession of the minutes and records of the board and shareholders and prepare needed materials?
30. Who will keep the books and accounts of the business and be responsible for all tax filings?

Postincorporation Checklist

Once you have set up the corporation, you are not finished. There are a number of critical housekeeping items which you have to take care of almost immediately. We include this list here because, if you cannot take care of these things after the corporation is formed, you should not incorporate in the first place.

1. File an application for a federal employer identification number, using IRS Form SS-4. (In some states, you need this number to incorporate, so you would apply for it after reserving the corporate name but before filing the articles of incorporation.)
2. Obtain worker's compensation coverage.

3. Designate an agent for service of process and file related papers with the state government.
4. Obtain key-person insurance and other forms of insurance needed to fund buy-sell and other stockholder agreements. (Stockholder agreements are covered in Chapter 11.)
5. Pay state taxes related to issuance of stock.
6. File for unemployment insurance coverage.
7. Obtain sales/use tax licenses.
8. Select a bank for corporate accounts and open the accounts.
9. Select and purchase appropriate insurance to protect your business. (See the Insurance Checklist at the back of this book.)

CHAPTER 9

The Costs of Incorporating

Forming a corporation is usually more expensive than forming a partnership or a sole proprietorship. Legal fees, state incorporation fees, start-up costs, and other expenses tend to be higher for the corporation than for other forms of business. (The costs of operating the corporation may also be higher than for another business form, because separate books must be kept, regular meetings of the stockholders and directors must be held, and annual fees and taxes must be paid.)

As a general rule, you cannot simply deduct all the expenses of setting up the corporation on the corporation's first tax return. Instead, they must be capitalized (treated as if you bought an asset and added to the corporation's capital) and in some cases amortized (written off) over a period of 60 months.* (A capitalized expense may or may not be amortized, but an expense must be capitalized in order to be amortized. Different types of expenses are handled in different ways. For example, the new corporation might incur $100

---

*The reader should be warned that how the costs of incorporating are treated is not a simple subject. "Capitalization," "capital," and "expensing" have slightly different meanings depending on whether the context is accounting, tax law, or corporate law.

in incorporation fees, $500 in legal fees, and a $2,500 fee for registering stock with the SEC. The $2,500 is capitalized, carried on the corporation's books, and not amortized over time. The remaining $600 can be amortized by the corporation in 60 equal installments of $10 a month.)

One crucial point must be kept in mind: for you to deduct *any* expenses, your business must make a profit; if your business has no income, there is nothing from which to deduct expenses.

There are three basic types of expenses involved in setting up a corporation: investigatory expenses, organizational expenses, and start-up expenses.

Investigatory Expenses

Investigatory expenses involve examining and evaluating the venture before you decide to go ahead. Typically, these costs involve market studies and meetings with potential investors and lenders.

Organizational Expenses

Organizational expenses include legal fees, state incorporation fees, and other costs directly associated with the creation of the corporation itself. The fees for setting up a corporation usually include the following items:

1. Reserving the corporate name: $2 to $10.
2. Filing the articles of incorporation: $25 to $75.
3. Advertising the formation of the corporation: $50 to $150.
4. Purchasing a corporate kit (printed stock certificates, sample minutes, preprinted bylaws, stock transfer journal, corporate seal, storage case): $50 to $100.
5. Attorney's fees in connection with the incorporation: $150 to $1,000.

These fees are amortized over a period of at least 60 months, beginning on the date that the business starts operations. You cannot, however, either deduct or amortize costs such as printing a prospectus, underwriting fees, and other expenses related to issuing and selling stock. These are capitalized and generally cannot be recovered until you liquidate the corporation.

Start-Up Expenses

Start-up expenses are those expenses incurred after the decision to incorporate has been made, but usually before the business actually begins operation. Such costs can include hiring and training employees, salaries, travel, telephone calls, and other similar expenses involved in starting up the business.

Handling the Costs

A key issue in handling the costs of incorporating is deciding when business actually begins. The position of the Internal Revenue Service is that a business does not begin until revenue is being produced. Thus, according to the IRS, no deductions are allowed until that time.

Many tax lawyers and accountants object to this standard. In recent years, the Tax Court has taken the position that the question is really whether the business expenses in question are capital or ordinary expenses, not when operations have begun. As long as there is a business or profit-making motive, the Tax Court takes the position that ordinary expenses are business-related and thus deductible against income when incurred.

In determining how to handle the costs of incorporation, there are several issues to consider. First of all, decide whether your business is a new venture or whether it qualifies as an expansion of an existing business. Investigatory and start-up costs of an expansion can be deducted on a current-year basis. In a new venture, these expenses are amortized over 60 months.

Secondly, determine when the corporation begins operations. If this is not clear, and if it is hard to differentiate between currently deductible operating expenses and those that are related to starting up the corporation, you have a choice. You can deduct the expenses on a current-year basis, starting with the start-up of the business or the beginning of profit-motivated activities, even though the corporation has not yet earned any money. If the IRS disputes this and wins, you may lose the chance to amortize these costs as well as to deduct them. On the other hand, you can amortize them up to a date when it is clear that the business had begun operations. Then you can deduct the costs as a business expense from that point on.

If you might have to abandon the corporation before its operations begin, having set up a corporation will allow you to take an ordinary loss deduction for pre-opening expenses if the project never gets off the ground.

If you may have to abandon the corporation *after* it has begun operations, but within 60 months of the start-up, the remaining unamortized expenses can be written off as a loss or carried over into reorganization, if necessary.

Abandoning a Risky Business

If you are forming a business that involves a considerable degree of risk, that is, if you could fail rather completely and quickly, incorporating the business can be to your advantage. If you incorporate and later abandon the business, you and the other stockholders can take deductions for ordinary losses associated with the organization of the corporation *if* (1) the corporation was organized as a small-business corporation, *and* (2) you paid for the stock of the corporation, as opposed to getting the stock in exchange for services. You can deduct only up to the amount of cash or property you actually paid for this stock.

These deductions can be obtained only by using Section 1244 stock. This type of stock is discussed more completely in Chapter 12.

CHAPTER *10*

Issuing Your Stock

Stock certificates are the instruments used to denote ownership of a corporation. Stock represents the money the owners have put into the corporation, and it is therefore described as an "equity" security.

Although stockholders own the corporation, they do not own the property of the corporation. Instead, the corporation owns its property. The stockholders have a right to receive dividends (money), and if the corporation is dissolved, the stockholders have a right to the value of the corporate assets when they are sold (after paying off the corporation's debts). They also control the corporation indirectly by voting for directors and on other key matters.

There are basically four types of stock. *Authorized shares of stock* are the shares of stock that the corporation is authorized to issue by the law of the state where it is incorporated and by its articles of incorporation. *Issued shares* are the authorized shares of stock that have actually been issued to stockholders for some consideration. The issued shares equal the outstanding shares plus the treasury shares. *Outstanding shares* are issued shares of stock that are currently held by the stockholders. *Treasury shares* are the issued shares of stock that have been repurchased by the corporation. They are held in the corporation's treasury.

It is to a corporation's advantage to have treasury shares, because these shares can be sold to new stockholders or distributed in other ways (such as through profit sharing). A corporation can also elect to cancel its treasury shares, which means that the shares no longer exist. Once a corporation has done this, however, it must go through all the formalities of issuing new stock in order to sell any more stock.

Authorizing and Issuing Stock

Stock must always be "purchased," either for money, for property, or for services performed for the corporation. When this happens, the stock is usually considered as fully paid and nonassessable. If the stock has been given away or sold at a very low price, it may be considered to be void. This means the stockholder could be prevented from voting or receiving dividends. Such stock can also be assessed by a creditor if the corporation becomes insolvent. This means the creditor could require the stockholder to pay what should have been paid when the stock was issued.

Even when stock is properly issued, the holders of the stock can still be subject to certain liabilities imposed by state law. For example, some states now have laws imposing personal liability on stockholders for wages due to employees of the corporation.

As previously noted, stock must be issued in return for something. The requirement that the corporation receive something for the stock it issues is called the requirement for consideration. This consideration can be defined in terms of kind and quantity.

The amount of consideration to be given depends on the par value of the stock. "Par" means that the value of the stock is stated on the certificate and not set by the board of directors. The par value is allocated on the corporation's books to its "capital." All other money received for its sale is considered as "capital surplus." The type of consideration given for stock with a par value is usually set by the state incorporation laws. These are almost always limited to money, services rendered, and property received by the corporation. This precludes issuing stock in return for future services.

In terms of quantity, the consideration must be no less than the par value of the stock being issued. The board of directors of a corporation is generally allowed to designate the value or the consideration that must be given in exchange for the stock. This is called the "good faith rule" and means only that the consideration received be designated by the board of directors in good faith to have a value no less than the par value of the stock being issued. In those states where the incorporation laws require a minimum paid-in capital, the capital represented by the shares that have been sold must satisfy that minimum capital requirement.

No-par stock is stock having no par value on its certificate. The stock sells at a price determined by the board. The money received on its sale is divided between capital and capital surplus as the board determines. The consideration given for no-par stock must be of the type permitted by state law, such as money, services rendered, or property received by the corporation. However, there are no stipulations regarding the amount of the consideration to be given in exchange for the stock, except in states with a minimum paid-in capital requirement, in which case the consideration must satisfy any such requirement.

The Mechanics

The steps involved in actually issuing the stock are as follows:

1. The corporation must have been authorized to issue this stock, in terms of both the class (preferred or common) and the number of shares. This is usually found in the articles of incorporation, or in the bylaws if the articles permit this to be handled there.

2. By a formal resolution, the board of directors accepts a written offer by a potential stockholder to purchase the stock, and, in the corporation's books, allocates the purchase price to capital or to capital surplus or both. This allocation affects both dividend payments and the ability to buy back issued stock. In many states, only capital surplus (and not capital) may be distributed as dividends or used by the corporation to buy back its own stock.

3. The potential stockholder turns over the cash or the property involved to the corporation. If cash, it is deposited in the corporation's accounts. If property, the corporation takes possession and executes all documents needed to transfer title to the corporation.

4. The secretary of the corporation prepares a blank stock certificate for issuing to the new stockholder. If there is a restriction on its transfer, the secretary ascertains that the restriction or a reference to it is printed on the certificate.

5. The blank stock certificate is filled in with the name of the stockholder, the number of shares it represents, and the class of stock represented by the certificate.

6. The completed certificate is signed by the president and the secretary of the corporation. The corporation's seal is embossed on the certificate.

7. The secretary then enters information about the stock certificate in the corporation's stock transfer ledger. This information shows the certificate number, to whom it was issued, for how many shares, and when. Typically, this information is indexed under both the name of the stockholder and the certificate number. This ledger is used to issue replacement certificates and as the source of names to be given notice of stockholder meetings.

8. The certificate is delivered to the new stockholder.

9. If the new stockholder wishes to transfer the certificate, the stockholder completes the back of the certificate, identifying to whom the certificate is being transferred, and returns the certificate to the corporation. The corporation issues a new certificate to the new stockholder and changes the entries in the corporation's books.

A typical provision in the articles of incorporation providing for two classes of stock would be as follows:

The Corporation is authorized to issue _____ shares of Class A common stock with a par value of $_____ and _____ shares of Class B common stock with a par value of $_____. Class A stockholders, as a class, have the right to elect one-half (½) of the members of the Board of Directors of the Corporation, known as Class A Directors, and to fill any vacancy occurring in this class. Class B stockholders, as a class, have the right to elect one-half (½) of the members of the Board of Directors of the Corporation, known as Class B Directors, and to fill any vacancy occurring in this class. Except as provided in this Article, each share of Class A common stock and each share of Class B common stock are in all respects equal.

Controlling the Business

When planning the issuance of stock, the key point is that the stock should be authorized and issued to correspond to an already-agreed-upon division among the stockholders. This division is usually based upon (1) equitable division of earnings, (2) equitable allocation of assets on dissolution, and (3) desired distribution of control (via special voting or other powers assigned to certain classes of stock).

When allocating control of the business by allocating stock, it is important to consider a number of other factors related to how the corporation is governed. These factors will influence who gets how much stock and with what powers. They include:

1. Control over the directors, if any, by permitting their removal on the broadest possible grounds.
2. Control over the conduct of directors' or stockholders' meetings by establishing low or high quorum requirements or greater-than-simple-majority voting requirements. Requiring a more-than-majority vote can protect the interests of minority stockholders in deciding on the dissolution and sale of the corporation, election of directors, etc.
3. Restrictions on the sale of stock of the corporation by current stockholders in order to limit new stockholders.

For example, even if you own 40 percent of the stock, you will not have much power if someone else has 60 percent and everything is decided by majority vote. But if your 40 percent is a special class of stock that grants the right of electing half the board of directors, you have considerable power.

CHAPTER 11

Stockholder Agreements

It is common to have written agreements among the principal stockholders of a corporation governing major aspects of how business will be conducted. These agreements are perfectly legal, provided they do not oppress the rights of minority stockholders and that they meet other provisions of the state incorporation laws. The agreements can cover how stock will be voted, how officers will be elected, how stock will be purchased upon the death of a stockholder (buy-sell agreements), and how stock will be transferred.

Voting Agreements

The owners of a new corporation can maintain control of the business by agreeing among themselves to exercise their voting rights in certain ways, as long as they are not oppressing the minority stockholders. For example, they could all agree that their shares will be voted together on certain issues, such as the election of directors. This means that if others become stockholders of the business, they will be unable to control the board of directors and the operations of the business. In addition, the stockholders' agreement can include buy-out provisions to provide a way out for dissenting stockholders.

One of the most important powers possessed by stockholders is the election of directors, because the management of the corporation is vested in the board. Any stockholder seeking influence at the board level either must have enough representatives on the board to vote his way or must control the board through director agreements.

Stockholder agreements requiring that the parties vote for certain directors are usually enforceable as long as the directors involved act in the best interests of the corporation. Stockholder agreements that call for the parties to vote for or consent to specific corporate actions that require stockholder approval (such as a merger or acquisition) are also valid, again as long as they do not result in oppression of the minority, nonparticipating stockholders.

Many state laws now let the stockholders elect officers of the corporation directly, instead of through the board of directors. If stockholders of a small corporation want control over how the business is run on a day-to-day basis, they should consider adopting this strategy. However, if this strategy is coupled with greater-than-majority voting requirements, it can result in the minority being able to block the majority's desires on hiring and paying officers.

Agreements Among Directors

While agreements among stockholders on how they will vote their stock on certain issues are routine, attempts to have the directors of a corporation agree in advance how they will act can cause problems. First, state law requires that the directors of a corporation cannot be unduly restrained by agreements. Second, the parties to a directors' agreement must anticipate those matters that will require collective action without dissent in the future. This is almost impossible.

Nevertheless, when the officers must be elected by the board of directors, the new stockholders should consider an agreement among the directors on electing and retaining officers. One way is to have the stockholders also serve as the directors. Then, as directors, they can agree to appoint and retain a particular person as an officer "so long as he (or she) is faithful, efficient, and competent." This permits the officer to serve until the necessary majority of stockholders subjectively conclude that the person is no longer useful. What makes this acceptable is that all the stockholders, even signing as directors, are parties to the agreement.

Employment Agreements

Another way to assure selecting and keeping particular persons as officers is through employment agreements between the corporation and the individual officers.

To prevent a majority of the board from imposing an unacceptable officer on the minority stockholders, the bylaws might require a greater-than-majority vote to appoint an officer. To protect an officer under an employment contract from being removed at the whim of a simple majority, the bylaws could provide that removal can occur only by a greater-than-majority vote, with the minority stockholders having the right of veto. If the officer with the contract is also a stockholder and director, this could provide him or her with a way of blocking any removal attempt.

The Buy-Sell Agreement

The death of a shareholder in a closely held corporation can leave a void that may result in reorganization or even dissolution. The buy-sell agreement, properly written and funded, ensures that the surviving shareholders will buy the stock, that the needed cash will be available, and that a price will be established for estate planning purposes.

Funding the Agreement

Binding the stockholders to buy the stock of a deceased stockholder presents a distinct liability to the corporation or remaining stockholders. At death, some sort of sinking fund must be made available to provide immediate execution of the buy-sell agreement and present the money to the survivors of the deceased stockholder. Several alternatives are available to the corporation to establish this sinking fund. If the stockholders are wealthy enough, they can make part of their own money available to supply this fund. A second alternative is to borrow the money at death. Finally, the parties can pay on the installment plan. Each alternative has severe drawbacks that could ultimately disrupt the normal operations of the corporation.

Another alternative, perhaps the best alternative, is to use life insurance. Through an advance installment plan, the future surviving stockholders can pay at pennies to the dollar for insurance to assure the proper amount of money at death.

Cross Purchase and Stock Redemption

There are two types of buy-sell agreements: the cross purchase and the stock redemption. Through the cross purchase agreement, each stockholder agrees to buy out the other's stock in the event of death. Under the stock redemption agreement, the corporation agrees to redeem the stock from the deceased stockholder's estate.

The choice between cross purchase and stock redemption is dependent upon a number of factors. Where the corporation has several stockholders, a stock redemption agreement reduces the number of policies that must be purchased. If there are four stockholders, for example, under a cross purchase agreement, each owner buys policies on each of the other three owners, for a total of 12 policies. Under a stock redemption agreement, the corporation buys the policies, and only four need to be purchased. If the stockholders want to retain the same proportionate ratio of ownership after the death of one stockholder, then a cross purchase agreement should be used. On the other hand, if ownership is projected to change, stock redemption could bring the desired results. A stock redemption agreement also has the benefit of equalizing the premium costs for insurance policies when there is a wide age variance among stockholders. For those who anticipate the disposal of their business after the death of a stockholder, the cross purchase method has an advantage in that it results in a higher "cost basis" for the purchasing stockholders than does stock redemption. The cost basis is what the IRS considers you to have paid for the stock. The result is more favorable capital gains treatment at the time of disposal of the corporation.

Who Benefits?

The surviving shareholders, the deceased shareholder's estate, and the shareholders while all living can all benefit from a buy-sell agreement. For the surviving shareholders, the buy-sell agreement ensures that there will be no disruption of the business operations. It also prevents the deceased's family from being brought into the business, which could cause undesirable management changes. The benefit to the deceased shareholder's estate is the full and prompt payment of the value of the deceased stockholder's share, enabling quick settling of the estate. The deceased's family is also relieved of the worry about being forced into an existing corporation.

The final benefit is to the shareholders while still alive. The business is stabilized for the stockholder as well as for the employees. If permanent cash value life insurance is used as a funding mechanism, it provides a further savings for emergencies.

Setting the Price of Stock

A buy-sell agreement funded by insurance entails a number of important commitments. There is a definite commitment that binds the shareholders to the deceased shareholder's estate. There is a definite commitment of the time payment for policies. The insurance policies must be maintained and updated. Finally, there must be a price set to be paid to the deceased shareholder's estate.

There are several methods of deciding on the price of the stock: book value, straight capitalization, and stated purchase price are the most common. The book value of the company is derived from the last financial statement of the company prior to the death of the shareholder. The book value can be adjusted for goodwill, if the parties agree. Straight capitalization is found from the average net profits over a specified period capitalized at a predetermined rate. The stated purchase price allows for no future adjustments unless the agreement requires periodic recalculations for inflation. These purchase prices also aid in establishing a price for estate planning.

Stockholder Agreements

Selecting and Paying for Insurance

The type of insurance plan to be used depends on the desires of the insureds. Obviously, some plan of permanent insurance will develop cash values or equity to provide a savings fund for retirement. Term insurance can provide a large amount of protection at very little cost. Sometimes, in the case of two stockholders, a joint life plan, which allows insurance on both participants but pays for only the first death, is desirable. However, the survivor is left with no insurance coverage, perhaps at an age when protection is very expensive.

In a cross purchase agreement, the shareholder owns the policies, and the beneficiaries are the surviving stockholders who are bound by the agreement. On the other hand, with a stock purchase agreement, the corporation should be the owner and the beneficiary of the policies. Naming an impartial trustee as beneficiary in either situation can be a satisfying way to complete the final details of collecting and paying the money to the right people.

Payment of premiums may be made by each stockholder on the lives of the other stockholders, by the corporation, or from a pool. In a cross purchase plan, disparities in age among the shareholders could cause one party to pay more than another. Under a stock redemption plan, the corporation will pay the premiums; the pooling arrangement allows all the shareholders to contribute according to their proportionate interest in the corporation or by adding the total life premiums and then dividing the costs among the shareholders.

The Disability Buy-Out

An aspect of the buy-sell agreement generally overlooked is the disability buy-out. People are usually aware of the consequences of death, but few ever recognize and examine the problems arising from disability. Simply stated, an accident or illness that prevents a shareholder from performing his or her duties can cause a loss of profits and make paying the individual very difficult. The solution is a disability buy-out agreement with insurance that guarantees that the disabled shareholder will be paid after a certain waiting period. The amount paid will be based on his or her monthly needs and the value of his or her stock. A policy of this nature should also provide a termination option if the disabled shareholder recovers. Premium payments for this product are not deductible, but the benefits are received tax-free.

Sample Buy-Sell Agreement

The following are sample portions of a buy-sell agreement that has been used by one of the authors:

1. On the death of any stockholder who is a party to this agreement, the Corporation shall purchase, and the estate of the decedent shall sell, all of the decedent's stock in the Corporation. The parties to this agreement shall take such action as may be necessary to permit the Corporation to make such purchase. Title to all of such shares shall be deemed to vest in the Corporation immediately on the death of any such stockholder. The purchase price of such shares shall be computed as provided in this agreement.

2. The value of each share of this Corporation is for all purposes fixed at \$_____ per share. Such value includes an amount representing the goodwill of the Corporation as a going concern. Within 30 days after the end of each fiscal year of the Corporation, the shareholders shall, by unanimous consent, redetermine the value of the said shares for the next fiscal year and endorse that value on the Schedule to this agreement. The Schedule is made a part of this agreement. In the event that, for any reason, the parties to this agreement have made no advance redetermination of the value of the stock for the next fiscal year, the value of the shares shall be the value last set under this agreement, increased or decreased as the case may be, by the proportionate amount, allocated to the shares being valued, of the algebraic sum of the net earnings and net losses, before all federal corporate income, state franchise, income, business, personal property, and municipal taxes, of the Corporation from the date of such last value to the date of the death of the shareholder.

3. The Corporation shall purchase life insurance on the life of each of the parties to this agreement, payable to the Corporation as beneficiary, and shall pay the premiums thereon, in the respective amounts shown below:_____.

4. All certificates of stock of this Corporation shall, in addition to any notice which the articles of incorporation or the bylaws require to

be placed on them, bear the following notice conspicuously on the front or the back: "Sale, assignment, mortgage, hypothecation, transfer, pledge, creation of a security interest in or lien on, encumbrance of, gift of, trust (voting or other) of, or other disposition of these shares is restricted by the terms of a shareholder agreement dated _____, 19___, which may be examined at the Corporation's offices.

Stock Transfer Restrictions

Before the 1982 amendments to the Subchapter S tax laws, the failure of the corporate bylaws or stockholder agreements to restrict transfer of stock meant that *any* transfer, voluntary or involuntary, could automatically result in the loss of the special status as a Subchapter S corporation. This was because the new stockholder had to agree to the status of a Subchapter S corporation within a very short time or the Subchapter S status would automatically be lost. This was a major impetus to adopting stock transfer restrictions.

The tax law has been changed to eliminate this automatic termination, but arrangements to restrict the transfer of stock should still be established either in the bylaws or by separate agreement among all the stockholders. There are still several reasons why these arrangements are necessary:

1. State securities laws may exempt from regulations corporations with a small number of stockholders. The sale by one stockholder of a closely held corporation to several new stockholders could result in a violation of state "blue sky" laws. These laws govern sale of stock to the public and usually define a public sale according to the number of stockholders.

2. The founders of the corporation may wish to keep the number of equity participants to a minimum, or to restrict stockholders to the active founders of the business.

3. If a stockholder can sell his stock, he can also pledge it. If that stockholder then defaults on a loan secured by the stock, the stockholders may find they have a bank for a partner.

4. In order to provide liquidity for stockholders for whom the stock represents a major asset in their estate, the corporation and

stockholders may wish to arrange for a buy-out on death. This requires a written agreement and stock transfer restrictions to control the transfer of the stock both before death and in the estate.

5. In a corporation with only two stockholders, the board of directors might only be required to have as many members as there are stockholders. A sale of stock by one stockholder to two persons could automatically raise the size of the board to three, one for each stockholder. This could mean that the remaining stockholder would be outvoted on the board, even if he or she had a majority of the stock in the corporation.

6. Some states permit corporations to be run by the stockholders, eliminating the need for a board of directors. Increasing the number of stockholders, particularly if some are not close to the corporate operations, could make this a difficult way to run the business. To establish a board of directors, stockholders must amend the articles of incorporation. Any problem in assembling all stockholders to vote for the amendments could make it difficult to adopt the board of directors format.

7. Some states permit stockholders and directors to conduct their official business by unanimous consent, that is, in writing without a formal meeting. The free sale of stock means that new stockholders (and directors) would be involved in running the corporation. Their consent to operating without formal meetings may be difficult to get.

Stock transfer restrictions are an integral element of control, since they assure that sudden changes in the makeup of the stockholders, and thus in the board, will be avoided. In addition, they can assure that a relative balance of power among the parties is maintained. However, this does not work all the time, as the following illustrates:

> In the Guardian Corporation, there are six stockholders, Mr. Sascha, Mr. Pansi, Miss Kali, Miss Gaiety, Ms. Hashi, and Mr. Prissi. Each owns 50 shares, or 16⅔ percent of the total amount of 300 shares of stock. All corporate action is taken by a two-thirds majority. Thus, it takes four stockholders to agree on any action. If Mr. Pansi and Ms. Hashi got married, they control 33⅓ percent of the stock, but they cannot control the corporation because of the two-thirds majority rule. However, if one of the stockholders, say Mr. Sascha, leaves and is required to sell his stock back to all other stockholders, pro rata,

then after the sale, each stockholder owns 60 shares, or 20 percent of the firm. Since two of them are married, together they now control 40 percent of the stock. This essentially gives them a veto over the corporation's actions. Due to the departure of one stockholder, their power in the corporation has increased.

In the above example, note that after the departure of the stockholder, the remaining stockholders still held equal numbers of shares, but their relative power had changed. This is why it is essential to work through the effect of stock transfer restrictions in terms of both stock ownership and control.

There are various kinds of stock transfer restrictions. The most common ones provide (1) that the stockholder must first offer the stock to the corporation and/or proportionately to the other stockholders before transferring it to an outsider, and (2) that the corporation and/or the other stockholders have an absolute option to buy the stock of any stockholder under specified circumstances, such as the death of a stockholder.

In general, state law provides that there can be no restriction on the transfer of stock by virtue of the bylaws or stockholder agreements unless that restriction is stated on the stock certificate. The portions of a stockholder agreement presented earlier in this chapter contain a longer form of stock transfer notice. But on the certificate itself, a legend such as the following is usually sufficient:

This is stock subject to a restriction on transfer as set forth in its bylaws (or in an agreement dated _____, 19__).

PART III

Financing Your Corporation

CHAPTER 12

Capitalizing the Corporation: Stocks and Loans

One of the most crucial steps in organizing a corporation is deciding how you are going to finance it. In general, most corporations are financed (capitalized) through a combination of (1) investments made by the owners in exchange for stock and (2) loans made by owners or other parties. This chapter covers how to determine your financial needs and how stocks and debt (loans) are used to capitalize the corporation. The next three chapters cover private and government sources of money.

Budgeting

Your first step in determining your financial needs is to set up a budget. Once you have a budget, you can see how much capital the corporation will require. The amount of capital you put in must be enough to allow the corporation to achieve its profit or sales goals within the budget that you have set.

A budget enables you to set a profit or sales goal and identify the steps necessary to reach that goal. Thus a budget helps you think about what you want your business to do and to be in the future. By planning, you are in a better position to act to prevent financial and management crises.

In its simplest form, a budget is a detailed plan of future receipts and expenditures—a projected profit and loss statement. Thus, once you reach the end of the period for which you have budgeted, you can compare actual results with anticipated goals. If some of your expenses, for example, are higher than you expected, you can start looking for ways to cut them. Conversely, if you have fallen short of your goals, you may want to look for ways to increase your business income.

As a budget maker, you can either start with a forecast of sales and work down or with a forecast of profits and work up. Most small service businesses use the latter method. In other words, you decide what profit you want to make and then list the expenses that your business will incur to make that predetermined profit.

Before you can use a budget as a plan for increased profits, you have to be sure that your present profits are what they should be. In a service business, the year-end profit should be large enough to make a return on your investment and a return on your own work (paying yourself a salary). Skilled crafts people who own service businesses are misleading themselves if they set as a goal firm profits that are less than they could earn working for someone else. Your net profit after taxes should be at least as much as you could earn if you worked at your trade for a weekly paycheck.

Return on Investment

The year-end profit is too low if it does not include a return on the owner/manager's investment. That investment includes the money you put into the firm when you started it and the profit from prior years that has been left in the firm (the firm's retained earnings). Make sure that the rate of return on your investment is what it should be. Your trade association should be able to provide guidelines about the rate of return on investment in your line of business. A copy of the *National Trade Association Directory* is available from:

Capitalizing the Corporation: Stocks and Loans

Office of Information/Associations
Office of the Chief Counsel for Advocacy
U.S. Small Business Administration
1441 L Street, N.W.
Washington, D.C. 20416

Your accountant and banker are also sources of help.

Target Income

After you know what you made last year, you can set a profit goal for the next year. Be sure that your goal includes a return on your services, a return on your investment, and an amount for state and federal taxes. For example, if you want to earn $10,000 after taxes, your goal before taxes should be about $13,000. You have to add this $3,000 (30 percent) to take care of state and federal taxes. Keep in mind that the larger your goal, the larger the amount that will have to be added to account for taxes. Your accountant can help you determine that amount more exactly.

Reaching the Goal

Once you have decided on your target profit, the next step in preparing a budget is to determine whether or not your business can attain the profit goal. To do this, project your fixed costs and your variable costs. From these three figures—profit, fixed expenses, and variable expenses—you can determine your targeted total income.

Fixed expenses are those that stay the same regardless of sales. Examples of fixed expenses are insurance, rent, property taxes, salaries, depreciation of equipment, interest on borrowed money, building maintenance costs, and office expenses.

Variable expenses are those that vary with sales. In some service businesses, the cost of labor is the biggest variable expense. Sales commissions, payroll taxes, advertising, and delivery expenses are other examples of variable expenses.

Service income is the difference between projected sales and the variable expenses necessary to produce these sales. When this difference equals fixed expenses and the desired profit, you have a workable budget.

In gathering figures for your budget, keep in mind that without accurate information, planning becomes guessing. The owner/manager who has never budgeted should talk with an accountant about a recordkeeping system. (An excellent book for beginners on the subject of accounting and recordkeeping is *Accounting Handbook for Nonaccountants* by Clarence B. Nickerson. The complete reference appears at the back of this book.) Even if you have a recordkeeping system now, look at it in light of the needs for planning and budgeting. It may be that your present system does not break down costs into fixed and variable expenses, or it may be that you need to have a profit and loss (or income) statement at more frequent intervals to determine the seasonal fluctuations of your revenues and expenses.

The forms in Tables 12-1 through 12-3 are designed to help you determine how much cash you will need to get your business started. Table 12-1 requires you to list all of the furniture, fixtures, and equipment that you will need to get started. When you have completed that form, you can enter that total on the next form (Table 12-2) as one of the starting costs that you must pay only once.

The forms in Tables 12-1 and 12-2 are not to be used verbatim, because the needs of every business are different. Instead they should be used as a format for considering *all* of the elements of starting up and operating the business *you* have chosen. Once you have completed them, you know your costs. Then you can consider how you can earn enough income to cover these costs and turn a profit. Remember, your sales should enable you to cover the estimated monthly expenses and contribute to paying off the starting costs.

To keep track of how you are doing, compare your estimate of expenses and income with the actual figures on a regular basis. Use a form like the one in Table 12-3 to do this.

Stock

Ownership of a corporation is designated by ownership of the corporation's stock. As mentioned in Chapter 10, stock is an "equity" security, that is, it represents money the stockholder has invested in the corporation. Among the methods of financing the operations of a corporation, stock is the first one to consider and is probably the most essential to understand.

After a stockholder puts money (or property) in the corporation, the stockholder no longer owns this money or property. The corporation owns its own property. The stockholder has the right to share in the profits of the corporation through dividends paid by the corporation. If the corporation makes no profits, the stockholder receive no dividends. In addition, as the corporation increases (or decreases) in value, the stock likewise increases (or decreases) in

Table 12-1. Cost of furniture, fixtures, and equipment.

(1) Item^a	(2) Amount^b	(3) Price^c	(4) Down- payment	(5) Amount of Each Installment	(6) Estimated Cash
Counters	$	$	$	$	$
Storage shelves, cabinets					
Display stands, shelves, tables					
Cash register					
Safe					
Window display fixtures					
Special lighting					
Outside sign					
Delivery equipment					
Total Furniture, Fixtures, and Equipment (enter this figure in Table 12-2 under Starting Costs You Have to Pay Only Once)					$

^{a}Leave out or add items to suit your business. Use separate sheets to list exactly what you need.
^{b}If you plan to pay cash in full, enter the full amount in this column and in column (6).
^{c}If you are going to pay by installments, fill out columns (3)–(5). In column (6) enter your downpayment plus at least one installment.

value. Essentially, the stockholders share in the growth or decline of the business, taking risks as owners. That means that they can make or lose a substantial amount of money. However, since the corporation has limited liability, the stockholders cannot lose more than they invested.

Stock is an important source of financing. However, since the stockholders share in the profits and losses of the business, they will want to know more about the business than a lender might. In addition, they will want to exercise their rights to vote, so that they can participate in the direction that the corporation takes. A lender does not vote.

Table 12-2. Cash needed for start-up.

Item	Estimated Monthly Expenses Based on Sales of $_____ Per Year	Safety Factor[a]	Estimated Amount of Cash Needed to Start Your Business
Salary of owner/ manager	$	×2	$
All other salaries and wages		×3	
Rent		×3	
Advertising		×3	
Delivery expense		×3	
Supplies		×3	
Telephone and tel- egraph		×3	
Other utilities		×3	
Insurance		Premiums due	
Taxes, including Social Security		×4	
Interest		×3	
Maintenance		×3	
Legal and other professional fees		×3	
Miscellaneous		×3	
Subtotal for This Page			$

Capitalizing the Corporation: Stocks and Loans

Starting Costs You Have to Pay Only Once	Source of Estimate	
Fixtures and equipment	Table 12-1	$
Decorating and remodeling	Contractor	
Installation of fixtures and equipment	Suppliers	
Starting inventory	Suppliers	
Deposits with public utilities	Utility companies	
Legal, accounting, and other fees	Lawyer, accountant, etc.	
Licenses and permits	City and state offices	
Advertising and promotion for opening	Your estimate	
Accounts receivable	Cash needed to purchase stock until credit customers pay	
Emergency cash	For unexpected expenses or losses, special purchases, etc.	
Other	Make separate list and enter total	
Subtotal		$
Add Subtotal from p. 96		$
Total Estimated Cash You Need to Start With		$

[a]The safety factor represents the number of months to be covered by start-up cash. Multiply the estimated monthly expense by this factor and enter the amount in the right-hand column. The factors listed here are typical for one kind of business; you will have to decide how many months to allow for in your business.

Debt

Another way to finance the operations of a corporation is to use debt, that is, to borrow money that the corporation agrees to repay with interest over time. Debt is generally designated by a note or a bond (a long-term promissory note). The bond shows that the corporation is obliged to repay that debt at some future time, usually at a specified rate of interest.

Since bondholders have loaned money to the corporation, they must be repaid. However, the bonds are a form of claim on the assets of the corporation, just as is stock, so that bonds are also considered as a security. Bonds are referred to as a debt security, in contrast to stock, which is an equity security.

Sometimes a bondholder has the option of turning the bond into some other security, such as common or preferred stock. This is a convertible security, and means that debt can be converted into equity. Also, a bond may be backed by the pledge of property, either real or personal. If the bond is backed by the pledge of real property (generally by a mortgage on the property), it is referred to as a mortgage bond. If it is backed by the pledge of personal property, it is called a collateral trust bond.

Any debt security issued to a stockholder (that is, any loan from a stockholder to the corporation), should be treated just like any other debt. If it is not, for example, if the stockholders are paid while other debtors are not, the stockholders run the risk that the IRS will consider it to be just another class of stock rather than a bond. This is because the payments being made to stockholders look like dividends: they are irregular and not made as a part of regular payments to all debtors. If your regular creditors find out about these stockholder loans, they may insist that their right to repayment preempt that of the stockholders. Due to the danger that stockholder loans may be considered to be stock by the IRS, you would do well to talk with your lawyer and/or accountant before issuing debt to stockholders if there will be other outstanding debt. This will prevent any problems with the IRS.

How Much Stock? How Much Debt?

There are no hard and fast rules concerning how much of the capital of the corporation should be in the form of stock and how much should be in the form of debt (loans). Nevertheless, answering the questions below will help you decide what kind of stock or

Table 12-3. Comparison of actual and budgeted sales and expenses.

Actual and Budgeted Sales for the Year Ended December 31, 19___

| | Actual Sales | Budget Sales | Variations from Budget (under) | |
			Quarterly	Cumulative
1st quarter	$	$	$	$
2nd quarter				
3rd quarter				
4th quarter				

Actual and Budgeted Selling Expenses for the Year Ended December 31, 19___

Budget This Month	Actual This Month	Variation This Month	Budget Year to Date	Actual Year to Date	Variations Year to Date	Remarks

debt to use. Following the questions, three subjects are discussed that may influence your decision: thin capitalization, Subchapter S corporations, and Section 1244 stock.

- Will you be dividing control of the business among several persons? Use common stock because it has voting power representing the relative interests of those investing in the corporation.
- Do you want a tax-free incorporation? Stay away from short-term debt because you might be subject to taxation in spite of your intentions. For more on this, see Chapter 7.
- Do you have assets you can lease to the corporation and that the corporation can rent? Consider investing cash in the corporation in return for stock and arranging a lease with the corporation for the asset. This permits the corporation to deduct all of its payments for use of the asset on a current basis. You will receive income from the rental on a current basis. If you turn over the asset to the corporation instead of renting it, the corporation will depreciate the asset over time, and no cash will come back to you from its use, except indirectly as dividends.
- Do you want a steady income in return for the cash you will put in? Use debt. Debt must be paid according to its terms, even if the corporation is not making a profit. This guarantees you a steady stream of cash (unless the business fails completely). With stock, you can receive only dividends, and payment of dividends might be erratic or nonexistent if the corporation is not profitable.
- Do you want the business to grow so you can sell it at a profit? Use stock. That way, the business can be sold by selling the stock, and you will receive a capital gain on the sale of the stock. If the business is not incorporated and you sell it, some of the sale price you receive will be in the form of ordinary income, which is taxed at a higher rate.
- Do you have an investor who wants to share in capital growth but also wants a steady income? Consider issuing the investor preferred stock without voting powers. This kind of stock can have a guaranteed dividend; in fact, the corporation can be required to make up for any dividend payments it had to skip

because it was not profitable enough. Being stock, any growth will be in the form of a capital asset, the sale of which will produce capital gains as opposed to ordinary income.

- Do you want your investment partially returned to you as the business grows? Put part in stock and part in debt. This way you receive money on a current basis (repayments of the debt) and share in the growth of the business through the stock's increase in value.

- Are you using the corporation as a way of setting up an estate for your spouse and/or children? Use common stock and set up buy-sell agreements to provide liquidity. This will permit the estate to sell your stock at a set price and put cash, not stock, in the estate for your family.

- Do you have investors who do not want to be involved in the management of the corporation? Use preferred, nonvoting stock. This way, they share in the capital growth of the business but cannot vote for directors. You may wish to set a minimum, a guaranteed, or a maximum dividend on this stock.

- Do you expect initial short-term losses that you could deduct if you were not incorporated? Use common stock in a Subchapter S corporation in the amount you think you might lose. That way any initial losses can be passed through directly to you. During the period that the corporation does not earn profits against which to offset these losses, you can deduct them from income you have received from other sources.

- Is there a possibility that the corporation will become worthless and be unable to repay you if you loan it money? Put your investment in the corporation as Section 1244 stock, not as debt. This way, if the corporation goes under, you can deduct the total amount of your investment as a current loss for tax purposes. If the corporation owes you money, you may have to prove to the IRS that there was a valid loan, that it went bad, and when it went bad.

- Do you want to be free to accumulate profits in the business in the early stages so that the business can expand? Use common stock and stay away from preferred stock or debt. That way any money you make can accumulate in the corporation. It does not have to be paid out as interest (on debt) or as guaranteed dividends (on preferred stock).

Thin Capitalization

There can be excellent tax advantages in issuing debt instruments as well as stock to the persons who organize the corporation. Financing through debt instruments is commonly known as "thin capitalization" since only a small portion of the corporation's capital is actually equity, and the rest is in the form of debt.

One of the main benefits of this kind of mixture of stocks and loans is that the repayment of the principal of the loan is tax-free to the stockholder and interest payments are a business deduction for the corporation. The stockholders, however, do pay tax on the interest income. A related benefit is that, since the interest paid on the debt instruments (loans) is deductible by the corporation, the corporation's overall tax liability is lessened (in contrast to dividends, which are paid with after-tax profits). If the same amount of money were paid in the form of dividends, the stockholders would pay taxes on all of it, after the corporation had already done so.

Another benefit is that repayment of loans can help avoid the accumulated earnings tax by removing cash from the corporation. This tax is paid by the corporation if it keeps too much cash or other earnings. If the corporation pays out the same money in dividends, it must first pay corporate income taxes on those funds, so repayment of loans is a preferable way to reduce accumulated earnings.

A final advantage is that if the corporation fails, members of the corporation are both creditors and stockholders. As creditors, they may be able to receive a portion of their loan back; if they are only stockholders they will receive nothing. For more details on the relative position of debtors and stockholders in the case of bankruptcy, see Chapter 18.

On the other side of the coin, there is a possibility that using thin capitalization will result in the IRS classifying everything as stock and not debt. The IRS does this to reinstate the very tax circumstances that you have sought to avoid—the taxation of withdrawals both at the corporate and individual level. If an IRS challenge is successful, both the corporation and the stockholders will be subject to a large tax liability. Before you consider thin capitalization, check with your lawyer or accountant and let them set it up. This may protect you later if you have a problem with the IRS.

To help assure that thin capitalization will not get you into trouble with the IRS:

■ The debt must be clearly shown on the corporation's books.
■ The debts owed stockholders should be treated like any other debt; repayment must *not* be delayed until other debts of the corporation are paid.
■ The debt should have a definite date for repayment.

Do You Plan to Lose Money?

Even with the best of plans, it may be clear that a business could lose money, or that it will lose money in the short run. You can take advantage of this with two differing devices, the Subchapter S corporation and Section 1244 stock.

Subchapter S Corporations

When you use a Subchapter S corporation, all of the corporation's profits and, more importantly, its losses are passed through to the stockholders. So if the corporation is going to lose money at the beginning, the stockholders might do well to form a Subchapter S corporation so that the corporation's losses can be deducted right away on the stockholders' individual tax returns. This can represent a substantial tax saving if the stockholders have income from other sources, such as another job, investments, or salary earned by a spouse. Once the tax advantage is over, the corporation can give up its Subchapter S status. Subchapter S is discussed in more detail in Chapter 4.

Section 1244 Stock

Section 1244 of the Internal Revenue Code recognizes that high risk is inherent in starting up many small corporations. Under Section 1244, the original stockholders in a small corporation can claim up to $50,000 per year in ordinary deductions for losses on stock classed as "small business stock." This means that the stockholder can deduct a loss if the stock is sold at a loss or if the stock becomes worthless.

To qualify under Section 1244, the following requirements of the Internal Revenue Code must be met:

1. The corporation can issue no more than $1,000,000 in stock.
2. The benefit can be available only to the original stockholders.
3. The stock involved must be common stock issued for money or property. Stock issued for other stock or securities cannot be Section 1244 stock.
4. The corporation must be an operating company. That means its income must not come primarily from sources that are "passive," such as royalties, dividends, interest, and rents.
5. The stock must be that issued at the beginning, when the corporation was organized. It cannot be stock issued later on.

To issue Section 1244 stock, at its organizational meeting the board of directors should adopt a resolution like the one shown below. Since there are no adverse consequences to issuing Section 1244 stock, most new corporations should consider issuing it.

RESOLUTION OF THE BOARD OF DIRECTORS: The Board of Directors of the Corporation has determined that, to attract investment in the Corporation, the Corporation shall be organized and managed so that it is a "Small Business Corporation" as defined in IRC Section 1244(c)(1), and so that the shares of stock issued by the Corporation are "Section 1244 Stock," as defined in that same section. Compliance with that section will permit the stockholders to treat the loss on the sale or exchange of their shares as "ordinary losses" on their personal income tax returns. IT IS RESOLVED that the proper officers of the Corporation are hereby authorized to sell and issue common stock of the Corporation in an aggregate amount of money and other personal property (contributed to capital and as paid-in surplus), which, together with the aggregate amount of common stock outstanding at the time of issuance, does not exceed $1,000,000, and IT IS FURTHER RESOLVED that the sale and issuance of this stock shall be conducted in compliance with IRC Section 1244 so that the Corporation and its stockholders may have the benefits of that section, and IT IS FURTHER RESOLVED that the proper officers of this Corporation are directed to maintain such accounting records as are necessary so that any stockholder experiencing a loss on the transfer of common stock of the Corporation may determine whether he or she qualifies for "ordinary loss" deductions on his or her personal income tax return.

CHAPTER *13*

Getting Private Financing

There are any number of reasons a business may need to seek additional financing. The company could be expanding, new equipment or facilities might be needed, or a successful business might have outgrown its local bank. In planning for the financial life of your business, you have a choice of several different means of raising additional capital:

1. Taking out a mortgage on the company's building.
2. Asking suppliers to extend credit on purchases.
3. Borrowing on the company's receivables and inventory.
4. Borrowing on a note basis from friends.
5. Borrowing the cash surrender value of life insurance policies.
6. Contacting an insurance company for a long-term loan.
7. Contacting the Small Business Administration for a business loan if you are eligible. In some areas you may be able to get financing from a small business investment company.
8. Selling a portion of the stock to the company's employees for cash.
9. Selling some of the stock to another company for cash. In a merger, you can use the other company's credit worthiness.

10. Contacting a regional investment banker who can privately find a lender by using the company's stock as collateral.
11. Contacting a national investment banker who would underwrite some of the company's stock. This is referred to as "going public."

The use of private sources of capital will be discussed in this chapter. The sale of stock to outsiders is covered in Chapter 14, together with "going public." The availability of public sources, principally the SBA's loan guarantee program, is covered in Chapter 15. In every case, you are essentially bringing "partners" into the business, since those who invest in your business or who loan you money will always take a special interest in what you do and how you do it. In some cases, they will even be able to tell you what you can and cannot do with the business. Their money has made them partners.

Commercial Financing Options

There are many alternatives to consider in deciding where to go for financing, and each alternative has its merits. There are federal government loan programs, state and local government programs, insurance companies that also lend money, quasi-government lenders such as local development companies, venture capital companies, and even private placement loan brokers. The viability of any of these depends in part on what the borrower plans to do with the proceeds of the loan. Whether the loan is used to purchase inventory or equipment, to support accounts receivable, to pay off existing debt, or to fund continued research and development frequently determines which lender is interested in your request and which program you qualify for.

In determining how much money you need and why you need it, consider the following questions. How you answer them will tell you (and your lenders) a lot about why you need money, how much you actually need, and for how long:

■ Are your sales adequate? Can your sales (or projected sales) support the expense of the business and the costs associated with the loan?

- Are you asking for a loan to bolster sagging sales volume? To buy additional stocks of high-volume merchandise that you feel has even greater potential? To create a new image by an advertising campaign? You should estimate how much income this will generate, when, and how much it will cost. Make sure that it will pay for itself on a timely basis.
- What is your receivables position? Are your accounts going uncollected and getting old? In effect, do you need money to carry old accounts? Perhaps you should consider sending these out for collection and also revising your position on granting credit. Also, if your receivables are old, they may not be worth their face value in a lender's determination of the worth of the business.
- Is your profit margin adequate? Are you doing a lot of business and showing a lack of profit, indicating that expenses are not being controlled? If so, consider whether borrowing is the solution. Perhaps you should consider changing your prices and attacking your costs. If you need help in reducing costs, a loan may be in order, but you should have already determined how much you need to reduce costs (by more automation, for example), how much this will save, and over what period.
- Is your market sufficient? What is your breakeven point for profits? If you do not know this, your lender may not have much confidence in your ability to repay a loan. This kind of analysis can help you decide not only how much money you need, but for what.
- What is your plan for repayment? Do you forecast your cash income and expenses realistically? If you do not estimate on a realistic basis, all you will do is get into additional difficulty. Borrowing on unrealistic assumptions can mean that your lender will eventually move in to protect its loan and take your business away from you.
- Can you lease instead of buy? In other words, have you looked at all alternatives, from the point of practicality and affordability?

Types of Money

When you consider borrowing, determine the *kind* of money you need. A business uses four basic types of money in its operations.

Your purpose in borrowing the money will determine the type of money you wish to obtain.

Trade credit. This type of money is not borrowed. It is money you owe your suppliers who permit you to carry your fast-moving inventory on an open account. A good credit experience is proven evidence of your ability to repay borrowed funds.

Short-term credit. This type of money is provided by banks and other lenders to support your purchases of inventory for special reasons, such as buying inventory for the next selling season. Such loans are self-liquidating because they generate the sales dollars needed to repay them. You repay short-term credit in less than a year.

Long-term credit. These are loans for more than a year and are used for expansion or modernization of your business. The loans are repaid out of accumulated profits. Usually, the evidence of this type of loan in a small business is a mortgage or a promissory note with terms.

Equity funds. This type of money is never repaid. You get it by relinquishing a part of your profits to an investor. That is, you sell an interest in your business.

Many owner/managers fail to recognize the differences among the four types of money. Keep in mind that borrowed money used for a temporary purpose should be used in the profit-producing areas of your business and repaid out of that operation (at least on your own books). Equity funds remain in the business and increase the net worth for the owner.

Types of Loans

To help understand financing options, we have outlined the basic types of commercial financing options available to you:

Short-term bank loan. This can be used for purposes such as financing accounts receivable for 30 to 60 days or for building a seasonal inventory over a period of 5 to 6 months. Banks grant such money either on your general credit reputation with an unsecured loan or on a secured loan against collateral.

Unsecured loan. This is the most common form of bank credit for short-term purposes. You do not supply collateral because the bank relies on your credit reputation.

Getting Private Financing

Secured loan. This involves a pledge of some or all of your assets. The bank requires security as a protection for its depositors against the risks that are involved even in business situations where the chances of success are good.

Term borrowing. This provides money you plan to pay back over a fairly long time. Some people break it down into two forms: (1) intermediate—loans for longer than one year but less than five years, and (2) long-term—loans for longer than five years.

Equity capital. Some people confuse term borrowing and equity (or investment) capital. There is a difference. You don't have to repay equity money. It is money you get by selling a part interest of your business.

Types of Collateral

When lending money, creditors usually want to make sure that the loan will be fully repaid. To do this, they evaluate the soundness of the business and its ability to generate sufficient means to repay the loan. They also want collateral—that is, something (or someone) they can turn to for money if the business does not repay the loan. Providing collateral traditionally means pledging an asset, which means the lender has the right to sell that asset if the loan is not repaid. There are other types of collateral in business, a number of which are discussed below.

Endorsers. An endorser is another person brought in to sign a note in order to bolster your own credit. Endorsers are contingently liable for the note they sign. If the borrower fails to pay off the loan, the bank expects the endorser to pay it. Sometimes the endorser may be asked to put up collateral or pledge some of its own assets.

Co-maker. This obligation is made jointly with the borrower. In this case, the bank can collect directly from either the maker or the co-maker.

Guarantor. This is where you have a person guarantee the payment of a note by signing a guaranty commitment. Both private and government lenders often require guarantees from officers of the corporation in order to assure continuity of effective management.

Assignment of leases. The assigned loan is similar to the guarantee. It is used in some franchise situations. The bank lends the money on a building and takes back a mortgage. Then the lease that the dealer and the parent company work out is assigned so that the bank automatically receives the rent payments. In this manner, the bank is guaranteed the repayment of the loan.

Warehouse receipts. Banks also take commodities as security by lending money on a warehouse receipt. Such a receipt is usually delivered to the bank and shows that the merchandise used as security either has been placed in a public warehouse or has been left on your premises under the control of a bonded employee.

Evaluating the Applicant

When applying for a loan, the borrower will usually be expected to provide the following documentation:

- A statement of current assets and liabilities
- A current profit and loss statement
- Profit and loss statements and/or corporate tax returns for the past three years
- Projected revenues and expenses

Trust receipts and floor planning. Merchandise such as automobiles, appliances, and boats must be displayed to be sold. A loan can be made against these kinds of items with a note and a trust receipt. This trust receipt is the legal paper for floor planning. It is used for serial-numbered merchandise. When you sign one, you (1) acknowledge receipt of the merchandise, (2) agree to keep the merchandise in trust for the bank, and (3) promise to pay the bank as you sell the goods.

Chattel mortgages. If you buy equipment such as a cash register or a delivery truck, you may get a chattel mortgage loan. You give the bank a lien on the equipment you are buying.

Once you have supplied the necessary information to the prospective lender, the next step in the borrowing process is the evaluation of your application. The processing officer, whether at a bank or in the SBA, considers a number of things when determining whether to grant or refuse the loan. These include the borrower's debt-paying record to suppliers, banks, home mortgage holders, and other creditors; the ratio of the borrower's debt to net worth; the past earnings of the company; and the value and condition of the collateral that the borrower offers for security.

When the Bank Turns You Down

Banks are the major source of financing for new corporations. However, many businesses experience difficulty in obtaining financing from banks. "Your bank has just turned down your loan request" is an oft-heard statement and helps reinforce the idea that bankers enjoy only foreclosures or repossessions.

Believe it or not, bankers actually look for reasons to say yes to loan requests. Logic dictates this. Take a look at any bank balance sheet—the largest income entries can be attributed to loan fees and interest. Turning down a loan also bothers bankers because it almost always loses a customer for the bank. No business, no matter what its product, likes to lose a potentially good customer.

When a banker does turn down a loan, it can be for a number of reasons. It may be for credit reasons. It may be that the banker is uncomfortable with your industry and its future. It may be that the banker is uncomfortable with your management ability. It may be that the banker has concluded that it is simply not worth taking the risk.

When the bank says no, there *are* viable alternatives. These are covered in the sections below and in the next two chapters.

Venture Capital Firms

One alternative to the more traditional sources of funding is venture capital. Venture capital firms are owners. They hold stock in your company, adding their invested capital to its equity base. Therefore, they examine existing or planned products or services and the potential markets for them with extreme care. They invest only in firms they believe can rapidly increase sales and generate substantial profits. The reason for this is that venture capital firms invest for long-term capital, not for interest income as banks do. A common estimate is that they look for three to five times their investment back in five to seven years.

Venture capital is a risky business, because it is difficult to judge the worth of companies in the early stages of operation, which is typically when venture capital companies get involved. Furthermore, their investments are not protected in the case of a failure. So, to reduce their risks, most venture capital firms set rigorous policies for venture proposal size, maturity of the seeking company, and evaluation procedures.

Most venture capital firms are interested in projects requiring an investment of at least $250,000 to $1,500,000. Of the over 1,000 projects submitted for consideration to these firms, 90 percent will be rejected immediately. Venture capital firms want to assume control and be able to rescue their investment if your corporation goes bad. They will almost always include protective covenants in their equity financing agreements permitting them to take over control and appoint new officers if your financial performance is poor.

Sources of Venture Capital

There are a number of different types of persons or businesses that may be willing to invest capital in a project that promises to be highly successful. These are described briefly in the paragraphs below.

Traditional partnerships. These are often established by wealthy families to manage aggressively a portion of their funds by investing in smaller companies.

Professionally managed pools. These pools include institutional money and operate like the traditional partnerships.

Investment banking firms. These usually trade in more established securities, but they occasionally form investor syndicates for venture proposals.

Insurance companies. These often require that their investment managers put a portion of their equity into loans to smaller companies as protection against inflation.

Manufacturing companies. Some of these companies look upon investing in smaller companies as a means of supplementing their own research and development programs. Some *Fortune* 500 companies have specific venture capital operations to help keep them abreast of technological innovations.

Getting Private Financing

Small Business Investment Companies. SBICs are licensed by the SBA. They may provide management assistance as well as venture capital. SBICs can be interested in an equity position, as venture capital, or merely in lending for the long term on a fully secured basis.

Elements of a Venture Proposal

The following list outlines the elements typically required in a proposal to a venture capital firm. In fact, similar information will have to be provided to the lender or investor, no matter what type of financing you seek. Provide as much of this information as you can.

1. *Purpose and objectives.* A summary of the what and why of the project.
2. *Proposed financing.* The amount of money you will need at the beginning and through the maturity of the project proposed, how the proceeds will be used, how you plan to structure the financing, and why the amount designated is required. ·
3. *Marketing.* A description of the market segment you have or plan to get, your competition, the characteristics of that market, and your plans for getting or holding the market segment you are aiming at.
4. *History of the firm.* A summary of organizational milestones, description of employees and employee relations, explanation of banking relationships, recounting of major services or products your firm has offered during its existence, and any other pertinent details.
5. *Description of the product or service.* A full description of the product, process, or service offered by the firm and the costs associated with it.
6. *Financial statements.* These would be needed for at least the past three years together with pro forma projections (balance sheets, income statements, and cash flows) for the next three to five years, showing the anticipated effect if the project is undertaken and if the financing is secured. This should include an analysis of the key variables affecting the corpora-

tion's financial performance, showing what could happen if the projected level of revenue is not attained.

7. *Capitalization.* A list of shareholders, how much is invested to date, and in what form (equity or debt).
8. *Biographical sketches.* The work histories of the owners and key employees.
9. *Principal suppliers and customers.*
10. *Anticipated problems.* A candid discussion of any contingent liabilities, pending litigation, tax or patent difficulties, and any other contingencies that might adversely affect the project you are proposing.
11. *Advantages.* A discussion of what is special about your product, service, marketing plans, or other elements of your project that give it something unique.

Employee Stock Ownership Plans

In 1974, Congress created the Employee Stock Ownership Plan (ESOP). Basically the ESOP is a profit-sharing plan that allows the company involved to make contributions to the plan in its own stock as well as in cash. That way, the corporation's contributions stay in the corporation, either because the fund buys stock from the corporation or because the corporation contributes treasury stock, not cash.

An important consideration is that, after the plan has been set up, the corporation making the stock contributions can deduct the value of the stock given to the fund. This means that at the 46 percent corporate tax rate, for each dollar of stock the corporation puts into the fund, it saves $0.46 in cash. The corporation can provide for profit sharing by its employees, and still free up operating funds for internal expansion, via the ESOP's tax benefits.

The ESOP also gives employees an incentive to work hard, for as the corporation prospers, the value of the stock in the profit-sharing fund will increase. Retiring employees will receive either cash or the stock.

For the employer who also owns stock in the corporation, an ESOP provides a market for his or her stock, since the profit-sharing fund can buy the stock it needs to acquire from the current

114

stockholders. This can be done without the adverse tax consequences of having the corporation actually redeem the stock of one stockholder. The transaction is a sale of stock, which is subject to capital gains taxes, rather than a partial redemption of stock, which is subject to higher ordinary income taxes.

Some business owners worry about the fact that the ESOP can end up owning the corporation. Although this is possible, the law permits the ESOP to be set up as a voting trust, with the employer having the right to vote the stock. Thus, although the ESOP might own a majority of the stock, the other stockholders can still maintain control of the corporation.

Setting up an ESOP is not simple, nor is it cheap. But for a corporation that foresees long-term growth, desires its employees to share in the profits, and needs large amounts of capital for expansion, the ESOP can be a valuable financing tool.

Promoters

Promoters are individuals who are involved in setting up new businesses in exchange for stock in that business. From their point of view, they will get stock in the new business for the services they performed before the incorporation. These services typically involve obtaining financing by locating both potential stockholders and sources of debt financing.

Special care must be taken in dealing with promoters. First, they will be acting on behalf of the corporation before it even comes into existence. This means the corporation must be very careful when it ratifies any contracts the promoters make on behalf of the corporation. Corporations often ratify and accept all contracts made for the corporation during the course of the first meeting of the board of directors. Do not do this. Ratify and accept only specifically identified contracts. Any contracts not ratified by the board are not binding on the corporation. You should no more give a blanket ratification to the actions of a promoter than you should give the promoter a blank check.

When deciding how much stock to give the promoter for his efforts on behalf of the corporation, remember that the value of the services to the corporation must be reasonably related to the value of the stock given the promoter. If it is not, then the promoter may have been given a gift by the corporation or the corporation may be considered to have "watered" its own stock. (Watered stock is stock given for little or no consideration. On the books the stock looks valuable, but in fact it is not supported by anything of value. If the value of the stock has been watered, or deflated in this way, a creditor might be able to force all the stockholders to pay in more money to the corporation to restore the value of the stock.)

Promoters can be helpful to corporations that have special financial needs at start-up. Since the corporation does not yet exist when the promoter begins work, the organizers of the corporation might want an agreement with the promoter stating what the promoter will be doing and what stock he will get, and agreeing to vote for ratification of any contracts that are made in accordance with the preincorporation agreement. Even with this, the acts of the promoter should be reviewed and contracts ratified individually as described above.

Without a clear agreement with the promoter outlining what the promoter is to do, what he cannot do, what the promoter will receive, and what the new corporation can expect to receive, disagreements and arguments will inevitably arise. This is because the parties are all acting to create and benefit from something that does not yet exist—the new corporation. Agreements with a promoter should not be entered into lightly. This is one situation when the advice of a lawyer should always be sought before the parties even begin negotiations.

CHAPTER 14

Selling Your Stock

When you start your corporation, or even after you have owned it for a while, you may find you need additional sources of financing. One way to get additional financing is to sell your stock, either to one or more individuals, who in effect become your partners, or to a wider public. Some of the important ramifications of selling your stock, either privately or publicly, are considered in this chapter.

Bringing in "Partners"

One way to tap a source of money is to bring in a rich "partner." Of course, what we mean is to bring in another stockholder. If you are considering this, remember that once you have someone else in the corporation, many things can change.

In deciding whether to bring someone in and who that should be, consider the following questions:

- What kind of a person do you need? Someone to provide money, customers, on-site assistance, or something else?
- Are the people you are considering compatible with you and with the business?

- If they are going to invest in the business, what are they going to provide: cash, property, other assets, their expertise?
- What do they want for their investment: a share of the corporation reflecting its capital growth (stock), a share of the corporation's current income (dividends), regular income from their investment (dividends on preferred stock), set income reflecting the size of their investment (interest on debt)?
- What are you willing to give up: voting stock, the right to guaranteed dividends, interest payments, a place on the board of directors, an officer's position, a veto over the corporation's activities?

The answers to these questions will help you determine who you want in and on what terms.

When you add someone else to your group of principal owners, you should undertake the same analysis about whether to incorporate and how to structure the corporation that you undertook when you started. That includes considering whether it should continue as a corporation, be a Subchapter S corporation, or have agreements among stockholders on the purchase of stock, and what kinds of stock should be created.

Selling Stock

In theory, any time you try to sell any stock to anyone, you have to have permission from the state and/or federal government. However, most transactions involving the stock of a small corporation are not subject to direct regulation.

For example, in most states, if you elect to be a close corporation, you will be agreeing to make no public offering of the stock of the corporation and to keep the number of stockholders in the corporation below a certain number. If you do this, you will not have to register the corporation and its securities with the state.

If you will be trying to sell the stock publicly, or expect to offer the stock to people who are not going to be real insiders to the business (that is, work there or have a personal knowledge of what the business will do), you must be careful not to accidentally "go public." You avoid going public (and being regulated) by using one of two devices: the private placement or the small offering exemption.

Basically these are exemptions from registration requirements imposed on corporations by the Securities and Exchange Commission. These exemptions are encompassed in what is called Regulation D, adopted by the SEC in 1982, replacing Rules 146, 240, and 242. (When using other reference materials on this subject, be sure they are current. If they are dated prior to 1982 or make frequent references to Rules 146, 240, and 242, they are out of date.)

Although Regulation D provides for exemptions, they are *not* automatic. You will have to apply for them and submit evidence that you are eligible for them. If you qualify, then you will be exempted from some of the more onerous requirements imposed on public corporations. The philosophy here is that small, closely held corporations should not have to meet the burdens imposed by the U.S. Securities Acts in order to get relatively small amounts of financing from small numbers of sophisticated investors, such as venture capital firms.

You will have to balance the costs of filing for these exemptions with the need for the capital that might be available only by making use of these exemptions. The major consideration here is that failing to seek an exemption from the SEC could result in an accidental violation of the Securities Acts, with severe penalties. Going through with the Regulation D procedures can be the way to open up new sources of financing to your business, beyond that available from persons you will bring in, and at less cost than comes from going public.

One good thing is that you do not have to go through the Regulation D process unless and until you are ready to seek private investors for your firm. If you think that this might be the way for you to go, check with a securities attorney who is an expert in this area.

Going Public

There are several key benefits to becoming a publicly traded corporation. First, it provides additional means of obtaining funds for use in the business, and being a publicly traded corporation can make it easier to borrow money at better rates. A public corporation can also show a proven market value for the stock held by the founders. Furthermore, the process of going public will require a more stringent management system. It forces a legal and accounting review of the operations of the business; it requires the installation of sophisticated accounting and management systems; and it can force a review of the future prospects of the corporation. All of this can be beneficial to the present and future operations of the business.

But there are major drawbacks to going public. Operating as a public company is a considerable change from operating as a closely held or private company. What the public corporation does is in the public eye. This means that a number of the private corporation's accustomed habits must change. For example, the corporation will have to disclose stockholdings, insider control arrangements, its dependence on particular customers or product lines, and the compensation of the top officers of the corporation.

The public corporation also must submit reports to the Securities and Exchange Commission at regular intervals and when certain events occur, such as the purchase or sale of stock by key insiders. Any future offerings of stock must be registerd with the SEC before it can be offered for sale. The costs of registering a public offering of stock are extremely high; they can include legal fees up to $100,000, a 10 percent underwriting fee, and a major commitment of time by senior management. Last but not least, the corporation's accounting practices must be revised to conform to SEC requirements. These go beyond generally accepted accounting practices.

Complying with the SEC and State Laws

Congress has passed and updated numerous laws pertaining to fair practices in the securities industry. They are generally administered by the Securities and Exchange Commission, an independent regulatory commission. The SEC issues rules and regulations under each act, and the practice in the securities industry is to refer to each act by its name and to index regulations under the act they are designed to implement. Some regulations are so important they are referred to by their own name, without reference to the authorizing act, e.g., Rule 10-b-5. These statutes and rules are broad in scope and cover virtually all of the activities of a public corporation related to the sale of its stock, including requirements that the public be notified of events that might impact the stock's price.

Selling Your Stock

Business owners have often made the mistake of assuming that, since a potential stock offering is subject to federal regulation, their concerns end there. That is wrong. In fact, compliance with federal regulations usually will not exempt the transaction from having to comply with state law.

The laws of the states in this regard are not uniform. But there is a common pattern to them. Before anyone can solicit the sale of stock or issue stock, a corporation must get permission to do so in almost every state (except Delaware and Nevada). State laws regulating the sale of a corporation's stock are enacted to protect the public from being defrauded and are known as "blue sky laws." The sale of stock that violates any of these laws is voidable; that is, it may be rescinded by the purchaser.

Compliance with these laws is costly and time-consuming, although the states have begun to routinely exempt small offerings of stock where the corporation is not really publicly held. However, unless you qualify under one of the exemptions, the corporation considering going public must fully and completely comply with these regulations, both in the state of incorporation and in any state in which it sells or offers its stock for sale.

CHAPTER 15

Getting Help from the Government

If you are a small-business owner and have had trouble getting a loan from commercial sources, you might qualify for a loan made directly by or guaranteed by the federal government. These federal loan programs are administered by the Small Business Administration (SBA). Other sources of money are the grants to small businesses made by individual government agencies for the research and development of products or processes needed by that agency. Most states also have programs to help local businesses, although the assistance offered is usually not financial. A few states, however, have small-business loan programs.

Small Business Administration Loans

The Small Business Administration assists small businesses with many programs and publications. What most businesses hear about are the loan programs. The SBA offers two basic types of loan programs:

1. Loans made by private lenders, usually banks, and guaranteed by the SBA. This type of funding is much more abundant and easier to obtain than direct loans from the SBA.
2. Loans made directly by the SBA. The availability of these loans varies from year to year, depending upon how much money is appropriated by Congress for this purpose.

By law, the SBA cannot make or guarantee a loan if reasonable commercial business financing can be found. If you seek funding and have been turned down by banks or private lenders, then you may apply directly for an SBA loan. However, the rules vary by area. For example, if you do business in a city with a population of over 200,000, you have to be turned down by two banks.

Your business must also be independently owned and operated for profit, must not be dominant in its field, and must meet certain standards of size in terms of employees or annual receipts. Loans cannot be made to speculative businesses, newspapers, or businesses engaged in gambling. Applicants for loans must agree to abide by SBA regulations that there will be no discrimination in employment or services to the public based on race, color, religion, national origin, sex, or marital status.

In addition to its basic loans programs, the SBA offers loans or loan guarantees for:

- Low-income and other disadvantaged persons.
- Small firms owned by handicapped persons.
- Small firms engaged in manufacturing, selling, installing, servicing, or developing specific energy conservation measures.
- Development companies for projects aiding small businesses in urban or rural communities.
- Loans and revolving lines of credit for export purposes.
- Guaranteed loans for qualified Employee Stock Ownership Trusts.

The SBA also licenses, regulates, and provides financial help to private firms called "small business investment companies." These companies supply equity capital and regular loans to small firms with unusual growth potential. These are discussed in Chapter 13.

In general, direct SBA loans carry interest rates that are slightly lower than those in the private financial markets. However, direct loans are available only to those who cannot get funding at reasonable terms elsewhere. If you find that banks and private investors will not support your business with a loan, instead of immediately applying to the SBA, find out why the banks won't give you a loan. Perhaps there is something in the way you have conducted your business that needs further thought. Bankers are usually willing to take the time to talk with you and go over your plans with you. Remember that it benefits a bank to have your growing company as a client.

Eligibility

At present, the eligibility for SBA loans varies by industry and by SBA program. As with any government-sponsored program, you should always check with the agency involved to make certain what programs are currently available and what the current requirements are. Some of the requirements for various industries are outlined below.

- *Manufacturing.* Maximum number of employees may range from 250 to 15,000, depending upon the industry in which the applicant is primarily engaged.
- *Wholesaling.* Yearly sales not exceeding $1 million to $22 million, depending upon the particular industry.
- *Services.* Annual receipts not exceeding $2 million to $8 million, depending on the particular industry.
- *Retailing.* Annual sales or receipts not exceeding $2 million to $7.5 million, depending upon the industry.
- *Construction.* General construction: average annual receipts not exceeding $9.5 million for the past three fiscal years. Special trade construction: annual receipts not exceeding $1 million or $2 million for the past three fiscal years, depending upon the industry.
- *Agriculture.* Annual receipts not exceeding $1 million.

The SBA is also interested in your soundness of character, your management ability, and the soundness of your corporation. Specifically, the SBA requires that a candidate for a loan be of good character, show that he or she is capable of operating a business successfully, and show that the business can operate on a sound financial basis. The candidate must demonstrate that, on the basis of past earnings (unless the corporation is brand-new) and projected future earnings, the firm has the ability to repay the loan and other fixed debts, if any, out of its profits. The loan must be secured (through collateral, for example) so as to reasonably assure payment. The candidate must also have sufficient personal assets to withstand possible losses, particularly during the early stages of a new venture.

Loan Terms

Loans made directly by the SBA have a maximum of $150,000. The guaranteed loan program permits the SBA to guarantee a maximum of $500,000. When neither private financing nor a loan guarantee is available, the SBA may provide loan funds on an "immediate participation" basis with a bank. The bank disburses part of the loan at market interest rates. The balance of the loan is disbursed directly by the SBA, at a lower interest rate. The SBA's share of an immediate participation loan may not exceed $150,000. These administrative limits are subject to change. Also, they do not always hold across the board. For example, a handicapped assistance loan made directly by the SBA is limited to $100,000. Local development company loans also carry a maximum of $500,000.

In general, the terms of an SBA loan are as follows:

1. Regular business loans have a maximum maturity of 25 years.
2. Working capital loans are generally limited to seven years.
3. Interest rates on direct loans and SBA's share of a medium participation loan are tied to the cost of money to the federal government and are adjusted periodically.
4. The interest rate is 3 percent for SBA's share of handicapped assistance loans.

As with any commercial loans, SBA loans, whether direct from the agency or through a bank with an SBA guarantee, require that the borrower put up collateral. Acceptable collateral for an SBA loan could be a mortgage on land, a building, and/or equipment;

assignment of warehouse receipts for marketable merchandise; a mortgage on chattels; guarantees or personal endorsements; or, in some instances, assignment of current receivables of the business.

Applying for an SBA Loan

To apply for a loan from the SBA when you are already in business, first prepare the following documentation:

1. A current financial statement (balance sheet) listing all assets and all liabilities of the business.
2. An earnings (profit and loss) statement for the current period to the date of the balance sheet.
3. A current personal financial statement of the owner, or each partner or stockholder owning 20 percent or more of the stock in the business.
4. A list of the collateral to be offered as security for the loan with an estimate of the present market value of each item.
5. A statement of the amount of the loan requested and what it is going to be used for.

Armed with all the proper paperwork, go to a bank and ask for a direct loan. If the bank turns you down, ask the bank to make the loan under the SBA's loan guarantee plan or immediate participation plan. If the bank is interested in making these kinds of loans, the banker will contact the SBA and will work jointly with you to process the loan. If a guarantee is not available from that bank, write or visit the nearest SBA office. If needed, an SBA representative will come out to your business and talk with you. It helps to have all the paperwork sent to the SBA in advance.

If you want to use an SBA loan (or SBA guarantee) to start a new business, do the following:

1. Describe the type of business you plan to start.
2. Describe the experience you have and demonstrate your management capabilities.
3. Prepare an estimate of how much you or others have to invest in the business and how much you need to borrow.

4. Prepare a current financial statement (balance sheet) listing all your personal assets and liabilities.
5. Prepare a detailed projection of earnings for the first year of operation of the business.
6. List the collateral to be offered as security for the loan indicating your estimate of the present market value of each item.

When you have completed all of the above items, go to your bank and the banker will either try to give you a commercial loan or contact the SBA and proceed directly with it.

Business Begins at Home

As you may have gathered from reading the preceding sections, the SBA is as interested in the soundness of your business proposal as a commercial bank would be. Furthermore, the SBA is usually a last resort, after private or commercial financing has been sought but not found. The following excerpt from an article by E. Ronald Watson in the Bucks County (Pa.) *Sunday Intelligencer* (March 6, 1983) is relevant in this regard. The article is titled "For Mom, Pop, Starting Business Begins at Home," and in it Mr. Watson quotes Daniel M. Sossaman, a representative of the SBA, who was responding to a question on where the small entrepreneur can go for help in starting a business. Here is Mr. Sossaman's answer:

"The first place to look is at home," suggests Sossaman. "We [the SBA] have to look to the private sector for help. When we're taking a business to the bank we're looking for a third down—it's not like it used to be when you'd plunk down 10 or 20% and get a loan. You have to go to the private lender, sell the bank that the business is an investment in the local community. If the local lender doesn't want to do it, why should we?"

And what if the local bank doesn't want to make the loan? There are many banks in any community that might make the loan, he added. "Just how committed is the Mom and Pop business to getting started? Enough to go to all the banks? And if nobody is going to finance you, well, you just save up," Sossaman said.

Government R&D Contracts

Recent legislation has made government R&D money available to small businesses on a regular basis. The program, known as the Small Business Innovation Research Program, requires almost every government agency to offer to small businesses contracts that will result in marketable products and processes. The contracts are for amounts up to $50,000. Each agency publishes a shopping list of the areas it wants researched. The variety of contract topics is immense, ranging from library cataloging services and surveys of data on family problems to research on high-impact materials.

For the small business seeking to expand in manufacturing, high-tech, or other areas, this program may become a new source of money. If a small business gets a contract to study and evaluate a new concept, follow-up federal funding to develop the product so that it can be sold commercially may also be available. Each agency administers its own programs, so you will have to contact each one separately.

State Programs

Today, virtually every state has programs aimed at assisting small businesses. They may be located in the governor's office, in the department of commerce or its equivalent, or in a state-level small business administration.

Typically the programs they offer include (1) advocacy at the state level before the legislature on behalf of small businesses; (2) information on filing requirements of the offices most small businesses deal with, such as the secretary of state or department of revenue; (3) intervention on behalf of small businesses with state bureaucracies to "cut the red tape"; (4) information on state programs of interest to small business, including small-business set-asides in procurement and loan programs; and (5) state-guaranteed loan programs for small or disadvantaged businesses, similar to those of the SBA.

Not every state has all of these programs. For example, very few have either direct loans or loan guarantees for small businesses. In those that do, their availability depends each year on the funding provided by the state legislature and the willingness of the governor's office to permit state agencies to spend money given them by the state legislature.

It is not likely that you will be able to borrow money directly from the state merely because you are a small business. However, if you are expanding your business, you may wish to find out more about industrial development authority operations in your state. In many cases, they can provide low-interest financing for major building and equipment purchases that will result in more jobs in the state.

From time to time, the SBA has put out materials on small-business programs in the states. Usually these materials are outdated as soon as they are prepared. The best thing to do to find out more on state programs is to contact the governor's office in your state capital and ask about small-business assistance. Even if the state's small-business programs are not supervised by the governor's office, that office can direct you to the correct agency.

PART IV

Operating and Dissolving the Corporation

CHAPTER 16

Operating and Updating the Corporation

How you run your business is not strictly up to you, especially if you have incorporated. Briefly, the things that govern the conduct of business are as follows:

- The corporation law of the states you incorporated in
- The articles of incorporation
- The bylaws
- The resolutions of the board of directors and of the shareholders
- Agreements made by the corporation with its shareholders and with outsiders

The order of these items basically reflects their relative importance. For example, the corporation law of your state may prevent a corporation from merging with another corporation without the approval of the shareholders. This is a limitation on the board of directors and the officers. State law may permit the corporation to appoint officers, and the bylaws may provide that the officers serve for a period of one year only. This means that they have to be reappointed each year. Finally, the corporation may have signed a loan agreement in which it is agreed that no assets will be sold without the prior approval of the lender. This too is a limitation.

In terms of authority, the articles of incorporation may permit the bylaws to be amended by the board of directors. This means they can change them without the approval of the shareholders as long as the change does not contradict the articles of incorporation or the corporate law. For example, the directors may provide that there will be a treasurer and an assistant treasurer. There is nothing in the corporate law or the articles of incorporation to prevent this. On the other hand, the directors cannot amend the bylaws to provide that the articles of incorporation can be amended by the directors instead of by the shareholders. Either state corporate law or the articles of incorporation will undoubtedly provide that the articles can be amended only by the shareholders. To give this power to the directors, the shareholders themselves would have to amend the articles and give the power of future amendment to the directors.

Corporate Records

After you have formed your corporation, you must keep it in working order, and this requires keeping the corporate records accurate and up to date. A corporation's records consist of several types:

1. The corporate book, which includes the articles of incorporation, bylaws, minutes of board of directors' and shareholders' meetings, and the stock transfer ledger.
2. Contracts and agreements that the corporation has made with other persons, businesses, or agencies.
3. The tax and financial records.

The first two items make up what we speak of as the corporate records. Anytime a major corporate action is proposed, these documents must be consulted ahead of time to make sure they do not prevent or impose special conditions on the action.

Failure to keep the corporation's books and records in order and adhere to them can have serious consequences. For instance, you might lose the protection the incorporation offers against lawsuits, you might suffer costly tax consequences, or you might violate the terms of a loan agreement.

Corporate Minutes

As far as the law is concerned, a meeting of either the board of directors or the shareholders is what the minutes say it is. For example, when the shareholders meet to take some routine actions about which there will be no discussion or dispute, it is not necessary to have a full-blown, parliamentary-style meeting. Whoever is in charge of the meeting should prepare the minutes ahead of time, as if they were an agenda. This permits needed resolutions to be adopted in the proper form and assures that the meeting will take care of all matters before it. If desired, the unsigned minutes can be distributed ahead of time so that everyone is familiar with them.

The minutes themselves should have some blanks in them, for the names of persons making motions and seconding them, as follows:

On the motion of _____, seconded by _____, it was resolved that the corporation enter into a lease for office space with ABC Landlord, a copy of which is attached to these minutes and incorporated in these minutes. The motion, after discussion, was passed by a vote of _____ to _____.

Notice that the exact terms of the lease are approved merely by attaching a copy of the lease to the minutes. (Do not, however, attach the original.)

In those cases where the resolution will be supplied by someone else, but the concept is agreed on, a different procedure is used. The most common case of this is opening a new bank account. The card signed by the corporation is actually a certification that the corporation, on a certain date, passed the resolution as drafted by the bank, authorizing the corporation's officers to open the account. These banking resolutions are basically the same, but each bank has its own version. Your minutes should read something like this:

> On the motion of _____, seconded by _____, it was resolved that the corporation adopt a banking resolution authorizing it to open an account with the _____ Bank in the form attached to these minutes and incorporated in these minutes. The motion, after discussion, was passed by a vote of _____ to _____.

In this case, you would use the date of the meeting as the date on the bank's signature card, and you should get an extra copy of the bank's resolution form for the minutes. When you have opened the account, the resolution form from the bank will be added to the minutes where indicated.

If the corporation is going to negotiate a major transaction, such as a loan, but you do not know the terms of the final package, the board of directors may wish to adopt a resolution granting the relevant officers authority to negotiate and sign the loan agreement. The resolution can provide that the final agreement, as signed, is later to be made a part of the minutes. This can be done as follows:

> On the motion of _____, seconded by _____, it was resolved that the President and Secretary of the Corporation are authorized to negotiate a loan agreement with the Local Bank and Trust Company, in the principal amount of $100,000 on such terms as the two officers shall find prudent and reasonable. After discussion, the motion was adopted by a vote of _____ to _____. A copy of the loan agreement, as finally signed, will be added to the minutes of the corporation following the minutes of this meeting.

Corporate Meetings

After your corporation is organized, each year a meeting of the stockholders should be held to elect the directors of the corporation. The new directors should then hold their annual meeting to elect new officers and to conduct other business. The following kinds of business activities should be handled in meetings either of the stockholders or of the directors and recorded in the minutes of the corporation:

1. The replacement of any director.
2. The sale or purchase of any of its stock by the corporation.

3. The purchase or sale of major assets of the corporation.
4. Entering into any loan.
5. The execution of any significant agreement by the corporation, such as a lease for office space, a long-term employment contract, opening new bank or investment accounts, or taking an option on another business.
6. Electing a new officer or replacing an existing officer.
7. Bonding officers or directors.
8. Authorizing the officers of the corporation to make certain contracts.
9. Indemnifying officers, directors, and employees against lawsuits.
10. Approving a stockholder agreement.
11. Changing any tax election made by the corporation, such as its election to be taxed under Subchapter S.
12. Any major action which could commit the assets or personnel of the corporation in any significant way.

In deciding who votes on what, you must be guided by the priorities established in the laws, resolutions, and agreements listed at the beginning of this chapter. In general, matters affecting the management and operation of the corporation are voted on by the board of directors. Matters affecting the long-range structure and future of the corporation (mergers, issuing new stock) are voted on by the common stockholders. Matters affecting the elimination of dividends or of voting rights for any class of stock are voted on by holders of that class of stock.

Here is another example of a resolution of the stockholders giving the directors authority to negotiate a contract for the sale of corporate assets. Note how broad it is. Always remember, unless the officers or directors can point to something giving them the power to take an act in the name of the corporation, they cannot commit the corporation to just any agreement they think is useful.

RESOLVED, that the Board of Directors of _____ Corporation is hereby authorized to sell or exchange all or any part of the Corporation's assets and property, including goodwill and franchises, on such terms and conditions and for such consideration, as the Board of Directors shall deem expedient and in the best interests of the corporation. More specifically, the Board may accept as consideration for the sale of such assets and property, in whole or in part, the shares of stock of any other corporation or corporations, including but not limited to the stock of _____, Inc.

Certifying a Resolution

At various times, the officers of the corporation may have to certify that the corporation has in fact adopted a particular resolution. This certification is often requested in major transactions when an outsider to the business wants assurance that the officers he is dealing with have the authority to commit the corporation to the transaction. Common examples are the opening of a bank account and the sale of major portions of the corporation's assets.

There are two ways the request for certification can be satisfied. First, a resolution may already have been adopted giving, say, the president the authority to sell a particular warehouse. In that case, it is necessary to certify the passage and good status only of that resolution. If a resolution has not yet been adopted, the other party to the transaction should be asked if the resolution must cover certain points or be in a certain form. Then the corporation would adopt it and certify it in that form. The certification usually takes the following form:

ATTESTATION: I, _____, do hereby certify that I am the duly elected and qualified (Assistant) Secretary of _____ Corporation, and that the above is a true and correct copy of a resolution duly adopted at a meeting of the (Board of Directors) (shareholders) of that Corporation, called and held in accordance with law and with the Bylaws of the Corporation on _____ 19__, and that such resolution is now in full force and effect. IN WITNESS WHEREOF, I affix my name as (Assistant) Secretary and cause the seal of the corporation to be affixed hereunto, this _____ day of _____, 19__.

_____
(ASSISTANT) SECRETARY

138

Amending the Articles of Incorporation and the Bylaws

Amending the articles of incorporation takes a vote of the stockholders (unless the original articles provided that the directors have the authority). Since bylaws set out the requirements for stockholder meetings, they must be followed. For example, stockholders would have to receive the advance written notice that they are entitled to receive under the bylaws. Or the stockholders can waive this notice by signing a unanimous consent, if that is permitted by your state's corporation law.

To amend the articles of incorporation, basically all that is required is that the stockholders adopt a resolution such as the following:

> On motion made, seconded, and duly adopted, the stockholders of the corporation have amended the Articles of Incorporation, Section _____, to read as follows: "[exact text of the new section.]"

After adopting the resolution, the officers of the corporation must file the necessary forms with the secretary of state, together with a filing fee, showing the amendment. The procedure is essentially the same as for filing the original articles. In fact, some states require you to advertise that the articles have been amended.

When the amended articles are returned to the corporation, they are to be filed in the minute book, together with the original articles. It should always be clear when going through the minute book what articles were in effect.

Amending the bylaws is easier than amending the articles of incorporation since most states do not require the bylaws or amendments to them to be filed with the secretary of state. Again, a meeting is held, usually of the directors, since they usually have the power to amend the bylaws. The meeting includes adopting the following resolution:

> RESOLVED, that Article _____, Section _____ of the Bylaws of this Corporation be amended to read as follows: "[the new language of the bylaws.]"

If the amendment is long, then the resolution should note that certain designated bylaws are being amended and that copies of the amendments are a part of the minutes of the meeting and filed with the minutes.

After adopting the amendment, the secretary of the corporation should take the set of bylaws kept in the minute book and change them. The best way to keep intelligible records is to paste over the old section with a copy of the new section. Then note in the margin next to the section being changed the date of the meeting at which the change was passed. This way, you will always be able to tell which bylaws were in effect at any particular time by starting with the first meeting at which the first bylaws were adopted. From there, you can go through the meetings and reconstruct the history of the bylaws. If the corporation is ever sold or goes public, the secretary of the corporation might have to certify that the buyer (or the stock underwriter) is being given an accurate copy of the current bylaws of the corporation.

Common Changes

The most common changes that corporations make in their articles of incorporation, bylaws, or working resolutions are listed below. Next to each is noted the related steps usually needed to make the change official.

1. Change the corporation's fiscal year (get IRS consent).
2. Change the corporation's name (amend the articles of incorporation and all tax and license filings).
3. Purchase real estate (sign the agreement of sale and other papers).
4. Elect to end the corporation's status under Subchapter S (notify the IRS).
5. Open a new account with another bank (close the old one).

In amending the corporation, it is essential to keep in mind that the corporation is an entity separate and apart from its stockholders, officers, and directors. Always act under the assumption that, at some point in the future, you will have to point to some *written* authority for what has been done in the name of the corporation. The source of your authority may be in the state corporation laws. If it is not, make sure it is in one of the following:

The articles of incorporation.
The bylaws of the corporation.
The minutes of the stockholders of the corporation.
The minutes of the directors of the corporation.
A written agreement executed by the corporation, either approved by the board of stockholders or signed by someone with the authority to sign such agreements and bind the corporation.

Insurance is another area that must not be overlooked as a corporation changes or expands. It is important to review your insurance coverages from time to time to be sure they protect your business adequately according to your current needs. To help in this review, use the Insurance Checklist in the back of this book.

Going Private

"Going private" is a major move for any corporation. It means the elimination or reduction of the number of public stockholders of a corporation so the corporation's stock is no longer freely traded or subject to registration with the Securities and Exchange Commission. The benefits of going private are that the corporation regains its privacy and the flexibility associated with the private status and escapes the costs associated with a publicly registered firm.

Returning to the status of a private corporation is not cost-free. In fact, SEC rules impose significant costs in terms of disclosures and dissemination of information.

The state law applying to going private is the law of the state in which the corporation is incorporated. Basically, whether by statute or by case law, the states have begun to establish a standard requiring that the stockholders in control of the corporation protect the interests of the outsiders or minority stockholders.

If a corporation decides to go private, state law may well give affected stockholders the right to enjoin the entire transaction because it is unfair to their interests. In fact, the courts seem to be holding that a transaction designed to freeze out minority stockholders is a breach of a fiduciary duty owed by the majority to the minority, leading to an action for damages against the majority stockholders.

CHAPTER 17

Dissolving the Corporation

There are several reasons a solvent corporation may wish to undertake the time-consuming chore of a voluntary dissolution. Perhaps there is no further purpose in continuing the business. Or a disagreement among the major stockholders of the corporation might be resolved only by dissolving the corporation and dividing up its assets. Another case would be when the owners of the corporation wish to operate as a partnership, passing through deductions and credits. If this is a motive, they should consider becoming a Subchapter S corporation, which provides some of the tax benefits of a partnership without requiring dissolution of the corporation.

It may also be necessary to dissolve the corporation in order to provide liquidity to settle the estate of a major stockholder. Being forced to dissolve the corporation under this circumstance is often not desired or welcomed by the remaining stockholders. Fortunately, certain sections of the Internal Revenue Code are geared to helping small, closely held corporations avoid dissolution upon the death of a stockholder. This is dealt with in greater detail in the section below.

Estate Planning

A corporation is sometimes dissolved to pay estate taxes on the value of the stock in a stockholder's estate. Since the requirement to settle an estate could force the dissolution of many small corporations whenever one of the stockholders dies, the Internal Revenue Code provides some relief. Section 303 of the Internal Revenue Code is designed to provide funds to estates of stockholders of closely held corporations where cash is needed. Under IRC 303, the corporation's redemption of stock is not taxable as a dividend. This permits the estate to redeem enough stock to pay taxes and final expenses without having to dissolve the entire corporation.

To qualify for special treatment under IRC 303, the stock owned must equal at least 35 percent of the adjusted gross estate. The adjusted gross estate includes the total value of the estate at death less final expenses, federal estate taxes, probate, and administration and executors' fees. If the stock represents less than 35 percent of the estate, the special provisions of Section 303 are not available. The death of a stockholder whose stock was a minor portion of the estate might still force a dissolution if the estate has only nonliquid assets and no cash. Life insurance owned by the corporation on the shareholder's life may be used to cover Section 303 expenses if money to redeem the stock is unavailable.

Section 6166 of the Internal Revenue Code offers deferred payments of federal estate taxes, again to help avoid the involuntary dissolution of a corporation just to get cash to settle the estate of a former stockholder. To qualify for Section 6166, the deceased stockholder's business interest must equal 35 percent of the adjusted gross estate. The total deferred period is 14 years. In the first four years, only interest payments are required. The balance, with interest, is paid thereafter in ten equal installments.

Voluntary Liquidation and Dissolution

An alternative to dissolution is partial or complete voluntary liquidation. A liquidation is a distribution of the assets of the corporation to its stockholders, but the stockholders do not turn in stock, nor does the corporation cease to exist (except in a complete liquidation). To undertake a partial liquidation, the distributions to the stockholders generally have to be made out of the corporation's unrestricted capital surplus. This means the distributions cannot be made if the corporation is insolvent or when they would make the corporation insolvent.

If its capital surplus is not sufficient to support the distribution of assets, a corporation can increase surplus by reducing the stated capital. (The stated capital is the total par value of any issued stock. If the corporation has no par stock, the stated capital is the value assigned by the board. The capital surplus of a corporation is basically the capital of the corporation minus the stated capital.) Reducing the stated capital is done by amending the articles of incorporation to reduce par value or by canceling treasury shares. (Once treasury shares are canceled, they no longer exist.)

The corporation may also be able to increase the available capital surplus by transfers from earned surplus (accumulated profits). Usually these actions require the approval of the stockholders.

A partial liquidation generally results in ordinary income to those receiving it. However, Section 346 of the Internal Revenue Code permits a partial liquidation to receive the more favorable capital gains treatment if one of the following conditions is met:

1. The partial liquidation is one of a series of liquidations resulting in a complete liquidation of the corporation.
2. The distribution is "not essentially equivalent" to a dividend.
3. The liquidation is the result of the termination of two or more active businesses.

A complete liquidation is available either before or after a corporation commences business. If a corporation has not yet commenced business, there are no tax problems or considerations. The corporation is liquidated by the approval of a majority of the stockholders, and articles of dissolution or liquidation are filed with the secretary of state. After filing the articles, the corporation's existence ceases.

When a corporation has already begun its business, approval for a complete liquidation can usually be obtained by the written consent of all of the stockholders, or by majority vote of the stockholders and directors at meetings considering the dissolution.

After a certificate of election to dissolve has been filed with the secretary of state, the corporation ceases business except for actions relating to winding up operations. Its corporate existence does not end. After the winding up is completed, articles of dissolution are filed and, on their filing, the corporation ceases to exist.

In a dissolution, the distribution of cash to the stockholders is usually a capital gain or loss. The amount of gain or loss is determined by the difference between the adjusted basis of the stock (that is, the tax acquisition cost) and the amount received in liquidation. If the liquidation is accomplished in installments, the payment of tax by the stockholder on any profit may be deferred.

There are two major cases when the liquidation can be partially nontaxable. First, Section 333 of the Internal Revenue Code provides for a partially tax-exempt "one-month" liquidation. Using Section 333 can be useful in situations where the business will continue in another form, such as a partnership. The stockholder realizes gain to the extent of his or her share of the corporation's retained earnings and profits, but not on the accumulated assets. The gains are either long- or short-term capital gains, depending on the extent of any money or securities of the stockholder that are held by the corporation.

Second, when a corporation is selling all of its assets and then liquidating completely, Section 337 of the Internal Revenue Code can be used to avoid a double tax. The double tax consists of a tax to the corporation on the sale of the assets and to the shareholders on the distribution of the proceeds. To qualify under IRC 337, the liquidation must be completed within a 12-month period beginning on the date the plan of liquidation was adopted. If IRC 337 is complied with, the corporation will not recognize any gain or loss on sales or exchanges of its property within the 12-month period.

Mergers, Acquisitions, and Consolidations

Other means of functionally ending a corporation are by merger, by acquisition, and by consolidation. The result of a merger or acquisition is sometimes, but not always, the dissolution of a corporation. In a consolidation, the original corporations cease to exist.

Statutory merger is the purchase of one corporation by another corporation, with the company that still exists after the merger designated as the surviving or acquiring corporation.

In a *statutory consolidation*, two or more existing corporations cease to exist on their own and a new corporation is formed in their place.

Asset acquisition is the purchase by one corporation of all the assets of another corporation. Technically there is no change in the legal existence of either corporation. Instead, the acquiring corporation has ownership of more assets, and the selling corporation has received cash, other assets, or income over a number of years in place of the assets transferred.

In a *stock acquisition*, both corporations continue to exist, but the acquiring company now owns controlling interest of the acquired company.

CHAPTER 18

If You Do It Wrong

Even in this best of all possible worlds, things can go wrong. Mistakes can be made in filing the papers for incorporation, or the owners and management might fail to operate the business according to regulations. If not corrected, these mistakes, whether inadvertent or not, can have unfortunate consequences for the owners. If your corporation is incorrectly organized or operated, your company could be viewed in the eyes of the law as an *unincorporated* business, and you will forfeit the benefit of the corporate "shield" in the event of a lawsuit.

These and other cases of "doing it wrong"—and what to do about them—are covered in the sections below.

Piercing the Corporate Veil

By creating a corporation, the stockholders expect to be insulated from liability for the actions of the corporation. However, there are circumstances under which persons injured by the corporation secure a judgment against the stockholders as well as against the corporation.

It is usually the closely held corporation that has the most difficulty in keeping the stockholders insulated from lawsuits. The most common reasons for ignoring the existence of the corporation and holding the stockholders liable (known as piercing the corporate veil) are the following:

1. The corporation does not have enough capital for the line of business in which it operates. For example, a company making toxic chemicals whose capital is $1,000 would be subject to this challenge, particularly if it did not have a reasonable amount of insurance.
2. The corporation was never properly incorporated. Incorporation means extra responsibilities for the stockholders. No one wants to find out when something is wrong that the incorporation is defective and therefore the corporation does not really exist.
3. The owners of the corporation do not treat it like a corporation. For example, if customers are not aware that the business is incorporated because bills, checks, and so on do not use a corporate name, your "corporation" may not be enough to protect you in court.

In each one of these situations, the stockholders can face personal liability for the actions of the corporation. To avoid this, make sure that the corporation is adequately capitalized. If it isn't, increase the corporation's capital base and consider additional insurance. Review the incorporation of the business. If you find there has been a problem, do not hide it and pretend it is not there. Correct it. Generally this means redoing the steps you missed previously, such as advertising the corporation's formation. In addition, consider adopting a resolution like the following to clean up the record and validate everything the corporation has done before:

Whereas it has come to the attention of the Directors of the Corporation that [describe the defect and the date it occurred], and the Directors today resolve that [describe the corrective action, e.g., file back annual reports with the state, correct a defect in the paid-up capital], and the Directors, having concluded that these errors were made in good faith, do hereby ratify and confirm all acts of the Board of Directors and officers of the Corporation taken since [date of error], and the Directors do hereby agree that the Corporation shall indemnify and hold harmless all past and present officers, directors, employees, and agents of the Corporation for any actions taken in the name of the Corporation [during the period in question or under the mistaken belief that they had authority to take such steps].

A similar resolution can be adopted by the stockholders, if the defect is one that can be corrected only by them, such as failing to elect directors.

If you have not been treating the corporation as if it is a corporation, stop it at once. You will fall under what lawyers call the "walks like a duck" rule. That is, if it walks like a duck and it talks like a duck, it is a duck. For the corporation, that means, if it looks like an unincorporated business, and it acts like an unincorporated business, then the courts will treat it like an unincorporated business.

Tax Issues

As was discussed in more detail in Chapter 7, an incorporation can be either tax-free or taxable. Unlike most cases with the Internal Revenue Code, it is difficult to make the incorporation a taxable one. Tax-free incorporation is the norm, and, assuming you want a tax-free incorporation, it is unlikely that you will accidentally make it taxable. If the unlikely occurs, and your incorporation was inadvertently a taxable one, then both you and the corporation will have to file amended tax returns for the year when the incorporation took place, paying the additional taxes required, together with interest on the back taxes.

If the mistake is that you tried to make the incorporation taxable and failed, what happens depends on the actual tax consequences. If you or the corporation actually owe taxes, you will have to pay. However, if you or the corporation accidentally overpaid taxes because of a mistake (either in a tax-free or in a taxable transaction), you may be stuck. There comes a time after which you cannot file for a refund, even if the overpayment was accidental and in good faith.

Unfortunately, the books close quickly on overpayments; it is hard to close them on underpayments. If you discover that you or the corporation owe money because of some mistake in the incorporation, and you do nothing about it, you open yourself or the business to fraud penalties, which are payments in addition to the taxes and accumulated interest you owe.

Bankruptcy

No one plans for bankruptcy, but it is always a possibility. And going into bankruptcy is a prime example of "doing it wrong." If you are facing bankruptcy, be aware that in 1978 Congress passed an entirely new bankruptcy law, repealing the former law that had been in effect since 1898. Make sure any references you use on bankruptcy are written from the perspective of the new law. Be aware, too, that Congress may make major amendments to this law during 1984 to replace portions of it (dealing with technical issues of judicial power) that the U.S. Supreme Court has declared unconstitutional.

It is important to know something about bankruptcy for several reasons. First, you should know that if you made a serious mistake in incorporating and do not have a corporation, the protections available to a corporation and its stockholders in bankruptcy will not be available at all. Second, if you have to go into bankruptcy, or your creditors threaten you with it, you should be prepared ahead of time. The possibility of bankruptcy might motivate you to fund your corporation more with debt and less with investments for stock. This is because you are better off as a debtor of the corporation than as a stockholder. A stockholder will probably lose everything in bankruptcy; a debtor may recover something. Another reason to learn something about bankruptcy is that if one of your customers goes bankrupt, you will want to know what, if anything, you can expect to get out of the proceeding.

Forms of Bankruptcy

There are two types of bankruptcy: involuntary and voluntary. For an involuntary bankruptcy to take place, either the corporation must have been unable to pay its debts as they came due or else a custodian was appointed or took possession of the corporation's property within 120 days before the petition for bankruptcy was filed.

An involuntary bankruptcy case can be brought against a corporation if three or more persons file a petition with the federal bankruptcy court. The total claims held by all these creditors must be at least $5,000 more than the amount of any liens they hold against the corporation's property. This is carefully supervised, and the persons filing against the corporation must abide by rather strenuous rules. An involuntary bankruptcy case also can be begun by one or more creditors (when there are fewer than 12 creditors of the corporation) if these creditors hold at least $5,000 in claims against the corporation.

In a voluntary bankruptcy, a corporation becomes bankrupt by filing a petition in the proper court. From that point on, the bankruptcy proceedings are virtually the same for both voluntary and involuntary cases.

Basic Rights and Procedures

In a bankruptcy proceeding, the corporation must file an inventory of all of its property and a list of all creditors, even if a debt is secured. This list must show what each creditor is owed. A statement must also be filed describing the financial history, volume of business, income, and related information. These statements must also claim any exemptions that the bankrupt corporation believes itself entitled to. If they are not claimed at this stage, they are lost forever. These statements are signed under oath.

To make a claim against a bankrupt corporation, a creditor uses forms developed for the bankruptcy courts. These claims must be filed in a timely manner with the court. A claim that has been properly filed is deemed to be allowed unless some party in interest objects. If an objection to a claim is made, the bankruptcy court, after a hearing, decides on the validity of the claim and the amount of the claim that will be paid.

The assets of the bankrupt corporation are distributed as follows:
1. Administrative costs, including fees for the attorney of the bankrupt corporation, the trustee, the petitioning creditors, and the receiver, as well as commissions for the trustee and receiver.

2. Unsecured claims arising in the ordinary course of the corporation's business after the case has begun, but before the appointment of the trustee (or before the court order declaring it to be bankrupt, if that is earlier).
3. Unsecured claims for wages, salaries, or commissions earned within 90 days before the date the petition was filed or before the corporation's business ceased (if that was earlier). There is a maximum of $2,000 claim per person.
4. Unsecured claims for contributions to employee benefits plans arising from services rendered within 180 days before the petition was filed (or the business ceased). These claims are limited to $2,000 per employee (less any money paid for wages).
5. Unsecured claims of $900 per individual for money deposited in connection with the purchase, lease, or rental of property, or the purchase of services for the personal, family, or household use of such individuals, that were not delivered or provided.
6. Tax claims.

Each class must be paid in full before any funds can go to the next class.

The discharge of the debts of the bankrupt corporation is the key feature of the bankruptcy proceeding. A bankrupt corporation is entitled to a discharge of most of its debts as a matter of right unless appropriate objections are made and sustained by the court. In the case of a corporation, an application must be made within six months after the corporation is adjudged bankrupt or the right to a discharge is forfeited.

Not all debts and liabilities are discharged in bankruptcy. The bankruptcy law provides that certain kinds of obligations will remain as liabilities of the corporation after it has gone bankrupt. This includes certain tort claims, fines, penalties, and liabilities for obtaining money or property by false pretenses.

Insurance Checklist

The points covered in this checklist are grouped under three general classes of insurance: (1) coverages that are essential for most businesses, (2) coverages that are desirable for many firms, but not absolutely necessary, and (3) coverages for employee benefits. For each of the statements, put a check in the first column if you understand the statement and how it affects your insurance program. Otherwise, check the second column. Then study your policies with these points in mind and discuss any questions you still have with your agent. Four kinds of insurance are essential: fire and property insurance, liability insurance, automobile insurance, and worker's compensation insurance. In some areas and in some kinds of businesses, crime insurance, which is discussed under "Desirable Coverages," is also essential.

	No Action Needed	*Look Into This*

Essential Coverages and Property

Fire and Property Insurance

1. You can add other perils, such as hail, windstorm, smoke, explosion, vandalism, and malicious mischief, to your basic fire insurance at a relatively small additional cost.   _____   _____

Insurance Checklist

	No Action Needed	Look Into This
2. If you need comprehensive coverage, your best buy could be one of the all-risk contracts that offer the broadest available protection for the money.	_____	_____
3. The insurance company may indemnify you—that is, compensate you for your losses—in any one of several ways: (1) it may pay actual cash value of the property at the time of loss, (2) it may repair or replace the property with material of the same kind and quality, or (3) it may take all the property at the agreed-upon or appraised value and reimburse you for your loss.	_____	_____
4. You can insure property you don't own. You must have an insurable interest (a financial interest) in the property when a loss occurs but not necessarily at the time the insurance contract is made. For instance, a repair shop or dry cleaning plant may carry insurance on customers' property in the shop, or you may hold a mortgage on a building and insure the building although you don't own it.	_____	_____
5. When you sell property, you cannot assign the insurance policy along with the property unless you have permission from the insurance company.	_____	_____
6. Even if you have several policies on your property, you can collect only the amount of your actual cash loss. All the insurers share the payment		

No Action   *Look Into*
Needed   *This*

proportionately. Suppose, for example, that you are carrying two policies, one for $20,000 and one for $30,000, on a $40,000 building, and fire causes damage to the building amounting to $12,000. The $20,000 policy will pay $4,800; that is, $20,000 ÷ $50,000, or $2/5$ of $12,000. The $30,000 policy will pay $7,000; that is, $30,000 ÷ $50,000 or $3/5$ of $12,000.

    _____   _____

7. Special protection other than the standard fire insurance policy is needed to cover the loss by fire of accounts, bills, currency, deeds, evidences of debt, and money and securities.

    _____   _____

8. If an insured building is vacant or unoccupied for more than 60 consecutive days, coverage is suspended unless you have a special endorsement to your policy canceling this provision.

    _____   _____

9. If, either before or after a loss, you conceal or misrepresent to the insurer any material fact or circumstance concerning your insurance or the interest of the insured, the policy may be voided.

10. If you increased the hazard of fire, by renting part of your building to a dry cleaner, for example, the insurance company may suspend your coverage even for losses that did not originate from the increased fire hazard.

    _____   _____

156

Insurance Checklist

	No Action Needed	Look Into This
11. After a loss, you must use all reasonable means to protect the property from further loss or run the risk of having your insurance canceled.	_____	_____
12. To recover your loss, you must furnish within 60 days (unless an extension is granted by the insurance company) a complete inventory of the damaged, destroyed, and undamaged property showing in detail quantities, costs, actual cash values, and amount of loss claimed.	_____	_____
13. If you and the insurer differ on the amount of loss, the question may be resolved through special appraisal procedures provided for in the insurance policy.	_____	_____
14. You may cancel your policy without notice at any time and get part of the premium returned. The insurance company also may cancel at any time with a five-day written notice to you.	_____	_____
15. By accepting a coinsurance clause in your policy, you get a substantial reduction in premiums. A coinsurance clause states that you must carry insurance equal to 80 or 90 percent of the value of the insured property. If you carry less than this, you cannot collect the full amount of your loss, even if the loss is small. The amount you can collect will depend on what percentage of the full value of the property you are insured for.	_____	_____
16. If your loss is caused by someone else's negligence, the insurer has the		

157

Insurance Checklist

	No Action Needed	Look Into This

right to sue the negligent third party for the amount it has paid to you under the policy. This is known as the insurer's right of subrogation. However, the insurer will usually waive this right upon request. For example, if you have leased your insured building to someone and have waived your right to collect from the tenant for any insured damage to your property, you should have the insurance company waive this subrogation clause. ———— ————

17. A building under construction can be insured for fire, lightning, extended coverage, vandalism, and malicious mischief. ———— ————

Liability Insurance

1. Legal liability limits of $1 million are no longer considered high or unreasonable even for a small business. ———— ————

2. Most liability policies require you to notify the insurer immediately of an incident on your property that might cause a future claim. This holds true no matter how unimportant the incident might seem when it occurs. ———— ————

3. Most liability policies, in addition to bodily injuries, may now cover personal injuries (libel and slander, for example) if these are specifically insured. ———— ————

4. Under certain conditions, your business may be subject to damage claims even from trespassers. ———— ————

158

Insurance Checklist

	No Action Needed	Look Into This

5. You may be legally liable for damages even in cases where you used "reasonable care." _____ _____

6. Even if the suit against you is fraudulent, the liability insurer pays court costs, legal fees, and interest on judgments in addition to the liability judgments themselves. _____ _____

7. You can be liable for the acts of others under contracts you have signed with them. This liability is insurable. _____ _____

8. In some cases, you may be held liable for fire loss to property of others in your care. This property would normally not be covered by your fire and general liability insurance. This risk can be covered by fire legal liability insurance or through requesting subrogation waivers from insurers of owners of the property. _____ _____

Automobile Insurance

1. When an employee or a subcontractor uses a car on your behalf, you can be legally liable even though you don't own the car or truck. _____ _____

2. Five or more automobiles or motorcycles under one ownership and operated as a fleet for business purposes can generally be insured under a low-cost fleet policy against both material damage to your vehicle and liability to others for property damage or personal injury. _____ _____

Insurance Checklist

	No Action Needed	Look Into This
3. You can often get deductibles of almost any amount and thereby reduce your premium.	————	————
4. Automobile medical-payments insurance pays for medical claims, including your own, arising from automobile accidents regardless of the question of negligence.	————	————
5. In most states, you must carry liability insurance or be prepared to provide other proof (surety bond) of financial responsibility when you are involved in an accident.	————	————
6. You can purchase uninsured-motorist protection to cover your own bodily injury claims from someone who has no insurance.	————	————
7. Personal property stored in an automobile and not attached to it (such as merchandise being delivered) is not covered under an automobile policy.	————	————

Worker's Compensation

1. Federal and common law requires that an employer (1) provide employees a safe place to work, (2) hire competent fellow employees, (3) provide safe tools, and (4) warn employees of an existing danger.	————	————
2. If an employer fails to provide the above, the employer is liable for damage suits brought by an employee and possible fines or prosecution.	————	————

Insurance Checklist

	No Action Needed	Look Into This
3. In nearly all states, you are now legally required to cover your workers under worker's compensation.	_____	_____
4. State law determines the level or type of benefits payable under worker's compensation policies.	_____	_____
5. Not all employees are covered by worker's compensation insurance laws. The exceptions are determined by state law and therefore vary from state to state.	_____	_____
6. You can save money on worker's compensation insurance by seeing that your employees are properly classified.	_____	_____
7. Rates for worker's compensation insurance vary from 0.1 percent of the payroll for "safe" occupations to 25 percent or more of the payroll for hazardous occupations.	_____	_____
8. In most states, most employers can reduce their worker's compensation insurance premium cost by reducing their accident rate below the average. They do this by being safety oriented and using loss prevention measures.	_____	_____

Desirable Coverages

Business Interruption Insurance

1. You can purchase insurance to cover fixed expenses, such as salaries of key personnel, taxes, interest, depreciation, and utilities that would

Insurance Checklist

continue if a fire shut down your business, as well as those profits you would lose. _____ _____

2. Under properly written contingent business interruption insurance, you can also collect if fire and other peril closes down the business of a supplier or customer and this results in an interruption of your business. _____ _____

3. The business interruption policy provides payments for amounts you spend to hasten the reopening of your business after a fire or other insured peril. _____ _____

4. You can get coverage for extra expenses you suffer if an insured peril, while not actually closing your business down, seriously disrupts it. _____ _____

5. When a policy is properly endorsed, you can get business interruption insurance to indemnify you if your operations are suspended because of failure or interruption of the supply of gas, light, heat, or water furnished by a public utility company. _____ _____

Crime Insurance

1. Burglary insurance excludes such property as accounts, fur articles in a showcase window, and manuscripts. _____ _____

2. Coverage is granted under burglary insurance only if there are visible marks of the burglar's forced entry. _____ _____

3. Burglary insurance can be written to cover, in addition to money in a safe,

Insurance Checklist

	No Action Needed	Look Into This
inventoried merchandise and damage incurred in the course of a burglary.	———	———
4. Robbery insurance protects you from loss of property, money, and securities by force, trickery, or threat of violence on or off your premises.	———	———
5. A comprehensive crime policy written just for small-business owners is available. In addition to burglary and robbery, it covers other types of loss by theft, destruction, and disappearances of money and securities. It also covers theft by your employees.	———	———
6. If you are in a high-risk area and cannot get insurance through normal channels without paying excessive rates, you may be able to get help through the federal crime insurance plan. Your agent or state insurance commissioner can tell you where to get more information on these plans.	———	———

Glass Insurance

	No Action Needed	Look Into This
1. You can purchase a special glass insurance policy that covers all risk to plate glass windows, glass signs, motion picture screens, glass brick, glass doors, showcases, countertops, and insulated glass panels.	———	———
2. The glass insurance policy covers not only the glass alone, but also its lettering and ornamentation, if these are specifically insured, and the costs of temporary plates or boarding up when necessary.	———	———

Insurance Checklist

3. After the glass has been replaced, full coverage is continued without any additional premium for the period covered.   _____   _____

Rent Insurance

1. You can buy rent insurance that will pay your rent if the property you lease becomes unusable because of fire or other insured peril and your lease calls for continued payments in such a situation.   _____   _____
2. If you own property and lease it to others, you can insure against loss if the lease is canceled because of fire and you rent the property again at a reduced rate.   _____   _____

Employee Benefits and Related Coverages

Group Life Insurance

1. If you pay group insurance premiums and cover all employees up to $50,000, the cost to you is deductible for federal tax purposes, and yet the value of the benefit is not taxable income to your employees.   _____   _____
2. Most insurers will provide group coverages at low rates even if there are ten or fewer employees in your group.   _____   _____

Insurance Checklist

	No Action Needed	Look Into This
3. If the employees pay part of the cost of the group insurance, state laws require that 75 percent of them must elect coverage for the plan to qualify as a group insurance plan.	————	————
4. Group plans permit an employee leaving the company to convert group insurance coverage to a private plan at the rate for his or her age, without a medical exam, within 30 days after leaving the job.	————	————

Group Health Insurance

1. Group health insurance costs much less and provides more generous benefits for the worker than individual contracts would.	————	————
2. If you pay the entire cost, individual employees cannot be dropped from a group plan unless the entire group policy is canceled.	————	————
3. Generous programs of employee benefits, such as group health insurance, tend to reduce labor turnover.	————	————

Disability Insurance

1. Worker's compensation insurance pays an employee only for time lost because of work injuries or work-related illness, not for time lost because of disabilities incurred off the job. But you can purchase, at a low premium, insurance to replace the lost income of workers who suffer

	No Action Needed	*Look Into This*

short-term or long-term disability
not related to work.

2. You can get coverage that provides
employees with an income for life in
case of permanent disability resulting from work-related sickness or accident.

Retirement Income

1. If you are self-employed, you can get
an income tax deduction for funds
used for retirement for you and your
employees through plans of insurance and annuities approved for use
under the Employees Retirement Income Security Act of 1974 (ERISA).

2. Annuity contracts can provide for
variable payments in the hope of giving the annuitants some protection
against the effects of inflation.
Whether fixed or variable, an annuity can provide retirement income
that is guaranteed for life.

Key-Person Insurance

1. One of the most serious setbacks that
can occur in a small business is the
loss of a key employee. But your key
employee can be insured with life insurance and disability insurance
owned by and paid to your company.

2. Proceeds of a key-person policy are
not subject to income tax, but premiums are not a deductible business
expense.

Insurance Checklist

	No Action Needed	Look Into This
3. The cash value of key-person insurance, which accumulates as an asset of the business, can be borrowed against and the interest and dividends are not subject to income tax as long as the policy remains in force.	_____	_____

Glossary

Accumulated earnings—Earnings accumulated by the corporation and not paid out as dividends. Accumulations above certain specific limits established by the Internal Revenue Code are subject to penalties.

Acquisition—In corporate law, there are two types of acquisitions. The first occurs when one corporation acquires all the stock of another corporation; the acquired corporation continues to exist as a subsidiary of the acquiring corporation. Under the second type of acquisition, one corporation acquires all the assets of another. In this case the acquired corporation continues to exist independently of the acquiring corporation, but is a "hollow shell'; the only assets owned by such a corporation are usually notes, bonds, and/or stock from the acquiring corporation, and cash.

Amortize—To pay off a bond or other debt over time in installments.

Asset—An accounting term used to describe things of value, measurable in monetary terms.

Basis—The cost of property, adjusted upward for installation charges, transportation charges, and substantial improvements and adjusted downward for subsequent depreciation. Also known as the tax cost of an item.

Blue sky laws—State laws governing the intrastate sale of stock, designed to protect potential investors.

Bond—A long-term promissory note issued by a corporation to persons who loan it money. The bondholders are creditors of the corporation.

Buy-sell agreement—An agreement among stockholders or between stockholders and the corporation, providing for the purchase and sale of the stock of the corporation, usually upon the death or departure of a stockholder.

Capital—The money or finances required to operate a business. In corporate accounting, the total assets of the corporation.

Capital expense—An expenditure in the nature of an investment for the future. In tax terms, a capital expense cannot be deducted when made; it can be deducted only over time, if at all.

Capital gains—Profits on the sale of a capital asset. Capital gains are taxed at a considerably lower rate than ordinary income.

Capital stock—Common stock.

Capital surplus—Property paid into a corporation by its stockholders in excess of the capital stock liability, that is, in excess of either the par value of the stock or the value established by the board of directors in the case of no-par stock.

Capitalization requirements—Requirements established by state corporation laws that permit a corporation to begin operation only after it has met a predetermined capitalization level, that is, after it has sold a set amount of stock.

Class (of stock)—A way of dividing stock into categories with differing rights to dividends and voting. The most common divisions of stock are into common and preferred.

Closely held corporation (close corporation)—A small private corporation with a small group of stockholders that does not sell its stock to the general public.

Common stock—Stock in a corporation that entitles the owner to vote with one vote per share and to participate in corporate profits through dividends.

Consolidation—Combining two or more corporations, terminating their individual existence, with a newly formed corporation carrying on their business.

Corporation—A separate legal entity, created as permitted by law under a certificate giving it certain rights, powers, and privileges in the conduct of business.

Cross purchase—A form of buy-sell agreement in which stockholders purchase the stock of a retiring or deceased stockholder in proportion to their current holdings of stock.

Debt—A fixed sum of money due under an explicit agreement.

Debt security—A security that gives the holder a right to repayment, but no ownership in the corporation. Such securities include notes, debentures, and bonds.

Demand note—An obligation to pay or repay money on the demand of the creditor, at any time after the note is signed.

Depreciation—If you buy business property that has a useful life of more than a year, you may be able to deduct only a limited amount of the cost as an expense for tax purposes the year you buy the property. The rest of the cost is spread over more than one year and deducted one part at a time. This is called depreciation by the IRC.

Dissolution—The termination of a corporation by its complete liquidation. After dissolution, the former stockholders have their proportionate share of the net assets of the corporation, which then ceases to exist.

Dividend—A distribution of cash, property, or shares of stock to the stockholders in proportion to their interests in the corporation (measured by their stockholdings).

Earned surplus—The retained earnings of a business.

Equity—A claim against the assets of a business. There are two types, liabilities and owner's equity. The former is debt, the latter is stock or equity security.

Equity security—Stock in a corporation.

IRC—The Internal Revenue Code of 1954, as amended. It is codified as Title 26 of the United States Code.

IRS—The Internal Revenue Service.

Liability—An obligation to pay, imposed either voluntarily or by the judgment of a court.

Liquid assets—Assets that are cash or that can be easily converted to cash, such as government bonds.

Liquidity—The ability of a business to meet its short-term financial obligations promptly and satisfactorily.

Merger—When one corporation is absorbed by, and into, another corporation. Its corporate existence is terminated.

Glossary

Natural person—A human being, as distinguished from a legal person, such as a corporation.

Nonassessable stock—Stock that has been issued for the proper consideration, as to both type and amount. "Nonassessable" means that the stockholder cannot later be required to provide additional consideration.

No-par (stock)—Stock with no par value associated with it. Its value is determined by the board of directors.

Ordinary income—Under the Internal Revenue Code, this is income that does not qualify for any favorable or special treatment, such as capital gains treatment, and is taxed at the established federal income tax rates.

Partial liquidation—The distribution of a portion of the assets of a corporation to its stockholders. After the distribution, the corporation continues to exist, unlike in a dissolution.

Partnership—A voluntary contract between two or more persons to place their money, assets, and labor in a business, with the understanding that there will be a proportional sharing of the profits and losses among them.

Par value—The designated value of a share of stock. This is the minimum amount that the purchaser must pay for the stock, but it may not correlate to the actual value of the stock.

Passive income—Income from sources such as rents and royalties. This is a category created by the Internal Revenue Code to differentiate types of income for corporate tax classification purposes.

Pledge—The delivery of goods, such as stock or assets, to a creditor as security for repayment of a debt.

Preemptive rights—The right of a stockholder to purchase a pro-rata share of newly authorized issues of stock before they are offered to others.

Preferred stock—Stock with a priority over common stock in the payment of dividends and in the distribution of capital on dissolution of the corporation. Generally, preferred stock is nonvoting stock.

Redemption—The buying back of property from the original purchaser by the original owner. In the case of stock, the corporation redeems its own stock from the stockholders.

Retained earnings—The total cumulative net income that a business earns over its life, less any funds that have been returned to the stockholders as dividends.

Return on investment—A measure of the earnings of a business in relation to the investment required to generate this income.

S corporation—The IRS's new name for a Subchapter S corporation.

Secretary of state—The official with whom all corporate papers are filed. In some states, this office may be known as the commissioner of commerce, the corporation commission, the superintendent of corporations, the director of regulation, the secretary of the commonwealth, or the department of assessments and taxation.

Security (securities)—Evidence of ownership in a corporation (stock) or of an obligation of the issuing corporation (debt).

Shareholder—A person who owns one or more shares of stock in a corporation.

Sole proprietorship—The most basic form of business enterprise, an individual operating the business alone. The sole proprietor retains all profits and bears all losses of the business. The sole proprietorship ends on the death or retirement of the owner.

Stock—The equity or ownership interest in a corporation.

Stockholder—*See* shareholder.

Subchapter S corporation—A business corporation that has elected to be taxed as a Subchapter S corporation under the Internal Revenue Code (Code Sections 1371–1374). This permits it to be taxed on a basis similar to that of a partnership.

Thin capitalization—Capitalizing a business using a relatively small amount of stock compared to debt to the stockholders. This is often done to make repayment of the investment of the stockholders tax-free.

Tort—A private wrong or injury for which the injured person can sue and collect monetary damages.

Trust—A legal device where possession and ownership of property is transferred to one person for the benefit and use of another.

Valuing (a business)—Determining what a business is worth if it would be sold. This involves several techniques, including a determination of a value as a multiple of earnings.

Glossary

Venture capital—Capital, or investment in a corporation, from outside sources. Typically these investments are designed to help the corporation to grow and to provide the investor with a substantial return on his investment in the corporation.

Voting stock—Stock in a corporation that carries a right to cast a vote in stockholder meetings. This is usually common stock, but preferred stock can also be issued with voting rights.

Voting trust—A trust created and managed to hold and vote stock in a corporation in order to maximize control over the affairs of the corporation.

References

Books

Buge, Edward W. *Business Financing Handbook*. Englewood Cliffs, NJ: Prentice-Hall, 1981.

Castle, Gray, et al., eds. *The Business Insurance Handbook*. Homewood, IL: Dow Jones–Irwin, 1981. Chapter 24 on valuing a business is a good treatment of the issue.

Gumpert, David. E., and Timmons, Jeffrey A. *The Insider's Guide to Small Business Resources*. New York: Doubleday, 1982.

Institute for Business Planning. *Lawyer's Desk Book—10th Edition*. Englewood Cliffs, NJ: Institute for Business Planning, Inc., 1984 (or latest edition). A handy reference for information on incorporating, including where to file incorporation papers, incorporating fees, and annual corporate taxes and fees.

Lane, Marc J. *Legal Handbook for Small Business*. New York: AMACOM, 1977. A basic primer for the business person who wants to become familiar with the legal issues facing a small business.

McGonagle, John J., Jr. *Business Agreements—A Complete Guide to Oral & Written Contracts*. Radnor, PA: Chilton Book Company, 1982. A complete guide to business contracts of all sorts, including agreements to sell a business. Special section on how to read and write contracts.

McGonagle, John J., Jr. *Managing the Consultant—A Corporate Guide*. Radnor, PA: Chilton Book Company, 1981. An overview of how to find, hire, contract with, and work with consultants. Written from the point of view of the client.

References

McGonagle, John J., Jr., Vella, Carolyn M., Davis, John, Jr., and Vella, Vito T. *Master Guide to Organization, Capitalization, and Control of Corporations.* Englewood Cliffs, NJ: Institute for Business Planning, Inc., 1984. Designed as a complete reference for legal, tax, and financial advisors to both public and privately held corporations.

Nickerson, Clarence B. *Accounting Handbook for Nonaccountants.* Boston: Cahners Books International, 1975. One of the best books on the subject, with many examples and sample documents for the entire accounting cycle.

O'Neill, F. Hodge. *Close Corporations*, 2nd ed. Chicago: Callaghan & Company, 1981. A reference book for lawyers.

Rao, Dileep. *Handbook of Business Finance & Capital Sources*, 2nd ed. New York: AMACOM, 1982. A useful guide to many financing possibilities, but not a basic "how to" for the novice.

Rausch, Edward N. *Financial Management for Small Business.* New York: AMACOM, 1979. Introduction to basic financial management issues. Chapter 5 on venture capital is a frank explanation of the shortcomings of using venture capital firms.

Sweeny, Allen. *Accounting Fundamentals for Nonfinancial Executives.* New York: AMACOM, 1972. A good, basic text, useful for those trying to understand how to prepare profit and loss statements and balance sheets.

U.S. Congress, House Subcommittee on Economic Stablization, Committee on Banking, Finance and Urban Affairs, 97th Congress, First Session. *Catalog of Federal Loan Guarantee Programs*, January 1982. Basic outline of the many federal loan guarantee programs. Given the rapid changes in policy, however, any such list is outdated before it is issued.

U.S. Small Business Administration, Office of Chief Counsel for Advocacy. *States and Small Business: Programs and Activities*, 1983.

Articles

Abbin, Byrle M. "Company Benefits vs. Estate Planning." *Boardroom Reports*, June 1, 1982.

Howard, Jim. "What's It Worth To You?" *INC.*, July 1982. An overview of valuing a small business.

Howitt, Doran. "Employee Ownership: A Capital Idea." *INC.*, April 1982. A study on how some businesses have used ESOPs to raise money from their own workers.

175

References

Millstone, Robert J., and Chester, Paula L. "Regulation D: New Opportunities for Small Business." *Barrister*, Spring 1982. One of the first summaries of the new SEC rules for private offerings.

Welsh, John A., and White, Jerry F. "A Small Business Is Not a Little Business." *Harvard Business Review*, July–August 1981. Discusses the difference between management of the smaller business and the larger business.

Periodicals

INC., Inc. Publishing Company, 38 Commercial Wharf, Boston, MA 02110.

The Business Owner, Thomar Publications, Inc., 383 South Broadway, Hicksville, NY 11801.

Venture, The Magazine for Entrepreneurs, Venture Magazine, Inc., 35 West 45th Street, New York, NY 10036.

IRS Publications

(Available from your local IRS taxpayer assistance center)

Pub. 15, Employer's Tax Guide (Circular E)

Pub. 334, Tax Guide for Small Business

Pub. 463, Travel, Entertainment and Gift Expenses

Pub. 527, Rental Property

Pub. 534, Depreciation

Pub. 535, Business Expenses

Pub. 538, Accounting Periods and Methods

Pub. 539, Employment Taxes

Pub. 541, Tax Information on Partnerships

Pub. 542, Tax Information on Corporations

Pub. 544, Sales and Other Dispositions of Assets

Pub. 551, Basis of Property

Pub. 583, Information for Business Taxpayers

Pub. 589, Tax Information on S Corporations

Pub. 1048, Filing Requirements for Employee Benefit Plans

References

Small Business Administration Management Aids

(Available from SBA, P.O. Box 15434, Fort Worth, TX 76119)

No. 1.001, The ABC's of Borrowing
No. 1.002, What Is the Best Selling Price?
No. 1.004, Basic Budgets for Profit Planning
No. 1.009, A Venture Capital Primer for Small Business
No. 1.014, Getting the Facts for Income Tax Reporting
No. 2.004, Problems in Managing a Family-Owned Business
No. 2.009, Business Life Insurance

Index

179

Index

Index

thin capitalization in, 102-103
voluntary liquidation of, 144-146
see also articles of incorporation;
costs of incorporating
costs of incorporating
amortizing, 69
deducting, 69-70
investigatory, 70
organizational, 70-71
start-up, 71
cross basis, 81-82
cross purchase buy-sell agreement,
81, 83

debt, 98-99
Delaware, flexibility of corporate
laws of, 47
directors, first meeting of, 63
domestic corporations, definition of,
48
double taxation, 11-12

Economic Recovery Tax Act
(ERTA), and Subchapter S corporations, 29
Employee Stock Ownership Plan
(ESOP), 114-115
Employee Stock Ownership Trusts,
and SBA guaranteed loans, 123
endorsers, as loan collateral, 109
equity capital, 109
equity funds, as type of money, 108
estate planning
advantages of incorporating for,
10-11
and avoiding dissolving the corporation, 144

foreign corporations, definition of,
48
fringe benefits
as advantage of incorporating, 8

options, when incorporating, 65
in Subchapter S corporations, 32
and Tax Reform Act of 1983, 1

going private, 141-142
going public
avoiding, 118-119
benefits of, 119-120
drawbacks to, 120
good faith rule, 75
government R&D money, 128
guarantor, as loan collateral, 109

incorporated pocketbook, as problem corporation, 45
insurance companies, as venture
capital source, 112
Internal Revenue Code
and collapsing a corporation, 46
and creation of Subchapter S corporations, 6
and dissolving corporations, 143
and estate planning, 144
and incorporated pocketbook, 45
and multiple corporations, 44
and partial liquidation, 145
and partially nontaxable liquidation, 146
and recapture provision, 56
Section 1244 of, 28, 103-104
and taxable incorporation, 55
and transfer of property to new
corporation, 53
and wage continuation plans, 9
Internal Revenue Service (IRS)
and bonds, 98
and closely held corporations, 27-
28
and collapsible corporations, 46
and corporations, 6
and cross basis, 81-82
and double taxation, 11

Index

partner, choosing, 117-118
partnership
  general, 16
  incorporated, *see* Subchapter S
    corporations
  and sole proprietorship, 15
par value of stock, 74-75
personal holding company, 45
piercing the corporate veil
  avoiding 149-150
  in closely held corporations, 28
  in multiple corporations, 42
  reasons for, 149
private placement device, to avoid
  going public, 118-119
professionally managed pools, as
  venture capital source, 112
promoters, 115-116
property, tax-free transfer of, 10
public corporations, *see* going public

Regulation D, of SEC, 119
requirement for consideration, 74-
  75
residency, and corporations, 40
resolutions, certifying, 138
retirement, and salary continuation
  agreements, 8-9
return on investment, 92-93

salaries, as advantage of incorporating, 8-9
salary continuation agreement
  cash-value life insurance to fund,
    8-9
  definition of, 8
S corporations, *see* Subchapter S
  corporations
Section 1244 stock
  and losses, 28, 103
  requirements for, 103-104

secured loans, 109
Securities and Exchange Commission
  and corporations going private,
    141
  Regulation D of, 119
  reporting to, by public corpora-
    tions, 120
  role of, 120
security
  convertible, 98
  debt, 98
  equity, 94-95, 98
short-term bank loans, 108
short-term credit, as type of
  money, 108
SIC (Standard Industrial Codes), 64
sinking fund, for funding buy-sell
  agreement, 80-81
Small Business Administration
  (SBA)
  applying for loans by, 126-127
  law regarding loans by, 123
  loan programs of, 122-127
  loans, eligibility for, 124-125
  loans through, 105
  and small business investment
    companies, 113, 123
  terms of loans by, 125-126
Small Business Innovation Research Program, 128
small business investment companies (SBICs), 113, 123
small offering exemption, to avoid
  going public, 118-119
sole proprietorship, 14-15
stated capital, 145
state laws
  flexability of, in Delaware, 47
  and going private, 141-142
  and public corporations, 120-121

183

Index

state small business programs, 128-129

statutory consolidation, 147

statutory merger, 146-147

stock
  assessing, 74
  authorized shares of, 73
  in closely held corporations, 24
  ESOP for ownership of, 114-115
  issued shares of, 73
  issuing, 75-76
  as method of financing corporations, 94-96
  outstanding shares of, 73
  no-par, 75
  par value of, 74-75
  regulations on sale of, 118
  Section 1244, 28, 103-104
  as source of capital, 7
  stated purchase price of, 82
  straight capitalization price of, 82
  transfer restrictions, 25, 85-87
  treasury shares of, 73-74
  types of, 73-74

stock acquisition, 147

stock redemption buy-sell agreement, 81, 83

stock subscription agreements, 64

stockholder agreements
  buy-sell, 80-85
  and directors' voting, 79-80
  and employment agreements, 80
  voting, 78-79

stockholders
  election of officers by, 79
  first meeting of, 63
  loans from, 98
  meetings, 136-138

Subchapter S corporations
  advantages of, 30-31
  and benefits, 32
  capital gains in, 36
  and close corporations, 29
  as compromise between corporation and partnership, 15
  Congress and, 29-30, 34
  creation of, by Internal Revenue Code, 6, 29
  disadvantages of, 31-32
  earnings in, 30-31
  Economic Recovery Tax Act (ERTA) and, 29-30
  income taxation in, 30-31
  IRS Form 2553 for, 33
  loans in, 35-36
  losses in, 35, 103
  and partners, 118
  qualifications for, 30
  Subchapter S Revision Act and, 30, 85
  and taxation, 11-12
  and Tax Reform Act of 1983, 1
  termination of, 34
  unreasonable compensation in, 36-38

Subchapter S Revision Act, 30

subsidiary, 41

taxable incorporation
  choosing, 55-56
  by mistake, 150-151
  regulations for, 55

tax advantages, of corporations, 9-10

Tax Court
  and incorporating costs, 71
  and unreasonable compensation in Subchapter S corporations, 36-37

tax(es)
  capital gains, 10
  consequences, and multiple corporations, 43-44
  double, 11-12

184

Index

and Economic Recovery Tax Act (ERTA), 29
  see also Internal Revenue Code; Internal Revenue Service
tax-free incorporation
  choosing, 55-56
  failed, 150-151
  and property transfer, 10
  regulations for, 54
taxpayer's number, 64
Tax Reform Act of 1983 (H.R. 4170, 98th Congress), 1
term borrowing, 109
term insurance, for funding buy-sell agreement, 83
thin capitalization
  benefits of, 102
  definition of, 102
  and IRS, 102-103
trade credit, as type of money, 108
traditional partnerships, as venture capital source, 112
treasury shares of stock, 73-74
trust receipts and floor planning, 110

unreasonable compensation
  in close corporation, 27-28
  guidelines for defending against, 37-38
  in Subchapter S corporations, 36-38

U.S. Congress
  and bankruptcy laws, 151
  and laws governing Subchapter S corporations, 29-30
  and tax law changes, 1
U.S. Securities Acts, 119

venture capital
  definition of, 111
  insurance companies as source of, 112
  investment banking firms as source of, 112
  manufacturing companies as source of, 112
  professionally managed pools as source of, 112
  proposal for, elements of, 113-114
  Small Business Investment Companies (SBICs) as source of, 113
  traditional partnerships as source of, 112
voluntary liquidation
  complete, 145-146
  partial, 145

wage continuation plans, 9
warehouse receipts, as loan collateral, 110
Watson, E. Ronald, on SBA loans, 127

DATE DUE

DEC 2 1 '87			
NOV 2 0 '89			
MAY 31 '90			
MAY 31 '93			
	261-2500		Printed in USA

THE
DARK COMEDY

THE DEVELOPMENT OF MODERN
COMIC TRAGEDY

BY

J. L. STYAN

CAMBRIDGE
AT THE UNIVERSITY PRESS
1962

PUBLISHED BY
THE SYNDICS OF THE CAMBRIDGE UNIVERSITY PRESS
Bentley House, 200 Euston Road, London, N.W. 1
American Branch: 32 East 57th Street, New York 22, N.Y.
West African Office: P.O. Box 33, Ibadan, Nigeria

©

CAMBRIDGE UNIVERSITY PRESS

1962

Printed in Great Britain at the University Press, Cambridge
(Brooke Crutchley, University Printer)

PREFACE

I hope that the title chosen for this book, *The Dark Comedy*, will not mislead readers into thinking that the drama of the twentieth century is dull, or necessarily gloomy: it is anything but this for the spectator. When it is stimulating, it is because it refuses to allow us to respond with preconceived notions of the tragic or the comic. I have therefore been at pains to lose in my title the associations belonging to the spurious term 'tragicomedy', which invites us to measure a play by two widely different yardsticks simultaneously, regardless of their possible irrelevance.

Once again I owe my very sincere thanks to Professor G. E. T. Mayfield, Mrs Pat Roberts and my wife for their most valuable suggestions and assistance. Grateful acknowledgement is also made to the owners of copyright material quoted in this book.

J.L.S.

UNIVERSITY OF HULL
June 1961

v

CONTENTS

vii

I cannot immediately determine whether or no I am dignified by the Title you have graciously conferred on me. You cannot but recollect the difficulties that have unceasingly arisen to prevent my discerning whether your Angels are black, white, or grey.

THOMAS BUTTS *to* WILLIAM BLAKE

ON TEARS AND LAUGHTER

DELMONTE. I play everything, classical and modern plays, tragedies
and comedies.

ISABELLE. And you never get them muddled, mix them up at all?

DELMONTE. Never used to in the old days! Comedy was comedy
and tragedy was tragedy! But with the plays we get served up
nowadays, of course....

JEAN ANOUILH, *Dinner with the Family*

FORM OR FORMULA?

García Lorca is reported by his brother as saying, 'If in
certain scenes the audience doesn't know what to do, whether
to laugh or to cry, that will be a success for me'.[1] Such a
statement by a playwright could not easily have been made in
any century but our own. We know that several great plays
from the past have called for an equally vacillating response
from their audiences, yet not until now, confronted by a pro-
lific line of modern plays which refuse to be pigeon-holed as
comedies or tragedies, are we being forced to rethink some
of the long-accepted categories which have traditionally helped
us to evaluate the play.

Over recent years, comments from critics have grown increasingly ambivalent and paradoxical, and we now flounder
in the near-meaningless terminology of the farcical tragedy
and the pathetic comedy, the *drame comique* and the *pseudo-
drame*, the 'charade' and the 'extravaganza'. The term 'tragicomedy' was equivocal enough in the past. On the other
hand, the enigma is far from resolved when a contemporary
writer, Ronald Peacock, states forthrightly, 'In the midst of

[1] Francisco Lorca, introduction to *Three Tragedies of Federico García Lorca*, trans.
Graham-Luján and O'Connell (New York, 1955), p. 13.

more intricate details of aesthetic analysis it is well to state a simple truth. Drama must be one of two things: either comic or intensely moving.'[1] It is partly to discuss how far such embarrassing words as 'comic' and 'moving' in themselves beg important questions that this book is written.

Drama, as a structure of shifting relationships between character and spectator, today ranges over largely uncharted fields of feeling; and it reveals itself in infinite variety. A traditional nomenclature is just no longer serviceable for the description or analysis of the relationships developed by Chekhov, Pirandello and Jean Anouilh. These are the three playwrights who best exemplify a new direction in the twentieth-century theatre.

It is time to call a halt to the Polonius-like mobilization of genres and sub-genres. Our standard is still to be the intensity of the reflection and the incisiveness of the comment the play calls up. But we shall recognize that a play may legitimately refuse to be a failed tragedy or a failed comedy—because the response it wants may be of neither kind, and the forms and conventions it uses may bear no relation to either. Ambiguous plays like *Hamlet* and *Major Barbara* are unique ways of speaking, devised to satisfy the demands of their own subjects, not to conform to preconceived patterns of thought or feeling explored elsewhere.

As early as 1775, Goethe saw the distraction of caring for form when it was merely fashion: 'It is well nigh time that people ceased talking about the form of dramatic compositions, about their length and shortness, their unities, their beginning, middle, and end, and all the rest of it; and that we now begin to go straightway to their contents, which hitherto, it seems, have been left to take care of themselves.'[2] We are but a step away from Coleridge. His reiterated demand was for

[1] R. Peacock, *The Art of Drama* (London, 1957), p. 189.
[2] Goethe, quoted by B. H. Clark, *European Theories of the Drama* (Cincinnati, 1918), p. 339.

2

our awareness of the relevance of the part to the whole, for our appreciation of the total pattern as it takes shape from within the work itself. The creative impulse which fixes the unity of the piece may take no account of fashion.

Ibsen's *An Enemy of the People* is an angry pamphlet play about a half-comic, hot-headed individualist, Dr Thomas Stockmann, who sacrifices everything in his fight against 'the compact majority'. It narrowly misses tragedy, and Ibsen admitted that he was not sure whether the play was comedy or drama: 'it partakes of the nature of either, or lies half-way between'.[1] *An Enemy of the People*, as is well known, was written in haste as an urgent personal statement: this accounts for its polemics, and also for its uncertain form, which Ibsen did not preconceive. He was instinctively tilting against the formal frontiers of drama in his imaginative effort to find a public analogy for his private battle.

Or consider *The Silver Tassie*, O'Casey's play about the callousness of war, which he calls uncomfortably a 'tragi-comedy'. It develops from farce to tragedy, adopting in turn the conventions of pseudo–realism and expressionism, in order to smite us with the grotesque ironies of the last act in which we see young Harry the ex-footballer soldier sit helplessly in a wheel-chair. As O'Casey felt the need to regulate our response in the audience, so he called into play first one, then another, expedient. Only the vehement drive of the play's theme fuses its several parts. We must recognize a distinction between form and formula.

Eliot's *The Family Reunion* is a more deceptive example. It is too easy to see this play in the pattern of tragedy: it invites our sympathy with a central figure Harry, Lord Monchensey, who cannot understand his agony of mind; this 'hero', in human suffering, traces a course through and beyond

[1] Ibsen, letter to Jonas Lie, 1882, quoted by J. Lavrin, *Ibsen: an Approach* (London, 1950), p. 85.

I-2

a universal human predicament; it incorporates elements of the *Oresteia* of Aeschylus, deriving its energy from the Greek concept of the curse, merged with a Freudian concept of heredity; Harry's impulse towards 'atonement' may even be taken as an equivalent to that intangible, the cathartic effect of classical tragedy. Audiences might be forgiven for faintly hoping to apply standards acquired from Sophocles's *Oedipus Rex* or Shakespeare's *King Lear*.

Second thoughts confirm that these elements of the 'tragic' are quite lost in another pattern which makes a stronger impression. This pattern is marked by differing manners of speech, by indicative action on the stage, by contrasting levels of characterization. These present an argument on two levels: the world of Harry and Agatha, his favourite aunt, is set against the lower level of the family chorus. The chorus persists vividly throughout the play even when not speaking as a formal group. It does not have the traditional function of explaining, anticipating, exciting, but, in a new way, it ironically accentuates the spiritual problems of Harry. The family is the negative to Harry's positive. Here is one view of an older generation who live and move in a narrow orbit of the past, who

> tighten the knot of confusion
> Into perfect misunderstanding,

who are 'ridiculous in some nightmare pantomime', who do not 'understand'.

In organizing this second pattern, Eliot has done more than write the 'tragedy' of Harry, Lord Monchensey: he has, perhaps inadvertently, written the melancholy comedy of those whose 'ordinary day isn't much more than breathing'. Amy, his mother, and the aunts and uncles together take our attention as much as Harry does, and Eliot has written neither tragedy nor comedy. The tensions between the two constituents present us with a *tertium aliquid*, and the author

4

rightly calls *The Family Reunion* 'a play', simply. Central to the play, as to *The Cocktail Party*, is the conception of the monstrous discrepancies between human minds.

More recently, an attack on Anouilh's play of St Joan, *The Lark*, is rooted in the wish to see the play as tragedy when it was conspicuously intended to be nothing of the kind, any more than was Shaw's *Saint Joan*. It is not considered that the 'scaling-down' process of Anouilh's treatment is important for our fresh response to a well-worn theme, and to help us to recognize man as a creature doing evil and doing good, created by God, as Anouilh says in the person of Joan, 'in that contradiction to make his difficult way'. Joan is presented to us in modest, human terms, not as the idealized saint of legend, nor as a Shavian and rationalized symbol; to say this, of course, does not mean that she is not also a fit subject for tragedy or for comedy in other hands. Is this humanizing treatment of Anouilh's really an attempt to introduce 'a form of realism which belongs to bourgeois comedy and drama, and which is completely out of place in this context and has no relevance to the theme'?[1] Within a patently simple theatrical convention, with the trial presented detachedly as a play-within-a-play, thus having a far from naturalistic impact, we are shown a Joan who is not a religious mystic, but a child in pigtails who *might have been* beaten by her father, as a girl who *might have been* easy in the company of earthy soldiers on their own level, who *might have been* mocked by other women and seduced by men like Baudricourt. Not a mystic, not a tragic, but a naïve, Joan is offered to us by mixing her with a selfish and pompous sensualist, a good-humoured brute, a fanatical psychopath, and other types of the 'experienced' beside whom Joan's simplicity glows. The transfiguration of Joan at the final curtain is not the ascension of Joan to heaven, but the

---

[1] J. Chiari, *The Contemporary French Theatre: the Flight from Naturalism* (London, 1958), p. 189.

coronation of the Dauphin; it is not there to send us off happily, not a misplaced attempt at a tragic irony, but an irony to impress upon us the presence of the mystery, the phenomenon of Joan, like 'the phenomenon', as Anouilh remarks in a programme note, 'of a daisy or of the sky or of a bird', of a lark uncaged.

The argument against *The Lark* is reinforced by formal preconceptions about tragedy which are commonly held:

Who ever heard of jesters or clowns at the foot of the Cross at the moment when the world rent itself in an eternal wound? Clowning and tumbling can certainly be moving homages to God, but they cannot take place at the foot of Calvary. The death of a saint, a hero or a myth-maker is part of the revelatory process of the very essence of life through death, and in order to be effective it can only take place in a setting of austere grandeur, which may include irony but not snivelling or tearful jocularity. A tragedy must have a style, a form or ritual which cannot include barracks life.[1]

But clowning and tumbling *can* take place at the foot of Calvary, and in as sober a Miracle Cycle as that from York there is evidence enough that the pinners took very much to heart the idea of the mockery of Jesus by the soldiers who crucified him, as the Gospel suggested. It appears first as a direct sarcasm:

> I KNIGHT. And since he claimeth kingdom with crown,
> Even as a king here have it shall he.[2]

Between the action of a very protracted crucifixion, the men quarrel among themselves with a fair sprinkling of comedy:

> I KNIGHT. Why chat ye so? Fasten on a cord,
> And tug him to, by top and tail.
> 3 KNIGHT. Thou commands lightly as a lord;
> Come help to haul, with an ill hail.
> I KNIGHT. Now certes that shall I do,
> Full surely as a snail.[3]

---

[1] J. Chiari, *The Contemporary French Theatre*, pp. 194–5.
[2] *The York Cycle of Mystery Plays*, version by J. S. Purvis (London, 1957), p. 284.
[3] *Ibid.* p. 285

Form or Formula?

After a natural modicum of advertisement to the crowd of their skill and trade, the business of casting lots for the garments while Christ is in his agony is abruptly concluded by the leader in this way:

> 3 KNIGHT. I rede we draw cuts for this coat;
> Lo, see how soon all sides to save.
> 4 KNIGHT. The short cut wins, that well ye wot,
> Whether it falls to knight or knave.
> 1 KNIGHT. Fellows, ye need not take offence;
> This mantle is my gain.[1]

The real interest of this drama lies in what these apparent contradictions contribute to the theatrical experience. Anouilh is ostensibly refusing us the austere grandeur of tragedy; the author of the York play is testing us by including barracks life. By oblique means these plays yield their meaning, and, unless we choose to read their attempts as ignorant structural errors and to ignore their effect on an audience, they bring sharply into question the so-called 'rules' that must be followed by the dramatist.

Before we consider the inadequacy of traditional theories of tragedy and comedy to identify and explain the characteristic tone of modern drama in general, we should remind ourselves quickly of those great, intuitive playwrights of earlier years who have upset the theories. Notably, these are Euripides, the anonymous authors of the English Mystery plays, Marlowe and, pre-eminently, Shakespeare and Molière.

[1] *Ibid.* p. 289.

7

On Tears and Laughter

It is no part of the argument to suggest that dark comedy is a new vogue, only that it has had its fullest expression in the last sixty years. It would be surprising should we fail to find a mixture of moods, comic and pathetic, and of responses, critical and sympathetic, at times earlier than the twentieth century, especially since the mixture can so well reflect the multi-coloured world of society or the soul. We do in fact find the dark note making itself heard subversively at particular moments in earlier ages of the drama. How far an unstable public or private temper, an uncertain climate of opinion or an uneasiness in the spirit of the writer from disturbing personal experiences, was responsible for the troubled drama we are describing, is for others to decide. Athens's declining years, England at the turn of the sixteenth century, Molière's France under Louis XIV, Russia at the turn of the nineteenth century, and Western Europe as a whole after the two world wars, seem to have in common that mood of unrest that permits a Judas drama.

Towards the end of Euripides's long life, Athens, previously confident and secure as the commercial centre of the Greek world, was a creature spent and frustrated by the exhausting Peloponnesian wars. After the fatal Sicilian expedition of 415 B.C. she was torn by factions at home. At the same time, scepticism at the old beliefs was undermining the Athenian sense of moral security, and rationalism, pervasive as scepticism is in educated society today, encouraged the fruition of an iconoclastic theatre, notably in Euripides and Aristophanes. With his comic eye, Aristophanes chose the way of burlesque, mercilessly satirizing the man whom one would have thought closest to his own mind.

As far as we know, Euripides, the restless Socratic questioner, chose to write largely within the given tragic form he inherited from Aeschylus and Sophocles, and it proved the more powerful weapon for that. Within the limits of tragedy he tried to depict the truth about the people of the old legends as he saw it. He makes a gesture, for example, towards showing two sides of Jason, towards explaining Clytaemnestra's sin, towards querying the popular religion that could find the matricide Orestes at once right and wrong. In Aristophanes's *The Frogs*, Euripides is made to explain that he taught men to talk with freedom, 'to fall in love, think evil, question all things'. And he adds,

I put things on the stage that came from daily life and business,
Where men could catch me if I tripped; could listen without dizziness
To things they knew, and judge my art.

A little later we hear,

I mingled reasoning with my art,
And shrewdness, till I fired their heart
To brood, to think things through and through;
And rule their houses better, too.[1]

In some of his plays Euripides is at moments within an ace of creating something of dark comedy by his modernity, and its presence may account for the arguments that have surrounded him in the past.[2] Thus although his first extant play, the *Alcestis*, was probably a type of Satyr-play, as Gilbert Murray argued,[3] we can recognize its contradictory nature. In it the story is told of the loyal wife Alcestis, who agrees to die in lieu of Admetus, not the best of husbands. Meanwhile Heracles, receiving hospitality in the palace of Admetus, has apparently got himself roaring drunk at the very time when Alcestis's funeral procession is moving off. So much so that the butler makes a complaint about him; but also, in order to shame him, the butler has told Heracles all about Alcestis.

[1] Aristophanes, *The Frogs*, trans. G. Murray (London, 1908), pp. 72–3.
[2] These positions are reviewed by A. R. Thompson, *The Dry Mock* (California, 1948), ch. 8.
[3] See the Introduction to *The Alcestis of Euripides*, trans. G. Murray (London, 1915).

This information not only sobers the reveller, but inspires him to go and rescue her forthwith, and thus the play ends as a 'comedy'.

The *Helen*, of *c.* 412 B.C., is a high comedy, satirical to the point of undermining the glory of the Trojan War itself, hallowed repository of the greatest among the Greek legends. The *Ion*, of about the same time, tells of the princess Creusa who was seduced by the god Apollo and bore him the child Ion. This child is exposed to die, only to be saved by Hermes. The play ends with a conventional recognition scene between mother and son, but in the meantime Apollo the seducer has been smoothly debunked.

The wit in this author was working against the greater single-mindedness of his famous predecessors, but also towards a greater resourcefulness in drama. As Murray suggested so long ago, 'Greek drama has always suffered from a school of critics who approach a play with a greater equipment of aesthetic theory than of dramatic perception'.[1]

Even more difficult to disentangle are the contradictory springs of feeling present in the popular drama of medieval times in England. We saw how the soldiers who are set to crucify Christ in the York Pinners' and Painters' Play performed their task well 'in character' as broad, insensitive sadists. The guilds' actors obviously also saw their function as one of amusing their audience with horseplay, in spite of the grim seriousness of the moment. This element of near-blasphemy is common to all the medieval Mysteries. Herod, the slayer of the Innocents, is the prize clown of the show; the devils and Satan himself contribute to the fun at the very moment when the sinners are thrown into the jaws of Hell, and especially when Hell is being harrowed. Years later, in Marlowe's *Doctor Faustus*, 'shaggy-haired devils' were still to be seen 'roaring over the stage with squibs in their mouths'.

[1] *The Alcestis of Euripides*, trans. G. Murray, p. vi.

Euripides, Mystery Plays, Marlowe

The reader may not need reminding of the joy evident at other, less pressing, times. The introduction of a wife for Noah in the Chester *Flood* is one of those happy opportunities for the male actor in his skirts to caricature some wifely aberrations, and in so doing unavoidably present God's chosen one as a poor pathetic creature easily led by the nose. Having teased Noah for as long as the farce will stretch, the wife is finally carried into the Ark by force:

> NOYE. Welckome, wiffe, in to this botte.
> NOYES WIFFE. Have thou that for thy note!
> NOYE. Ha, ha! Marye, this is hotte!

Mrs Noah's blow as she passes him, however, is abruptly forgotten as the Ark begins to float, and we hear from her no more.

Of most unusual interest, Joseph in the York Mysteries supplies a very earthy comment on the Immaculate Conception, for Joseph is the unsophisticated peasant of medieval England. He makes his entry primarily to establish for the spectator that Jesus will shortly be born, but he speaks like the old cuckold who cannot trust his young wife:

> For shame what shall I say,
> That thusgates now in my old days
> Has wedded a young wench to my wife,
> And may not well stride over two straws?[1]

So Mary for a brief instant is delightfully seen as a 'wench', with all the connotations of the word.

The story of Mak and Gyll in the notorious Second Shepherds' Play from Wakefield undoubtedly parodies the birth of Jesus in the manger. The play is jolly with the coarseness of the clowning of Mak, the *extra* shepherd who turns out to be a sheep-thief, and with the raucous groaning of Gyll who hides the stolen sheep in the cradle by her assumed childbed. After

---

[1] 'The Pewterers' and Founders' Play' in *The York Cycle of Mystery Plays*, trans. Purvis (London, 1957), p. 86.

Mak's crime has been discovered and he has been suitably tossed in a blanket, it is not surprising if we are today startled to hear a ready Angel break into a 'Gloria in Excelsis'. But the play must go on. This example is in no way explicable as illuminating by contrast the holy event. Nor would one think that any 'restlessness' in the audience of this time could in this case account for such strange phenomena in the drama. These instances, however, do strongly suggest that it is natural and human for an unfettered popular audience to be willing to undergo surprising contrasts of feeling and to joke about what is deeply revered.

The mixture of 'hornpipes and funerals', to use Sir Philip Sidney's phrase, was very much to the public taste. As if to spite the exertions of Renaissance critics, English drama of the sixteenth century brazenly flourished the peculiar tragicomic legacy of medieval drama. In *Doctor Faustus* Marlowe made an incomplete attempt at comic parody in the subplot of the servant Wagner with whom Faustus makes a mock compact of seven years to echo his own of twenty-four with Lucifer. However, the set-piece scenes of Faustus's jests with the great and the not-so-great belittle the hero and detract from the dignity of his impending doom. The clowning makes for a heterogeneous play: it hardly controls the light and shade of the drama of the soul in its hell on earth. Not until Marlowe's *The Jew of Malta* does the racy temper of the age translate itself effectively into drama. In this play in particular, its author's own wild, robust temperament added a special unity of spirit to the whole; this unity has been difficult to recognize, probably for the simple reason that the play is never seen on the stage. We remember T. S. Eliot's firm diagnosis in 1918 of the play's piquancy:

If one takes *The Jew of Malta* not as a tragedy, or as a 'tragedy of blood', but as a farce, the concluding act becomes intelligible; and if we attend with a careful ear to the versification, we find that Marlowe develops a tone to suit this farce, and even perhaps that this tone is his most powerful and mature tone. I say farce, but with the enfeebled humour of our times the word is a misnomer; it is the farce of the old English humour, the terribly serious, even savage comic humour.[1]

It was perhaps typical of the time to choose a Jew to be at the centre of a blood-curdling play, but it was especially typical of Marlowe to work so hard to make the Barabas we first meet as sympathetic as he is. Barabas has much of Tamburlaine's vast vitality and faultless logic:

> What, bring you Scripture to confirm your wrongs?
> Preach me not out of my possessions,

he answers to the Governor who is robbing him. His hatred of the Christians is justified, and he stands upright amid his calamities. But quite early on, hints are supplied for another, more farcical, view of him, as when with the help of his daughter Abigail he manages to recover his wealth from his house, requisitioned as a nunnery. As she throws his money-bags down to him, he cries, 'O girl! O gold! O beauty! O my bliss!' In this attitude he repels us, till the figure of heroic stature is steadily dwarfed to the caricature of a 'bottle-nosed knave'.

The character of Barabas is also instinct with Marlowe's evident delight in the outrageous conduct of a monster:

> As for myself, I walk abroad a nights
> And kill sick people groaning under walls:
> Sometimes I go about and poison wells,

which suggests Marlowe's grotesque, teeth-dripping interest in the fascination of fear. Our sympathy does not long survive Barabas's cruel use of Abigail's feelings and the sacrifice of her lovers for the sake of his revenge, however just, but the defiant note of a superman warring against inevitable defeat is heard even to the end when he curses his enemies from his boiling cauldron: 'Die, life! fly, soul! tongue, curse thy fill and die!'

[1] T. S. Eliot, 'Christopher Marlowe' in *Selected Essays* (London, 1932), p. 123.

13

On Tears and Laughter

Marlowe's 'acid humour', as F. S. Boas calls it,[1] remains strong in *The Massacre of Paris*, his tale of the Duke of Guise and the murky slaughter of the Huguenots. 'The Guise' is yet another Tamburlaine and very like Barabas; all are men of 'policy'. He commits a short series of gruesome murders on stage, giving a quick impressionistic view of the general massacre supposedly taking place off-stage. But each killing is conducted with a grim mockery of the victim and a short parody of his belief. Thus he mimics a Protestant preacher with 'Dearly beloved brother—thus 'tis written' as he thrusts his dagger home. The horror is streaked with a vein of perverse humour, and farcical cruelty is a mood we do not truly feel again, after the Jacobean drama of Marston, Webster, Jonson and Middleton, until Jean Anouilh and Samuel Beckett arrive in the theatre three hundred years later.

SHAKESPEARE

So to Shakespeare, the most intuitive writer of them all. So much has been written about his tragicomic spirit, that a cursory view of his position as a whole would seem useful. The simple fact is inescapable that Shakespeare's exploration of his experience in terms of the stage led him quite often, though of course not always, to touch his comedy with the tragic and his tragedy with the comic. Especially in the relatively new fields we are pleased to call 'histories' and 'problem comedies', he obeyed his most profound impulses to mix the two. In Dr Johnson's words, he 'caught his ideas from the living world', and it was this that produced his exciting results.

Shakespeare could draw a broad comic character and situation with the best of them. But again and again we notice that special power of his to observe, reflect and reassess which sets in motion a conflicting, even sobering, undercurrent. It

[1] F. S. Boas, *Christopher Marlowe* (London, 1940), p. 159.

is this which restrains our unharnessed submission to the potential comedy of Shylock and Jaques. In little we see the process at work in our picture of the justices Shallow and Silence, for example. On one level they are comic because they are utterly serious about themselves. But on another they are serious for us too because we know we have that within us which can find two pathetic old men comic. In these two creations Shakespeare displays his delicious sense of people growing old and thinking of their lusty youth; but they are also aware that their acquaintances are dying, and that 'we shall all follow'. However, punctuating these troubled thoughts on the great eternal verity, are other more material troubles like the price to be fetched by 'a good score of ewes'. As when King Hal's procession passes Falstaff by and the old man turns to his friend with an ambiguous 'Master Shallow, I owe you a thousand pound', so in the Shallow and Silence exchanges Shakespeare touches exquisitely a true nerve of comedy.

In another department of comic pleasure we must place, for example, the rare portrait of Rosalind on which so much of our enjoyment of *As You Like It* hangs. Rosalind lacks the single-minded strength of a Célimène or a Millamant, the larger-than-life creatures of Molière's and Congreve's comedy; it is her weaknesses that make her more compassionate and warm than either of these. Our moments for laughing at her are balanced by the times when we laugh with her. Thus, caught in the stutters and hesitations of romantic love, she cannot drag herself away from Orlando's presence, for all an embarrassed Celia pulls at her sleeve:

> ROSALIND. He calls us back: my pride fell with my fortunes,
> I'll ask him what he would: did you call sir?
> Sir, you have wrestled well, and overthrown
> More than your enemies.
> CELIA. Will you go coz?
> ROSALIND. Have with you: fare you well.

On Tears and Laughter

When she hears that Orlando is there in the forest with her, her agitation is that of an articulate canary:

ROSALIND. Nay, but the devil take mocking: speak sad brow, and true maid.

CELIA. I'faith, coz, 'tis he.

ROSALIND. Orlando?

CELIA. Orlando.

ROSALIND. Alas the day, what shall I do with my doublet and hose? What did he when thou saw'st him? What said he? How look'd he? Wherein went he? What makes he here? Did he ask for me? Where remains he? How parted he with thee? And when shalt thou see him again? Answer me in one word.

Yet this same Rosalind can advise her Orlando when in a similar condition that 'men have died from time to time, and worms have eaten them, but not for love', and describe the meeting of brother Oliver and Celia with the perceptive diagnosis of a wise old aunt:

For your brother, and my sister, no sooner met, but they look'd: no sooner look'd, but they lov'd; no sooner lov'd, but they sigh'd: no sooner sigh'd but they asked one another the reason: no sooner knew the reason, but they sought the remedy....

As a result of this treatment, the spectator is placed in the position of one who feels sympathy with the chicken that might have been hatched from the egg he is relishing.

The dramatic pattern of *As You Like It* as a whole exemplifies those qualities of comic balance found in *A Midsummer Night's Dream*, *Much Ado About Nothing* and *Twelfth Night*. The play's pattern is again one of the frivolous pulling against the serious, felt in the opposition between the picture of social disruption and the affairs of the heart, between the 'desert inaccessible' of 'melancholy boughs' and the concept of 'the golden world' of Arden. The love stories themselves explore the 'tyranny' of the pretty passion, Phoebe teasing Silvius, and Rosalind teasing Orlando, while the harmony brought by Hymen may only descend after the trials and torments of harsh experience. Already a Pirandellian questioning of earthly values is felt in this most gentle of comedies, where we are invited to see, in the words of old Corin the bystander, 'a pageant truly play'd' by those who wear their masks quite lightly. In the structure of his scenes Shakespeare conceals another of his mysteries. The contrast and continuity of mood and tone forbids and welcomes us by turns; and for us to pass between the worlds of Silvius, the absurd lover, and of Corin, the plain man, from Orlando's noble but rather rhapsodical sentiments to Audrey's slap-and-tickle substantiality and Rosalind's bright sanity, to pass from Jaques the pessimist to Touchstone the realist, is to build rhythmically within the mind the balanced image of a unique play.

This oblique approach to dramatic meaning found in the earlier comedies marks that salty style that defies final analysis. Though we would not say that such roseate comedy contains more than a tinge of grey, the manner of its keeping its equilibrium is recognizably that of other Shakespearian comedy in which the complexion is darker. The last comedies, and in particular *The Winter's Tale*, stagger us with a more brazen disregard of 'form'. This tragedy of Leontes's jealousy is turned face-about, and yet remains extraordinarily stable for its sheer vitality. In his effort to translate a portrait of ugly human caprice into one of regeneration and hope, Shakespeare uses a series of outrageously successful tricks of theatre: planting an ironic Paulina at the heart of the tragedy, introducing clowns into the emotional storm into which the child Perdita is cast, having the irresistible realist Autolycus take our whole attention with his delightful 'coney-catching', inviting us to jump from one generation to another that is young and infinitely lovable, and demanding daring leaps in tone that make the sheep-shearing feast of IV. iv the enduring piece of legerdemain it is.[1]

[1] An interesting analysis of the tragicomic mixture in this play will be found in S. L. Bethell, *The Winter's Tale: a Study* (London, 1944). See especially 'Antiquated Technique and the Planes of Reality', pp. 47 ff.

On Tears and Laughter

How far is such a technique truly distinguishable from that which Shakespeare introduces with extraordinary effect into some of the tragedies? In a tragic context rarer and deeper passions are plumbed by the presence of the commonplace and the trivial, the comic and the absurd. We are confronted by a tragedy like *King Lear*, the peak of Shakespeare's achievement, at whose point of crisis is conceived the scene of the mad trial. 'The core of the play', writes Wilson Knight, 'is an absurdity, an indignity, an incongruity.' Webster's *The Duchess of Malfi* and Middleton's *The Changeling*, at whose climax madmen touch off the mordant mood of the drama, seem to have borrowed some of *King Lear's* feverishness for the next generation. The peculiar tensions of Shakespearian tragedy arise not only from the total irony of the events in their course, but as well from the many and detailed moments misleadingly called comic 'relief', moments carefully thrust into the tragic action to make the pain the more acute.

The facilities offered by Shakespeare's neutral stage lent themselves to his special dramatic rhythm of ironic contrasts. A virtual absence of scenery encouraged an exceptional fluidity in the structure of scenes, affecting the pattern of responses demanded from the spectators. A possible intimacy between the actor and his audience permitted a wide and flexible range of playing from rhetorical declamation to the naturalistic confidence of a whisper, affecting the pattern of tone in speech, scene and sequence of scenes. These patterns are especially likely to be missed in reading: in performance we become immediately aware that a scene in Shakespearian tragedy is written always as a stage in the cumulative extortion of feeling from an audience, a well-planned turning of the screw.

The simply constructed, early apprentice tragedy of *Romeo and Juliet* may serve as our example. In this play Shakespeare tested the scope of his stage, and explored the powers

18

of tragedy by balancing scene against scene. He found that by mixing the spectator's moods within the continuity of the narrative line of the story, he could add immensely to our sense of the lovers' isolation and the poignancy of their difficulties. He prepares us for the balcony scene, otherwise surely one of the sweetest of saccharine love-scenes in drama, by the coarseness of Mercutio's ribaldry:

> I conjure thee by Rosaline's bright eyes,
> By her high forehead, and her scarlet lip,
> By her fine foot, straight leg, and quivering thigh,
> And the demesnes, that there adjacent lie...

In jest Mercutio invites Romeo to 'cry but ay me': 'ay me' is the very note we hear echoing joyfully from Juliet a moment later. 'Pronounce but love and dove', cries Mercutio, mocking the hollow clichés of the love-songs: soon after, we hear the soft exquisite music of 'Oh speak again bright Angel'. So the beauty of the love-scene is itself enhanced by contrast, while the total dramatic flavour we retain is that of a bitter-sweet prelude to the more distasteful action to come. Similarly, the Nurse's banter to Juliet about the preparation of her 'bird's nest' to receive her lover, echoes in the mind long after the old shrew has left the stage, sounding right through the frightening and portentous scene in which Tybalt is killed and Romeo banished.

The play moves towards its climax of feeling. The lovers are to have their last secret assignation 'at the window', but not before old Capulet and the County Paris, Juliet's betrothed, boorishly plan the wedding below:

> CAPULET. ...bid her, mark you me? on Wednesday next.
> But soft, what day is this?
> PARIS. Monday my Lord.
> CAPULET. Monday, ha ha, well Wednesday is too soon,
> A'Thursday let it be, a'Thursday tell her,
> She shall be married to this noble Earl:
> Will you be ready? Do you like this haste?

On Tears and Laughter

...what say you to Thursday?
PARIS. My Lord, I would that Thursday were tomorrow.
CAPULET. Well get you gone, a'Thursday be it then.

Nudging his future son-in-law in the ribs, Capulet exudes his vulgar *bonhomie*, casting over the succeeding love-scene a finer feeling of purity and simplicity than it would otherwise have, but nevertheless leaving us with the ominous impression that time is hounding its victims. We come finally to the controversial 'burlesque' of mock-mourning, the simultaneous expression of the comic and the tragic, performed by the quartet of Lady Capulet, the Nurse, Paris and Capulet, with their awkward concatenation of apostrophes to the 'woeful day' and the rest of it. This is of a piece with, and perhaps a tiresome introduction to, the farce of Peter (the Second Quarto has 'Enter Will Kemp', who was the company's clown) and his request to the musicians to play 'Heart's Ease'. Here Shakespeare is, if less successfully, attempting another and bolder withdrawal of sensation before the onset of his catastrophe.

Who can doubt that it was a trial of this kind that led him, with a subtler pen, to introduce into the mature tragedies scenes like those of Macbeth's Porter, Hamlet's Gravediggers in their discussion over Ophelia's grave, Lear's Fool, Cleopatra's Clown? In these tragedies, however, Shakespeare was careful to make the comic element less obtrusive.

Only faintly does the quality of parody and burlesque appear in these plays, in, for example, the verbal insistence of Mercutio's mockery, in Lear's mad trial of his absent daughters, in the disrespectful love-play of Charmian and Alexas which follows the heroic exchanges of Antony and Cleopatra themselves: 'Lord Alexas, sweet Alexas, most anything Alexas, almost most absolute Alexas....' But parody was the likeliest form of mockery for the less trammelled 'history' plays, in which not a tragic but a narrative form was uppermost in the author's mind in the writing, and in which a lucky balance was struck between the comedy of Eastcheap and the noble deliberations and enterprises of the kings and princes of the realm.

Falstaff and Eastcheap, one can guess, were first introduced to mark the point of departure from which the audience was to trace the development of Prince Hal from rogue to monarch, and for more fashionable reasons than to provide meaningful parody of the glorious by the inglorious. Falstaff, who can move freely among both, grows to represent more than the common clown before his death in *Henry V*: he is felt to embody a common humanity. This function of a unique character creation has been excellently stated elsewhere; and D. A. Traversi makes the point succinctly:

At one time, in his account of his own exploits at Eastcheap, he parodies the heroic boasting to which the more respectable characters in their weaker moments are given; at others, he provides a comic version of the moral lectures addressed by Henry IV, not without a strong hint of political calculation, to his son (1 *Henry IV*, II. iv) or comments bitingly at Shrewsbury (v. i and iii) on the true meaning of the word 'honour' so freely invoked by dubious politicians to urge others to die in their interest. Working sometimes through open comment, sometimes through parody, his is a voice that lies outside the prevailing political spirit of the play, drawing its cogency from an insight that is the author's own and expressing itself in a flow of comic energy.[1]

It remains only to estimate for ourselves the joy with which the Elizabethan spectator of *Henry IV*, *Part I* must have heard the bright irony of 'Honour pricks me on. Yea, but how if honour prick me off when I come on? how then?...', and the mixed feelings with which he heard the lugubrious irony in *Part II* of 'Peace, good Doll! do not speak like a death's-head; do not bid me remember mine end'.

The so-called 'problem comedies', *Troilus and Cressida*, *Measure for Measure* and *All's Well that Ends Well*, are dramas

---

[1] D. A. Traversi, *An Approach to Shakespeare*, 2nd ed. (London, 1957), pp. 30–1.

of such romantic form that in them Shakespeare feels himself even more at liberty to swing between the *pièce rose* and the *pièce noire*. They are plays demonstrating as original a dramatic exploration of experience as anything in the canon. Each has, too, a special interest as an experiment in controlling an audience's quality of attention; it may be that this is one of the reasons why so many playgoers declare roundly how much they dislike them. Few of their characters are endearing; their behaviour is less so. Yet the force of their drama is irresistible, and the peculiar pungency of dark comedy is strong within them.

We no longer bother to face the impossible task of deciding whether *Troilus and Cressida* is a tragedy, a comedy or a history. Nowhere in Shakespeare are riotous gyrations of style so complete as in this play. The swinging of the tone between tragedy and mockery persists throughout, though it is not introduced to intensify its potential tragedy, but to extract that special flavour of bitterness we associate with it.

The acrid taste of the play is partly due to its anti-romantic subject, which is the disintegration of social and personal values under certain stresses; it is partly due to its ugly imagery; and partly to a deliberate confounding of the audience—the play sets the classical heroes of traditional romance over against the coarseness of Thersites and Achilles, and contrasts our romantic ideal of Helen and her world with the crude reality of Pandarus and Cressida. In the outcome, Cressida finds another lover and Troilus both loses Cressida and his horse. But the particular quality of our dramatic experience arises from the range of styles and juxtapositions through the play, deliberately kneading our every reaction, in spite of the jocularity of the Prologue's

> Like, or find fault, do as your pleasures are,
> Now good, now bad, 'tis but the chance of war.

The keynote is struck at the outset of the play, where we meet a despondent and introspective Troilus wallowing in his love, but under fire from a bantering Pandarus—it is clear we are not to take this Trojan hero seriously. In this same spirit of mockery we are invited to watch the chieftains at their counsels. So through to the end, where Pandarus, our irresponsible guide through the play, walks downstage like Laudisi in Pirandello's *Right You Are If You Think So*, and half laughs, half spits at the spectator to whom he says he will 'bequeath' his 'diseases'. There can be no mistaking that we are to respond in a mood of acute scepticism.

This scepticism is enacted in the language of the play: the poetry directs the inflexion of our mind. Thus we are prepared for the scene in which Cressida is to play her part as 'daughter of the game' by, of all things, a conventional expression of sentiment in a Petrarchan manner from Troilus. Troilus, it seems, has spent a last impassioned night with her, though we may have noticed that 'the busy day/Wak'd by the lark' also 'hath rous'd the ribald crows'. But Troilus's romantic rhetoric is set sharply against Cressida's keen psychological naturalism and Pandarus's coarse prose. So, too, after the fine public speeches of the Greek politicians, we drop with startling frankness into Ulysses's private tone, and have our misgivings clinched by the unequivocal voice of Thersites. The conflict and uncertainty in the spectator's mind is thus given shape and authority. Changes in the language of this play anticipate amazingly those changes in convention more commonly met with in twentieth-century drama.

Measure for Measure tells the story of the chaste Isabella who is invited to sell herself, sinning to save her brother Claudio, himself under sentence of death for a sin of the flesh. This is a situation we should declare today to be of pure Pirandellian irony: a seduction for a seduction. This raw and grotesque plot is further coloured by the garish presence of a gang of comic supers, who coarsely restate the moral points of the theme throughout. Thus the words of the wit Lucio,

spoken to his friend Claudio who has just expressed his somewhat belated regrets at finding himself in prison, are spliced
with ambiguity: 'I had as lief have the foppery of freedom, as
the morality of imprisonment.' The comic bawd Pompey, upon
being apprehended by the comic lord Escalus, asks gently,
'Does your worship mean to geld and splay all the youth of the
city?' The macabre interlude before the anticipated execution of Claudio is taken up, first, with a light-hearted discussion between the executioner Abhorson and the bawd on the
'mystery' of hanging, then with Pompey's merry comments on
the assortment of criminals he finds with him in the prison,
and, third, with a clown's performance from Barnardine who,
because he is drunk, 'will not consent to die this day, that's
certain'. Though this fooling may have assured the Elizabethan audience that a happy end was to be anticipated,[1] we
cannot fail to hear the distorted echo of Claudio's own
agonized

> Ay, but to die, and go we know not where;
> To lie in cold obstruction and to rot...

In this profound and constantly engrossing play, Shakespeare
compels us to weigh in one scale the meaning of life, as
illuminated by death both tragic and comic, against, in the
other, the meaning of 'honour' as illuminated by lechery both
tragic and comic; then he coolly asks us whether it is God or
man who holds the scales. Having posed an insoluble problem,
he promptly cuts the knot with a facile *dénouement*: he scan-
dalously and contemptuously has the Duke of Vienna marry
Mariana and Julietta to their seducers Angelo and Claudio.
Mary Lascelles comments on the easy intervention of the Duke
that, when a writer of tragicomedy 'propounds a situation
from which no happy issue seems possible', he 'then deploys
a power strong enough to avert the expected ill'.[2]

[1] M. Lascelles, *Shakespeare's Measure for Measure* (London, 1953), p. 111.
[2] *Ibid.* p. 146.

24

Shakespeare

The matter of *All's Well that Ends Well* offers a similarly cold analysis, without solution, of the problem of the battle of the sexes in relation to class. Can the woman who loves a man of higher rank than herself chase him, and remain virtuous? Can she chase him knowing that he loves her not, and remain virtuous? Even though she is technically married to him, can she substitute herself in bed for her husband's mistress, and remain virtuous? It seems she can; and live happily ever after. But to accept this, we are asked to question the precepts on the nature of honesty in woman that we previously held dear. That Shakespeare, in approaching the technical problems of this interesting task, faced insuperable difficulties, is clear from the awkward mixture of the real and the unreal among the characters. Thus the Countess, mother of Bertram the rake of a husband, is sympathetically real, while Bertram himself is ugly and unnatural. Helena, the embarrassing lady who initiates the problems of the play, is both real and unreal: like Cressida and like Isabella, she must behave as a puppet when Shakespeare is not warming her to life by his poetry.

In this play again there is a running *badinage*, this time from Parolles, Bertram's self-opinionated follower, and from Lavatch, clown to the Countess; and again the calculated mixing of scenes and styles. Thus as Helena plans her campaign to sleep with Bertram against his wishes, stressing the 'wicked meaning in a lawful deed' and suggesting the ambivalent values in the trick, Bertram is simultaneously preparing to ambush his friend Parolles to test his valour and prove him a liar in a scene reminiscent of the baiting of Falstaff. With these two scenes juxtaposed in performance, we receive an oblique mockery of our objections to the motives behind Helena's action. The moral pattern of the play is thus defined. The honest justice in deflating Parolles is scaled against Helena's instinctive and justifiable immodesty in deflating Bertram.

On Tears and Laughter

The degree of horseplay and the casual and irresponsible endings of these 'romantic' plays seem to belie their seriousness. Is it that Shakespeare did not quite know what he was about, taking up popular stories in haste and finding too late that their form was unsuitable? Their poetic strength denies uncertainty in their tone, though an uncertainty might have been presupposed from a recapitulation of their plotting. The tone is as deliberate and serious as any in Shakespeare. Mary Lascelles should have the last word for the moment when she says that 'the logic of tragicomedy may seem slack', but 'it is capable of gratifying a natural and proper desire to ruminate modes of human experience other than our own'.[1] But: *other* than our own? The Jacobean drama is uneasy with doubt, and its troubled heart reflects its feelings about a questionable world. Significantly, there has been a marked revival of interest in the problem comedies since 1946.

MOLIÈRE

Having adopted the comic form and made it delightfully his own, Molière was quick to find that any comic character and any comic situation pressed hard enough can turn a comedy towards tragedy. At times he seems to slip into the limbo inadvertently; but at his best he is working consciously to secure that fine balance of attraction and repulsion, that partial identification of the spectator with a character who would otherwise be viewed detachedly. In doing this, he roused a new excitement in the theatre of his time which survives today, and at times he touched depths of painful feeling which puts *The Misanthrope*, for example, in a class far above the more farcical comedies deriving from the *commedia dell'arte*. The intimate backstage reasons for his special understanding of the enormous potential and the enduring fascination of a

---

[1] M. Lascelles, *Shakespeare's Measure for Measure*, pp. 157–8.

comic-pathetic picture of life have been repeatedly traced to the misery and uncertainty of his private life with Armande Béjart, his young leading actress. More attention is needed now, not upon the causes, but upon the effects in the auditorium, of his dramatic wisdom.

Molière's own statements of his intentions indirectly offer some little help in this. There are the well-known comments of Dorante–Molière in *La Critique de l'école des femmes*. With eminent common sense, it is suggested that the dramatist should make his final reference to nature rather than to forms and rules. Dorante declares,

When you portray heroes, you may treat them as you please: they are imaginary portraits in which one does not look for a likeness, and you have only to follow the promptings of a soaring imagination, which often abandons the truth in order to attain the miraculous. But when you portray men, you must paint from nature.[1]

Again and again in Molière's art, it is nature which sharpens the edge that cuts deeper into our sensibilities.

Nature takes a firm hand in *The School for Wives*, the prototype for Anouilh's *Colombe* and other plays of innocence betrayed. Beginning as an exercise in pure comedy, the presence of natural forces introduces that inescapable note of tragedy which makes it the first of Molière's great dramatic *causes célèbres*. Arnolphe has tried to educate his young ward Agnès to be the perfect wife for himself. He has kept her in ignorance to ensure her innocence. The point of the play becomes plain after a few moments; this same ignorance must leave a void which may be filled by bad as well as good, and her sweet inexperience of life lays her especially open to impulses over which Arnolphe can have no control. What is more, we are completely won over by her spontaneous joy when she innocently tells Arnolphe of her encounter one warm evening with the charming Horace: 'Such a handsome young

[1] Trans. A. Tilley in *Molière* (Cambridge, 1936), p. 93.

27

man. When he saw me he immediately gave me a deep bow.
I didn't want to seem less polite, so I curtsied in return. So
promptly he gave me another bow; then I did the same
again....' Under the lyrical influence of the simplicity and
the poetry, we are ready to see Arnolphe as the comic villain
of the piece and Horace as the knight errant, and we respond
lightly.

But with the crisis of the last act our mood is changed for
us. Agnès tells how much she loves her Horace, and cannot
love the angry Arnolphe:

AGNES. Don't blame me. Why didn't you make yourself loved like him?
I didn't try to stop you as far as I know.
ARNOLPHE. I did the best I could, but I've been wasting my time.
AGNES. Then it's clear he knows more about such matters than you,
since he had no difficulty at all in making himself loved.

So Arnolphe discovers, too late, that he is really devoted to
her, and in a speech full of pathos we are given a glimpse of
the other side of the coin. The play hovers for an instant
on the brink of a precipice, one we approach frequently in
dark comedy; then Molière quickly resolves the difficulty.
Arnolphe is made to sheer over to safety with the 'rolling
eyes, ridiculous sighs and childish tears' of Pantalone from the
commedia dell'arte. With this and a facile *dénouement*, Molière
saves the play, spares his audience and avoids the issue.

In the second half of *Tartuffe* the action totters crazily
between farce and tragedy. If we feel discomfort, it derives
largely from the conception of the central character and the
impossibility of his actor's keeping a balance in performance.
Is Tartuffe a clown or a monster? At first 'his red ears and
his red face' of Dorine's description, his manifest hypocrisy,
his greed and his piety, would seem to stamp him as a buffoon.
For him to hurt others would stifle our sense of comedy, but
the laughable fanaticism of Orgon helps us feel that no great
harm could come to such a patron. Yet as the play progresses,

the true Tartuffe emerges to show himself a vile and sinister scoundrel, determined upon marriage to the guileless daughter Mariane, ready to insult Orgon's wife, resolved to turn his benefactor and his family penniless into the street. The spectator watching this rugged and unlovely play must feel that Molière's sense of congruity has been sacrificed for an ulterior motive. His desire to make a reckless frontal attack on sanctimonious cant rends his comedy from top to bottom. Boileau may well have had a point when he suggested that Molière was forced to make Tartuffe a viper to ensure that we recognized the evil in him in time to correct earlier misjudgments, but the artistic failure seems unmistakable in every performance.

Don Juan, like *Tartuffe*, swings between farce and tragedy. We laugh when Juan makes love simultaneously to Charlotta and Mathurine; we laugh when he flatters and out-talks M. Dimanche who comes to ask for the repayment of Juan's debts. But his scurvy desertion of his wife Elvire and the cheating of Don Luis his father leaves him a despicable and far from romantic hero. He is merely the atheist whose appropriate end is for the earth to open and swallow him with rolls of thunder and flashes of lightning. The Statue is a *deus ex machina* who serves only to bring down the curtain on a dramatically purposeless mixture.

In *Amphitryon, Georges Dandin, The Miser* and *The Imaginary Invalid* the case is different again. In each the initial 'humour' of the central character makes for broad comedy, and though in excess it is always ready to slip into pathos, the tone of the play is kept largely under control. Indeed, a submerged pathos tends to strengthen our response. Amphitryon's jealousy of the king of the gods who seduces his wife is mixed with his shame as a dishonoured husband. Dandin is another unhappy husband presented in terms of explosive farce, but whose despair is just allowed to show itself. The miser Harpagon, in the pursuit of his love of money, runs the risk of hurting his family, and the exchanges between Harpagon and his son Cléante repeatedly introduce a strong suspicion of serious comment into the broad comedy of the plot. Thus because of the oscillations of feeling in this play particularly, we cannot be as sure of the direction in which Molière is taking us, or that the contrary elements of the play have been blended with assurance. The story of Argan the hypochondriac might have been the tragedy of a man whose carefully preserved life is hardly worth preserving anyway. But the element of tragedy is almost completely hidden. Only in the brief moment when his daughter thinks him dead is there any hint of another point of view. Rightly, the plays in this group are generally performed with all the weight on the farce, in the confidence that this will outweigh our doubts.

The Misanthrope justly deserves its place at the head of Molière's work, if only for the reason that nowhere else does his writing display so beautifully that comic-pathetic poise which has us rooted to our seats. Those who think with Bergson that comedy is more like life than tragedy because the latter must sublimate life, might think that here at least is the justification for that loose remark. The truth is that *The Misanthrope*, in touching life more closely, has run the risk of ceasing to be comedy. It successfully remains a comedy, but then it is a very exceptional play.

Alceste is a bear and a prig; yet we love him for his faults. Without moderation and without that indispensable sense of humour needed to ease the rigours of social life, he will not tolerate the insincerity and cheap flattery he hears about him; yet our conscience tells us he is right. Thus the direction of sympathies in the auditorium is carefully prescribed in the first place by the ambivalence in the central character. He is weighed against his friend Philinte, who seems shallow by comparison. He speaks his mind fiercely about the poor sonnet of the poetaster Oronte, and this honesty is justified in our eyes to a great extent, not only because the verses are bad, but also because that same sonnet is addressed to the lady Alceste loves. In all this we are with him in spirit. But he is also in love with an enchanting creature, Célimène, and as soon as he is seen to apply his rigid standards of social morality to her, we know that the man is impossible.

Célimène's part is the second key to our understanding of the complexity of the piece. She is admittedly the queen of coquettes, and by Alceste's standards she deserves more than censure; we may even pity his infatuation. Nevertheless we love her too, because we know that there are qualities in *nature* again that justify such behaviour in a young girl. Though she lacks the sincerity of her rival Eliante, she is contrasted cleanly with the prudish Arsinoé to exemplify her truly feminine merits, and her wit and her engaging ease in society —the pleasure she gives us as social beings ourselves—must plead her cause. Molière has arranged it that the man who hates the ways of society is hopelessly in love with the idealized woman who has them all. The situation is a nice development from that of *The School for Wives*, where Arnolphe in his way also mistrusts society, and his inflexibility is similarly belied by our common sense; but both Alceste and Célimène lack the innocence of Arnolphe and Agnès, and their more human errors accentuate the more human problem, stressing the conflict between heart and head and between the male and the female principle.

Elasticity and compromise is the secret of happy human relations; without them, as Bergson suggested, there inevitably follows either laughter or tears. The great scene of the play, Act IV, scene iii, calls up both, because it is alive with the vitality of two characters, perfectly balanced, whose natural opposition we have been made to feel and understand. Like

On Tears and Laughter

Strindberg's eternal query 'Man or woman, who is master?', like Shaw's life force in *Man and Superman*, like the inevitable opposition of Marcel and Albertine in Proust's great novel, this quality elevates the scene to become symbolic of the battle of the sexes itself.

In the face of Alceste's blind rage at having discovered her letter to Oronte, Célimène remains completely in command of herself. At first she calmly comments, 'This is certainly a remarkable method of love making.'[1] Her frankness continues to disarm: 'Why should I blush?...Why should I disown a letter in my own hand?' She begins to draw our sympathy in spite of the justness of Alceste's accusations. She suggests that the letter might have been written to a woman—but she is careful to avoid saying that it has. Then in apparent anger herself, she encourages him to believe what hurts him most, that the letter was addressed to Oronte, but again she concedes no secrets:

No, it's to Oronte. I'd rather you thought that. I delight in his attentions, enjoy his conversation, esteem his qualities—I'll agree to anything you like. Go on, pursue your quarrel, don't let anything deter you...so long as you plague me no longer.

She shows her strongest weapon, but we are less in sympathy with her for this feline subterfuge, though we cannot avoid some momentary amusement at her craft. Célimène now has him in thrall, and he pleads with her to relieve him of his doubts in passionate words which win us completely.

Yet to keep the equilibrium, Molière has her answer ready: 'You are mad when you are in these jealous fits, and don't deserve the love I have for you....I ought to bestow my affections elsewhere and give you reason for legitimate complaint.' Incensed, Alceste goes so far as to declare his feelings in outrageously paradoxical terms characteristic of the man we know:

[1] Trans. J. Wood, from *Molière, the Misanthrope and Other Plays* (London, 1959).

ALCESTE. Ah! My love is beyond all comparison! Such is my desire to make it manifest to all the world that I could even wish misfortune might befall you—yes, I would have you unloved, reduced to misery or born to indigence, without rank or birth or fortune so that I might in one resounding act of loving sacrifice repair the injustice of your fate and enjoy the love and satisfaction of knowing that you owe everything to my love.

CELIMENE. A strange way of showing your goodwill!...

Which promptly thrusts her back where she previously stood in our esteem. So the balance is re-established and the only 'uproarious' scene in the play, the farcical interlude with the servant Du Bois, consolidates the position.

In the following act Molière repeats these tricks at the expense of the spectator. The reading of another communication from Célimène reduces her in our eyes to a scandal-monger who respects no one. This time she pathetically admits her guilt, but in spite of Alceste's confession that he loves her still, it is he who rights the balance of our affections once again by condemning himself out of his own mouth. Du Bois had planted the idea in his mind that, as a result of a lost lawsuit, he should decamp. Thus he now offers to forgive her everything, 'provided you'll agree to join me in my plan of fleeing from all human intercourse and undertake to accompany me forthwith into the rustic solitude to which I have sworn to repair'. Her reply is the one we might have made ourselves: 'Me? Renounce the world before I'm old and bury myself in your wilderness!...The mind shrinks from solitude at twenty....' She sweeps out and is gone for ever. The separation of these two was the only 'happy ending' for both, and the growth of our image of the play's meaning has been marvellously held in check for the last twenty minutes of the play.

In the last analysis, however, there are no shocks in Molière. The eruption of savage farce always possible with his predecessors dies down during the seventeenth century; it belongs to a less classical age, and is not felt again until the licence of our own. Wyndham Lewis reaches the conclusion about Molière that 'we realize from the beginning that he is on our side',[1] and the truth is that we are reasonably safe in distinguishing the villain from the victim. With the possible exception of *The Misanthrope*, we are largely at ease with ourselves, and we in the audience who share Molière's common sense and humanity need to fear little for our personal security, compared with the risks we run when we watch, say, Pirandello's dark comedy of the twentieth century. To say this is in no way to discredit a dramatist who primarily offers other things; it is only to stress that the ancestry of Chekhov's muddled families, Pirandello's introspective fanatics and Beckett's helpless clowns, if traceable at all, is certainly hybrid and probably illegitimate.

TRAGEDY AND TRAGICOMEDY

It is understandable if today we are inhibited in our diagnosis of tragedy and comedy. The vexed question of what properly constitutes the tragic is accentuated by our often muddled preoccupation with an appropriate dramatic formula and correct playing convention for the play. We may too readily anticipate as the form for a tragedy what should grow out of the content of the play and not be imposed upon it: recent efforts to resurrect the ancient Greek tragic chorus on the modern stage, or to find a verse pattern for the lines, or to contrive a modern equivalent for the soliloquy and other conventional devices, or to employ a mythological framework within which to work, are symptomatic. The elements by which we tend to identify tragedy are generally conventional ones: verse, in preference to prose, that the diction may be suitably 'heightened'; kings, princes, heroes and their rarefied circumstances shall provide the characters and their situations, that the play may be

---

[1] D. B. Wyndham Lewis, *Molière: the Comic Mask* (London, 1959), p. 205.

34

suitably elevated in tone; the plot shall lead remorselessly
towards disaster, that the spectator shall be properly edified,
sometimes by pity, sometimes by fear, sometimes by both.
Each of these agencies is artistically equivocal.|

Drama is not to be heightened by verbal dexterity alone—
burlesque gains some of its peculiar force by being grand with
the words when the situation or the character explicitly lacks
grandeur. The words take their substance from the action to
which in turn they give rise, and prose dialogue which is
functioning fully within the play may be reinforced as well
by the action on the stage as verse. The unaffected language
and the exquisitely simple expression of Lear's grief in the
lines,

> Why should a dog, a horse, a rat, have life,
> And thou no breath at all? Thou'lt come no more,
> Never, never, never, never, never!
> Pray you, undo this button. Thank you, sir,

gathers its power chiefly because of its context: it comes
quietly at the end of a great rush of feeling, and it marks the
reversal of the King's former attitude and his complete
humility. Nor could the magnificent appeal of Lear's

> O, reason not the need; our basest beggars
> Are in the poorest thing superfluous...

reach its intended degree of poignancy out of the mouth of the
Fool or of Edgar.

The heroic character is dependent for its dignity upon the
world in which it moves: Hamlet grows taller in our eyes in
proportion as Ophelia, Gertrude, Claudius or Laertes by
their presence raise him and in consequence grow smaller
themselves. But the commonplace world can have its relative
nobility too, and can be equally fearful and pitiful, just as a man
can attain heroic proportions in his own circle or in his own
eyes. Provided that circle is recognizable and brought close

enough to us, and provided his eyes are our eyes, with our absorption in the play intense and complete, the character can be exalted for us too. For the quality of the heroic on the stage must always lie within the imagination of the audience: Nora, the child-wife of Ibsen's *A Doll's House* who defies the world of respectability, or Maurya, the fisherwife of Synge's *Riders to the Sea* who faces nature itself, can rise above her littleness to the solemnity and grandeur of a queen; Willie Loman, Arthur Miller's salesman in his tough territory, can have the temporary dramatic stature of a king on his uncertain throne. Theatrical convention dictates that the stature of the hero is relative to the setting in which he is placed, and if the dramatist is capable of passing a character into our experience, that character may also be capable of assuming tragic proportions.

A sense of 'the remorseless' in the drive of the plot towards the dethronement of man in his pride by forces beyond his control is what induces the emotion characteristic of tragedy. This remorselessness is felt by ironic implications which must lie within the structure of the play: a snare is set by the dramatist for the protagonist, and we wait breathlessly for the trap to be sprung. Yet the spectator must not feel that the trap is there by accident, that it is arbitrarily planted to rouse his excitement: his natural sense of unfairness must not betray his dramatic sense of the just subjugation of his deputy on the stage. Whether Fate, Necessity, or the Gods, or the short-sightedness of the hero himself, shall set and spring the trap, punishment must be in one sense explicable: it must be justifiable. Here too convention plays its part. If any audience is to declare, 'Yes, this outcome is fitting', it must have some moral presuppositions; by common assent there must be some scale of judgment. Thus unless we are prepared to share imaginatively the convictions of the Greek world, we may doubt whether we can today know the catharsis of which

Tragedy and Tragicomedy

Aristotle speaks after we witness, for example, the *Oedipus Rex* of Sophocles. Nor is the glory of Thomas à Becket's martyrdom in Eliot's *Murder in the Cathedral* likely to be fully meaningful outside Christendom. This is not to say, of course, that the pity or fear felt about our mortality, which is common to ancient Greek, modern Christian and all men alike, may not persuade us to an emotional response in the theatre satisfying in itself.

Today the ethical conventionalism of tragedy seems impossible to adopt. If an implicit moral valuation must contribute to the understanding and enjoyment of the play, the dramatist must share it with his audience, and a homogeneous theatre seems a prerequisite for successful tragedy. In his researches as a playwright since the war in plays like *The Cocktail Party*, Eliot has trusted his audience less and less: he does not deploy religious counters about his play; he merely implies a vaguely Christian reference which may be felt or not only after the characters have suffered a particular secular experience. Writing in France during the same period, Sartre sets up his own framework of values in order to lend moral significance to the events of his play. But the obsessive inevitability of tragedy is lost in *Men Without Shadows*, his play about men of the French Resistance who discover an existentialist meaning in their sufferings, or *Crime Passionnel*, the play which invites us to question whether its hero has acquired existentialist grace, because we are too busy questioning first premises to attend to conclusions; we think too much to be passionate. The important 'universal human predicament' may exist within Celia Coplestone of *The Cocktail Party*, the society girl who suffers a change of heart sufficient to sacrifice herself as a missionary, or within Hugo Barine of *Crime Passionnel*, the new party member who asks to be allowed to kill a traitor in order to prove himself a man; but the universal impact is dangerously softened by our asking with simple pagan sentiment whether Celia has not wasted her talents, or whether Hugo did not die a rather selfish death.

The Elizabethans had no need to ask whether Romeo and Juliet died worthwhile deaths: they defied the irrepressible powers of society to the glory of a greater cause, and a limited sexual encounter became a spiritual triumph in an age which admitted individualistic experiment. Tragedy, like any drama, should be a reflection and interpretation of life—on this it stands or falls; but it may argue from a silly philosophical standpoint even though it may have much of 'life' in it. If Eliot's philosophy is too narrow, or Sartre's incomplete, there is no reason why it may not be dramatized successfully, though this may yet not prove the value of the philosophy: it merely proves that it may be dramatized. Tragedy may escape. Both Eliot and Sartre have nevertheless done us a service by implying within the body of the play a code by which to reason and evaluate its meaning; they have shown again that it is possible to evolve a serious drama, given meaning by what may be a selected, fantastic and subjective ethic, in a play which is, however, neither tragedy nor comedy.

In these ways at least 'tragedy' is precariously balanced on variously ephemeral conventions of theatre or audience, and it is not surprising that the tragic of one age may not easily be revived in another with any assurance. Especially where the appositeness of earlier conventions is in doubt, a parochial near-tragedy is likely to follow. Thus Arthur Miller's *Death of a Salesman* is arguably a lesser creation than the *Agamemnon* of Aeschylus; but if criticism, in order to make sense of such a play as Miller's, continues to employ a term associated with a set of conventions no longer in use, it invites confusion.

Perhaps the most tiresome instance in modern times has been the drama of Ibsen. Those who missed the ritualistic heroism in his mature plays found it necessary to say he was writing a solemn form of satirical domestic tragicomedy based on personal psychology but having social reference. Oh, dear. We see more clearly now that the movement towards realism of subject and manner in the nineteenth century was one which simply modified the conventions of classical tragedy and produced another kind of play. The tragic individual superseded the tragic hero, but had the power to be no less moving and no less significant. Ibsen was raising important issues for drama: What are the near limits of the tragic world? May the spectator's <u>intelligence</u> be used with his emotions to help rationalize his interest and yet allow the flow of the play to be preserved? Dare the dramatist risk hearing us laugh when he would wish us to weep? Can he risk diminishing the stature of his hero in order to ensure his individuality, as happens with Dr Stockmann of *An Enemy of the People*, whom Ibsen variously declared to be 'muddle-headed' and 'an extravagant immature fellow and a hot-head'? Might not the narrowing of the frame and setting of the play limit the width of its appeal, as seems to have happened with *A Doll's House*, but not with *The Master Builder*, concerned with those who will not accept the limitations of middle-age, and so touching us all? As Desmond MacCarthy justly said of Hjalmar Ekdal of *The Wild Duck*, Hjalmar the small man and our representative of illusory happiness, 'Hjalmar is a wide shot that hits half the world'.[1] We may sense tragedy here, but we may not find it: we may be looking for the wrong evidence.

Thus tragedy 'in the full sense of the word' is missing today. Our present-day mongrel conventions, interbred with the spirit of naturalism, can better do other things, and do not encourage the exclusive consistency of purpose we ask of

[1] D. MacCarthy, 'The Wild Duck', 1905, reprinted in *Specimens of English Dramatic Criticism, XVII–XX Centuries*, selected P. C. Ward (London, 1945), p. 237. In his essay on 'Tolstoy: Tragedian or Comedian?', 1921, Shaw later suggested that 'Ibsen was the dramatic poet who firmly established tragicomedy as a much deeper and grimmer entertainment than tragedy'.

tragedy. Twentieth-century currents of contradictory thought and the mood of audiences do not permit it; the laws of tragedy belong to a world which is religious in its affirmation of human greatness. Today we hear only the uncertainty and the whimper of the ending of Jean Cocteau's Oedipus story, *The Infernal Machine*, as Creon and Tiresias watch the blinded king led away by his daughter Antigone and the ghost of his wife Jocasta:

CREON. And even supposing they leave the town, who will look after them, who will admit them?

TIRESIAS. Glory.

CREON. You mean rather dishonour, shame....

TIRESIAS. Who knows?

Curtain.[1]

The play slips imperceptibly into 'tragicomedy'. In an age when tragedy is submerged in moral indifference, we may expect a kind of tragicomedy to come into its own.

The line between tragedy and its hybrid partner tragicomedy is often difficult to draw, and is a central concern in this essay. A technical point, however, invites attention here. The ironies which enforce the dialectical conflict of tragedy are simple in formula: each step the hero takes towards a supposed triumph is a step nearer his death, each step one which strengthens the audience's sense of a necessary end. The spectator, knowing or feeling this outcome, is wholly in the confidence of the author and the secret of the play; the characters are not. The spectator stands where the Gods themselves stand, in a happy position of omniscience. Therefore his excitement during the performance does not arise from a simple chemical mixture, as it were $x + y$, where x is each decision arising from the hero's wish to assert his personal responsibility, the positive element, and y is the tightening of the net of inevitable destruction, the negative element; but its source is in an active chemical

[1] J. Cocteau, *The Infernal Machine*, trans. C. Wildman (London, 1950).

compound, where the resulting passion is xy, imaginatively irreducible, a new substance with fierce properties of its own. It has even been given a name of its own: 'tragic irony'.

Yet its counterpart, 'comic irony', is not very different in kind. It may indeed merge at times into the more easily recognizable irony of tragedy. The spectator is equally omniscient, able by his presence in the comic theatre to perform a chemical experiment like his fellow in the tragic theatre. Within his mind he mixes the positive image of a character wishing to be and to assert himself, x, with another aspect of necessity's power to destroy—its power to belittle and under-mine by suggesting commonplaceness and triviality, y. Comic irony, however, can prick with a thousand pins in the course of a play, and in its way be as all-pervading and relentless and irresistible in its effect as tragic irony itself. Nor need we assume that such tragicomedy as emerges carries less weight than tragedy, is any the less moral, or bears any the less relationship to the society which promotes it. Its philosophy may come equally from profound laws of feeling and under-standing, just as important in themselves for our apprehension of the quality of life.

Both experience of life and familiarity with the best of twentieth-century drama constantly compel us to be aware of the blood relationship of the tragic and comic senses, of the interbreeding of tears and laughter. In an earlier essay, Ronald Peacock had declared with more justice that both tragedy and comedy 'spring from the tension between our imperfect life and our ideal aspirations. They exist together in their dependence on the contradictions of life. They are parallel expressions, in different keys, of our idea of what is good.'[1]

---

[1] R. Peacock, *The Poet in the Theatre* (London, 1946), chapter on 'Tragedy, Comedy and Civilization', p. 126.

On Tears and Laughter

We may gladly defer to the sound judgment of Dr Johnson in his familiar defence of Shakespeare's tragicomedy:

Shakespeare's plays are not in the rigorous and critical sense either tragedies or comedies, but compositions of a distinct kind; exhibiting the real state of sublunary nature, which partakes of good and evil, joy and sorrow, mingled with endless variety of proportion and innumerable modes of combination; and expressing the course of the world, in which the loss of one is the gain of another; in which, at the same time, the reveller is hasting to his wine, and the mourner burying his friend; in which the malignity of one is sometimes defeated by the frolick of another; and many mischiefs and many benefits are done and hindered without design.[1]

Dr Johnson is of course the last man to invite anarchy in literary or dramatic standards: the play must disclose its design if life will not. But even he allows that 'there is always an appeal open from criticism to nature': we must be well prepared to admit an endless variety of proportion and innumerable modes of combination.

TYPES OF COMEDY

The recognized theories of comedy do not help us any the more to understand the characteristic drama of the twentieth century. Ideas about the comic have never been expressed as abundantly as those about tragedy, both because the seriousness of comedy has not been as evident to writers as its more impressive high-toned counterpart, and because the ways and intentions of comedy may be more tiresome to explain. Up to the beginning of this century, comedy suffered a hardening in its arteries and its critics had grown further and further away from the practice on the stage. Certainly, no theorist seemed capable of putting forward an explanation sufficiently all-embracing, and the philosophical and the psychological approaches have both been wanting.

[1] Johnson, *Preface to Shakespeare*, ed. W. Raleigh (London, 1908), pp. 15–16.

42

Types of Comedy

The diagnosis of comedy presents many difficulties. Laughter, a recurring and therefore an evidently important ingredient, seems to arise from a great variety of sources: we laugh at other people's bad luck, or at relief from embarrassment, or at a little flattery, or even when we do not want to laugh. We laugh heartily, or smile gently, or at some comedy we may not laugh at all. There are so many uses to which laughter can be put, from the promotion of a cold vindictive sarcasm to that of the empty gaiety of knock-about. There is considerable discrepancy between the things we find comic in life and those contrived on the stage: a man falling on his face in the street may be an object of pathos, but on the stage an object of derision. There is confusion between the techniques of comedy designed to raise laughter and the use to which the laughter is put: why should an anticlimax make us happy, or a clown make us sad? There are too many 'types' of the comic, and we plague ourselves by trying to sort comedy from burlesque, satire and farce, notwithstanding that in Shakespearian comedy elements of each seem to be present, and the points where they overlap are none too clearly defined. We are often at a loss to assess a total impression: even where in Molière the play's parts have been largely sweet and farcical, the whole when swallowed can leave a bitter taste in the mouth.

We find that when a joke is dissected, it abruptly ceases to be funny, which is disconcerting to say the least. It is also notorious that a 'sense of humour' is an unreliable quality, and what will seem laughable to an English audience will not necessarily seem so to a Scottish. As a psychologist has written, 'If members of a social group observe that their own objects of laughter do not produce laughter in another social group they are inclined to express this fact by saying that the second group has "no sense of humour"'.[1] From the world of the

[1] R. H. Thouless, *General and Social Psychology* (London, 2nd ed., 1937), p. 209.

On Tears and Laughter

theatre we might add that what will seem laughable on Monday may be damned on Tuesday. It is, moreover, a nuisance that what is comic to one age is not to another: Shylock was a butt for the Elizabethans, but not for the Victorians; Richard III was played for comedy by Irving, but for pathos by Olivier. Fashions in laughter change too readily, and we are in some doubt today whether to laugh at or sympathize with a Falstaff or a Tartuffe or a Sir Peter Teazle. Furthermore, should we begin by studying crowd psychology or the particular successes of a particular writer? And if we are to set our standards by one author, who shall it be?—Aristophanes, Shakespeare, Molière, Shaw?

For Hazlitt[1] the essence of the laughable was 'the incongruous', a distinction between 'what things are and what they ought to be'. This happily enough explains what we may call 'satirical' laughter, the laughter by which the spectator refuses to acknowledge the propriety of the fop and the coquette in Restoration comedy, when he recognizes the affectation in their gesture and speech, or by which he knows to ridicule the seriousness with which the characters in *The Importance of Being Earnest* pursue their absurd ends. But Hazlitt lets fall a damning admission: 'It is perhaps the fault of Shakespeare's comic muse that it is too good-natured and magnanimous. We sympathize with his characters more often than we laugh at them.' It is a *fault*!

For Meredith[2] 'the test of true Comedy is that it shall awaken thoughtful laughter', but he too can only comfortably explain the *raison d'être* of the 'high' comedy of intellect: 'The laughter of Comedy is impersonal and of unrivalled politeness.... It laughs through the mind, for the mind directs it.' And though in another place he suggests, attempting to distinguish between comedy and humour, 'The stroke of the

[1] Hazlitt, Introduction to *The English Comic Writers* (1818).
[2] Meredith, 'On the Idea of Comedy and of the Uses of the Comic Spirit', a lecture delivered in 1877.

great humourist is world-wide, with lights of Tragedy in his laughter', he will not admit that this quality can also appear in the greatest forms of comedy. Shakespeare is again the stumbling-block: because Shakespeare paints 'humanity' rather than 'manners', he does not begin to explain Shakespeare's eye for the comic. 'Jaques, Falstaff and his regiment, the varied troop of Clowns, Malvolio, Sir Hugh Evans and Fluellen—marvellous Welshmen!—Benedick and Beatrice, Dogberry, and the rest, are subjects of a special study in the poetically comic.' So we move on to safer ground with Molière, some of whose success he can account for.

After Meredith has named this glittering variety of the ostensibly comic, should he not have tried to understand them? Neither Hazlitt nor Meredith can explain the warm comic success of these and others like Rosalind and Touchstone and Quince and Bottom and that great host of Shakespeare's comic creation which reflects so closely the 'English' sense of humour. Moreover, they cannot help us to sense the nature of the achievement in plays like *The Wild Duck*, *The Cherry Orchard*, *Major Barbara* and *Waiting for Godot*, ambiguous plays of the modern theatre which challenge our laughter, as we shall see.

Bergson[1] with every good intention turned to example after example to establish his precepts, but concerned himself too much with first causes and with the detail of technique rather than the odd results produced in the theatre. He further remained rather parochial in drawing too much on the kind of comedy which has so admirably set the standard for the French comic stage, that of Molière. It is noticeable that his examples are drawn chiefly from the farces and farcical moments of Molière and Labiche (author of such plays as *Le Voyage de M. Perrichon* and *Un Chapeau de paille d'Italie*)

---

[1] Bergson, *Laughter, an Essay on the Meaning of the Comic*, trans. C. Brereton and F. Rothwell (London, 1921), first French ed. 1889.

or the comical-absurd of such works as *Don Quixote*. He diagnoses comedy as arising from the incongruity of 'something mechanical encrusted on the living': 'the attitudes, gestures, and movements of the human body are laughable in exact proportion as that body reminds us of a mere machine'. He thus cites as laughable the forms and movements of the puppet, and in the same way Molière's Sganarelle and his kind. Sganarelle, *The Doctor in Spite of Himself*, is enjoying his new-found power as a man of medicine, when he is accused by Géronte of reversing the position of the heart and the liver:

GERONTE. ...the heart should be on the left side, and the liver on the right.

SGANARELLE. Yes, it used to be so, but we have changed all that.

Likewise, Dr Bahis of *Love's the Best Doctor*, provides an excellent example of professional automatism when he advises that 'It's better [for a patient] to die through following the rules than to recover through violating them'. This argument of course helps us to explain the fun in much of Molière, and the comedy of snobbery in Lady Bracknell, and how in Fry's *The Lady's Not For Burning* Tyson's pomposity as mayor is belied by his having a frightful cold in the head. It explains all manner of caricature in character and action on the stage. It explains the prohibition of much emotionality from the comic theatre. It does not explain the force of its *presence*, and emotion is often present to great purpose in comedy. Bergson declares rigidly 'laughter is incompatible with emotion', when we know well enough from experience, if not from countless moments on the comic stage, that we *do* have the faculty of laughing and feeling at one and the same time. It must exclude Shakespeare once again, and, what is more, it cannot approach our true sense of Molière's greatest achievement, *The Misanthrope*. Bergson's laughter is a 'social corrective', as Meredith's was an 'agent of civilization', but it trades on the debased and degraded in human nature and cannot respond to the warmth of comic humanity which remains after the eccentricities have been skimmed off.

The argument was not quite over. Freud[1] arbitrarily narrowed his field to include only what he pleased to call 'wit', and satisfactorily explains to us, after much belabouring, that wit serves as an escape from authority just as nonsense serves as an escape from critical reason (with occasional help from alcohol). Having said this at great length, he has said little that we did not know already. Others have since taken up the challenge, and J. B. Priestley's essay on humour[2] was a hopeful advance on his predecessors. Where Freud started from minimal instances, with little wish to move into the wider world of comedy, Priestley saw all the limitations and difficulties and perhaps would embrace too much. He would admit Shakespeare into the ranks, and goes some way to explaining his humour as the product of the close observation of human character and behaviour in its incongruities.

Among all the hints offered by these writers, certain recurring elements in the comic stand out. A sense of incongruity, with a resulting release of tension, is felt within the mind. Whether by the laughter of success or of failure, whether arising from the recognition of a friend or a tune, or from Santayana's 'little triumph' of the mind when it receives an illumination, whether by the laughter that follows upon bathos or upon the loss of a lady's dignity when her hat is blown off by the wind, some bulwark of our natural resistance, little or big, is broken down, and a weapon of unquestionable power is in the hands of the one who can effect this artificially. The comedian is suddenly free to pour his shafts through the gap, rebuffing us with mockery or drawing us with tears. Whatever the technique he employs he has his audience captive.

On the other hand, that a comedy *should* make you laugh is

[1] Freud, *Wit and its Relation to the Unconscious*, trans. Brill (London, undated, ?1906).
[2] J. B. Priestley, *English Humour* (London, 1929).

not admissible as an argument: incongruity is not necessarily laughable. There are too many plays, patently not tragedies, which clearly evoke no laughter, or little that is perceived as laughter; too many fine plays end in questions and by sobering us, from *Troilus and Cressida* and *The Misanthrope* to the comedies of Pirandello. The interested reader should look into that excellent discussion initiated by L. J. Potts in a more recent essay on our subject.[1] Where it does arise laughter can be a means to a greater end than itself, creating the conditions for the dramatic achievement of other things. The values of the comic attitude appear only when we measure the *uses* to which it is put. Nor should we deceive ourselves into thinking that its uses are not infinitely variable. The evidence suggests that the conventions of the comic stage readily admit an admixture of seemingly extraneous elements like the tragic and the pathetic, whereas tragedy has its fabric dangerously stretched to admit the comic or the farcical. What then are the traditional uses of comedy?

Broad comedy had contrived the release of laughter for partly satirical purposes by a relatively uncomplicated incongruity. Just as we laugh at the clown who sacrifices his self-respect by wearing trousers that are excessively too big for him, or at Charlie Chaplin for his exaggerated delight in a 'house' whose wall afterwards collapses when he leans on it, so we laugh at Harpagon, grotesque in his avarice, faced with the costly processes of being in love; or we laugh at the newly honoured Lord Foppington's airs and graces as he incongruously rehearses his part for the evening's *levée* while still in his nightgown: 'Well, 'tis an unspeakable pleasure to be a man of quality—Strike me dumb—My Lord—Your lordship—My Lord Foppington....' Of course, it is the situation which the dramatist may complicate, and the wink at the audience can be very much more subtle when, say, Lady Bracknell finally succumbs to hard cash in lieu of the desirable attributes of an

---

[1] L. J. Potts, *Comedy* (London, 1948), esp. pp. 18–22.

elegant lineage, or when Volpone the fox out-foxes himself. The bookworm is funnier and more like a bookworm on a dance-floor than in a library, the flirt funnier and more of a flirt in a library than on a dance-floor.

Even at the level of the near-farcical, where the merely physical sensationalism of the laugh is uppermost in the playwright's mind, such drama can sometimes justify itself morally by being acutely pointed in its object of derision. The contrivance of derisive laughter by the exaggeration of some affectation of human behaviour is a time-honoured method used since the days of Aristophanes. Thus the learned Meton of *The Birds* arrives in Cloudcuckooland to 'subdivide the air into square acres':

METON. Observe:
    The conformation of the air, considered as
    a total entity, is that of a conical damper.
    Very well. At the apex of this cone we apply
    the ruler, bracketing in the dividers to allow
    for the congruent curve. Q.E.D....

But his notions are not received as gratefully as he expected:

PISTHETAIROS. ...we've passed a law
    that charlatans shall be whipped in the public square.
METON. Oh. Then I'd better be going.
PISTHETAIROS.   You're almost too late.
    Here's a sample, God help you!   (*Knocks him down.*)
METON.   My head! My head![1]

One would not of course think that there were a majority of learned mathematicians in the Greek audience to make the satirical and corrective point of this very far-reaching. Nor would Molière have expected to find too many hypochondriacs like Argan in the court of Louis XIV. These comedies can nevertheless give us, perhaps incidentally, many tiny and momentary insights into human nature through the agency of puppets like Meton and Argan. We all share a little of Meton's

---

[1] Aristophanes, *The Birds*, version by D. Fitts (London, 1958).

desire to make order of fantasy, to stiffen what should be flexible. Even if we would not confess to being, each of us, a little of the hypochondriac with a natural fear for our health, we must feel just a touch of fellow-feeling for Argan when M. Purgon the doctor wreaks his rage like this:

M. PURGON. I foretell that within four days you'll be in an incurable condition.

ARGAN. Oh mercy!

M. PURGON. You'll fall into a state of bradypepsia.

ARGAN. M. Purgon!

M. PURGON. From bradypepsia into dyspepsia.

ARGAN. M. Purgon!

M. PURGON. From dyspepsia into apepsia.

ARGAN. M. Purgon!

M. PURGON. From apepsia into diarrhoea and lientery.

ARGAN. M. Purgon!

M. PURGON. From lientery into dysentery.

ARGAN. M. Purgon!

M. PURGON. From dysentery into dropsy.

ARGAN. M. Purgon!

M. PURGON. And from dropsy to autopsy that your own folly will have brought you to.

ARGAN. Oh my God! I'm dying.[1]

Here character, situation and dialogue are 'artificial' and the playing demands a special degree of stylized speech and movement, all apparently earnest in manner. The characters' behaviour tends to puppetry, and the situations, though still recognizable, may be outrageous: the ways of the actors are deliberately shown at some 'distance' from normal behaviour in order that the spectator can freely laugh across the gap at what he believes different from his own. The classical methods of comedy, whether broad and low, romantic and pastoral, or high and mannered, have always been anti-naturalistic. A stage extravagant in word and deed permitted those excesses which still compel us to deride certain characters and their

[1] Molière, *The Imaginary Invalid*, in *The Misanthrope and Other Plays*, trans. J. Wood (London, 1959).

attitude to life. To talk of 'stylization' equally to cover *As You Like It*, *Volpone*, *The Way of the World*, *The School for Scandal*, *The Importance of Being Earnest* and *Man and Superman* is perhaps an impertinence, but in each of these plays the dramatist invented a world to different degrees fantastic the better to compare our own. Artificial characters in an artificial situation gained him more freedom and more force for his dramatic effects. It is only after we have laughed spontaneously that we perhaps perceive that the laugh has rebounded upon us, and that the artificiality was all a snare. In the same way a simple verbal witticism can leave some permanent mark upon us—if it includes some quality of illuminating humour too.

Thus the best comedy teases and troubles an audience; it *can* be painful. Comic method can serve to create an imaginative but dispassionate attitude; to create the conditions for thinking; to free the dramatist in his attempt to tap certain rational resources of mind in his audience. Derisory laughter may be used for this and it may arise from this; it may not. Clearly it must do so in mannered comedy like Shaw's *Arms and the Man* or *Heartbreak House*, where we are encouraged for the most part to keep our critical distance from the central characters Raina and Ellie the better to recognize their whole significance. It may do so in surrealistic comedy like Samuel Beckett's *Waiting for Godot*, where the slapstick convention of the play deceives us most of the time into thinking that we are not looking at ourselves. It probably will not do so in *King Lear*, where an ironic joke from the Fool, laughable out of its context, is the more caustic in context because we feel our sympathies are too directly its butt. The urgent fact remains that, whether we laugh or not, the 'comic' attitude may be present in any genre of play. The best jokes are not only compatible with the most solemn intention, but are likely to be the best jokes for that reason.

On Tears and Laughter

As the gap narrows so that what remains incongruous is still funny, but too close to the bone to laugh at, then we move swiftly across the frontier into the realms of the tragic. We have seen that plays with large measures of sympathy felt through the laughter, like Shakespeare's romantic comedies, were inconvenient to the theorists. Similarly, plays which came near to closing the gap between the normality of the audience and the abnormality of the stage, plays like *Measure for Measure* or *The Misanthrope*, have been regarded as on the suspect fringe of the comic tradition, unwelcome exceptions to the rule. The presence of the comic eye in the midst of tragedy, as in *King Lear* or *Hamlet*, was put down to the licence of genius. Now, in the work of Chekhov, Pirandello and Anouilh, and many others, it is the rule and not the exception to mingle the laughter and the tears; large numbers of plays today merely *use* the mechanism of laughter without granting its expected release of tension.

For our overall understanding of the comic in drama today, we should turn, not to Hazlitt and Meredith, nor to Bergson and Freud, but to Pirandello, whose essay *L'Umorismo* offers the key to the comedy of our own times. In this he suggests a brilliant example, which demonstrates among other things how flexible and serviceable for serious purposes is the comic attitude once the dramatist can evoke it. Imagine, he says, an elderly lady: we are immediately predisposed to be sympathetic. But she is overdressed, her face painted, her hair dyed like a girl's: we find this comic and we are ready to laugh. Yet suppose she is aware of the figure she is cutting, and is behaving in this way in order to hold the affections of her husband: we are sobered. The old lady seems pathetic again, and the laugh is 'on us'. The comic may be no laughing matter.[1]

---

[1] Pirandello, *L'Umorismo*, 2nd ed. (Florence, 1920), p. 179. The original reads, 'Vedo una vecchia signora, coi capelli ritinti, tutti unti non si sa di quale orribile manteca,

52

Types of Comedy

Pirandello in 1908 was feeling for those qualities demanded by the modern stage in acknowledging with some finality the flexible nature of the theatre as a medium. Through it an audience could, and should, be drawn, repelled and drawn again, the 'gap' closed, opened and closed again. Since the comic view has always been instinctively felt to be an indispensable, if not quite respectable, prophylactic in drama as in life, so the methods of broad and artificial comedy were devised to make the comic view presentable. Now Pirandello insists that the comic view is a powerful and essential element in the effective control of an audience and an immensely serviceable corrective for its image of the play in the process of its formation. The fidelity of the drama to truth of feeling, and its accuracy of understanding in its handling of life on the stage, may depend upon the command the author has of the comic view and the keenness of his comic eye. How the comic may make of the drama a world living and flexible, and yet one unnaturally confined within the strict bounds of the stage, is also our concern in this study.

A simple short example for analysis is chosen to demonstrate the way impressions flow from actor to spectator with the kind of ironies most typical of the drama of recent times. In *The Rose Tattoo*, Tennessee Williams is catching at the incongruities of life by overtly setting them on the stage in their barefaced opposition. The scene is the home of Serafina delle Rose, who lives in a Sicilian colony on the coast between

e poi tutta goffamente imbellettata e parata d'abiti giovanili. Mi metto a ridere. *Avverto* che quella vecchia signora è *il contrario* di ciò che una vecchia rispettabile signora dovrebbe essere. Posso così, a prima giunta e superficialmente, arrestarmi a questa impressione comica. Il comico è appunto un avvertimento del contrario. Ma se ora interviene in me la riflessione, e mi suggerisce che quella vecchia signora non prova forse nessun piacere a pararsi così come un pappagallo, ma che forse ne soffre e lo fa soltanto perchè pietosamente s'inganna che, parata così, nascondendo così le rughe e le canizie, riesca a trattenere a sè l'amore del marito molto più giovine di lei, ecco che io non posso più riderne come prima, perchè appunto la riflessione, lavorando in me, mi ha fatto andar oltre a quel primo avvertimento, o piuttosto, più addentro: da quel primo avvertimento *del contrario* mi ha fatto passare a questo *sentimento del contrario*. Ed è tutta qui la differenza tra il comico e l'umoristico' (Pirandello's italics).

53

New Orleans and Mobile. The cottage is presented as a sectional 'frame', set in the semi-tropical vegetation of the place and in 'extremely romantic' lighting; this method of stage-setting is one that Williams has practised carefully both in order that we should retain a sense of environment throughout the play by actually seeing it, and that we should feel some initial detachment from the persons of the play. The characters are to be both typical and particular: we are to spy on them without joining them, and Serafina is to be 'a strange beast in a cage'.

Against the romantic setting and lighting we see the odd details of the living-room, introducing both Serafina and the incongruities of feeling that are to ensue. Serafina takes in sewing, and in a room cluttered with 'at least seven' dress-maker's dummies 'in various shapes and attitudes', as the author's production notes tell us, we see

an interior that is as colourful *as a booth at a carnival.* There are many religious articles and pictures *of ruby and gilt*, the *brass* cage of a *gaudy* parrot, a large bowl of *goldfish*, cutglass decanters and vases, *rose-patterned* wallpaper and a *rose-coloured* carpet.... There is a small shrine against the wall between the rooms, consisting of a prie-dieu and a little statue of the Madonna in a *starry blue* robe and a *gold* crown. Before this burns always a vigil light in its *ruby* glass cup. [The italics are mine.]

This is the passionate but limited world of the heroine of the play, bold in its contradictions. Williams significantly adds the comment, 'Our purpose is to show these gaudy, childlike mysteries with sentiment and humour in equal measure, without ridicule'.

Serafina, fiercely in love with her truck-driver husband, learns in the course of the play that not only has he been killed, but that he was, in spite of her love, unfaithful to her. She has regarded her marriage with the same kind of reverence that she reserved for the Madonna, and now her worship of her dead Rosario is turned to bitter grief, in its expression a kind of blasphemy. This little tragedy is presented to us against the incongruous details of her ordinary life, which includes the chase of a symbolic goat around the house by Serafina dressed in high-heeled slippers and a tight silk skirt, frequent screaming matches with the neighbours and their children, and the grotesque intrusion of the two prostitutes, Flora, 'tall and angular', and Bessie, 'rather stubby'. It is these who reveal the husband's infidelity against a background noise of a Souza march indifferently played by the band of her daughter's high school. Every ironic impression is a signal to the audience to revalue its estimate of Serafina's importance. Curiously she grows more weighty the more her simple dignity is undermined, and the strength of the ironic method Williams uses carries the play through many of the crudities of the theme's heated overstatement.

In the second act, the man who is to replace the magnificent Rosario arrives: 'He is short in stature, has a massively sculptural torso and bluish-black curls. His face and manner are clownish; he has a charming awkwardness.' Serafina's first comment upon him when she is alone sums up the whirling mixture of our own image: 'Madonna Santa!—*My husband's body*, with the head of a *clown*! (*She crosses to the Madonna.*) O Lady, O Lady! (*She makes an imploring gesture.*) Speak to me!' But Alvaro Mangiacavallo, for that is indeed his name, is, we learn, hardly sincere in his feelings for Serafina in the way that she wants him to be.

The following, finally, is the kind of sequence with which the play impresses itself upon its audience. The last act begins with both the widow and the wooer prepared ludicrously for their assignation. Serafina has put on an intolerably tight girdle, which she has only just managed 'with much grunting' to strip off again before the arrival of her lover. Alvaro has soaked rose oil in his hair and has had a rose tattooed upon his chest, reminder of the dead Rosario, and the better to appeal, as he thinks, to Serafina's sensibilities. Now—horror!—a contraceptive drops from his trousers' pocket—their ludicrous passions thus merging into the repulsive.

SERAFINA. ...You think you got a good thing, a thing that is cheap!

ALVARO. You make a mistake, Baronessa! (*He comes in and drops to his knees beside her, pressing his cheek to her flank. He speaks rhapsodically.*) So soft is a lady! So, so, so, so, so *soft*—is a lady!

SERAFINA. Andate via, sporcaccione, andate a casa! Lasciatemi! Lasciatemi stare!

(*She springs up and runs into the parlour. He pursues. The chase is grotesquely violent and comic. A floor lamp is overturned. She seizes the chocolate box and threatens to slam it into his face if he continues towards her. He drops to his knees, crouched way over, and pounds the floor with his fists, sobbing.*)

ALVARO. Everything in my life turns out like this!

SERAFINA. Git up, git up, git up!—you village idiot's grandson! There is people watching you through that window, the—strega next door....

So Alvaro is humiliated, though not as much as Serafina herself.

If we examine the impressions passed to us by the actors within this short space of time, we may begin to feel something of the way modern dark comedy operates. First, any sympathy we felt for Serafina in her grief is taken up and strengthened by her new agony, much as she had brought it upon herself. Her implication that she is not a 'thing' to be bought so cheaply, spoken with all the ferocious dignity of her Sicilian birth, is entirely as we would have her speak. To this extent we are self-composed, a relaxed audience, and Alvaro's abasement in his half-drunken state, with Serafina's spitting and lashing abuse of him, comforts us in our need to raise the widow as someone worthy of our commiseration. She has been outraged enough already.

But at this point in the play, Serafina's own baser instincts begin to emerge, though she cannot this time begin to elevate her new relationship to the holy level of her intimacy with her

late husband. In all her self-righteous fury, she is already un-
bending a little, and in her 'Lasciatemi stare', 'let me be', we
hear the old note re-enter her voice. We feel some of her
willing pity for this fool who presumes to take the place of
Rosario. And in her one ironic gesture of *running* from him,
inviting his pursuit, our composure is shattered by a contradictory impression, and our image of the play once again turns
turtle. Instead of growing to a nobility, Serafina, with the
incongruous rose in her hair, shrinks to be another clown with
Alvaro: 'The chase is grotesquely violent and comic.' She
fights with the box of chocolates he had brought her, he drops
to the floor sobbing like a frustrated child: 'Everything in my
life turns out like this!' We might say that here an incipient
tragic convention has become a comic one by inversion.

This is the way that Serafina's romantic obsession is punc-
tured. We know her humiliation more than she knows it herself, since we have the complete situation in view and the whole
counterpoint of the action violently registered in our minds.
And it seems even Serafina has some sense of objective appearances, feeling her indignity, when she draws attention to the
'witch' next door: 'There is people watching you.' As she
says this she knows the eyes are on herself.

This is a play about human illusions, about a simple woman
who believes too much in herself; it is about her sin of pride.
It is not about the man Mangiacavallo, who has few illusions
and no pride. He is introduced into the action, this man with
the head of a clown, simply as an agent of destruction, not so
much to destroy Serafina as to destroy our image of human
worth. But, oddly, the heroine in her simplicity and in spite
of her littleness and nakedness, is given by this author an
ineluctable stature by her very weaknesses, warmly comprehensive and curiously close to us. The summation of the
individual ironies of the play's action is the huge particular
irony of the total image the play leaves with us. We do not now

deal in tragedies, nor in comedies, nor indeed in the non-descript 'tragicomedy'. There flourish—what?—dramas of 'mood'. These are not necessarily plays calling up a peculiar atmosphere, but plays which attempt to control the exceptionally disparate audiences of modern times by teasing the mind and the emotion this way and that, making the one deceive, encourage and contradict the other.

What follows is not intended as a history of modern drama, nor indeed can it deal justly, if at all, with individual playwrights of major status, like Ibsen, Hauptmann, Shaw, O'Neill, Eliot and Sartre, writers who do not always display to advantage the dark characteristics of twentieth-century dramaturgy. But it may illuminate some of the drama that has flourished in the theatre of paradox, and trace a development in this most disturbing technique of dramatic communication which is recognizably of our time.

2

NATURALISTIC SHADING

Choose something ordinary and greyish, without bright colours and superfluous noises. In general construct your life in a stereotyped way. The more grey and monotonous the background the better.

IVANOV to DR LVOV

Incidentally, as we're not likely to meet again, I'd like to give you a bit of advice, by way of farewell: stop throwing your arms about! Try to get rid of that habit of making wide, sweeping gestures!

TROFIMOV to LOPAKHIN

EARLY NATURALISM

Naturalism in the theatre is hardly the invention of Ibsen, Strindberg and Chekhov, but its vigorous exploitation by these great dramatists marks the resuscitation of European drama in the second half of the nineteenth century. With its emergence and astonishing progress over a short period, the dark tones are heard again for the first time since the seventeenth century.

'Naturalism' as a dramatic convention should be distinguished from 'realism', the content of the drama. Euripides, in trying to reproduce more commonplace human feelings, lays claim to being a great realist, though his plays are founded on the most artificial set of stage conventions Western drama has known. *Hamlet* investigates the mind and spirit of man with deeper psychological realism than the theatre had known before, but only because the free Elizabethan pattern of action and the supremacy of the soliloquy permitted it. Shaw is an outstanding realist in the sense that he directs all his art against the romantic attitudes of his contemporaries, but he nevertheless writes as mannered a comedy as he pleases. It is

59

clear that realism bears no direct relation to the manner of performance.

On the other hand, it is very questionable whether some 'realists' of their own time, like Eugène Scribe in France and Arthur W. Pinero in England, playwrights very advanced by their own standards in the skills of uncovering skeletons in private cupboards,[1] succeeded in fact in getting any closer to the flavour of human life and its social relations. Pinero at the close of *The Second Mrs Tanqueray* composes dialogue like this:

AUBREY. Curse him! My poor, wretched wife! My poor, wretched wife! (*The door opens and Ellean appears. The two men turn to her. There is a moment's silence.*)
ELLEAN. Father...father...!
AUBREY. Ellean?
ELLEAN. I—I want you. (*He goes to her.*) Father...go to Paula! (*He looks into her face, startled.*) Quickly—quickly! (*He passes her to go out, she seizes his arm, with a cry.*) No, no; don't go!
(*He shakes her off and goes. Ellean staggers back...*)

Actors 'hurl' things to the floor, actresses 'faint' upon convenient ottomans, and it is apparent that those who are given the task of embodying such clichés of thought and feeling can do little more than 'register' the improbable emotions of improbable beings. Meanwhile a self-satisfied, if titillated, audience is unlikely to respond with the kind of anguish dark comedy provokes.

Realism, or truth to life, is therefore always the legitimate end for a good playwright; naturalism intends truth to life only as a method of presentation, using what is likely to be said and done as a way of reaching out to us. Naturalism, as a technique and a convention in its own right, does not necessarily imply realism. If it did, we should soon find unbearable

[1] The reader is recommended to read Shaw's formula for the 'well made' play in his preface to *Three Plays by Brieux* (London, 1911), p. xxiii. He suggests that 'the situation of an innocent person convicted by circumstances of a crime may always be depended on. If the person is a woman, she must be convicted of adultery, etc.'

the slaughters sustained by cowboys and Indians or by cops and robbers as seen on the cinema or television screen. Naturalism is serviceable for drama, but only as the stylizing of the Greek or Elizabethan theatres is serviceable. Indeed, 'naturalistic drama' is a fine contradiction in terms, since drama can never reproduce life with complete fidelity; in the end it must always cheat us to serve some ulterior purpose. The stage must always supply meaning and form to what is otherwise meaningless and formless, and it does this knowing that we are quite willing to be cheated.

The advent of *realistic* naturalism brought with it many new problems for the writer, and placed many new pressures on the actor and his audience. The play's dialogue had to do all it had done before, carrying character and movement, exposing the past and furthering the plot, but it had to do this while seeming casual and conversational. Elements of triviality and a lightness of touch had to be presented together with elements of importance and seriousness, if the illusion was to be sustained. Instead of distracting the attention of the spectator from the true aims of the play, paradoxically such dialogue tended to intensify and 'hold the attention by supplying the gentle ironies implicit in everyday intercourse. Even more striking changes appeared in dramatic construction. Because of the shape and structure of naturalistic plays, events followed one another more reasonably and less theatrically, and dramatists quickly discovered the enormous asset of a scene or a portrait rendered with the contrasting lights and shades of nature. All the great naturalists found it helpful to equate stage time more with chronological time, telescoping the action to start the play near the crisis of events. Here again, they tended to cause new and unexpected juxtapositions of feeling. But the sharpest changes occurred in the depiction of character. For a character to be sufficiently rounded, his background and past had to be granted a more detailed history; he needed a memory and he needed roots; his relationships with others had to be implicit in every speech and action. Thus the actor found himself a student of psychology, and devised elaborate systems to aid him in his art. But notably, a three-dimensional creature like the central character of a dark comedy showed more than one side of his nature: if comic, he could also be serious; if serious, he could also be comic. He was especially comic if he lacked a sense of humour.

It followed that audiences, in reconstructing the image of a naturalistic play from a great wealth of impressions, found themselves compelled to supply a newly sensitive response. The new drama was not only complicated for them by demanding an honesty of assessment and judgment: they found themselves more and more having to ask the question 'why?' of the events of the play. Interest became centred on causes and not effects, and in the best of the naturalistic plays that old cliché 'the irony of life' acquired the reality it deserved. Reality became the test of the play and the audience, and cast the grey shadows characteristic of the labyrinth of ordinary experience. Yet a microscopic view of experience which was also a prismatic one was to reveal a surprisingly full range of colour within the small areas of domestic life, as it had previously done in the novel.

The new playwright tried to keep to conventions suggested by ordinary behaviour, carefully eschewing the unnatural in his stage devices. This policy left great voids to be filled where, for example, a more direct expression of feeling had been possible before. Alternative tricks, of the inoffensive stage letter, the casually adroit use of servant or telephone, the innuendo in conversational dialogue, even tell-tale properties deposited about the stage and persuasive suggestions in costume and *décor*, became the unnatural clichés of the naturalistic theatre in their turn. Nevertheless, the general suppression of rhetorical language and the striking gesture left a surface so smooth and unruffled that the gentlest emphasis broke the calm with an illuminating splash. Like the parent brooding over her family, the spectator was expected to be eagle-eyed for signs of unrest, and he was prompt with laughter and ready with compassion. Effects were possible which might have passed unnoticed in the boisterous theatres of other times. The toning down of feeling, the merging of farcical and tragic exaggeration, in fact required the spectator to be more alert to overtones of tragicomedy. Admittedly the switches in mood and feeling in modern naturalistic drama, moving as it must through narrower channels of expression, will be less bold and colourful. But more delicate effects may be none the less impressive and efficient in agitating our mental image of the play's meaning, if they are woven into an appropriately fine-spun texture. The ironic effect when Hedda Gabler subtly destroys Lövborg is as exciting in the close context of Ibsen's play as when Iago succeeds in destroying Othello in the openwork pattern of Shakespeare's.

The naturalistic playwright wished to point the incongruities he observed, but without having to distort the truth of life as he saw it. He aimed therefore at avoiding the cardinal principle of the old comedy—of that exaggeration which had guided the creation and presentation of comic characters from Bottom and Harpagon to Lady Wishfort, Mrs Malaprop and Miss Prism. As a result of this, he was not able entirely to exclude the audience's tearful response as writers had done before. Nor perhaps did he wish to; but he could command it at will. Essentially, only the details of life as it was lived were to be his raw material: he chanced upon a variety of the so-called 'domestic comedy' which has since his time been vastly abused by the countless dramatists who wrote a melodrama spiced with a handful of cardboard characters drawn from artificial comedy: sniffling maids, pompous aunts, well-bred fiancés, absent-minded grannies and comic policemen.

Naturalistic Shading

By a constant reference back to life, the good naturalistic playwright had us appreciate the chaotic emotions and the feel of life beneath the surface of his drama. It remained for him only to perfect a method whereby incongruities could be presented in the theatre intelligibly. We meet an acquaintance in the street: 'How nice to see you,' we say; while we think, 'What wretched luck to meet him at this moment!' We come down to breakfast with the conventional early morning greeting and comment; we would perhaps be happier to say nothing at all at such a time. From one point of view this duplicity can be pathetic, but from another it is very funny.

The microcosm of everyday life was the ground over which a drab tragicomedy seemed to be most fruitfully worked. In this the drama received many stimuli from the novel, particularly its nineteenth-century achievements, and Mario Praz has written illuminatingly of the 'democratization of the heroic'.[1] Since Chaucer, the domestic world had provided unlimited sources for the exciting details which go to make up life, but with the work of Jane Austen, Flaubert, Tolstoy and others, the novel had deliberately used this apparently restricted field in order to reveal the ways of humanity at large. The worst of the novelists narrowed their subject by so doing; the best infinitely widened it. The worst made the novel mean and bourgeois; the best made it universal. For already the novelist had faced the problem which twentieth-century dramatists have not yet completely solved: how to make what might otherwise sink into domestic cosiness or sordidness rise to be representative. Professor Praz wrote of Trollope,

Just as the seventeenth century Dutch painters, in their *genre* pictures, did not so much tell stories as present types of men and women who were in no way exceptional, just as they presented pictures of social life, constantly repeating themselves, so also does Trollope obtain his results through a slow accumulation of little pictures of ordinary life, with nothing

[1] M. Praz, *The Hero in Eclipse in Victorian Fiction*, trans. Davidson (London, 1956).

64

spectacular about them—often, in fact, varied by only slight alterations. And both the Dutch painters and the English novelist knew how to make monotony lively, and how to bring a universal character into the portraiture of everyday things.

The novel provided a direction, even supplied a pressure, for the dramatist, but it did not solve the distinctive dramatic problem of turning reality to significant theatrical account. Eventually, many dramatists adopted symbolism as their aid to greater expression, but many, like Ibsen, Strindberg and Chekhov, who resorted to symbolic methods themselves, in fact spent much time in perfecting the typical reaction, the typical behaviour, in reproducing the typical tempo of life in given circumstances, in order to solicit our attention. They discovered that their plays had to create what is a verisimilitude rather than an exact replica of life.

A quick comparison between the function of Natasha in *The Three Sisters*, the young lady who succeeds in marrying brother Andrey and eventually in taking over the family home, and that of Lopakhin in *The Cherry Orchard*, the embarrassed overseer who almost accidentally buys up the family estate, may show how a correct balance in the structure of a naturalistic comedy can help it to suggest its universal quality.

In the first act of *The Three Sisters* it seems that Chekhov does not wish us to make up our minds about Natasha. We meet her first only through Masha's eyes: 'The way she dresses herself is awful!...And her cheeks look as though they've been scrubbed, they're so shiny! Andrey's not in love with her—I can't believe it; after all, he has got some taste....'[1] But do we accept at face value the criticisms of one woman of another? Natasha with her scrubbed cheeks may be out to deceive Andrey, but, we tell ourselves, this is his jealous sister speaking. So now we anticipate her entrance, prepared to scrutinize every detail of her behaviour to confirm or deny

[1] Chekhov, *Three Plays*, trans. E. Fen (London, 1951).

Masha's statement. Thus we see her wearing a pink dress with a green belt...but, after all, isn't she a young girl? She preens herself before the mirror...but isn't this what all women do before a party? She gives Irena an ostentatious kiss...but isn't Irena of her own age, and isn't it her saint's day? May not all these things be an expression of her nervousness? Then Olga cruelly criticizes her clothes, and the company teases her at dinner: Natasha may have no sense of humour, but we are prepared to sympathize with the little outsider, even to the point of hoping she will capture brother Andrey. Thus at the end of Act I we remain neutral and uncommitted: Chekhov's character-drawing is brilliant, like his control of our sympathies.

After this the control relaxes. For the rest of the play Natasha treats her new husband Andrey abominably, ruthlessly takes charge of the household, puts on superior airs, uses her child as a whip to dominate the family, abuses the old servant Anfisa, persuades Andrey to mortgage the house and herself holds the money. She even has a child by another man. By the end of the play she has completely turned the tables and is incarnate selfishness. By this time the character has so nettled us that, rather than conclude that the sisters' own lethargy has brought this upon themselves, we place her in our picture no longer as the 'balanced' character of Act I, nor as the comic *haus-frau* of Act II, but as an insensitive amorality, even an unmotivated evil; in Andrey's own words, 'a mean blind thick-skinned animal'. For this reason this play is a lesser achievement than *The Cherry Orchard*: the play tends to be small without becoming a microcosm. True, there are such women as Natasha, and perhaps Chekhov is right to emphasize that the less sensitive, the less imaginative, people usually win the day. True, the sisters and their brother Andrey make a substantial, human and universal core for the play. But such a Natasha in this particular framework of helplessness risks toppling the play into melodrama.

Early Naturalism

By contrast, Chekhov is careful to remove any sense of evil from *The Cherry Orchard* which followed. His only potential villain is Lopakhin who buys up the house and the orchard rather out of a mistaken sense of duty, through a failure to realize the propriety of the situation, than through any desire for revenge. His forebears had been serfs on the estate, and the tables are as effectively turned by Lopakhin as by Natasha; but we feel sympathy for both parties in the transaction. The family lose their beloved orchard because they are themselves, and no external moral pattern of malevolence is introduced into the structure of the play to distract us.

Thus by excluding the cliché, Chekhov extends his *Cherry Orchard* to include 'all Russia'. Even the largely farcical characters, Epihodov, Charlotta, Pishchik and Gaev, have their sympathetic side. Everyday life is permitted to carry its own message by his careful adjustment of our critical with our sympathetic faculties throughout the play, balancing laughter and tears. The great discovery of modern drama was that an arrangement of the tiny elements of life could do this. Says Maddy Rooney, the old Irishwoman in Beckett's *All That Fall*, realistic in conception if non-realistic in convention, 'Oh I am just a hysterical old hag I know, destroyed with sorrow and pining and gentility and church-going and fat with rheumatism and childlessness...'. This little catalogue of human ills epitomizes that ironic alertness required of today's audience; we are to weep at the sorrow and pining, but laugh at the gentility and church-going; laugh at the fat and rheumatism, but weep at the childlessness. The little things are mixed with the bigger, the social pressures with the personal agonies. The irony of the whole is the overwhelming insight we take away with us.

Naturalism on the stage gave great impetus to the creation of a fresh structure of character, and thereby made a powerful assault on one of drama's indispensable agencies for affecting

5-2

its audience. The dark comic hero has an inner life of great and contradictory variety. In naturalistic drama it is more a case of representing outward behaviour and events in order to point to this confusion and complexity than one of shaping a character in order to exemplify a particular sequence of events. The outer world of events loses interest for us and gives place to an inner world with which we live in intimacy. Events sink into the background when the drama of human personality is shifted into the spotlight. Naturalistic drama is less concerned to illustrate external ethical and religious values and more to analyse and evaluate personal worth. In proposing the personal view in terms of the particular instance, it permits a new freedom to express an individual vision; in this sense an indeterminate and unstable Peer Gynt or Miss Julie has as much to offer us as an Orestes or a Tamburlaine. We may not go so far as to say, as Strindberg does, that 'the naturalist has abolished guilt by abolishing God', but we may well agree that, in the naturalistic theatre, God assumes no importance and holds no interest unless a character specifically admits Him.

In the preface to *Miss Julie* of 1888, an astonishingly precocious statement of the aims of naturalism for its time, Strindberg distinguishes between 'character' as an expression for 'automaton', and 'character' as an expression for a 'soul-complex':

An individual who had once for all become fixed in his natural disposition, or had adapted himself to some definite role in life—who, in fact, had ceased to grow—was called a 'character'; while the man who continued his development, the skilful navigator of life's river who does not sail with sheets set fast, but veers before the wind to luff again, was called 'characterless'. In a derogatory sense, of course, since he was so difficult to catch, to classify, and to keep guard over.

He goes on,

I do not believe, therefore, in simple characters on the stage. And the summary judgments on men given by authors: this man is stupid, this one brutal, this one jealous, this one stingy, etc., should be challenged by naturalists, who know the richness of the soul-complex, and recognize that 'vice' has a reverse side very much like virtue....My souls (characters) are conglomerations from past and present stages of civilization; they are excerpts from books and newspapers, scraps of humanity, pieces torn from festive garments which have become rags—just as the soul itself is a piece of patchwork.[1]

The chameleon character is now installed and domesticated.

In the characters of some dramatists, like Strindberg and Chekhov, the variegations are less apparent to the eye. In others, like Pirandello and Anouilh, the colour without may vary with the colour within. Thus every character in *The Cherry Orchard* of Chekhov, whether more or less comic to the beholder, suffers inwardly and has a sense of isolation. Lopakhin knows the value of money, works hard, is an efficient overseer and keeps a close eye on the clock, but he is also delighted and troubled by trees and fields and poppies in bloom, and cannot possibly cope with a girl in tears. Charlotta the governess is full of fun and parlour tricks, and eats cucumbers as though they were bananas, but she declares that she aches with loneliness for a family and a home she cannot remember. And so on through the long list of parts in this play.

A character in Pirandello, on the other hand, finds that his inner self can rarely communicate with the person he shows to the world at large. Pirandello has his Cecè, in the play of the same name, say, 'Is it not tormenting to think that you live diffused into a hundred thousand individuals who know you and whom you do not know?' Again, 'I am sure that you agree with me that we are not always the same. According to our humour, moments, relations, we are now one way and then another; happy with one, sad with another, serious with this man, funny with that one.'[2] In his sequence of great plays in

---

[1] Strindberg, preface to *Lady Julie*, trans. C. D. Locock, in *International Modern Plays* (London, 1950), pp. 8–9.

[2] Quoted from D. Vittorini, *The Drama of Luigi Pirandello* (New York, 1935), p. 76.

the 1920's, Pirandello puts this principle of personality to dramatic use many times. Thus Ersilia Drei in *Naked* tries by attempted suicide to clothe her dull life in a dress of her own making, while every one of those about her accepts only his own view of her personality until in despair she decides for a second time to take her own life. In the age of Freud and Joyce and Pirandello we explore more deeply into human personality, and have come up against one of the immediate frontiers of drama.

The last attribute of dark comedy in naturalistic drama would seem to be something more than universality, something closer to timelessness. It would seem to exist in direct contradiction to the particularity of naturalistic and trivial detail, which would tend to limit the subject, individualize the character, identify the moment in time. But, in making the play infinitely immediate, the very normality of behaviour extends the application of the play's theme. While its highest common factor remains human, it demonstrates the simple arithmetic of all ages. Thus Shaw thought he found twentieth-century England in Chekhov's nineteenth-century Russia: 'Just as Ibsen's intensely Norwegian plays exactly fitted every middle and professional class suburb in Europe, these intensely Russian plays fitted all the country houses in Europe. . . .'[1] In one sense Shaw was right. Halvard Solness and Uncle Vanya, like Willie Loman and Maddy Rooney and Archie Rice, are permanently amongst us.

Pirandello in his early phase expresses the doubts of the naturalist about his chances of capturing and communicating the timelessness of his subject. He said that 'art, too, like all ideal or illusory creations, tends to fix life: it fixes it into one moment or into various definite moments: the statue in one gesture, the landscape in one momentary aspect, unchangeable. But what of the perpetual movement of its successive aspects?

---

[1] Shaw, preface to *Heartbreak House*.

What of the continuous fusion in which life is found?'[1] One can guess that such doubts encouraged Ibsen, Strindberg and Chekhov to introduce suggestive symbolism more and more into their plays. The Master Builder's steeple, which he must climb in spite of his years, for example, takes on a life of its own and becomes the prototype of all foolhardy aspirations and ugly refusals to know thyself. A cherry orchard binds us all to the beauty we like to find in our past and blinds us to the realities of the present. But even without such symbolism the naturalistic playwright who managed to capture and fix his landscape or his statue in one intensely true, if momentary, aspect or gesture held the same secret of timelessness which the sculptor Praxiteles himself discovered.

For in naturalistic drama of the best kind no laugh is conclusive, no tears are the final expression of emotion. There is no finality about the dramatist's statement, although the statement may be complete. Chekhov's family groups end as they began, or nearly so, and have still to live out their lives. Pirandello's people stick themselves upon their own pins and remain wriggling, while we dare do no more than hold our breath lest we commit ourselves similarly. To imagine a continuation of the lives of Anouilh's characters is to ride further into the blind impasse of life where the optimist will only rub off more of his shine.

PORTENTS IN IBSEN

Ibsen, Strindberg and Chekhov are not equally dark nor evenly dark. While the dark tones are noticeably present in Chekhov, Ibsen is often more prepared to heighten his colours in the traditional way of Dumas and Augier to suit a more

---

[1] Pirandello, *L'Umorismo*, 2nd ed. (Florence, 1920), p. 222. The original reads, 'Anch'essa l'arte, come tutte le construzione ideali o illusorie, tende a fissar la vita: la fissa in un momento o in varii momenti determinati: la statua in un gesto, il paesaggio in un aspetto temporaneo, immutabile. Ma, e la perpetua mobilità degli aspetti successivi? e la fusione continua in cui le anime si trovano?'

traditional purpose. Thus *Hedda Gabler* is a plausible attempt to shine a bright light broadly on a social and spiritual malaise, but Hedda's neurotic boredom is presented by methods deriving from Scribean melodrama. Even the emphatic death of innocent Hedvig, the pathetic residue of *The Wild Duck*, Ibsen's darkest and most modern comedy, is highly contrived in the manner of the 'well made' play. When Ibsen uses the conventional frameworks of the period, one cannot be sure that the comic elements are not ultimately incidental. In comparison with Chekhov's best comedy, the laughter at, say, Jörgen Tesman, Hedda's thick-skulled bridegroom, or at his pathetically silly Aunt Juliane, provides little of the true driving force behind our response to *Hedda Gabler* as a whole.

Nevertheless, different styles encourage different kinds of incongruity, and Ibsen's satirical edge introduces comedy at illuminating moments. Perhaps it is not too far-fetched to argue that in Ibsen, the most sober of modern dramatists in many ways, his earlier attempts at vaudeville comedy took a long time to die in him. They are turned to account in the unique *Peer Gynt*, a morality in which Peer is a figure standing for Norway and mankind itself, carefully mixed in temperament to be at once loved and despised. But in spite of moments of warm intimacy in the play, the methods of poetic fantasy somewhat smother our sense of being implicated. Emotional infection does not spread.

Even when Ibsen writes his so-called 'social' and satirical plays, the new element is not clearly present. In *The Pillars of Society*, *A Doll's House*, *Ghosts* and *An Enemy of the People*, the subjects are presented in terms of simple conflict between an individualist on the one hand, and the community with its codes of behaviour on the other. Such a division must make for a degree of satire, but the essence of Ibsen is not found in this conflict. His deep interest in human motives and ultimately in the spiritual state of human beings gave the lie to such a thesis as Shaw's *The Quintessence of Ibsenism*. Ibsen's increasing attention to the accurate depiction of human psychology and suffering showed a grimmer side of the problems in question. Thus in *Ghosts*, the satirical conflict between human feeling and correct social behaviour is strongly present in the exchanges between Parson Manders and Mrs Alving. However, our real interest is soon drawn to Mrs Alving's depth of self-knowledge, and Parson Manders remains a rather easy caricature. He is the comic butt for the attack on bigoted views: his horror at finding Mrs Alving reading books of advanced ideas, or at Oswald's 'irregular union' in Paris, so conditions us that the actor today is hard put not to raise an unwanted laugh on his curtain line 'It wasn't insured' when the fire at the orphanage is reported. This is hardly calculated to accentuate, rather to belittle, the vital and tragic slant of the play.

An Enemy of the People, while lacking the depth of feeling of *Ghosts*, manages however to strike a more even tone. The battle between the Doctor and his brother the Mayor over the contamination of the baths is fought out over a fairly even ground of lively satire. But even in this most social of social plays, the artist is exploring human personality, and Dr Stockmann lives and makes the play live. Natural man is personified in him by making him poor, yet lavish with food and drink and childlike in his pleasure at luxuries; by making him exuberant with high spirits at one minute, yet self-righteous the next; by making him Quixotic and idealistic, yet also untidy and immature and muddle-headed. A whole man emerges, and the man has a meaning in the pattern of the play: honesty is recognizably human in its opposition to hypocrisy and humbug. The play cannot rise to tragedy: in the end we think more than we feel. But neither is it comedy. It 'lies half-way between'. As a play it does not impose beliefs before it invites experience, and the naturalistic observation of Stockmann's character and the play's intensely personal interest lend warmth to cold satire.

Though it follows this play, *The Wild Duck* parodies all that Stockmann stood for. Hjalmar Ekdal is much less a 'hero' than he: Hjalmar is the cheerful, natural man who is this time *not* so honest, and our sense of personal feeling and kinship is warmer still. Many feel this play to be Ibsen's greatest achievement, and the play's exquisite balance of feeling may account for this. Hjalmar is the inoffensive egoist who can only live by the white lies he feeds on. The subject of the play, the relativity of personal happiness, is as wide as anything Ibsen attempted before or since. More important, the enemy is not in a 'compact majority' this time, but in himself. The spirit of the play, therefore, is one of deep understanding and incisive and painful criticism. If it were not for this balance, the old attic in which Hjalmar and his father go 'shooting', and the comic parallelism of Old Ekdal with his son, like the parallelism of Fodal with Borkman in *John Gabriel Borkman*, would seem merely an intrusion from farce and destroy our sense of natural life in the play. The attic in its conception daringly risks a breach in the play's structure in order to make us smile and then remember our own limitations.

The play could well have dropped into melodrama, and from the start Ibsen is working to avoid this. The idealistic busybody Gregers, Hjalmar's friend, has the knowledge and the wish wherewith to break up Hjalmar's and Gina's happy little home, but luckily Hjalmar is too real and too weak to decide for honour and leave his comfortable wife. He can never be the melodramatic sort, though he tries to be. When his father was put in prison, Hjalmar had considered suicide:

HJALMAR. ...I thought the whole creation should come to a stand, as in an eclipse.
GREGERS. I felt like that, too, when my mother died.

HJALMAR. It was in such an hour that Hjalmar Ekdal held the pistol to his own heart.

GREGERS. You, too, thought of—!

HJALMAR. Yes.

GREGERS. But you didn't shoot.

HJALMAR. No. In that moment of supreme trial I won the victory over myself. I went on living. But you can well believe it takes courage to choose life in those circumstances.[1]

Especially when the child Hedvig shoots herself, her naïve self-sacrifice could have been appalling and harrowing if Ibsen had not provided for this by the presence of the realist Dr Relling, who deftly pricks the melodramatic bubble in time. In the last sequence of the play we pass from Hjalmar's hysterical shriek, 'Ah, Thou above! If Thou *art* there! Why hast Thou done this thing to me!' to its undermining by the drunken theological student:

MOLVIK. Praised be the Lord. Earth to earth. Earth to earth.

RELLING. Shut up, you fool; you're drunk.

until our last illusion about Hjalmar is finally collapsed by the Doctor's dry comment, 'Before the year is out little Hedvig will be nothing more to him than a fine subject to declaim on'. Ibsen turns our eyes from Hedvig to Hjalmar, and reminds us of the strong element of self-sympathy we saw in him when he spoke to Gregers about Hedvig's approaching blindness, 'It's terribly hard for me, Gregers'. So we sit rebuked at the fall of the curtain.

Without quite breaking the naturalistic form, Ibsen sees us, like Hjalmar himself, slung between the attitudes of Gregers and Relling. The dialectic of the action, the farce taking its life from the pathos and the pathos from the farce, to use Eric Bentley's neat statement,[2] the tears and the laughter interpenetrating the discussion—this keeps the spectator wide

[1] Henrik Ibsen, *Three Plays*, trans. U. Ellis-Fermor (London, 1950).
[2] E. R. Bentley, *In Search of Theater* (London, 1954), p. 45.

awake. The delicious paradox is that Hjalmar is so like our-selves, but too like ourselves to be fully sympathetic.

With the achievement of *The Wild Duck*, we may fairly leave Ibsen. Hedda Gabler's horror and disgust at Judge Brack's amused and sinister account of Lövborg's ugly death—'shot through the bowels',[1] when Hedda had so wanted him to die a noble and graceful death to satisfy her romantic perver-sions—is an echo of the ironic douching given by Relling to Gregers and Hjalmar. But an almost total lack of sympathy with the heroine, in spite of the singularly ill-matched marriage she has made, takes its toll of subtleties in *Hedda Gabler*. Brack's irony hits Hedda only, and cannot be turned upon the spectator. The somewhat kinder portrait of Solness in *The Master Builder* is wholly tragic, and in the plays of his last years, Ibsen never repeats the technical complexity in manipulating the audience which he approached in his inimitable play *The Wild Duck*.

STRINDBERG'S NATURALISM

Nor need we stay too long in this chapter with August Strind-berg, but for other reasons. This enigmatic, lunatic genius, obsessed for the most part (excluding the religiose dream plays) with the giant problem of sex, quickly found that naturalism was inadequate to communicate the convolutions of his mind, though he reverted to a quasi-naturalistic manner intermittently throughout a career in which he tried almost every theatrical style known to the modern theatre. We shall return, therefore, to see him at work later in such surrealistic-expressionistic plays as *To Damascus* and *The Ghost Sonata*.

It is difficult, first, not to suggest that the theories of naturalism outlined in his fine preface to *Miss Julie* are mostly conceived 'cold', without direct relevance to the drama he was

---

[1] Archer's translation, rather more pointed than 'in the stomach'. The original suggests more nearly our word 'belly'.

in fact writing. We should be unwise to turn to them for help in understanding his kind of realism. Looking back, we have, secondly, to accept that the better-known plays of intense realism, like *The Father*, *Miss Julie* and the terrifying *Dance of Death*, are properly not naturalistic at all, and it may be impertinent to see them as naturalistic dark comedies. Their *manner* of presentation is in the last analysis independent of their matter; they depend very little on the detail of ordinary life for their expression. *The Father* asks as properties only a table-lamp for the enraged Captain to throw at Laura his wife, and a strait-jacket to be slipped over him at her moment of victory. To capture the play's demonic strength, it would be better played on a naked stage, as others have suggested—'his action is of the soul, not of the body'.[1] Strindberg preferred *Creditors* to *Miss Julie* because it is simplified to 'three characters, a table and two chairs, and no sunrise',[2] a statement reminiscent of Alexandre Dumas's dramatic essentials, 'three planks, two actors and a passion'.

These plays suggest an incipient expressionism. They emerge as natural tragedies lacking the restraints of naturalism, domestic agonies lacking life's comic compensations. The thoughts and feelings of the characters scream aloud, their emotions flying 'like bullets at the enemy' and demanding what Eric Bentley considers to be 'Dionysiac' performance.[3] Strindberg displays realism in a cloak of personal melodrama: his tales are raw and macabre and his characters are fanatical and unbalanced. Surface manners are sometimes natural, but a symbolic war of sex is always raging just beneath, quickly to boil up and destroy the irony of appearances.

It is strange that the battle of the sexes, a primary source of comedy in the past, should so little reveal its comic and social

[1] A. Nicoll, *World Drama* (London, 1949), pp. 553–4.
[2] See M. Lamm, *Modern Drama*, trans. K. Elliott (Oxford, 1952), pp. 139–40.
[3] E. R. Bentley, *In Search of Theater* (London, 1954), p. 135.

side to Strindberg. Profoundly concerned with spiritual issues, Strindberg's approach tends to suppress the treatment of genuine social problems in these plays. He seems time and again to argue against the emancipation of women, and in *Miss Julie* even seems to concern himself with the rise and fall of the classes. Yet the subject of 'the new woman', as it is for Shaw, is only a springboard into deeper waters, and Miss Julie is ostensibly mistress, and Jean is servant, only to reinforce the real theme of the drama, which demonstrates that Jean is 'sexually the aristocrat', as the author says in the preface, and that the loser in the war of sex shall be the spiritual slave. For Strindberg the question of sex is, then, a personal and not a social one, and in general the fierce drive of these plays prohibits any sense of the monotony which might have killed them. The crude, head-on conflict between man and woman is inexorable and capable of no solution; its expression can only be tragic. As in *Ghosts*, the rising of the sun at the end of *Miss Julie* casts long, fateful shadows.

Yet there is another Strindberg who sees with an ironic eye at lucid moments: there appears also a kind of wan smile of grim self-relief which few would care to identify as comedy. We might recognize it in the country Pastor in *The Father*, with his ineffectual 'everyone has his burden', and the provincial Doctor, innocent tool of Laura, with his remarks on 'the sanctity of family life'. We might recognize it in Kristin the cook in *Miss Julie*, whose normality is there to set off the miseries and frustrations and the wretched guilt of Julie and Jean. She is the 'feminine slave' who is 'stuffed full of morality and religion, which she makes her cloaks and scapegoats. She goes to church as a simple and easy way of unloading on Jesus her household thefts, and of taking in a fresh cargo of guiltlessness.'[1] The simplicity in her attitude to the

---

[1] Preface to *Lady Julie*, trans. C. D. Locock, in *International Modern Plays* (London, 1950), p. 11.

nature of the sexual attraction, as shown in her mime of curling her hair with a hairpin, contrasts grotesquely with the aphrodisiac influence of the midsummer-eve dance and the insinuations of the others; the 'ballet' of the peasants dancing drunkenly and singing bawdily while Jean and Julie are alone in Jean's room is a unique effect of ugly incongruity.

Strindberg insists upon calling *Comrades*, a play which precisely echoes the theme and spirit of *The Father*, a 'comedy'. The title at least is ironic: the wife who destroys her artist husband's talent and self-respect is no comrade. *Creditors* he calls a 'tragicomedy'. In it another female vulture first preys and feeds upon the strength of her two men, the first a teacher and the second an artist, each of them her husband in turn. The second dies in an epileptic fit. It is hard to see how Strindberg could declare this play to be 'human and amiable'. There is, however, a kind of implicit comic irony in the play, as when the first husband meets his former wife again for the first time after long separation. They commence their interview with the politenesses of convention which we know cannot survive the questioning of motives:

TEKLA. Sit down a moment. You don't offend me, for you possess that rare gift—which was always yours—of tact and politeness.
GUSTAV. It's very kind of you. But one could hardly expect—that your husband might regard my qualities in the same generous light as you.[1]

There is present first the attraction on all levels. Gustav talks of 'my secret longing to see her whom I used to love more than my own life', and when he pinches her ear he says, 'That tiny ear!—Think only if your husband could see us now!' 'Wouldn't he howl, though!' is her reply. But the masks are soon off:

> TEKLA. Vindictive wretch—shame on you!
> GUSTAV. Dissolute wretch—shame on you!
> TEKLA. Oh, that's my character, is it?

[1] A. Strindberg, *Plays*, *Second Series*, trans. E. Björkman (London, 1913).

GUSTAV. Oh, that's my character, is it?—You ought to learn something about human nature in others before you give your own nature free reign.

The ironic tone becomes more evident in such a play as *Debit and Credit*, which with grim humour tells the sorry story of a scholar and explorer who is now persecuted by those who helped him reach his present fame and position. His brother and his brother's wife, his old teacher, his mistresses Marie and Cecilia, and Cecilia's former fiancé, all have their claim on the victim. These characters are presented with a slightly farcical touch, and luckily the hero for once is a bachelor. A point is made simply: 'What a peaceful, unassailable position he holds who has nothing to lose!', but the theme of 'eat or be eaten' is the same as before. In all these plays, abnormality stifles potential comedy.

By far the more interesting is *There are Crimes and Crimes*, another 'comedy'. This introduces an ironic note more incisive than any that had gone before, and this play with its odd mixture of naturalistic detail and symbolic undercurrents is the link with the ironic dream plays to come.

Maurice is a struggling playwright in Paris. With his faithful mistress Jeanne and their little daughter Marion, he is hoping for some financial success with his latest venture in the theatre: we see them all meet first in a cemetery. When success comes he neglects Jeanne, and fame brings with it a predatory female, Henriette, who has a 'scent of blood' and whose father 'melted away like wax before a fire in the hatred of her mother and sisters'. She is the complete antithesis to the forsaken Jeanne, who is an irreproachable angel; but 'the victor's wreath seems worthless if you can't place it at the feet of some woman'.[1] This is a Paris which smells of sin, whose 'air is poisoned', and when Maurice learns that his child has died and that his love for Henriette was a destroyer,

[1] Trans. E. Björkman in August Strindberg, *Eight Famous Plays* (London, 1949).

his sense of guilt grows to monstrous proportions, and the figure of the Commissaire of Police stands by like a symbol of death.

Maurice is cleared of the charge of murdering his child, who died naturally, but the terrors of nightmare begin: 'There are crimes not mentioned in the Criminal Code, and these are the worse ones, for they have to be punished by ourselves, and no judge could be more severe than we are against our own selves.'

In the Luxembourg Gardens, standing significantly beside the group of Adam and Eve, Maurice and Henriette prepare to take their own lives. 'The wind is shaking the trees and stirring up dead leaves, straws, and pieces of paper from the ground.' In accusing each other they are 'driving each other insane', 'torturing each other to death'. But the park is closed before their position can be resolved, and Maurice has second thoughts. Furthermore, now that his name is cleared, success returns to him. It is true he has apparently learned his lesson, since he declares that 'Honour is a phantom; gold, nothing but dry leaves; women, mere intoxicants', and he will reckon with himself through the help of the Curé at the church. But before the curtain is down he decides not to forsake entirely the good things which a renewed material success offers him. From hell, Maurice ascends again to heaven, and finds it rather cosy.

Strindberg's ironic twist in this is less of character and action and more an arbitrary and superimposed twist of mind and conscience: the audience is specifically invited to feel the pressure of guilt and then evaluate the incongruous outcome. The spectator is suddenly pushed to arm's length by a hero who should have renounced worldliness for the cloister or the grave, but who simply does not. The play suddenly shudders to *normality*, Maurice steps out of melodrama into a clear sane light, and judges us in return. 'Tonight I'll meet you at the Church', he tells the Abbé, 'but tomorrow evening I go to the theatre.' Strindberg is playing cat-and-mouse with us as only the comedian can do.

His attempts to express the inarticulate objectively on the stage led him further and further from naturalism into the symbolism of the last plays. Perhaps it is also true to say that the insoluble, destructive position in which he found himself by such probing into problems of the sexual struggle led him, too, into a dry, bloodless drama in which expression is only possible through a cadaverous grin. In *The Devil's Disciple*, Shaw's Minister Anderson tells his muddled wife Judith, 'After all, my dear, if you watch people carefully, you'll be surprised to find how like hate is to love'. John Osborne used this to initiate some of the momentum in his Jimmy Porter, but Strindberg's attempts to understand and express the ambiguities of the love–hate relationship between the sexes led him deeply into dramatic territory in which the irony is wholly individual and, one would think, inimitable in tone. If there is laughter in this, it is the most toothy and rasping laughter in modern drama.

CHEKHOV

We arrive at the achievement of Anton Chekhov, the most natural of the naturalists, and the first truly dark comedian. Chekhovian drama is nearer to the naturalism of the 'neo-realism' of the post-war Italian cinema, especially that of De Sica in *Bicycle Thieves*, *Miracle of Milan* and *Umberto D*, nearer to the English and American play of 'mood', to the television plays of Paddy Chayefsky, even to the realism of the 1950's in John Osborne and Arnold Wesker, than to the naturalism of Ibsen and Strindberg. It is a mistake to suppose that Chekhov's attempts to divide his audience against itself are really different from Osborne's to bring us to a state of awareness. Chekhov is able with an unruffled surface to reconcile all his contradictions, but beneath lies a ferment as troubled as anything Osborne is working for. In *The Seagull* and *The Cherry Orchard*, we are made to smile at both youth and age while we see ourselves as the young and the old; and we may not avoid resenting our laughter, since it is modified by pity. In some essentials the method of these two authors is very similar: where it differs is in the stance the author takes, and the place where he stands. Osborne gesticulates at us from an unassailable point in the wings, which may account for the external contrivances of his plotting and the icy finger that touches his situations, while Chekhov sits with us in the stalls, accepts his own bruises and understands their pain for having suffered them himself.

The supreme difference is that Chekhov's fundamental concern is to give us the feel of life by showing us the balance of life. Every character and every attitude shall be seen from two sides or more; every posture of body or mind is its own critic, and this is to be demonstrated without distorting the truth. We are to understand this ambiguity as well in the tiny detail as in the structure of a play as a whole. So Medviedenko, the schoolmaster in *The Seagull*, declares his love to Masha: 'I love you. I can't stay at home because of my longing for you....'[1] To which Masha responds thus: 'I feel touched by your love, but I can't return it, that's all. (*Holds out the snuff box.*) Have some snuff.' Simply done, this gesture tells us all we need to know of Masha's mood at this point, and Chekhov with a quick stroke effectively kills for the audience the pathos in the episode, though Medviedenko will whine on to the end.

So Natasha, the sister-in-law in *The Three Sisters*, comes upon her husband reading a book: 'What are you doing, Andriusha? Reading? It's all right, I only wanted to know....'[2] Recognizably commonplace, this tiny episode is implicit with

[1] Anton Chekhov, *The Seagull and Other Plays*, trans. E. Fen (London, 1954).
[2] Anton Chekhov, *Three Plays*, trans. E. Fen (London, 1951).

6-2

information and ironic feeling. Act I had just brought the curtain down on a 'shy' little Natasha busily capturing her man. Within a moment of the rise of the curtain on Act II, we know not only that they are married, but what sort of marriage it is, and will be. Andrey has lost his liberty and gained a domestic tyrant for a wife. Meanwhile, at another level, there lies implicit in Natasha's query the suggestion that touches off the next dramatic development: she is making the indirect approach of a woman who has something other on her mind and who means to speak of it. So our gorge rises slightly; we feel a sympathy with poor Andrey; and yet—the incongruity between what Natasha says and what she means is irresistibly funny on the stage. Our comic sense of human behaviour is tickled, and Chekhov has achieved his object of forcing upon us the gentle pangs of an ambivalent response.

'It is necessary,' declared Chekhov, 'that on the stage everything should be as complex and as simple as in life. People are having dinner, and while they're having it, their future happiness may be decided or their lives may be about to be shattered.'[1] At about the same time, Maeterlinck was saying:

There is an everyday tragedy which is more real, deeper and more in keeping with our true existence than the tragedy of great adventures.... I have come to think that an old man, seated in his armchair, simply waiting beside the lamp, listening, without knowing it, to all the eternal laws that reign about him, interpreting, without understanding it, what there is in the silence of the doors and windows and in the small voice of the light...I have come to think that this motionless old man was living in reality a deeper, more human and more general life than the lover who strangles his mistress, the captain who wins a victory or the husband who avenges his honour.[2]

These two writers approach the same goal from opposite sides, Chekhov as the comedian, Maeterlinck as the tragedian.

[1] Quoted by D. Magarshack, *Chekhov the Dramatist* (London, 1952), p. 118.
[2] Maeterlinck, *Le Trésor des humbles*, quoted by M. Lamm, *Modern Drama*, trans. K. Elliott (Oxford, 1952), pp. 155–6.

Chekhov

Neutralizing the pathetic with the comic and vice versa grows to be the sharpest weapon of the twentieth-century dramatist, incisive in effect, but all too easy to abuse. The swing of the pendulum within our minds sets up a fresh dramatic impulse over which the author has sole control. There seems to be a general principle to be observed here. The opposites must be so balanced as not to destroy, but to sustain, each other. We may be inclined to judge particular effects in Brecht and Tennessee Williams as both discordant and unbalanced when we feel the pendulum shudder.

Thus in Brecht's *Galileo*, we are, through our special knowledge, aware of the revolutionary implications of his telescope, and we sympathize with him as he tries to report on his vision of scientific development. But, for arbitrary reasons of uncertain satire, Galileo's genuine passion is echoed by the stupidity of the counsellors who see only amusement or personal gain in the invention. The spectator can react only with irritation, not against the counsellors who should offer the pleasure of derisory laughter, but against the ingenuous clumsiness of the balance in the scene.

The naïve concluding moments of Act II of Williams's *Cat on a Hot Tin Roof* follow these lines:

BRICK. How about these birthday congratulations, these many, many happy returns of the day, when ev'rybody but you knows there won't be any!

(*Whoever has answered the hall'phone lets out a high, shrill laugh; the voice becomes audible saying:* 'no, no you got it all wrong! Upside down! Are you crazy?')

The evident intention here is for outside trivialities to grate sharply on the strung-up nerves of Big Daddy at precisely this moment of his disillusion. We are to resent the intrusion of the voice at the telephone to the same extent as we feel with Big Daddy the agony of his son's disclosure. But at this, the crisis of the scene, the horror of the father's self-deception has

85

already made its mark: it offers an extreme of irony in itself. The irreverence of the family chorus at this point can only be gratuitous, and increasingly so:

BRICK. You told *me*! I told *you*!
(*A child rushes into the room and grabs a fistful of fire-crackers and runs out again.*)
CHILD (*screaming*). Bang, bang, bang, bang, bang, bang, bang, bang, bang!

Williams seems at present unable to judge when his play stands at the edge of the precipice—in *A Streetcar Named Desire*, too, he wrote one scene too many, unnecessarily sending Blanche to the madhouse as Kowalski shuffled the cards.

This effect of dramatic punctuation is not to be compared with the upstage laughter of Soliony and Tuzenbach, interpolated between the declarations of false optimism from Irena and Olga at the opening of another anniversary scene, Act I of Chekhov's *The Three Sisters*:

OLGA. ...Oh, Heavens! When I woke up this morning and saw this flood of sunshine, all this spring sunshine, I felt so moved and so happy! I felt such a longing to get back home to Moscow!
CHEBUTYKIN (*to Tuzenbach*). The devil you have!
TUZENBACH. It's nonsense, I agree.

If the device is not delicate, at least the balance is precise, perhaps because at this early place in the play we do not resist the ironies as they are established, perhaps because they are created too subtly to disturb the naturalistic convention. Naturalism admits apparent irrelevancies. Who does not feel that Williams's presentation of Big Daddy's agony of mind is larger than life, and that the offstage interpolations tip the balance of credibility? *Cat on a Hot Tin Roof* drops too easily into melodrama.

Chekhov the dramatist learned his craft from two exacting masters, the short story and the one-act vaudeville sketch, the former being of especially great importance. He learned from Flaubert and Maupassant, Turgeniev and Tolstoy the detachment of the realist, and he taught himself to work from the minute observation of the raw material of everyday experience. He taught himself how to *see*. As J. Middleton Murry recognized, in the early days of Chekhov's introduction to the English literary world, 'immediate consciousness' was the criterion, and Chekhov strove to assemble 'those glimpses of reality which in themselves possess a peculiar vividness, and by virtue of this vividness appear to have a peculiar significance'.[1] The linking together of such glimpses in a particular and suggestive sequence accounts for the odd sense we carry away from both story and play of an implied, indirect statement; we know that 'nothing has happened', but we feel that a great deal has been 'said', and moreover said in a personal way and with a personal vision. For want of a better term, this manner of communication has been called 'impressionism'; at least the word rejects the idea that Chekhov, the supreme naturalist, was a mere photographer.

Through writing his stories, too, he learned to make his characters inseparable from their surroundings: people and places gently merge into each other. He learned to convey personality by what the person does not do as well as by what he does, and in the enforced economy of the short story the briefest touch must do this. He found this method invaluable for his drama, which accepts a similar physical economy. A multitude of quick, slight brush-strokes paint a complete portrait of the character as we see him, as he sees himself and as others see him. Chekhov perfected a kind of shorthand of communication. Through fine details he achieves a special precision, and apparent trivialities acquire a cumulative power of meaning we cannot resist because we have already swallowed so many so easily. He tells his story simply, without artificial devices, and we are left with recognizable experience, all of it essentially real and normal.

[1] J. Middleton Murry, *Discoveries* (London, 1924), pp. 142–3.

Naturalistic Shading

Chekhov insists, in a letter to a woman writer, 'You may weep and moan over your stories, you may suffer together with your heroes, but I consider one must do this so that the reader does not notice it. The more objective, the stronger will be the effect'.[1] Any such objectivity makes it almost impossible for us to find the author in his characters, and the technique tears down all barriers between ourselves and his subject. This is, of course, the way of Shakespeare and of all good dramatists. The author enters his narrative only to control the ironies which are to control us. Yet, as we shall see, these same ironies ensure that his vision of life is present and is felt. The loneliness of man, the illusions he treasures, the mutability of his brief existence, are Chekhov's special province, and such methods as we have described make of such improbable material possible subjects for the artist.

This clipped account of his short-story writing has also indicated some of his qualities as a dramatist. In comparing play with story, we usually think of the differences: the physical limitations of the theatre as against the freedom with time and space possible to the story; the need to provide for the spoken word and bodily action of the actor, as against the power of the story-writer to make words think and tell. But the short-story's call for unity and economy is that of the play; and the short-story's answer in the use of impressionistic suggestion is the play's too. From both, we the audience deduce, we contribute and we create. As well as describe, naturalistic detail can hint and evoke, and the evocation can be that of poetry. The more we work, the less ground we cover, but the deeper we delve.

From pot-boilers and vaudevilles, like *The Proposal*, *The Bear* and *The Anniversary*, which seem simple but which Chekhov found fully demanding, he learned to create what he called 'a special kind of mood', admittedly 'a mood full of

[1] Quoted in W. Gerhardi, *Anton Chehov, a Critical Study* (London, 1949), p. 110.

high spirits'.[1] These are plays entirely of situation, comic through a bald incongruity. *The Proposal* is an account of a gentleman who comes to make a proposal of marriage, but instead finds himself making an argument. *The Bear* is an account of another gentleman who comes to make a demand for payment of a bill, but instead finds himself making a proposal of marriage. And so on. There is great fun and mimicry and gusto here, and much apparently inconsequential dialogue and 'business'. But come to play one of these little plays, and one quickly finds that nothing is wasted, and that many minor incongruities are employed to enforce the major contradiction upon which the play turns.

When Chekhov found his dramatic 'conscience' and evolved a final convention within which to write, he was well prepared. *The Seagull* seems to be about a boy whose series of frustrations and failures in his writing and in his love for Nina eventually drive him to suicide. But the play is properly a comedy of time passing, of youth and idealism wryly countered by age and experience. For Treplev is weak and lacks faith in himself, and we cannot admire him; he is no hero and no one in the play gains by his loss. His mother, Mme Arkadina, is an ageing actress, and she simply grows older. Trigorin, the successful writer who steals Nina from him, is no villainous roué; he just makes himself unhappier. Old Sorin yearns for his youth as before. Masha, though still in love with Treplev, marries the dull old schoolmaster after all, but regrets it from the start. Her mother Paulina loves Dr Dorn, a man who virtually remains unaware of her. With this procession of negatives, the play cannot be a tragedy: it could well, however, have been a farce. Yet *because* the drama is enacted with delicate, springing touches for the most part, and not with brash and heavy jolts upon our sensibilities, the totality of the play is extraordinarily acceptable even today.

[1] D. Magarshack, *Chekhov the Dramatist* (London, 1952), p. 54.

Naturalistic Shading

The naturalism of the play is not so restrictive that it does not allow room for a suggestive symbolism, and the imagination blossoms under its spell. The moonlight of Act I captures the dreamy, autumnal mood in which the characters are at first held; the thundery weather grows to a storm; the derelict stage of Act IV is a mark of thwarted ambition and a sad reminder of a gayer mood; the seagull itself is a symbol of a mother trampling over her son, of a young girl nearly ruined, of beauty disfigured. More organic than the symbols, the pattern of relationships works itself into our minds: the young turn to the old for understanding; the old, with the sole exception of Paulina and Dr Dorn, are concerned only for themselves.

All characters and all relationships play variations on the theme of 'I want', but every individual hunger, however trivial, offers a killing contrast to every other. Thus when Nina is speaking the earnest words of Treplev's play, Paulina is thinking of her beloved Doctor, Arkadina is in reality thinking of herself:

NINA. '[The Devil] is bored without Man....'

PAULINA (*to Dorn*). You've taken off your hat. Put it on before you catch cold.

ARKADINA. The doctor's taken his hat off to the Devil, the father of Eternal Matter.

TREPLEV (*flaring up, loudly*). The play's over! Enough of it! Curtain!

When Paulina speaks, Arkadina looks and so we all look, and Treplev's reproach is addressed to actor and to audience too. Again, when the family group nonchalantly plays lotto towards the *dénouement* of the play, each character is engrossed in his or her own interests: Arkadina in her reception at Kharkov, the bailiff Shamrayev in money, Masha in her wounded feelings for Treplev, Paulina perhaps in the worries of her daughter, Trigorin in his position as a writer faced by younger competition, and Sorin snores in his chair. Meanwhile a tragedy is being enacted off-stage. Treplev, alone, is playing a melancholy waltz and considering the taking of his own life. This is an orchestration of discordant instruments which only harmonize within our own imagination.

Yet amongst all this there is no sentimentality. There are better people, Paulina, Dorn, Nina, and there are worse. Arkadina is a little vicious and egotistical, but we are compelled to laugh, for example, at her gift of one rouble to be shared between three servants. Masha is heart-broken at losing Treplev, but she can still play cards with zest. We love Medviedenko for his concern for his baby and his four-mile walk home, yet his teacher's tones and his obsession at all times with his salary are ludicrous. So we smile at all these people. Masha's initial appearance in black, and her statement 'I am in mourning for my life', funny and pathetic together, strike the note heard through the whole play. With *The Seagull*, Chekhov properly inaugurates the dark comedy of modern times.

This play did not satisfy Chekhov's demand for perfect balance: the final suicide of Treplev displayed the vestigial remains of another way of playwriting. *Uncle Vanya*, which followed, did not, however, take him much further forward. Vanya also wishes to kill, but this time the target is missed with a 'Damnation!' and a 'Devil take it!' His drama of hatred for his unfeeling brother-in-law the Professor, and of desire for the Professor's indifferent young wife Elena, thus ends in nothing. But the framework of the play is still conventional, the mood is more heavily handled than in any of the last great plays, and the balance of critical sympathy is not achieved without sentiment.

The Three Sisters truly marks another departure. We meet another family, living a provincial life which torments them, and all yearning for Moscow as their means of escape. Like Beckett's tramps, they do not, of course, go. Irena, the youngest and weakest, declares irresponsibly, 'Oh, how good it must be to be a workman', and does not turn a hand. She seeks marriage as the only way she knows to broaden her life, but her lover is killed meaninglessly. Olga is bored to exhaustion with teaching in school, but she finally accepts a permanent position and resigns herself to stay where she is. Masha has married another dull schoolmaster, and consequently has fallen in love with the idea of falling in love with Vershinin, colonel of the regiment lately garrisoned in the town. The regiment moves on; Masha stays behind. Their brother Andrey wanted to be a professor and so goes to Moscow, but he makes the mistake of marrying a girl who saps his strength. She has a baby by another man and sells the house over their heads. But this recital of a 'plot' hardly suggests the spirit of the play. For the play is not about externals, but about a pattern of feeling which weaves itself in a felicitous design of delicate human entanglements.

To weave the strands together and adjust an equal emphasis on each of the four central characters draws attention to their meaning as a family group. 'Events' occur only to reorient the group as a whole, and a mood spreads through the whole company, modified and recast as it is touched by each of their idiosyncrasies in turn.

At the rise of the curtain, we learn that it is Irena's saint's day. Cheerful midday sunshine shines on to the stage. Olga is thinking of the past, and this makes her happy, if in a quaveringly nostalgic way: 'I remember so well how everything in Moscow was in blossom by now, everything was soaked in sunlight and warmth.' It is a bright, warm memory, and it is associated with beloved Moscow. Masha, absorbed in a book, has heard all this before and whistles a tune under her breath; she is not unhappy, but her whistling serves to underline the indirect comment on Olga's remarks made by the men laughing upstage. This touches off a more unpleasant sensation in poor Olga: 'Masha, do stop whistling! How can you? (*A pause.*) I suppose I must get this continual headache because I have to go to school every day and go on teaching right into the evening. . . .' Her mention of Moscow has meanwhile set in motion Irena's series of thoughts, pushing vaguely into the future: '. . . Sell the house, finish with our life here, and go back to Moscow.' A few minutes later the arrival of Vershinin starts a new train of feelings, and high spirits all round become irrepressible. Yet we are already made to feel the nostalgia and to judge the equivocal quality of their lives. There is a warm, dry humour in this detached view of simple human behaviour.

It is simple without being simplified: that is Chekhov's genius. As in life, we dare take nothing at face value. How far is Masha's love for Vershinin in reality a reproach to Kulyghin, her mild little husband? How far is Vershinin's love for Masha the sexual vanity of the male looking for pity? How far is Natasha's marriage with Andrey a social revenge for the ill-manners of the sisters? Are Kulyghin's feelings for his wife, his attempts to amuse her by wearing a comic beard, for example, fit for our laughter or for our tears? Is Irena's resolution to marry Tuzenbach selfish or unselfish? How real is her grief when he is killed in the duel with Soliony? These and countless other questions that flash through our minds during performance are all of the intangible mysteries of human relationships, each complicated by two or more variable human factors, denying any complete solution.

There are countless small moments, like the following, when the feelings of the characters cannon off each other like so many balls on a billiards table. Tuzenbach has suggested that Masha should play in a public concert in aid of the victims of the fire which occurs in Act III. Kulyghin, so very proud that his own wife is being praised, agrees joyfully that she plays 'wonderfully well!' Irena provides a dry comment which shatters the atmosphere and reminds us of the forlorn creature under discussion: 'She's forgotten how to! She hasn't played for three years...or maybe it's four.' Then a comment from Kulyghin unwittingly hints at a reason for this: '...But would it be quite proper for her to play in a concert?' A devastating pause, carefully planned by the author, marks his narrow slavishness, and during the raw silence which follows, we and each of the characters feel the appalled reaction of everyone else. Even Kulyghin feels an irritation, and he flounders for an apology till we feel there can be no harm in him: 'I don't know anything about these matters, my friends. Perhaps it'll be perfectly all right. But you know, although our director is a good man, a very good man indeed, and most intelligent, I know that he does hold certain views....Of course, this doesn't really concern him, but I'll have a word with him about it all the same, if you like.' Our affectionate animosity thaws him into life.

The play ends as it began. But the sisters now stand huddled together as the military band fades into the distance, declaring with vehemence that 'life isn't finished' for them yet. And into this still, ironical microcosm of life the neutral indifference of everyday flows as before. Kulyghin bustles in with Masha's hat and cape, happy to have her to himself again. Andrey, the would-be professor, pushes out the pram for the baby's constitutional. The useless old doctor sings quietly to himself:

CHEBUTYKIN. Tarara-boom-di-ay....I'm sitting on a tomb-di-ay....
(*Reads the paper.*) What does it matter? Nothing matters!
OLGA. If only we knew, if only we knew!... (*Curtain*)

It is difficult to describe and explain the drama of Chekhov in terms other than those of the plays themselves, and this is especially true of his crowning achievement, the most complex and perhaps the greatest of all modern plays, *The Cherry Orchard*. For this reason, some extended analysis of the play's last act has been attempted in the next section.

'The Cherry Orchard', Act IV

ANALYSIS: 'THE CHERRY ORCHARD', ACT IV

The Cherry Orchard is a play which represents an attitude to life under stress and a way of life in transition. The orchard itself summarizes the hopes and regrets, the desires and ideals of this way of life. Just as the orchard with the town on the horizon epitomizes all Russia, so the play in its structure at once encompasses the range of social class from landowner to domestic serf, and brings the past hard against the future in its three or four generations. It achieves in its design as wide a statement as a naturalistic play could hope to do.

In the last act of the play, this structure of change and decay is welded into a firm whole, both because its parts are here drawn together and because the sympathies of the audience are under careful restraint and precise control. In this act the crescendo of finely chosen discords is heard and felt with inimitable impact. The following account is written, not to repeat what is well known, but to discover how the impact is caused.

The mood of the act is conjured immediately with the rise of the curtain. It is late autumn and the cherry trees stand bare outside the window. The nursery is in a pitiful state of nudity, with fade-marks on the walls where the pictures were, furniture stacked or covered with dust-sheets, luggage waiting for removal. 'There is an oppressive sense of emptiness.' It was a brilliant stroke to have this final scene played in the nursery of Act I rather than in the drawing-room of Act III, not only to balance the arrival of the family with their departure, but also because a setting of birth and childhood challenges the affections of *all* the generations, young and old.

Lopakhin isolated

In the desert spaces of this room stands waiting the new master of the cherry orchard, now an embarrassed and rather lonely man, Lopakhin. Embarrassed because the family has always been unable to forget his peasant origins; lonely because he now realizes how he has hurt those he loved by taking from them what they loved. He waves his arms a little in nervousness; beside him stands Yasha with a tray of champagne, Lopakhin's offering of farewell, according to Russian custom. He has done what is expected, but coming from him this same champagne needles them all, except Yasha.

We in the audience take in the situation at a glance: this is a situation we can recognize and know from experience. We can fully understand, and thus sympathize with, this man in this position, but if we see him only at the level of one who has to speed the parting guest, the irony of his situation keeps us from a complete identity. We now see him as the merchant away from his merchandise, the shopkeeper out of his shop, fish out of water, for all that, as Chekhov told Stanislavsky,[1] 'he must behave with the utmost courtesy and decorum, without any vulgarity or silly jokes...it must be borne in mind that such a serious and religious girl as Varya was in love with Lopakhin; she would never have fallen in love with some cheap moneymaker'. We see him in his 'white waistcoat and brown shoes' (this is Chekhov to Nemirovich-Danchenko now), taking long strides when he is lost in thought, stroking his beard back and forth. At this moment the comedy of his characterization half rises to the surface.

The irony of his situation is accentuated, too, because Chekhov so carefully contrasts this scene with the last. Act III bustled visually to an emotional climax; Act IV is toned so much lower as to be almost an anticlimax. It offers a pause in its first few minutes for us to soak up its bitterness. We left Lopakhin in a drunken hysteria, proclaiming half in joy, half in self-reproach, 'Here comes the new landowner, here comes the owner of the cherry orchard!' He is now involved in the complexities of sentiment which surround the departing

[1] Quoted by D. Magarshack, *Chekhov the Dramatist* (London, 1952), p. 275.

family, unable fully to grasp what we in our Olympian seats assimilate in a flash.

His helplessness is enacted when Mme Ranevsky, with her brother Gaev, enter feverishly, cross the stage quickly, and go off, leaving him standing there perplexed, offering them the champagne they have ignored: 'Have some champagne, please do, please!' We balance this gesture against the depth of feeling in Mme Ranevsky; yet, in its own way, it too commands our sympathy.

The exchanges which follow with Yasha and Trofimov are all to explore the nature of Lopakhin's embarrassment with that clinical eye which is to keep us alert to the meaning of his suffering. The same Lopakhin is there displaying his classical comic obsession: business-like in his appreciation of the cash value of the wine—'eight roubles a bottle', he tells Yasha; business-like in his time-keeping—'there are only forty-six minutes before the train's due to leave'. Though Chekhov uses him to supply one of his illuminating moments of the mood and atmosphere in the house with his 'It's devilishly cold in here', the practical man with his feet on the ground must add, 'Good building weather'.

Thus by suggestion we are told that Lopakhin is floundering, and the more he turns for reassurance to matters of money, of time and of business, measurable, accessible, firm and concrete things, the more we smile. Should we have wept to see him unable to cope with the huge and complex agony of a lost cause? So he puppets it back and forth across the bare stage, obeying the little laws of his own habits, while we weigh his inadequacy with mixed amusement against tender impressions sustained over three acts.

Naturalistic Shading

Trofimov and Lopakhin: twin clowns

The image grows denser when Trofimov, with an incongruous air of efficiency and youthful egotism, enters echoing Lopakhin: 'I think it's time to start. The horses are at the door.' We begin to notice now how Chekhov applies pressure to our sense of time in this last act, squeezing out our sympathy for the general distress on the stage, while at the same time neatly indicating how little the 'eternal student's' assumption of command for the operation of departure is justified. Against Lopakhin's 'We must start in twenty minutes. Hurry up' is set the dubious 'I think...' of Trofimov. Especially since he is chiefly bothered because he cannot find his goloshes; and in a personal flutter he calls to the one least likely at this time to be able to help him—Anya (it is Varya who throws a pair of goloshes at him a few minutes later). The humble detail derides the total appearance.

However, Lopakhin is grateful to have someone, even someone he in his soul despises, to talk to at the moment. Without being asked, he pours out his heart with an abrupt, 'And I must be off to Kharkov...'. Then follows a long speech during which he is talking only to himself. Meanwhile Trofimov continues to hunt among the luggage and ignore him, until a breathless pause from Lopakhin brings Trofimov to a halt. With a bitter look and a curt reply, Trofimov puts him in his place: 'We'll soon be gone, then you can start your useful labour again.' Trofimov can be cruel in a way that the family itself would never dare to be.

Lopakhin now begins to draw on our sympathy more warmly, and it is Trofimov who comes more under scrutiny. Lopakhin in a sudden gesture of friendship, prompted perhaps by guilt, offers some of the champagne which Yasha is busily quaffing alone upstage. He is curtly refused. A little quarrel flashes out, and the sparks of their slight differences in social class and their greater differences in wealth catch fire, reminding us dramatically that behind the emotionality of the farewell unquenched antagonisms still burn:

LOPAKHIN. Well, well...I expect the professors are holding up their lectures, waiting for your arrival!

TROFIMOV. That's none of your business.

LOPAKHIN. How many years have you been studying at the university?

TROFIMOV. I wish you'd think up something new, that's old and stale. Incidentally, as we're not likely to meet again, I'd like to give you a bit of advice....

He goes on to criticize the 'wide, sweeping gestures' of Lopakhin's talk about building villas. We know that his criticism is really a criticism of himself, since he is the one who speaks in wide, sweeping gestures. We know, furthermore, that a Lopakhin who can buy the cherry orchard can also calculate precisely the profits from its summer residents. This is a farcical quarrel of tit-for-tat, but one with an ugly gist.

As if he suddenly realizes that he is dealing with a man of different calibre from himself, indeed that he may be saying things he will regret, Trofimov lets his anger die quickly. He sees that his comments on Lopakhin's personal behaviour have hurt far more than any criticism of his business methods: this attack on Lopakhin's social graces is of course a direct thrust at his class background. So Trofimov retracts and intuitively says the right thing, incidentally illuminating a little the mystery of the most complex character in the play: 'When all's said and done, I like you, despite everything. You've slender, delicate fingers, like an artist's, you've a fine, sensitive soul...'. We are reminded of Lopakhin's dreams in Act II, that men should be 'giants' to live in consonance with a country of 'vast forests, immense fields, wide horizons'.

They would then have parted friends, and the moral would have suggested itself, we may suppose, that there is a basis for progress and co-operation between opposing classes on grounds

7-2

of human tolerance, and so on, and so forth. Chekhov indeed hints at the need to link industry with culture and culture with industry, as he does less obliquely in the mouth of Vershinin in *The Three Sisters*. But here Chekhov doesn't allow us any such immediate response. Lopakhin, in a final mistaken gesture of friendship, offers the younger man money for his journey—the sort of offer he might have valued himself in earlier days perhaps, an offer that makes sense to the practical man he is. Trofimov is of course touched on another raw spot. He sees Lopakhin's generosity as a further sign of the vulgarity that distinguishes them, and the quarrel again flares up. He tells a lie about having had a translation accepted in order to refuse with dignity. They are, we recognize, two of a kind in matters of personal pride.

So Trofimov the idealist speaks. He is a free man, money can mean nothing to him, and, with the grand, abstract sweep of the arm of one who has nothing to lose and everything to gain, he drops into cliché:

> Humanity is advancing towards the highest truth, the greatest happiness that is possible to achieve on earth, and I am in the van!
>
> LOPAKHIN. Will you get there?
>
> TROFIMOV. Yes. (*A pause.*) I'll get there myself, or show others the way to get there.

In that pause Chekhov allows just time enough to let the insidious irony seep back. During that moment of hesitation, Chekhov permits us to pin down all youthful revolutionary leaders with their own doubts: pathetic Trofimov becomes comic again, and Lopakhin makes his point. The vision of a glorious future clouds slightly, but it does not disappear, for we hear of it again with Anya. As if to mark the impression, the first sound of an axe cutting into a cherry tree is heard distantly off-stage. 'Life is slipping by', says Lopakhin in a real gesture of shared sympathy, and irreverently identifies Trofimov's grand rhetoric, as we have already done, with infinite numbers of us, and not merely in Russia: 'how many people there are in Russia, my friend, who exist to no purpose whatever! Well, never mind, perhaps it's no matter.' He at least feels happier for working hard—he slips into the pragmatic view of the practical man again.

These two in their characteristic duologue embrace the conflict in our own minds. They offer not merely a restatement of a class difference in society, or of youthful idealism corrected by a maturer wisdom, though this symbolism is there. For it is a mark of the darkness of the comedy that both of these characters are specimens of broken-hearted clown: neither can therefore teach us a complete truth or give us a final answer. In the acumen of the one and the optimism of the other, Chekhov points to a rooted error of judgment. Behind them both lies the fading nostalgic beauty of all the cherry orchard stood for when circumstances were different. Chekhov is not indicting the Russian merchant or the Russian intellectual, any more than he is telling us what fools Lopakhin and Trofimov are: Chekhov is more subtle than this. There is some truth in Lopakhin's view and some in Trofimov's. We are to imagine a blend of Lopakhin and Trofimov, perhaps together with a little of Anya's lack of affectation and a good deal of Mme Ranevsky's heart. He is pressing us, in other words, to take a more balanced view. We are to discover that these two confused men are, like us, groping in a dark room while an unknown hand moves the furniture. Their differences of pragmatism and ideality are those that struggle within ourselves with each new experience that comes. If Chekhov leaves us in uneasy doubt about the righteousness of either, it is to encourage us towards impartiality; it is to induce a greater awareness of serious comic meaning in the extraordinary series of little episodes, particularities and attitudes that make up the *dénouement* of the play.

Naturalistic Shading

Infinitesimal tragedy: Yasha and the servants

As if suddenly to reduce the scale of our view, Chekhov now places the manservant Yasha centre-stage and completes the little story of the triangle Epihodov–Dunyasha–Yasha.

Yasha would be the one unsympathetic character in the play were he not also a little comic, and one must ask the reasons for this. As Lopakhin represents the new aristocracy of business-men, so Yasha represents a new breed of underlings, the smart servants who cheat their masters and lord it over their equals. They astutely take advantage of the social changes that only bewilder their superiors. They grease their hair, Chekhov is saying, and, when they can, they smoke cigars and ape their betters. They can mesmerize silly girls like Dunyasha, and, for what they are worth, break their hearts. They despise the genuine affection towards the family of a domestic serf like old Firs. For Chekhov they sum up all that is *poshlost*, vulgar.

Somewhat indirectly, Yasha is to suggest what might happen to the minds of the other young people of the same generation, like Anya and Trofimov, had they too to fend for themselves in a commercial world. In this he is the complement of Lopakhin, illuminating a side of this character we would not otherwise see, the Smerdyakov facet of Dostoevsky's Ivan Karamazov, the Svidrigailev of his Raskolnikov. He is denied any of Lopakhin's sensitivity and generosity of spirit. Now a little drunk from champagne, he speaks with casual disrespect to Anya when she inquires whether Firs, his foil, has been taken to hospital: 'I told them to take him this morning. He's gone, I think.' But Anya knows Yasha too well, and calls to Epihodov, 'Semyon Panteleyevich, will you please find out whether Firs has been taken to hospital?' Yasha is not concerned. With the gentlest of touches, we are told incisively that the man is wholly egocentric and contemptuous of all about him.

This is confirmed when Varya calls that his mother has come to say goodbye to him before he returns to Paris. This reminder of his former life is unwelcome, and he shrugs off her old-fashioned sentiment with a superior air: 'She just makes me lose patience with her.' We may criticize this as altogether too strongly contradicting psychological truth: a rejection of a mother by her son shocks. It condemns him, and illuminates the impression that was dim before, that there is an amoral and destructive aspect of progress. Like Lopakhin's unwitting negation of what is personally delicate and living in the cherry orchard home, like the eliminating of the Mme Ranevskys who have their own contribution to make to the harmony of existence, subtle changes in the social order can tear up what is deep-rooted and valuable in human life.

Unlike some farcical intrusions into modern domestic comedy, Yasha's presence in the play is relevant to the whole. His part faintly echoes that of Lopakhin, for it shows us how silly ignorance may injure silly innocence. This is done lightly: the regrets and distress of Dunyasha, the pert maidservant, are her just deserts; there is no real suggestion that Epihodov's love for her has been mortally wounded—no melodrama here. In their miniature comedy, played very much in the remoter background, Epihodov is the sort who can say how much he envies Firs because he is 'beyond repair' and must soon 'join his ancestors', and this part, written for brittle comedy, written for the Russian comedian Moskvin,[1] must exclude bitterness. In the same way, Dunyasha is quite an accomplished actress: she shams 'delicacy', falls too easily in and out of love, powders her nose, faints at appropriate moments, and so on. Her story must exclude tragedy, although it allows for pathos.

Nevertheless, all that Yasha stands for is thereby effectively diminished. He drinks his champagne in spite of the fact that

[1] N. A. Toumanova, *Anton Chekhov* (London, 1937), p. 201.

'it isn't the real thing', dreams of the journey in the express train, and longs for Paris where something is always 'going on', where there is less 'ignorance'. In view of the character who purveys these ideas, they are received by us only with scepticism. This is given open expression in laughter when Gaev enters, fixes one look on Yasha's hair, and says, 'Who's smelling of herring here?'

Mothers and babies: Lyubov, Anya and Charlotta

The late owners of the cherry orchard, Lyubov (Mme Ranevsky) and Gaev, are two lovable fools, held in affection by all around them. They now re-enter. 'In ten minutes we ought to be getting into the carriage...', and again we are reminded of time. Time was dogging us through the scene of the party in Act III, and now we realize that its pressure is not only of dramatic hours and minutes, but a poetic urgency fixing a paralysed attention on the treasure that is escaping. The loss of the orchard, prefigured from the outset, has grown in the imagery of the play to mean the loss of a whole way of life, with all the particularity of its hopes and frustrations, all the living experience of its memories and its expectations. There are ten minutes left for us, as it were, breathlessly to savour its sadness.

In the grip of a genuine nostalgia and a deep regret, Mme Ranevsky takes a last look round her nursery: 'Goodbye, dear house, old grandfather house.' With the simplest of epithets, Chekhov paints a picture of generations, while directly expressing the character's emotions. It would seem we are to expect an emotive sequel, flushed with sentiment. Yet there is an ironic edge to every gesture and statement which is to follow. Our view of the play remains carefully under control.

Lyubov's ardent kissing of Anya, with all her desire for her future happiness, hardly conceals the dilemma of a woman caught between her uncertain regret for the past and her uncertain hope for the future. She is not happy, but perhaps her daughter is:

> MME RANEVSKY. Are you glad? Very glad?
> ANYA. Yes, very. Our new life is just beginning, Mama!
> GAEV (*brightly*). So it is indeed, everything's all right now.

Anya unaffectedly sees no past standing over her like a judgment as her mother does: she unknowingly clouds the nostalgic image of the dear past, and looks fearlessly forward to a bright future. But we sense that Anya is her mother as she was, and Lyubov is as her daughter will be.

Gaev's effort of gaiety confirms the ambiguities beneath the surface of their mood. Our impression of the inadequacy of Mme Ranevsky, for all her unselfishness, is here as elsewhere reinforced by the greater weakness of her brother. This man who has no money-sense at all, who let the orchard slip between his fingers also, is simulating happiness as obviously as she: we immediately recognize his instinct to console himself. He tells us that he is to become a bank-clerk, of all things, 'a financier'.

Passionately embraced and passionately embracing, Anya, the innocent who has yet to face the world of hard experience, dreams of Mama's return, of passing examinations and working hard...'We'll read during the long autumn evenings, we'll read lots of books, and a new, wonderful world will open up before us...'. For a perceptible moment seventeen-year-old Anya reverses their roles; she is the little mother comforting Lyubov, till she relaxes into golden fancies. Almost symbolically the child curls up on the dust-sheet over the sofa, seeing with the bright eyes of youth, reassured by the caresses of the mother who tells her she will come back. We have the authority of the play's cumulative ironies to doubt what we see and hear.

In case we too grow sentimental over this imaginary prospect, too reassured by the archetype of mother and child,

Naturalistic Shading

Chekhov plays an ace. He had brought in Charlotta, the German-bred governess, and has had her downstage, looking with our eyes at the scene. Now, half to cheer the company, it would seem, half to express her and our scepticism, she plays one of her tricks:

> (*Picking up a bundle that looks like a baby in swaddling clothes.*) Bye-bye, little baby. (*A sound like a baby crying is heard.*) Be quiet, my sweet, be a good little boy. (*The 'crying' continues.*) My heart goes out to you, baby!

This must strike us as a naughty burlesque of the pathetic exchange we have just seen, belittling and colouring the impression the other three have created. The burlesque is offered with less of the gentle, shaded touch so familiar in Chekhov, and more with that callous juxtaposition to be found later in works like Anouilh's *Point of Departure*. Chekhov feels it necessary to give a more severe shock to dispel the more subversive sentiment. It is Chekhov's command to us to return to earth, and it is enacted when Charlotta almost viciously throws the bundle down and says, 'Are you going to find me another job, please? I can't do without one.' She is practical, for we remember what she told us on the garden seat in Act II, that she does not know who her mother was, that she has no past, that she is alone—as Anya may well be.

By the matter-of-fact tone of her last remark, a moment of farce is turned to wormwood. 'You should only sit down to write,' Chekhov told Bunin, 'when you feel as cold as ice.'[1]

Enter Simeonov-Pishchik, fatalist

Pishchik, 'strong as a horse', eternally penniless, high with blood-pressure, puffing and sweating, is most part clown. He is an ineffectual landowner from another cherry orchard, and we are really unable to take his financial distresses seriously. His constant borrowing of money is his comic 'gimmick', and

[1] W. H. Bruford, *Chekhov* (London, 1957), p. 15.

Gaev by his scuttling exit reminds us of Pishchik's apparent role in the play. He will enter now to provide us with some crazy horse-play perhaps, a little knock-about relief, 'what a phenomenon!' But he too has a calculated place in the pattern.

He blusters in, out of breath as usual, greeting Mme Ranevsky and Lopakhin, pouring a glass of water, fumbling in his pocket, swallowing a mouthful. Between his gasps for air and comic business with the tiresome glass, he drags from his pocket—a handful of notes! Too late he repays money that might have paid the mortgage interest on the unhappy estate. For in bewilderment he has found that science and progress have overtaken him unawares, to his advantage and amazement. In joy and confusion he explains what has happened: 'Wait a moment...I'm so hot...A most extraordinary thing happened. Some English people came to see me and discovered a sort of white clay on my land...'.

His perpetual simple astonishment at the phenomena of life around him is now given real cause for expression. Foreign capital was in fact being invested in Russia in the 1890's. Now indeed he can ridicule his naïve search for a philosophical justification for the forgery of banknotes—or taking one's own life. 'Just now a young fellow in the train was telling me that some great philosopher or other...advises people to jump off roofs. You just jump off, he says, and that settles the whole problem....Fancy that!' Thus subtly, farcically, does the author drop a thought among the audience, brushing it off as soon as it has settled. The sequence of the dialogue suggests that Pishchik had thought for a gossamer moment of a resort to suicide: now providence has relieved him of the need, just as it had left her token, ignored, with Mme Ranevsky. Could this same thought have occurred to her?—oh, but no—we dismiss the idea: Chekhov is teasing.

As if to strengthen our feelings, Pishchik has dashed about

the room, sat down, stood up, drunk his water and gone—at such a pace that we have hardly had time to assimilate the impression he leaves us with. He has gone without noticing that the family is on the eve of departure. Lyubov calls after him, and the pace abruptly halts as he turns back and looks unhappily about him. He sees the bare room at last. Something did not 'turn up' for them this time. His tone changes: 'Well, never mind. (*Tearfully*.) Never mind....These Englishmen, you know, they're men of the greatest intelligence....Never mind....I wish you every happiness, God be with you. Never mind, everything comes to an end eventually.' Jumping off the roof was not so outrageous a notion after all—'everything comes to an end eventually'. What was stated in jest is now echoed with deep embarrassment; the puppet becomes a man.

Pishchik's little scene, brief and funny and pathetic as it is, fits into the design. The comedy misleads us momentarily, but the contrast in the tempo of playing between the time of Pishchik's entrance and that of his exit again reorients by a fine degree the play's whole meaning. Pishchik's primary function is to introduce that recognizable element of fatalism into the structure of the life being demonstrated, though we remain free to dismiss it. The chance purchase of Pishchik's clay by the astonishing Englishmen is the counterpart of the sale of the cherry orchard: the positive and the negative of the same picture. Are we equally subject to chance? Only death is inevitable. Comic Pishchik epitomizes mankind faced with insoluble problems: in bewilderment he blusters with joy, and in the same bewilderment he frets in misery. It is all very droll.

Characteristically, Chekhov allows his good-hearted Pishchik a tender moment before he takes his departure from the play. This is quoted in all its subtlety, and without comment:

And when you hear that my end has come, just think of—a horse, and say: 'There used to be a fellow like that once....Simeonov-Pishchik his name was—God be with him!' Wonderful weather we're having. Yes....(*Goes out, overcome with embarrassment, but returns at once and stands in the doorway.*) Dashenka sent greetings to you. (*Goes out.*)

A proposal does not come off: Lopakhin and Varya

The tiny tragedy of Charlotta is followed by the tiny comedy of Pishchik, and this in turn is followed by the tiny tragedy of Varya. But just as Charlotta could never of course have risen to any real stature, neither can Varya. Chekhov wrote to Nemirovich-Danchenko that she was to be 'a little nun-like creature, somewhat simple-minded, plaintive'.[1] Plaintive, but still a comedienne: 'she is a crybaby by nature and her tears ought not to arouse any feelings of gloom in the audience.'[2]

Yet the sequence[3] which follows that of Pishchik's exit moves into the friendly territory of common experience far enough to colour the action with a sufficient tincture of pathos.

First Mme Ranevsky gives us another reminder of time: there are but five minutes remaining. However, as she insists, there is still time enough to settle a final problem, that of Varya's future. It is firmly in the mother's mind, in spite of many protestations from the parties concerned, that Lopakhin must propose to her. 'We have another five minutes or so...' A moment later: 'You'll hardly need more than a minute, that's all.'

Much of the comedy, and much of the pathos, of this episode rests upon counterpointing two senses of time: on the one hand, that which presses from without, the waiting carriage and the approaching train; and, on the other, the inner reluctance of Lopakhin, whose emotional indigestion makes it so impossible to hasten the passing of this most embarrassing

---

[1] *The Selected Letters of Anton Chekhov*, ed. L. Hellman, trans. Lederer (London, 1955), p. 316.

[2] D. Magarshack, *Chekhov the Dramatist* (London, 1952), p. 274.

[3] This scene is discussed in more detail in the author's *The Elements of Drama* (Cambridge, 1960), pp. 73 ff.

moment. His scene with Varya is to be played so slowly as to
make an audience conscious of an intentional dramatic meaning
through tempo. The contrast with the quicker pace of Pishchik's speech and movement is to make us feel Lopakhin's
own confusion of mind about time. When he looks at his watch
and when he finally leaves the room in unseemly haste, we
must be made to ask ourselves, were these actions the result of
his anxiety for the family's prompt departure, or for his own?
If this scene is to illuminate one more facet of the agony of the
relentless advance of tomorrow, we must feel the state of
Lopakhin's shuttlecock mind in wanting the moment to fly,
and yet wanting it to stop. He asks only that human relationships may resolve themselves in natural harmony, for they
will not obey the clock.

Chekhov's dialogue for this episode is masterly. With
brevity, and yet with an adroit mustering of points in favour
of a marriage, Mme Ranevsky is made to use all her feminine
wit to accomplish a mother's last duty to a daughter. She
excuses her for looking thin and pale. But this is only because
she has no work to do—an appeal to a Lopakhin who would be
expected to want an industrious wife. She tells him that her
Varya cries a lot—an appeal to his protective sympathies.
Finally she tells him that Varya loves him—an appeal to his
masculine pride. '...And I just don't know, I just don't know
why you seem to keep away from each other. I don't under–
stand it.' She implies a question: what reason can you give
for your delay?

What reason *can* Lopakhin give? We guess: although Varya
is only adopted into the household to earn her keep as a house-
keeper, perhaps an illegitimate daughter of Lyubov's husband, nevertheless, like Lopakhin's purchase of the cherry
orchard, his marriage to Varya would perhaps be a glancing
blow against social tradition, which he has always instinctively
accepted. Lopakhin could never aspire to the manners and

graces Varya has acquired in her years with Lyubov. A social barrier, however, is hardly used by Chekhov as a dramatic crux: there is to be no melodramatic gesture of defiance. The mother wants the marriage, as does the foster-daughter; but how strong are the ties that bind Lopakhin to the older respect for class? There is no defiance in his proposal, and Lopakhin remains human, humble, and no puppet. But he is equally reluctant to make a proposal of marriage because he is as shy as any man might be. Thus with sure control, Chekhov presents a socially symbolic situation under a wholly naturalistic guise, as he had done with Trofimov's poverty, Yasha's pertness, Pishchik's unexpected wealth. Neither Mme Ranevsky nor Lopakhin are aware of the forces present on the stage with them at this moment of decision.

MME RANEVSKY. ...I don't understand it.
LOPAKHIN. Neither do I myself, I must confess. It's all so strange somehow....

We feel Lopakhin's emotional immaturity and awkwardness compared with Mme Ranevsky's experience and grace. But the practical man will at last face the situation, and other members of the family are ushered out of the room, and Varya is called, while Lopakhin waits alone on the stage.

We are prepared for comic relief by the interminable pause that holds us in suspense after the exit of the mother. It is a pause redolent of the agony of making an irrevocable personal decision. We are held until we are ourselves self-conscious and Lopakhin's discomfiture is ours. So we are ready to laugh when we hear the 'suppressed laughter and whispering' of the others behind the door, and when in even greater embarrassment Varya enters pretending to hunt among the luggage: 'It's strange, I just can't find....' It is with this new pause that the character of the scene begins to change, and a warmth of feeling begins to spread over it.

In a series of false starts, Lopakhin tepidly endeavours to

make the bright opening gambit which might lead to the happy embrace of a potential bride and groom. But each time his leading questions only stress the misery of Varya's present position, and because she is the 'simple-minded, plaintive' little creature presented in the play, they lead her quickly to tears. He asks where she will go now that the family is leaving—she will go to the Rogulins to be a house-keeper. What is worse, her post will be seventy miles away—it might as well be in the antipodes. Husband and home will be left far behind, and for both Varya and Lopakhin a marriage must be contracted now or never. 'So this is the end of life in this house. . . .' Upon Lopakhin's saying this, Varya, in the anguish of nostalgia and longing, buries her tears furiously among the luggage. She has not dared to look at him.

Lopakhin has said the wrong thing, and he must start again. But the same nostalgia grips him too. As he looks out of the window, he sees the cold sun of autumn and feels the frost descending. With another of his fine imaginative strokes, Chekhov invokes the weather to epitomize the mood of the scene and at the same time extend and make articulate the feelings that surround the characters. The irony of Lopakhin's estimating the degrees of frost with the accuracy of a farmer, and of Varya's exasperated retort that their thermometer is broken, echoes painfully through a further long pause. Time rushes onwards.

Suddenly a voice, perhaps Epihodov's, calls his name, and Lopakhin is gone, his dilemma resolved for him. Varya is left to weep uninhibitedly with her face in a bundle of clothes. The precious moment is destroyed. How? By fickle accident, by the pressure of extraneous situation, certainly by a human inadequacy, perhaps by a deeper power of birth and blood, by all these things, by Chekhov's seeing life like this in such moments of time.

The idea of the mutation of things emerges through a

succession of innumerable minute insights that are discovered to us. It will depend on what we contribute to the interpretation of this episode, however, and what these characters have grown to represent to us, if we are to see the scene as something more than an unhappy little fragment in two small lives that do not matter so very much; the rather pathetic surface of the action on this level will fail to affect us or the play. However, we are so well prepared for the anticlimax when it comes, that we must pay another kind of attention to its meaning.

The false starts and proprieties of the man, the gentility and discretion of the woman, our sense of the limitations of a conventional behaviour in such a situation as this, must vividly illuminate human weakness. Varya and Lopakhin, if indeed the busy man ever really wanted marriage, cannot make a sufficient adjustment to the requirements of change. Two small people who cannot see their position except subjectively, are shown buffeted by forces they cannot recognize, even less control. With an appalling irony, Varya, virtual mistress of the house, who had thrown her keys at Lopakhin's feet in Act III, must now go to the Rogulins 'to be their housekeeper, or something'. While she becomes a servant, he will be master. Against such a reversal, Lopakhin's well-meaning decorums are wholly misplaced, almost laughable. A pathetic loneliness, half-conscious maybe, is balanced by a comic awkwardness.

Chekhov is saying to us in as positive a way as he can without breaking his naturalistic convention, that the smashing of one order need not necessarily comprehend the end of an existing harmony of relationships, certainly not of individual happiness. He is inviting us to see the position with an objectivity denied to his characters. He does it by enlarging and emphasizing their feelings, and presenting these in the white light of their comic littleness.

Naturalistic Shading

Ensemble

Chekhov now crowds his stage in order to empty it at the curtain. This is his last opportunity to bring together his small host of characters with the cumulative impact of all their petty, but overwhelming, little troubles. Before he finally dismisses the world of the cherry orchard, its fragmentary impressions are to be blended into a total image.

The room fills with people, as it did in Act I when it was a springtime, happier time of homecoming: Varya, Mme Ranevsky, Anya, Gaev, Charlotta with her dog, Yasha, Epihodov, Dunyasha, with other servants and coachmen. Trofimov and Lopakhin will enter in a moment. The house bustles with life and urgency once more, but it is the urgency of departure. The attitudes characteristic of this or that generation, each with a contrasting outlook fixed upon the future or the past, are by simple strokes compressed into a tone of voice, a gesture, a familiar form of words, which seem to echo and re-echo from the far walls of the play till they merge into its sombre reverberations.

The mother who resigned herself so quickly to the failure of her plan that we suspect that she had hardly anticipated its success, says flatly, 'Now we can start on our journey'. But her heart is in the past. Anya, representative of a younger generation, happy at new prospects and widening experience, echoes her joyfully: 'Yes, our journey!' Equally unrealistic, she is living in the future. Gaev, overwhelmed with personal memories, is least in command of his feelings, and after his habit slips from sentiment into rhetoric: 'My friends, my dear, kind friends! Now as I leave this house for ever....' Here it is dear old Gaev whom Chekhov permits to strike the seemingly false note of comedy, and it is emphasized by the girls who implore him to stop.

Amid all the activity of preparation and dressing and

gathering of personal luggage, Mme Ranevsky sits centre-stage, silent and alone in a pool of quietness. By her stillness she catches our eye: 'I'll just sit down for one little minute more. I feel as if I'd never seen the walls and ceilings of this house before, and now I look at them with such longing and affection. . . .' She is sincere and articulate about her emotions, and suddenly this apparently feather-weight heroine becomes solid for us: Chekhov uses her as his spokesman for the suffering, conscious and unconscious, of all. But only for that moment: she will be once more fussing about the luggage as soon as she hears her brother's voice take on the oratorical tone again. She tears herself out of her mood: 'Have they taken out all the luggage?' For us, the serious mood remains and continues under the surface of trivialities.

Now with inspired cunning, forcing us to enter into his peculiar war of nerves, the author has the most obvious comedian in the play, Epihodov, register his one truly fetching moment of pathos. As a result of Lopakhin's 'See that everything's all right, Epihodov', we digest the following exchange:

EPIHODOV (*in a husky voice*). Don't worry, Yermolai Alexeyevich!
LOPAKHIN. What are you talking like that for?
EPIHODOV. I've just had a drink of water. I must have swallowed something.
YASHA (*with contempt*). What ignorance!

Like Pishchik, Epihodov is allowed his feelings, however limited, before the end. But precisely because he has never before done other than make us mock at his emotion, his present frog in the throat startles us, just as it surprises Lopakhin and challenges Yasha. Yasha asserts his difference from the peasant by a characteristic remark of derision. This mild friction between the two servants adds nearly the last of the pieces to the jigsaw of class rivalries, here well thrust home by pressure of exceptional circumstances.

Naturalistic Shading

The limelight shines on Lopakhin too, for a last time. Again, Chekhov cleverly serves a double dramatic purpose by a single expedient.

MME RANEVSKY. When we leave here there won't be a soul in the place....

LOPAKHIN. Until the spring.

Hearing the despondency in Lyubov's voice, he tries to respond with a brightly engaging comment. Like the realist he is, he is concerned with the present. But again he has said the wrong thing. In his odd effort to make amends, he has intensified her distress. Spring is when strangers will live where they live; spring is when the orchard would have been in blossom; spring was when they came home, only to leave again.

At this moment, Varya pulls an umbrella from a bundle. It flies up, and she seems to be about to strike him. In a gesture that catches our eye immediately, an echo of the incident with the billiards cue in Act III, Lopakhin's reaction summarizes in a flash his place in the pattern: he raises his arm to ward off the blow, and we are reminded of his peasant relationship with the family. Yet it also reflects his essential lack of confidence and the guilt he feels surging up as soon as he has spoken, that of his outrageous presumption in buying the estate. With a laugh, he promptly turns his instinctive fear into a little pantomime that relaxes the tension between himself and Varya and makes them friends again. Like the whole play, it is a token of confused emotions.

As a gesture, it is also a signal for renewed activity by everyone. Trofimov takes charge and orders the party into the carriage. Varya finds his goloshes at last—Chekhov leaves no detail unfinished. Trofimov has to put them on while still giving his orders—Chekhov deflates even his last assumption of dignity. Lopakhin efficiently counts the heads. Anya and Trofimov, the younger ones, leave first, hailing the future:

'The Cherry Orchard', Act IV

ANYA. Goodbye, old house! Goodbye, old life!
TROFIMOV. Greetings to the new life!

The older ones leave their lives behind them; youth has the world before it. The rest follow, Varya unwillingly, Yasha willingly, Charlotta coldly, Lopakhin warmly. Lyubov and Gaev are left alone, two small figures clasping each other in grief in the centre of the bare, blank stage.

Vacuum

With unparalled simplicity of effect, Chekhov has his two forlorn puppets stand motionless in the deserted nursery. The cherry orchard is already forsaken, and they are the life that used to be. The lightness in Mme Ranevsky is now heavy, her feelings squeezed dry: and she says what the orchard and the house mean to her in explicit terms. They express the salt and bitter taste, the uneasy ache of the experience of the whole play: 'Oh my darling, my precious, my beautiful orchard! My life, my youth, my happiness...goodbye!...Goodbye!' The orchard is the symbol for just those things: life, youth, happiness, and their passing. The symbolism is not a loose sentimentality: it is recognized in the astringency of our criticism.

They listen, as we do, to the excited cries from Anya and Trofimov impatient outside the house in the carriage, impatient to plant another cherry orchard. A world outside is calling, and another beyond that. Inside, the sobs of regret are counterpointed with the shrill calls outside, until Lyubov and her brother leave: 'We're coming...(*Both go out*).' The play is over; the point is made.

But is it? The curtain refuses to fall, and Chekhov tries his most daring stroke. For an age we sit looking at empty, half-lit space, while the master of pauses employs the longest pause of his career. We are to assimilate the implications of the drama by the tempo he ordains: '*The stage is empty. The sound of doors being locked is heard, then of carriages driving off. It grows quiet. The stillness is broken by the dull thuds of an axe on a tree....*' The spirit of the cherry orchard is allowed time to seep into us, and by sheer radiogenic dramatics, we learn what it is to be left in a house when all have departed; we learn what it is to *be* that house and to feel the axe in our soul. There is no comedy here now: it is all twilight.

We wait again for the curtain to fall, but again it does not. We hear instead the shuffle, the slow shuffle of old feet, and we dimly discern Firs as he creeps in. The old servant has been left behind in the general confusion. He moves with difficulty to the door that has just been bolted, tries it unsuccessfully, and stumbles to the sofa covered with its dust-sheet. He sits. 'They forgot about me. Never mind....' He is content, for the world outside no longer has any call upon him. Those of his generation cannot lose their cherry orchard now. At his age, neither past, present nor future have much meaning. With a final prick of comedy, almost a lifetime is compressed in his speech: 'I don't suppose Leonid Andreyevich put on his fur coat, I expect he's gone in his light one....These youngsters!' He lies still, while once more we await the fall of the curtain.

Yet even now there is a last bold trump to play: '*A distant sound is heard, coming as if out of the sky, like the sound of a string snapping, slowly and sadly dying away.*' Just as Chekhov had gathered together his players for their last *ensemble*, visually gathering together the joy and the sadness, hope for the future and regret for the past, so he attempts to epitomize the mixture of all our feelings in one unearthly and inexplicable sound, the sound we heard, unexplained, in Act II. To interpret it is to interpret the whole play. The curtain falls slowly with this in our ears, this and the sound of an axe striking a tree in the orchard far away.

The teasing structure of *The Cherry Orchard* easily accounts for its misinterpretation by producers from Konstantin Stanislavsky onwards. Where Chekhov's effect rests on a knife-edge balance of comedy and pathos in so many details, it is only too easy to tip the play towards one or the other. By inclination the sentimental majority of us leans towards the emotionality of the passing of an order. The substitution of one world for another is an excuse for melodramatics. Yet Chekhov was constantly making a plea to redress the balance: 'I am writing about life...this is a grey everyday life indeed... but not an eternal whimpering.'[1] He believed that a full, objective statement of what he saw of the behaviour of people would be sufficient to paint the unbiased picture he wanted. Although some may feel he should have made more direct statements, relying less on the vagaries of arbitrary mood of the audience, less on the caprices which abound in the theatre, to the end he preferred, as he said, to *show* us horse-thieves rather than condemn them.

Chekhov put on the stage a group of people. He made this the centre of attention; not events, unless they affected the characters; not characters, unless they were to disturb or cast a reflection on the group. His group lives by the commonplaces of life they display, and these carry the weight of the play. Thus he found a form for drama suited to the stage. He is accused of having no plot, but it is not the absence of plot, rather the presence of many little plots, suggestive phases of many little lives woven intricately together, that gives his play its careful, taut pattern in which every detail is intensely relevant. Every detail is relevant, that is, to the creation of that particular balance of sympathies which can recreate for an audience the fluid feel of life. It is not a gallows humour he offers, nor mere exuberance, but it embraces each of us in its restless appeal to truth.

[1] Quoted by N. A. Toumanova, *Anton Chekhov* (London, 1937), p. 201, from V. Feider, *A. P. Chekhov, Literaturny byt* (Leningrad, 1928), p. 450.

Naturalistic Shading

Chekhov is the master and the measure of a large variety of lesser dramatists, and indeed of film and television script-writers, in the twentieth century. The English-speaking theatre alone provides a good sample. Some incline towards melodrama, like Elmer Rice (*Street Scene*), Eugene O'Neill (*The Iceman Cometh*), Terence Rattigan (*The Deep Blue Sea*), John Osborne (*Look Back in Anger*) and Robert Bolt (*Flowering Cherry*); some towards comedy, like John van Druten (*I Am a Camera*), N. C. Hunter (*A Day by the Sea*), and William Inge (*Picnic*). Some achieve a good balance in a narrow field, like Granville-Barker (*The Madras House*), though he would not have known of Chekhov at the time, Carson McCullers (*The Member of the Wedding*), Paddy Chayefsky (*The Bachelor Party*) and Ray Lawler (*Summer of the Seventeenth Doll*). Some, like Tennessee Williams, introduce a raw and forcing symbolism through the naturalistic surface, which suppresses the Chekhovian warmth and gentleness. Shaw in *Heartbreak House* makes an excursion into the Chekhovian world and emerges with a Shavian fantasy in which Chekhov is unrecognizable. The list could be extended indefinitely. All aim at a realism of statement which makes some use of a colouring of naturalistic presentation and a fair splash of human psychology in order to hold our interest. All stand or fall with the authenticity of their characterization and the conviction of their feeling. None is really concerned with 'telling a story'; all wish to show us a 'state of affairs', paint a 'mood'. It is an indicative mood.

From two opposite poles the word 'mood' has gained currency as a critical term in modern drama. It is used by Christopher Fry of his own comedies, *The Lady's Not For Burning* and *Venus Observed*, his April and October plays, plays of free poeticism.[1] And it is used by John van Druten in discussing plays with an underlay of Chekhovian naturalism.[2] Perhaps van Druten borrows the concept from Princess Toumanova, who first identified *The Seagull* as a 'drama of mood'.[3]

For Fry, a 'comedy of mood' is a play in which 'the scene, the season, and the characters, are bound together in one climate'—in other words, there is a quality which is directing all three elements, which may be governing the whole play. Fry naturally uses his poetry to establish and maintain that mood throughout, and the playgoer has the strong sense that the play was conceived as a poem of quasi-lyrical feeling which is in fact developed and explored dramatically.

Van Druten wrote, 'If there is a new-born creature in the theatre of the past thirty years, I would say that it is the play of mood, the play whose main quality—far more important than its story or its plot—is the maintenance and communication of a certain mood, through which the entire action is presented'. It is likely to be a play of close, and occasionally witty, observation, which attempts by subtle overtones to evoke a specific atmosphere as precisely as possible. That atmosphere, rather than a sequence of events, provides the unity of the play. Usually the setting, the social environment, often the season, is strongly established in order to compel that atmosphere, as, the Bronx and other New York locales (*Marty*, *The Iceman Cometh*), the Deep South (especially favoured by Tennessee Williams in plays and films like *The Rose Tattoo*, *Baby Doll*, *A Streetcar Named Desire*), the English country house (N. C. Hunter's *Waters of the Moon*, *A Day by the Sea*), high summer (*Picnic*, *Summer of the Seventeenth Doll*), and so on. *Street Scene* was a play about the interaction of an apparently motley collection of families living in a New York tenement, enacted on the doorstep. Elmer

[1] C. Fry, in *Theatre Newsletter* (London, 11 March 1950).
[2] J. van Druten, *The Playwright at Work* (New York, 1953), pp. 36 ff.
[3] N. A. Toumanova, *Anton Chekhov* (London, 1937), p. 117.

Rice said of it, 'I conceived the home as the real protagonist of the drama, a brooding presence, which not only dominated the scene, but which gave a kind of dramatic unity to the sprawling and unrelated lives of the multitudinous characters and lent the whole whatever "meaning" it may have'.[1]

Van Druten and Fry can be brought together in this context because it seems clear that the play of mood is at its best a poetic structure, that at its best it is prompted and bound by an impulse from within, an attitude, a state of mind in the author which is in a sound tradition of drama. It follows that our critical approach to these plays must be to estimate the efficient value of that state of mind, and to judge where and when the dramatist has slipped into broad generalities of character or of sentiment which are untrue, when the confidence of the author in his own purpose has failed, where a public convention of feeling has settled on the play to blur its precision. We may recognize the superiority of Tennessee Williams's *The Glass Menagerie* over his *Summer and Smoke;* of the first version of Act III of his *Cat on a Hot Tin Roof* over the second; of *The Bachelor Party*, with the exception of the declaration of love at the tail, over *Marty*, also by Paddy Chayefsky, which glamorizes what it sets out to de-glamorize, the likelihood of a Marty ever finding his partner; of *The Member of the Wedding* over *A Day by the Sea;* of Terence Rattigan's *The Deep Blue Sea* over his *The Browning Version*.

It is not so much the form of these plays as the subjects that demand that form which tends to make them somewhat unpopular with the public. It is not a question whether these assertions of mood and atmosphere could not be 'better dealt with in the novel than in the theatre', which is quite an irrelevant hypothesis: the nature of our experience of the novel is of course different from that of a play in the theatre. Delicate subjects like those of the maladjusted, of the solitary

---

[1] Quoted from *Radio Times* (London, 13 November 1959).

The 'Mood' Play

adolescent, of sexual awakening, the frustration and loneliness of old age, the decadence of a way of life, the claustrophobia of a home or village, of the need for love or self-respect, all demand that a hot light shall be shone on the soul of the play-goer. To evoke a state of nerves on the stage, it is necessary to play upon the nerves of the spectator, and without an easy line of development to follow, without a comforting 'right' or 'wrong' to recognize, any subject tends to be unpleasant.

The scale of the play of mood is necessarily small, and its action cramped. Details must be uncommonly accentuated, like these of Archie Lee's room so carefully collected, each to underline one aspect of the husband's sterile life in *Baby Doll*: 'On the bed table behind him is a half-empty bottle of liquor, an old alarm clock, ticking away, a magazine called "Spicy Fiction", and a tube of ointment.' Environment and character in the drama of mood will be unmistakably intertwined.

This is true of those plays of Eugene O'Neill in which a romanticized naturalism is the dominant mode, plays in which the author uses a careful excess of 'local colour', insists upon almost a rhetoric of tough dialect, where he stresses his characters' psychopathology at the expense of their psychology. *The Iceman Cometh* is, for example, a play about a large and mixed bunch of men each hugging his personal illusion to his breast in appalling futility. O'Neill characteristically gives them a detailed and sordid setting in which to get drunk, sober up and get drunk again:

The back room and a section of the bar of Harry Hope's saloon.... In the left corner, built out into the room, is the toilet with a sign 'This is it' on the door. Against the middle of the left wall is a nickle-in-the-slot phonograph.... The walls and ceilings once were white, but it was a long time ago, and they are now so splotched, peeled, stained and dusty that their colour can best be described as dirty.

To steal Michel Saint-Denis's phrase from its context, this is indeed the mud of naturalism.

Naturalistic Shading

Not only has Chekhov's method of shading together effects of the pathetic and the comic by their ironic implications killed the instinct to write the formal comedy for which we remember the drama of Ben Jonson, Molière and the Restoration in England, but the new play of mood is notoriously difficult to write well. Failures and part-failures abound, on two counts: because the sensibility of the writer must to a high degree be tuned to the subtle discordances of everyday; and because the art of presenting them to an audience so that the fine balance is struck between laughter and tears, cannot be achieved by following a set of rules, but can be forged only from the materials of the specific subject chosen, and with a suggestion of the rhythms the subject imposes. The element of life the author has selected for treatment must determine the form the play will take. Chekhov is a hard master.

Television may contribute to the growth of this kind of writing, just as the film encouraged the growth of melodrama. The intimacy of the television medium, the unavoidable visual tightness of the scene and its detail which encourages the domestic subject, the dominance of the actor in close-up, the necessity for his sustained performance and the slow motion of television action and editing, with its general sense of actuality—all these elements will make for the dark and shaded grey comedy of small contemporary life. At its worst the medium could produce hour upon hour of thin kitchen-sink drama; at its best, an immediate and exciting reflection of ordinary life under the pressures of our society. Already American television has produced one fine writer in Paddy Chayefsky, whose plays *Marty* and *The Bachelor Party* are almost documentary with detail of American home life.

Chayefsky has been helpfully articulate about his intentions, and in his notes on *Marty* and *The Mother* he says, 'I tried to write the dialogue as if it had been wire-tapped, I tried to envisage the scenes as if a camera had been focused upon the

124

unsuspecting characters and had caught them in an untouched moment of life'.[1] The implied use of the hidden tape-recorder and the candid camera indicates precisely the new techniques of spontaneous naturalism. A sense of immediacy is to be one of the objects of the new television comedy, an extension of the dramatized documentary programme in which principles of strict 'impartiality' are to be pursued. These are the new techniques; what are the new directions? Assuming that actuality has been caught, the dramatizer is still faced with the need to make actuality *creative*.

Chayefsky suggests that a particular interest in psychological subjects is likely to follow. 'Television drama', he says in his notes to *The Big Deal*, 'cannot expand in breadth, so it must expand in depth. In the last year or so, television writers have learned that they can write intimate dramas—"intimate" meaning minutely detailed studies of small moments of life...the digging under the surface of life for the more profound truths of human relationships.'[2] The dramatic action will be vertical and not horizontal. Later, he goes on,

In television, you can dig into the most humble, ordinary relationships: the relationships of bourgeois children to their mother, or middle-class husband to wife, of white-collar father to his secretary—in short, the relationships of the people....We relate to each other in an incredibly complicated manner. Every fiber of relationship is worth a dramatic study. There is far more exciting drama in the reasons why a man gets married than in why he murders someone....[3]

The thought of a larger and larger number of psychoanalytical case-studies of no relevance to general life, or of no interest beyond the satisfaction of a morbid curiosity, is not encouraging. But one thing is certain. The excerpt from the tape-recording, the shots cut from the camera's film, the actual or assumed blur of fragmentary details, must still be

[1] P. Chayefsky, *Television Plays* (New York, 1955), p. 173.
[2] *Ibid.* p. 132.
[3] *Ibid.* p. 178.

selected and arranged for dramatic meaning. In this we shall doubtlessly defer to Chekhov once again.

However, it has been evident that Chekhov's own plays do not televise well, principally because his family groups are larger than the narrow lens of television can include. In *Uncle Vanya*, the camera eye, concerned to pick up individual reactions to the Professor's announcement that he intended to sell the estate, gave us nothing of what his speech meant to the group as a whole, nor of its dramatic shape, which could only be communicated by our seeing the emotional response of all the family.

A final judgment on plays of mood must turn on the use or abuse of their peculiar nervous vitality. Should the playwright impress his atmosphere upon the spectator by a steady intensification of feeling, to ensure that his audience is at one with the mood? Or dare he keep his audience sober enough to have the ability to assess the values of the world he is painting? Too many of these plays, in their anxiety to capture the sympathies of the spectator, stamp their way into melodrama and sensationalism or try to win us with sentiment (Terence Rattigan's *The Deep Blue Sea*, William Inge's *Come Back Little Sheba*, Tennessee Williams's *A Streetcar Named Desire*, Robert Bolt's *Flowering Cherry*). The best retain a splendid compassion by an equally strong evocation of detail and mood, while yet with delicate wit modifying our sympathies: certain moments in Ray Lawler's *Summer of the Seventeenth Doll*, Chayefsky's *The Bachelor Party* and Williams's *The Glass Menagerie* for this reason suggest at least that they are in the tradition of *The Cherry Orchard*.

Nevertheless, with the play of mood we are today merely drifting along one stream in the history of the twentieth-century theatre. Elsewhere the wit was soon to oust the compassion, and in the 'twenties we were jerked into the territory of Pirandello and Anouilh; in the 'fifties, of Beckett and Ionesco.

3

TOWARDS TRAGIC INVERSION

Yes, my dear fellow, you wear a cook's hat! And you beat eggs!
And do you think that, having these eggs to beat, you then have
nothing more on your hands? Oh, no, not a bit of it....You have
to represent the shell of the eggs that you're beating!

PIRANDELLO, *Six Characters in Search of an Author*

A NEW FREEDOM OF FORM

The twentieth-century theatre has offered the dramatist a
dizzy variety of forms and conventions within which to work,
with infinite opportunities to break the continuity of one mode
to startle us with another. The historian of modern drama will
remark on the one hand the movement towards overt theatrical symbolism at the end of the last century, with its concomitant
adventures into surrealism and the 'dream' play, into expressionism, 'epic' drama and verse fantasy; and on the other,
surviving elements of the high comedy of manners, melodrama
and grotesque farce. Woven through all these is an irrepressible interest in the naturalistic experiment, as we have seen.
Moreover, the playwright has had at his disposal all manner of
media through which to speak, from the expert sorcery of the
theatre of illusions, whether behind a proscenium arch or on
a cinema screen, to the theatre of free imagination, the bare
stage, the open stage, theatre-in-the-round or theatre on the
air. It is small wonder that today's serious audience at times
seems to be a tormented creature with masochistic tendencies.

Thus the dramatist has had an unprecedented freedom to
mix his effects and discover new responses in us. Where,
before, the laughter and the tears had been so shaded together that they were effectively indistinguishable, now they

have been thrust upon us in deliberately incongruous, jarring arrangements. If once we could be made to accept some realm of fantasy, then the dramatist could juxtapose his impressions in innumerable combinations and in innumerable varieties of proportion. He hoped that the general act of synthesizing which had taken place more on the stage might now take place inside the mind of the spectator. The success of the new comedy would rest upon our exceptional 'suspension of disbelief' if the fusion was to occur, just as in neo-impressionistic art the pointillist anticipated that small splashes of pure unmixed colour would blend behind the eye to create a consistent effect of extraordinary vividness and luminosity, if the spectator stood far enough away.

Outrageous effects were to free the imagination of an audience trained by tradition to judge plays by their likeness to life. A new stylization in drama was to permit the contrasts necessary to project those monstrous ironies of life which are the great subject and the world theme of the modern stage. An exaggerated chiaroscuro was the intention—but each writer had an immediate problem to select a form to match his own statement and to manhandle effectively a reluctant audience.

Shifts of style and tone could be gentle or violent. Thus Dylan Thomas, with a wicked ear, takes full advantage of the loose form of his radio play *Under Milk Wood* and embraces an astonishing range of tickles and shocks, from the purely theatrical trick to a subtle impregnation of the mind. With ease he can sway us to sleep with the musical sounds and rhythms of his narrator's voice crooning, 'The sunny slow lulling afternoon yawns and moons through the dozy town...', and then jerk us awake as the knife-edged voice of Mrs Pugh jerks her husband:

> MRS PUGH. Persons with manners,
> VOICE. snaps Mrs cold Pugh,
> MRS PUGH. do not nod at table.

Equally effectively he can paint a conventional backcloth of spring and then slyly pursue a development of feeling through a rapid series of differentiated attitudes. Spring in Llaregyb becomes vital to us as it is felt vividly in Evans the Death, Gossamer Beynon, Jack Black, Captain Cat and Mary Ann Sailors, each in his or her own way; it grows the more alive as impressions are gently played off one against another. Undertaker, school-mistress, cobbler and ship's captain in contrasting ways feel the dignity of winter slipping from them 'in the young sun', solemnly, childishly, puritanically, bawdily, until Mary Ann Sailors can declare with a natural reverence for life, 'It is Spring in Llaregyb in the sun in my old age, and this is the Chosen Land'.

Some variations of tone and complexion have their place in most drama. On the other hand, jumps in convention, leaps from one 'plane of reality' to another, are readily accomplished where an author has boldly adopted an artificial convention for playing. His motive for doing this may be as different as Eliot's in *Murder in the Cathedral* and Brecht's in *The Caucasian Chalk Circle*.

In the former, the reasons have often been discussed for the surprise of switching from the stylized heightening in verse and gesture of the murder of Thomas, stressed by the near-hysterical, terror-stricken language of the Women of Canterbury, to the colloquial clichés of the Knights as they turn on the audience in direct address. Breaking the convention of playing and of language serves a number of purposes, but above them all is the extraordinary spur felt among the audience. We are made abruptly aware how contemporary and relevant in an age of political murders is this apparently remote martyrdom.

No different in kind, perhaps, is Brecht's method of telling his tale, only with Brecht the little thumps and raps persist through the play until we take a general concussion, and feel only that chill in the air that we associate with his 'realism'. Thus, in *The Caucasian Chalk Circle*, after Grusche has melodramatically moved us in her heroic, if fairy-tale, crossing of the rotten bridge in the storm with the child, and after the Story Teller has soothed us with the bland and measured, if somewhat cynical, lines,

> 'When I enter my brother's house', she thought,
> 'He will rise and embrace me.'
> 'Is that you, sister?' he will say,
> 'I have been expecting you so long.
> This is my dear wife...',[1]

we are suddenly and ironically introduced to 'a fat peasant couple', the characters of farce. The sister is a garrulous hypocrite and the brother a weak, self-centred hypochondriac, and they offer her neither rest nor food, though she is barely able to stand. A few minutes later, after Grusche has decided to give the child a name and a roof, sacrificing herself in becoming a wife (albeit to a man nearly dead), her pathos is sharply eclipsed by uproarious farce once more. The guests hope to celebrate simultaneously both a wedding and a funeral. A tipsy monk must conduct the twin services. The dying man abruptly recovers when he hears it said that the war is over. This odd structure of mixed slapstick and melodrama is cumulative in its effect. It allegedly stimulates us to a state of unsentimental alertness while proposing a naïve and simple Sunday-school sermon. How far Brecht's much discussed effect of 'alienation' results in superficial sensation, how far it *does* leave us unemotionally free to think our way through his play, and how far it falls within a strong tradition of the comic-pathetic, must be scrutinized.

Very different in intention is the drama of Anouilh, who mixes the tragedy of *La Sauvage* Thérèse with the buffoonery of old Tarde her father, the tragedy of Orpheus and Eurydice

---

[1] Trans. E. R. and M. Bentley (London, 1956).

with the farce of their Father and Mother, the tragedy of Ardèle and her hunchback lover with the mannered comedy of the Count and the Countess, the tragedy of the marriage of Julien and his Colombe with the cartoon characters who surround them, the tragedy of Général St Pé with the vaude-ville of Emily his wife and Ghislaine his one-time mistress. It is different because in these instances a volatile element of tragedy is distilled from a comic situation. The author prac-tises a cruel deceit, and condemns us for our laughter after we have laughed to order: he is using the freedom of convention that comedy grants him. Francis Fergusson has recently diagnosed a comic success and a comic failure: 'when Scara-mouche gets a beating, we do not feel the blows, but the idea of beating, at that moment, strikes us as funny. If the beating is too realistic, if it breaks the light rhythms of thought, the fun is gone, and the comedy destroyed.'[1] Anouilh beats his 'Scaramouche' realistically hard, wrenches and rends the light rhythms of thought—and yet brings off a success. Comedy is certainly destroyed—if we must call it comedy— and the dramatic impact of the fission is tremendous. It may be beyond articulate analysis to say how this happens; only an examination of the intangible impressions an audience re-ceives in performance could do it, and this is attempted below.

What happens when the writer takes an element of the ridiculous and thrusts it into tragedy? When the tragic heroine bursts her stays, when the tragic hero trips over the carpet? A laugh will kill a tear, we may say, but does it then remain a laugh? If hot steel is plunged into cold water, there is a tempering; if yellow is poured over blue, there is a new colour, the brighter for the brightness of the originals.

In dark comedy there are moments when, in counterpoint-ing his effects, the author takes his play to the very edge of disintegration. So in our minds the image grows perilously

[1] F. Fergusson, *The Idea of a Theater* (New York, 1954), p. 191.

brittle, and we the audience are on the point of making a destructive analysis. But a synthesis and reconciliation of the parts will follow if their dramatic chemistry has been perfectly calculated.

Counterpointing the pathetic and the comic within the same experience by demonstrating their object from more than one angle must have the effect of sharpening the awareness of the onlooker. Shaw had us mock his Eliza Doolittle by the high comic trickery of the tea-party scene; he reduced her natural dignity to the level of a shabby music-hall turn, in order that the shock of the fourth act, where the insensitive soul of Professor Higgins is revealed by his treating her as if she were still at the tea-party, should be felt by us as a personal recrimination. Nearly fifty years later, with the experience of Anouilh's black comedy, of Brecht's violent juxtapositions of styles and effects, and of Beckett's grim–gay nihilism behind him, John Osborne leaps wider and crazier gaps to have us denounce ourselves. The music–hall turn presented by Archie Rice in *The Entertainer* flashes upon us intermittently with the false abandon of coarse songs like 'Why should I care?', 'We're all out for the good old number one' and 'Thank God we're normal', and then the author drops us callously back to the sordid subnormality of domestic life or else to the whimsical nostalgia for the Edwardian days of Billy Rice: 'They were graceful, they had mystery and dignity. Why when a woman got out of a cab, she descended. Descended....'

The swinging of the pendulum within our minds, the dialectic of laughter and tears with its energizing effect on the spectator, is to be observed through much of the drama of our time. In the sections that follow, a sample has been selected of those playwrights whose influence has been or is likely to be strongest, and whose forms and modifications of dark comedy are most striking, namely, Strindberg in his expressionistic manner, the Irishmen Shaw, Synge and O'Casey, pre-eminently Pirandello, and then Eliot, Brecht, Anouilh and Tennessee Williams, with Beckett and Ionesco from the Parisian theatre of the 'fifties.

STRINDBERG'S DREAM PLAYS

Strindberg was very quick to break the rules of naturalism, as we saw briefly in *There Are Crimes and Crimes*. His increasing need to strip the soul naked, uncover its illusions and at the same time make his meaning as transparent as possible led him more and more to adopt the methods of symbolism and expressionism. Neither of these terms is really adequate to describe the processes of stage representation that are found in the apparently slack structures of *To Damascus*, *The Dream Play* and *The Ghost Sonata*. In each the symbols are virtually so private and the order of the action so subjectively ordained that commentators may be forgiven for passing over them quickly and missing in them the sardonic logic of feeling which binds them.

As Strindberg declared in his programme note to *The Dream Play*, 'anything may happen; everything is possible and probable. Time and space do not exist. On an insignificant background of reality, imagination designs and embroiders novel patterns, free fancies, absurdities and improvisations.'[1] But the fragmentation of character and all the other eccentricities of his method should take our attention less than the ends in view. Strindberg hastens to add that the dreamer of the dream remains the 'one consciousness' for whom the kaleidoscopic impressions make sense, and we should fasten on this. For the one consciousness must not be the author's alone: it must be no less than the spectator's in the theatre.

Yet none of these plays obeys the rules of comedy or of

---

[1] Quoted from A. Nicoll, *World Drama* (London, 1949), p. 562.

tragedy: they make their own laws, directed and unified, if at all, by a total feeling to be traced through the details of the action. Any complexity that follows is to be seen as the intrinsic complexity of personality, of life and reality, not merely the complexity of a wild dream or a nightmare. The inarticulateness of an individual mood and attitude must be made articulate, and the darker mysteries of human personality illuminated.

In his religious morality play *To Damascus*, comic methods of intensification and exaggeration of character are replaced by those of character distortion. These distortions are chiefly of facets of the 'Stranger's' own personality as he wanders through the play in search of himself. For this reason, standards of judgment familiarly applied to either farcical or naturalistic characterization are useless for the estimation of the audience's response. The numerous ghosts whom the Stranger encounters in his travels are all fragmented aspects of his own soul, and thus suffer from being almost depersonalized. While they indeed assume nightmarish qualities in this way, they yet remain cold and rather unmanageable phantoms.

Equally embarrassing is the shaping of the action in the long series of rich expressionistic scenes. Strong, bold and simple in their manner of presenting several stages in the condition of the mind on its road to redemption, nevertheless they risk losing much of the usual willing compliance of the spectator with the action, because he is largely asked to inspect it without the usual guides to feeling. He is granted little with which to identify the experiences on the stage as normal experience, and Strindberg makes little effort to draw the spectator into the play. These of course are faults endemic in any expressionistic drama.

Symbolism of character and situation such as is used in *To Damascus* is there to make articulate what is thought and felt; it can add a depth and complexity to a thought and feeling which might otherwise reveal itself rather nakedly in a new framework, but only if the symbolism is linked with traditional concepts common to the playgoer; it can be intensely illuminating if a narrow and seemingly personal sensation can in this way be connected with universal human experience. Thus the dramatist who uses symbolism takes upon himself an added responsibility: if the symbols are not sufficient in their own right, he owes it to his audience to teach it, within the context of the play, how to understand them. The play must build its meaning, else it sinks into private language. Strindberg scarcely establishes his symbols in this play, but continues relentlessly to take us through territory well-known to himself, but for us uncharted. Precision of communication at times is therefore very much at a premium, while at others we move in vaguely recognizable regions on the fringe of our consciousness. When this happens, the effect is overwhelming.

One short episode must suffice to suggest the play's style, and also bring into focus the uneasy ironies to which the enforced link between present reality and the chimerical shapes of the past give rise.

The first banquet scene of Part II of the play (Act III, scene i) enacts the slow destruction of a particular self-delusion, but here in the fantasy of the theatre and the telescoped sensation of nightmare it is accelerated to a pace where horror turns to hysteria, and the pattern of disillusionment is seen in crude outline by an effect of glaring myopia. The Stranger, an Everyman, finds himself at a sumptuous repast. Tables are set with golden goblets, and weighed down by dishes of peacocks, pheasants in full plumage, boar's heads, entire lobsters, oysters, salmon, bundles of asparagus, melons and grapes. By degrees this luxury is to vanish. There are four tables set, and the Stranger sits resplendent at the highest among frock-coated civic dignitaries; but he sits where he cannot see a crowd of beggars sitting at the fourth table. Among them are people from his former life, at once his victims and aspects of his own identity. To the solemn accompaniment of chords from Mendelssohn's 'Dead March', a Professor acclaims the Stranger as 'the greatest man of a great century',[1] places a laurel crown upon his head and hangs a shining order round his neck. For the Stranger has seemingly manufactured gold, symbol of the material achievement and earthly success which he desired in order to restore his self-confidence and kill his doubts.

Against the fine rhetoric of the Professor's speech and the Stranger's reply, the mutterings of subversion and disruption are already to be heard from the beggars' table. The banquet is slyly removed, the rich tables become trestles with bare boards, and the beggars take the places of the frock-coated gentlemen. As the Stranger's soul is stripped, poverty, ugliness and bareness surround him. Gradually his creative achievement is belittled, questioned and finally destroyed by the figures from his past: 'Is it true he's made gold?' 'So it's said. But it's certain he left his wife while she was in childbed.'...'I don't know whether he's succeeded in making gold. I don't worry about that, and I hardly believe it.'...'Did you ever hear anything so impudent? That we should honour a mystery man, an arch-swindler, a charlatan, in good faith.' Further, the Stranger is told that the civic reception was a mockery, in fact organized by the Drunkards' Society. A slut accuses him of having indirectly corrupted her mind as a young girl. The bill for the whole banquet is thrust upon him. And upon his being unable to pay, he is dragged off to prison as a thief and an impostor amid the hurrahs of the beggars.

The complete transformation takes place in less than ten minutes, a transformation of social status, of self-confidence, of health of mind. As all the external signs of riches are turned to those of poverty, a poverty of spirit strikes the agonized

---

[1] *The Road to Damascus*, trans. G. Rawson (London, 1939).

consciousness of the hero while he protests with the pathetic dignity of a tramp. With the half-amused shudder of one just woken from a bad dream to the safety of cool daylight, we observe all this from without. We sit omniscient with the gods and see and coldly criticize the mortal pretensions and sufferings of our representative. The speed of the change and the startling deflation of the man in his blank dismay borders on the ludicrous. Yet we cannot laugh. 'To think I've been so duped', he utters in black despair. Scene after scene of this tormented play presents a view of human experience refracted and contorted because it lies just below the uneasy surface of consciousness. Popular audiences will never thank Strindberg or his successors for trouncing them with a fierce and often private surrealism.

An interest today in the dream plays, and especially in *The Ghost Sonata*, could be justified by the successful virtuosity of Samuel Beckett's fantasies of the 'fifties. *The Ghost Sonata* of 1907 curiously anticipates elements in *Endgame* of 1957. Both have the disconnected form of dream in which 'everything is possible and probable' and in which 'time and space do not exist'. Both draw characters which are intended to be facets of a single consciousness, suited to an 'intimate' theatre. Both deal in deliberately half-explained symbolism. Both appear bizarre before their real horror is assimilated. They echo elements found in Maeterlinck's *The Interior* and *The Intruder*, in which the momentous terror of destiny and of Swedenborg's unseen universe surrounds those who live either in innocence or ignorance. They reproduce the stripping action with which Pirandello habitually attacks his characters. Their drama is of waiting and of self-discovery, a drama of silences and immobility without quiet or repose.

The action of *The Ghost Sonata* is bound together by the one view of the young Student, an idealist who has selflessly saved human life and who has bright visions of the future. It is his misfortune to meet old Jacob Hummel, a man whose inherent evil is not apparent at first, though hints of his power to poison the lives of others are dropped early in the play:

STUDENT. Do you speculate in houses? [*sc.* homes]
HUMMEL. Mmm-yah! But not in the way you mean.[1]

A little later the Student speaks to Hummel's servants:

STUDENT. Is this man to be trusted?
JOHANSSON. You may trust him—to do anything!
STUDENT. What is he doing around the corner now?
JOHANSSON. Watching the poor...dropping a word here and a word there...loosening a stone at a time...until the whole house comes tumbling down, metaphorically speaking.

In the first scene Hummel squats in his wheelchair before the façade of a two-storey house; in the second, the scene of the 'ghost supper', the façade is literally and figuratively removed, and the reality of his power to corrupt is revealed.

It is a house of pollution and degeneration: 'a house gets mouldy when it gets old, and when people are too much together, tormenting each other all the time, they lose their reason.' The house symbolizes life itself, in all its monotony and recrimination and pathos. Its ghosts, day in and day out, say nothing to each other for fear of facing the truth, but each is tied to the other by his sins against the other's humanity:

(*The company is seated in a circle, no one saying a word for a while.*)
COLONEL. Shall we order the tea now?
HUMMEL. What's the use? No one cares for tea, and I can't see the need for pretending.
(*Pause.*)
COLONEL. Shall we make conversation?
HUMMEL (*speaking slowly and with frequent pauses*). Talk of the weather, which we know all about? Ask one another's state of health, which we know just as well? I prefer silence. Then thoughts become audible, and we can see the past. Silence can hide nothing—but words can....
(*Long pause during which everybody is subject to silent scrutiny by all the rest.*)

[1] Trans. E. Björkman in August Strindberg, *Eight Famous Plays* (London, 1949).

Hummel, who is so willing 'to tear up the weeds' and unmask the horrors of their sins, is then terrifyingly unmasked himself: the insane wife of the Colonel reduces his speech to that of a grotesque parrot, in the way she herself had spoken before, and the 'death screen' is placed in front of the closet into which Hummel has been ordered. Even the voice of the vampire who 'sucked the house of all nourishment' must become outlandishly lifeless; the vampire must suffer annihilation himself.

For the very reason that *The Ghost Sonata* is a play of indirect communication, to say the least, it can infect us and leave us aghast with the fear of the half-apprehended. The eternal oppositions of illusion and reality, innocence and experience, youth and age, are seen in the shuddering light of monstrous delirium. The final words of the Student to the Young Lady, illegitimate daughter of Hummel and the Colonel's wife, and a girl who is dying from exposure to the truth, are partly addressed to the troubled spectator: 'You poor little child—you child of a world of illusion, guilt, suffering, and death—a world of eternal change, disappointment, and pain—may the Lord of Heaven deal mercifully with you on your journey!' These are sentiments that echo through the serious drama of the years that follow this strangely premonitory play.

THE SHAVIAN TOUCH

The Shavian touch can at times leave a distinctly dark stain. It was Shaw's avowed intention to disturb us. In his preface to *Man and Superman* he declared, 'It annoys me to see people comfortable when they ought to be uncomfortable; and I insist on making them think in order to bring them to conviction of sin'. This very proper attitude to his complacent *fin de siècle* audiences led him into extravagances of theatre which justify his place in the pattern we are tracing. Desmond MacCarthy observed in Shaw what he called his 'high-spirited agility in modulating out of serious and even poetic comedy into intellectual farce'.[1] If we look into Shaw again we will find him modulating freely from intellectual farce into serious comedy too. Shaw behaves instinctively, guided by what adjustment of mood he feels his play demands, aiming at a dominant tone of audience recrimination. He will allow us no romance and no tragedy: the 'alienation' of the stage from the auditorium by some surprise in the tone of the play is his favourite device for controlling the processes of our thoughts and responses. The resulting image we conceive of the plays has generally been called 'satirical', a loose term revealing a need for closer and theatrical analysis.

The Shavian play is still an unexplored field, and this is not the place to explore it. But certain issues have to be recognized. Shaw the politician and Shaw the philosopher, now mostly dead, have bothered us for too long. Shaw the dramatist has hardly been noticed: we persist in looking for the ideas-monger and do not see the artist. Yet the plays remain very much alive because they display the sure touch of the theatre-wise dramatist. Eric Bentley a few years ago called the Shavian play 'dialectical', a play not *of* argument, but *about* argument, a particular and individual approach possible to any theme under the sun, an approach which has rightly become associated with Shaw's name. All good plays are 'plays of ideas', but few are dialectical in structure. In the nature of drama, all good plays are 'problem plays' too, but some are plays insisting upon a thesis, putting an ultimately comforting case like Wilde in his 'serious' moments, or like Galsworthy most of the time. Whereas Shaw does not recognize an easy distinction between good and bad, with Wilde and Galsworthy and their kind we can sit back and relax,

[1] D. MacCarthy, *Shaw* (London, 1951), p. 150; reprint of a review written in 1943.

knowing that the play will satisfy our consciences. With Shaw, the audience may have no rest. Critics tend to look in the wrong direction, towards the characters who remain for them 'ventriloquist's dolls' and towards the plots which are merely the 'manipulation' of ideas. They would do better to look out into the house, at the unique activity in the auditorium during performance. For something new happens in the Shavian theatre, and the play will seem to have stopped on the stage when it is most alive in the audience, static in its physical action while intensely disturbing in the mind.

We forget that the comic artist must in the first instance understand his audience, how its mind works, how to flog it on when it is lazy. 'Nobody will trouble themselves about anything that does not trouble them', reiterated Shaw, and the indispensable basis of his comedy is a knowledge of the attitudes and prejudices, the beliefs and illusions of the average spectator. However, the average spectator will shut his ears if he suffers a frontal assault, and methods must be devised to woo him to laugh at himself and think again, and yet applaud the author who makes him do it.

Shaw's effort to keep his audience alert and its mind itching determines again and again the particular inflection of a line of his dialogue, the shaping of a scene and the form of a whole play. Each is constructed in its particular way as an indirect guide to us. Thus Robert de Baudricourt in the first scene of *Saint Joan* sits 'magisterially' in his place, scowling hard while he waits for Joan to enter: Shaw has built him up punctiliously by setting him baldly against the 'trodden worm' of his Steward. Joan breezes in, bobs a curtsy and all in a rush says, 'Good morning, captain squire. Captain: you are to give me a horse and armour and some soldiers, and send me to the Dauphin. Those are your orders from my Lord'. If Robert is taken aback, so are we. The whole of the scene is a steady deflation of poor Robert, its purpose to give us the first of many insights into the kind of power Joan exercises over her contemporaries, and to prepare us to see her face bigger game. The scene is also to set an initial tone for the play as a whole, a tone which is to be subtly turned against us. It is also to give us to believe we are dealing with a real girl, naturally flushed with the excitement of quick success, the better to have us accept the heroic and symbolic Joan who is to resist the religious and social order of the times.

This is not a medieval play, but a play with a strictly modern reference, one which is not fully explicit until the much-criticized Epilogue arrives. 'We are lifted on waves of emotion', said MacCarthy, 'and dashed on thought', much as in the earlier *Major Barbara*. We are deceived into the pleasure of suffering 'tragic' feelings, only in order to be shown our self-indulgence by the sudden return to farcical fantasy. After our sympathetic identification with Joan in her trial, abruptly we are given Charles, the most obviously comic character in the play. He is sitting up in bed in his nightcap, leaping in fear, hiding under the bedclothes, a pure figure of fun; yet it is he who becomes our new and mocking representative. With cool comic calculation all the attitudes of the players assembled in Charles's bedroom are seen again in the light of our passionate feelings about the burning. The play risks cracking its back-bone, but the best art takes such risks.

Pygmalion, to select another well-known play from the canon, is a fine example of a switching of styles in a reverse order from that of *Saint Joan*. The exquisite tea-party is generally felt to be the crux of the play—it is certainly the crux of the laughter. We cannot fail to notice in retrospect that our laughter is here directed equally against the astonish-ment of the Eynsford Hills as against the simplicity and in-congruity of Eliza in her new social role. To laugh at the earnestness of her account of 'the shallow depression in the west of these islands', at the incongruity of the story of her aunt who was 'done in' for the sake of her new straw hat, is irresistible. But we have been trapped. We have quite forgotten the now lifeless humanity of the Covent Garden Eliza of Act I, and we are liable to forget what Mrs Pearce in Act II had advised: 'She should think of the future'; and what Mrs Higgins in Act III calls 'the problem of what is to be done with her afterwards'; and the dilemma Eliza in Act IV finally recognizes when she cries, 'What am I fit for?' The live woman has been turned into Pygmalion's cold, dead marble: transplanting this natural flower into strange soil has withered it with the dry laughter of farce.

Act IV is to show us the results of Higgins's thoughtlessness and our blindness. In fully theatrical terms we see Eliza revived. This is no paradox, no trick of illusion, but a simple expedient to revive the audience too. Eliza returns from the ball a successful duchess, but in an agony of mind. As she sits apart from Higgins and Colonel Pickering in silence, she listens to the selfish insults of their yawns: 'Thank God it's over.'...'The whole thing has been a bore.'...'No more artificial duchesses. The whole thing has been simple purgatory.' When Higgins at last leaves her to go to bed, the storm in Eliza's brain breaks, and when he is heard looking for his slippers outside the door, she throws them at him viciously and with intent to kill. Then watch: the tempo of the scene changes, comedy is submerged, and the true climax approaches. We stand accused of ignorant romancing, and, to crown our guilt, Eliza marries Freddie the fool in outright preference to Higgins himself.

Shaw takes an Irish delight in refusing us comfort. Eliza ought to be thrilled at the new opportunities open to her, but she is not. Caesar will have none of Cleopatra, because he is 'too busy'. Louis Dubedat dies to the comic chorus of the doctors, and Mrs Dubedat's grief is marked by the persistent Newspaper Man who wants 'a few words on How It Feels to

be a Widow'. Candida chooses to mother her apparently solid
clergyman husband rather than the sickly poet Marchbanks.
Dick Dudgeon emerges as a natural hero, but will not love the
pretty heroine Judith Anderson. Delicious heroines in their
masses of Edwardian frills and flounces talk hard about hard
cash and have hard heads screwed firmly on. Ann Whitfield in
her mourning costume of black and violet silk, and softly
framed within her feather boa, has all the hidden strength of
tempered steel; the brash idealist Jack Tanner crumples
before her. Violet, the married version of Ann in the same
play, openly defies the rules of propriety from her position of
marital infallibility.

Such characters are unashamed puppets speaking the restricted language of artificial comedy. Shaw's scenes are built
up as contrasts and contests of attitudes to life in which
neither side is necessarily in the right: Ann and Tanner,
Undershaft and Barbara, Joan and Bishop Cauchon. The list
is almost inexhaustible, for frequently the duellists are re-
deployed within the same scene, as in the first act of *Man and
Superman* Ramsden is matched with Tavy, Tavy with Jack,
Jack with Ramsden. Somewhere in the struggle we shall find
our own fine champion and our own precious notions taking a
beating.

That ragbag of a play which so many admire as Shaw's
most timeless work, *Heartbreak House*, suggests his powers of
audience control as well as any. It is written to show us a
portrait of society, sweet like 'rotten fruit', and drifting towards a rugged catastrophe. We are to see it through the eyes
of an innocent, Ellie Dunn. But our view is not allowed to be a
simple one. Heartbreak House is for Ellie and for us 'this silly
house, this strangely happy house, this agonizing house'. The
mixture of her nostalgia and her hope is universal. The disorder of the drunken ship offers a disastrous gaiety.

Ellie is given an eccentric education in the play. She is

brought from ignorance to apparent wisdom, and then retreats to irresponsibility. She is told the truth about her romantic Hector; so she turns to the practical man Mangan until she is told the truth about him too. She learns finally that Captain Shotover, on whom she rested her faith, is a rum-soaked dreamer, no different from herself, only happy when 'stripped of everything, even of hope'. The last scene is a shock-treatment of crazy behaviour and painful humour. The family sits in the blazing lights of the house in an air-raid. 'A dull distant explosion is heard': Hector dashes to turn on more lights and tear down all the curtains at the windows, crying, 'It shall be seen for a hundred miles'. 'Another and louder explosion is heard': Hesione Hushabye and Ellie 'throw themselves into one another's arms in wild excitement'.

MRS HUSHABYE. Did you hear the explosions? And the sound in the sky: it's splendid: it's like an orchestra: it's like Beethoven.
ELLIE. By thunder, Hesione: it is Beethoven.

Lady Utterword refuses to go down to the cellars, but tells Randall to play 'Keep the home fires burning' on his flute, and we note the ironies in the choice of melody, and indeed in the choice of instrument. 'A terrific explosion shakes the earth. They reel back into their seats, or clutch the nearest support. They hear the falling of the shattered glass from the windows.' Then slowly the danger passes. Shotover calls, 'Turn in, all hands. The ship is safe', and promptly falls asleep. Ellie cries out in disappointment, 'Safe!' But the war is not yet over:

MRS HUSHABYE. But what a glorious experience! I hope they'll come again tomorrow night.
ELLIE (*radiant at the prospect*). Oh, I hope so.

A few years ago, John Fernald said of his production of the play,

In *Heartbreak House* Shaw has done something...which the limitations of 'real' characters would have prevented him from doing. He has made a synthesis of human attributes and has examined them in conflict with the whole gamut of problems which face civilization. Hector, Hesione, Shotover and the rest, each present a particular aspect of humanity: regarded separately they are not 'human beings', but looked at together they express the complete comical-tragical paradox of Man, the animal who can think but who has yet solved few of the problems that really matter.

The symbolism of this muddled group of lovable people is not far to seek. Shotover is a poet of wisdom, and at the same time a clown and a fraud. Ellie is a wide-eyed Desdemona who discovers that 'there seems to be nothing real in the world except my father and Shakespeare'. All of them are summed up by Hector as 'heartbroken imbeciles'. The modulations of tone within characters are echoed by the farcical modulations of the style, concluded by this leap into the perverse and lunatic scene which ends the play. This was a deliberate distortion to point his moral: 'Heartbreak House, in short,' we read in the preface, 'did not know how to live, at which point all that was left to it was the boast that at least it knew how to die: a melancholy accomplishment which the outbreak of war presently gave it practically unlimited opportunities of displaying.' In this play Shaw offers us a new dialectic, a dialectic of feeling, and it places him squarely in the twentieth century.

SYNGE AND O'CASEY

Within a tradition more or less their own, the Irishmen J. M. Synge and Sean O'Casey were among those who were quick to strike the fantastic note and through our willing imagination try to undermine our self-satisfaction. The riots over Synge's plays are readily explained by the political and religious feelings running strongly in a country enamoured of nationalism; but we should not forget that his kind of comedy was written with the same intention of disturbing his audiences as was Shaw's in a different social context. The shock of Synge's first play *In the Shadow of the Glen* lies in the curious mixture of cynical kitchen comedy and seductive lyrical feeling, and the author is being logically merciless to us when he rejects the anticipated punishment of Dan's erring wife for an imaginatively just ending. Nora, the wife who lives on another level of feeling, shall escape from her spiritually dead husband.

Synge brought with him from Paris a sophisticated approach to life and a comic and ironic eye which mingled oddly with the peasant Ireland he wished to rediscover. It is his French wit which introduces into his plays what Yeats called 'a new kind of sarcasm' and which did so much to invigorate the Irish Dramatic Movement after Yeats's own romantic start. Nora of *In the Shadow of the Glen* shares the romantic and the materialistic qualities of us all, and her cynical story hangs between tragedy and farce, like the styles within the play. Synge was refusing to be a propagandist for the Movement: 'the drama, like the symphony', he says in his preface to *The Tinker's Wedding*, 'does not teach or prove anything'. But there was more to it than this.

His idiom in *The Well of the Saints* beautifully splices with wit the pathetic story of the old blind beggar and his old blind wife. In blindness they think each other lovely; granted their sight, they see only ugliness and part in anger. In Act III their blindness has returned, and they can begin again to be happy in each other's company: 'Well', says Martin, 'we're a great pair, surely.' Yet when the 'Saint' who cured their eyes before is heard approaching, Mary cries, 'The Lord protect us from the Saints of God!' When the Saint raises his can of holy water, Martin sends it rocketing across the stage with our full consent. Though their vindictive neighbours lack understanding, we acknowledge that human illusion is a sacred treasure which Martin and Mary will not easily part with. Synge has his own way of reading his lesson.

The superbly simple piece which marks the maturity of

Synge's gaunt mood is, of course, *The Playboy of the Western World*. From the beginning we are carefully put in two minds about the blasphemy of its subject: that Synge should make his parricide such a figure of admiration to his audience in the shebeen, and hence such a charmer to his audience in the theatre, was a naughty sarcasm indeed. As Yeats said, the outcry against the play was an outcry against its way of seeing. The last sequence in the play was more than a way of seeing, it was a spit in the eye, or, to be more precise, three or four of them.

When Mahon, Christy's father, arrives very much alive to drag his son back home, Christy turns on him with real viciousness, another loy in hand. He has so enjoyed the praises of the girls that he will earn them again, and in earnest this time. We observe that the first response of the crowd is now 'half-frightened, half-amused'. Then, convinced that the actuality of parricide is less admirable in hard practice, and led by his beloved Pegeen, they rope him fast: 'there's a great gap between a gallous story and a dirty deed.' Synge brings sharply home to us the ugly reality of the situation by having Pegeen herself burn Christy's leg with a lighted sod. Yet we are shocked in another way when the father returns once more, proud to claim a son who has such gristle in him. And Pegeen's own famous last words, cried out alone under her shawl and in the despair of one seeing her illusions shattered, echo back over the comedy of the play, a lament for a girl's lost love and a lament for the lost vision of a whole community. We may admit that Pegeen, and all she stands for, deserves to lose Christy, and all he stands for, and yet dare we place blame when we know the human mind to be so fallible? In this masterpiece, the pattern of ironic feeling at least is unequivocal.

That Synge's drama reflects the spirit of the age in some degree is suggested by the way in which Sean O'Casey takes up the challenge where he left off. Whatever we may think of

Synge and O'Casey

O'Casey's uneven work, with its frequent lapses into blatant unsubtlety of tone and its ungoverned spells of affected rhetoric, with its final reliance on the melodramatic situation to justify itself to us, his plays continually fascinate as experiments. As we might expect of any good, developing dramatist, each new play he wrote was an experiment, not by any winning achievement in the expressionism he attempted, but in exploring his peculiar territories of feeling. The special irony found in *Juno and the Paycock* and *The Plough and the Stars* must seem to us now entirely appropriate to the unrest of his time and place, and indeed as relatively simple in conception. It provides an extension of the Chekhovian shading in his use of the everyday scene, and echoes Synge's alternating farce and poetry; but he adds a fair larding of melodrama of his own.

The violent contradictions of the pathetic and the comic in *Juno and the Paycock* are not preposterous, but they are too flagrantly juxtaposed at the level of naturalism their author has chosen, and the mechanism creaks. The resulting effect is sometimes merely hysterical. In its violent context of civil war the comedy of Fluther, Peter and the Covey in *The Plough and the Stars* mingles more naturally with the near-tragic feelings of Nora and Jack Clitheroe, Mrs Gogan's daughter and Bessie. Its setting and mood encourage us to accept a caricatured and categorical ordering of life's incongruities. The play's overcharged sentiment and its sensationalism are saved only by the injection of laughter. The interwoven tragicomedy he arrived at in this play guided O'Casey towards the arresting form he devised for *The Silver Tassie*.

The daring in the structure of this play is unmistakable. But our interest in it today does not rest on its method of sliding between the naturalistic and expressionistic manners from Act I to Act II, and then doggedly back to naturalism for the last two acts. Nor does it rest on its curious attempt to show the particular ugliness of war in the general and imper-

sonal terms of an unidentified bunch of common soldiers. It
chiefly impresses in its attempt to enlarge the audience's
vision by effects of calculated irony. These grow as the play
proceeds: the expressionism gives them an anti-naturalistic
licence for grotesquerie.

The battlefield scene of Act II introduces the first bold
stroke which marks O'Casey as a writer of real originality.
Into the ugly picture of 'jagged and lacerated ruin', with its
heaps of rubbish and spiky stumps of trees and its barbed
wire, dominated by the sinister outline of a squat howitzer
in giant form, into the exhausted and bitter soldiery who
themselves serve to decorate this setting, he pitches two figures
of pure caricature. One is the Visitor, 'a portly man with a
rubicund face', 'dressed in semi-civilian, semi-military
manner', who can utter only Blimpish clichés of the parade-
ground fighting spirit: 'Penetrate a little deeper into danger.
Foolish, yes, but then it's an experience; by God, it's an
experience. The military authorities are damned strict—
won't let a...man...plunge!' The other is a Staff Officer,
'prim, pert, and polished', who moves with a clownish springing hop. He enters only to wake the sleeping men and to order
them to attend a lecture on the 'Habits of those living between
Frigid Zone and Arctic Circle'.

The audacity smacks of the sensational and its effect is
somewhat unsure. But the introduction of raw farce into a
scene of desolation and human misery is an expedient designed
to unsettle an audience with a vengeance. It may well induce
that cynicism of mind which is to be a prelude to a series of
'false notes' and a preparation for the dramatic argument to
follow.

As the stretcher-bearers carry off the wounded, the
'Corporal' hands the '3rd Soldier' a parcel from home. It is
a prayer-book. The '2nd Soldier' meanwhile is also opening
a parcel from home. It is a red and yellow coloured rubber

ball with a note attached: 'To play your way to the enemies' trenches when you all go over the top. Mollie.' By juxta-posing these two gifts and showing them in this setting, the author reduces them both to a level of callous stupidity and suggests a gruesome irony. The scene closes with the soldiers singing a litany to their gun, with the Corporal as priest—an effect repulsive in the extreme.

Act III is set in a hospital. The stylization of Act II does not in this act wholly slip back to the naturalism of Act I, but remains half in evidence. The clowns of Act I, Simon and Sylvester, semi-choric at first, are easily identified again. The shadowy figures of the exhausted soldiers become human, though they remain the 'numbers' of a military hospital ward. The nurse is not the Susie we knew, but a cold, mechanical creature, like the Surgeon in charge. This is a most remarkable device within the play to make us recognize the particular individual in the general symbol. Further, this act is success-ful for having boldly juxtaposed the farcical discussions of Simon and Sylvester on having a bath or an operation, with the sobering entrance of once athletic, now legless Harry in a wheelchair, the cold cruelty of Jessie his former lover, and the unfeeling atmosphere in the hospital.

In the last act, O'Casey mixes his contradictory ingredients with a vicious piquancy. The war is over, and the stage is exuberantly gay with decorations of coloured lanterns and streamers. Off-stage, a dance-band plays a fox-trot. The scene bristles with people dancing and passing, wearing 'fantasti-cally shaped paper hats'. We see the reverse side of the battle-field scene. Naturalistic drama would have thought it enough to present the football club dance simply: the weight of feeling from the rest of the play would itself have suggested the irony of the image, as it does with the ball in Act III of *The Cherry Orchard*. But O'Casey makes his point unequi-vocally: lost in this bright festivity is a blind Teddy Foran who cannot see its brightness, and a legless Harry who must watch his girl dancing with other men.

There is no question of action to further the story in this last act. The incongruities make the dry statement:

HARRY (*singing softly*). Swing low, sweet chariot, comin' for to carry me home....

VOICE. Balloons will be given out now! Given out now—the balloons!

MRS FORAN (*excitedly*). They're goin' to send up the balloons! They're goin' to let the balloons fly now!

HARRY (*singing*). Swing low, sweet chariot, comin' for to carry me home....

Even to cap the blatancy of this trick, Surgeon Maxwell closes the scene with a song as he waltzes Susie in his arms:

> Swing into the dance,
> Take joy when it comes, ere it go;
> For the full flavour of life
> Is either a kiss or a blow.
> He to whom joy is a foe,
> Let him wrap himself up in his woe;
> For he is a life on the ebb,
> We a full life on the flow!

It does not need to be more than the doggerel it is; the dance tune gives the author licence to speak in almost direct address to us. Unsubtle though this is, yet it is strong in its dramatic effect, a stageworthy comment on the callousness of war. Perhaps O'Casey's satirical eye was never so jaundiced as when he wrote *The Silver Tassie*.

O'Casey since the 'twenties has signally failed to find a form to make his moralizing dramatically objective. The bald, balletic expressionism in *Within the Gates*, with caricatures for its characters and a naïve story of a 'Bishop's' lost daughter who for consolation turns from prostitution to the 'Dreamer' in preference to the Church, is instinct with ironic but ill-articulated ideas. *Red Roses for Me* also assumes an expressionistic freedom, but for all its vivid splendours of speech and feeling, its humour and its pathos, the strict discipline of form that expressionism demands is lacking.

Cock-a-Doodle Dandy will serve to illustrate the sad demise of the later O'Casey. The play has the same passionate vitality he has retained throughout his long apprenticeship of a career. It presents the worlds of the spiritually dead and the physically alive, the worlds of those who hate and those who love the Cock, symbolic of young vigour, which appears from time to time through the play. Michael and Mahan are crabby little Irish capitalists eaten up with lechery while their distemper is cloaked in the dogma of religion deriving from the parish priest, Father Domineer. With a pious vindictiveness and brutality, the priest, 'a green glow enveloping him', halts the happy sensual dancing of the girls with the villagers. Shame replaces their abandon. With a blow he murders the man 'living in sin'; he tells Michael to pack his daughter Loreleen off to America and hounds her out of the village in rags with Michael's consent; he sends the crippled girl Julia ceremoniously to Lourdes only to return in pitiful despair 'without even a gloamin' thought of hope'. Here is indeed a crude portrait of all the 'base-born' 'life-unbelievers', if we may use D. H. Lawrence's terms. The presentation of this sombre subject is intermittently counterpointed with the mad antics of pantomime which almost manage to relieve the starkness of the pulpit from which O'Casey is preaching. Yet we may guess that no stage tricks could make much difference to a play so black and white in its conception.

PIRANDELLO

The finest plays of Luigi Pirandello are those in which a gentle, naturalistic introduction is the prelude to a violent wrench as the rational world of the audience is questioned. So it is in *Each in His Own Way* (*Ciascuno a suo modo*) which begins with a quiet and respectable tea-party. The guests discuss whether one's opinions are true if one can change them according to circumstances. In particular they discuss the tragic conduct of the beautiful courtesan Delia Morello and the feelings of others towards her. But in two interludes we are staggered to find that Delia is given an existence apart from her character in the play. After Act I a 'real' Delia is under discussion apparently by members of our own audience, so that, as Pirandello has put it, the first act now assumes the shape of a fiction. Later the opinions of the 'spectators' themselves are thrust back a remove into fiction when the 'real' Delia leaps on to the stage from the stalls where we sit and flies at the actress who is playing her part. In the confusion, the 'third' act is not played at all, and we wonder whether we are not in fact players ourselves, subject to the observation of another and more omniscient audience. At each step the spectator's image in the mirror of the play is distorted until he is forced to adjust his own position. When the balance is restored, the image is distorted again.

In *Six Characters in Search of an Author* the curtain of the magic world of the play has no need to rise, for a rehearsal is in progress. In other words the actors and actresses in the theatre are as real as we are. This world of conventional reality is paraded long enough to relax us comfortably. Then six creatures of a half-composed fiction come upon the stage, creatures apparently as far from reality as Pirandello is able to devise. But in the course of the play they grow to such proportions of conviction that their make-believe becomes a reality and the reality of the original actors becomes make-believe, until we dare not try to distinguish the two. *Henry IV* encourages us tamely to accept the statement of Henry's insanity, only to discover that his madness is too cruelly sane. In *Right You Are If You Think So*, one statement is taken for truth, until it is flatly contradicted by another. We attempt each time to solve the problem by rational conjecture, only to find that another contradiction is proposed. We either press our reasoning to its limits, or admit a temporary insanity to gain relief from the satanic taunts of the author. These devices are designed to call up with a vengeance Pirandello's *sentimento del contrario*, the sense of the opposite.[1]

Pirandello's drama is a contest with the feelings of an audience as to whether these are to be preserved or destroyed. A play of his is often in the first place given its peculiar form to make us think, feel and comment, and then revise our feelings and comment on our commentary. We are to see from a new viewpoint, just at the moment when we thought we had established with some certainty the vantage point we had gained. Like each section of Browning's *The Ring and the Book* or each episode in the Japanese tale of *Rashomon*, each thrust in the action of Pirandello's comedy undermines our respect for what has gone before and for the decisions we made. We analyse and re-analyse the logic of our thought and feeling until we can neither think nor feel, nor even laugh. If we sit and gape perplexed, this is our tragedy, since we are the anti-heroes of the drama.

Pirandello's output has been very large, and somewhat mixed in quality. At his best he achieves the dark effect, not so much by the naughty arrangement of incongruous parts, but rather within the frame of the play set up as a whole. His theme does not suffer contradictions in its elaboration; it is contradictory in its conception. He conceives a tragedy and writes it as comedy. Domenico Vittorini tells us that Pirandello declared *Man, Beast and Virtue*, an early play, to be a tragedy stifled by comedy.[2] In this play a lady married to a sea-captain finds herself pregnant by her lover, and an aphrodisiac has to be devised to induce her husband, who usually

---

[1] Pirandello, *L'Umorismo*, 2nd ed. (Florence, 1920), p. 178.
[2] D. Vittorini, *The Drama of Luigi Pirandello* (New York, 1935), p. 369.

locks himself away from his wife, to spend a night with her. Here is a subject of traditional farce. In Pirandello's hands it becomes a bitter play in which the sin of the beast in man can only be covered by his own beastliness, and morality is used to hide his immorality.

Pirandello shows us human suffering and turns its tragic note of exultation from triumph to humility and from dignity to indignity. We are shocked. Legislating for himself, he has explained his work in these terms: 'Ordinarily in the conception of a work of art, reflection is like a form of feeling, almost a mirror in which the feeling is watching itself. Pursuing this idea, one might argue that, in the conception of humour, reflection is, yes, like a mirror, but of icy water in which the flame of the feeling is not only watching itself, but plunges and extinguishes itself.'[1] Emotion is to be douched by the cold scrutiny of the reason.

Pirandello's intention is to show man the contradictions within life and within himself, but especially to transmit to the spectator his own obsessed interest in man's erratic and impermanent mind, with its capricious motives and behaviour. In a state of near-hysteria, man will break into painful laughter, and the twin impulses of ridicule and pathos will come together in a completely felt, but pessimistic image of the human condition. We know that what is funny to us is often misery to others; Pirandello will have us live in two or more minds together, objectively and subjectively at once. Laughter as well as tears is an expression of grief, and as a character in *Each in His Own Way* says, 'That's my way of laughing and my laughter hurts me more than anyone else'. Pirandello's 'humourism' suggests an attitude limited in breadth but pro-

---

[1] Pirandello, *L'Umorismo*, 2nd ed. (Florence, 1920), p. 186. The original reads, 'ordinariamente, nella concezione d'un'opera d'arte, la riflessione è quias una forma del sentimento, quasi uno specchio in cui il sentimento si rimira. Volendo seguitar quest'imagine, si potrebbe dire che, nella concezione umoristica, la riflessione è, sì, come uno specchio, ma d'acqua diaccia, in cui la fiamma del sentimento non si rimira soltanto, ma si tuffa e si smorza.'

found in insight. It recognizes that man may hold within himself at the same time the power to mock and the power to sympathize. Humour for Pirandello is the exquisite coition of laughter and grief.

Aspect after aspect of commonplace human behaviour offered Pirandello his subject-matter: our instinct to preserve youth and to hold on to the youthful image we have of ourselves, to fix in immutable shapes the essentially fluid thing we know as life; our tendency to apply to others the attitudes we cherish ourselves, and to live in a world of dreams reinforced with all the logic in our power; our need to 'build ourselves up' and to create the 'reality' of ourselves from our own imagination; our intuitive way of presenting one appearance to one person and another to another, with our horror when we realize that we have grown so accustomed to using multiple masks that we may never know the face beneath; and our inevitable terror when we realize that we do not know where actuality ends and fantasy begins, and that at the end we are enshrined among our carefully hoarded illusions, naked and utterly alone. This is Pirandello's limitless mine of dramatic material.

Naked (*Vestire gli ignudi*) is the story of a girl, Ersilia Drei, who attempts to poison herself partly out of remorse for the death of her charge, a child who fell from a terrace, and partly out of despair at the emptiness of her life. Sentimentally, but humanly, she had desired only a modest enough success in life, and had fallen in love with a young naval officer who had jilted her. She thus wishes it to be known that she died for love. In hospital she recovers, however, and tells a reporter a lurid version of her story; in the sensation that follows she is befriended by a novelist. While seeming to help her out of pity, in fact he wishes only to use her for 'copy'. The officer returns to her apparently out of compassion, but in fact he too had been jilted by a second fiancée, and is coming to her on the rebound. Then we learn that her former employer was in fact her lover, and that it was through their joint neglect that the child had fallen to her death. No one is as he seems, and poor Ersilia recognizes this at last. She tells them that she had not lied in order to live, but in order to die, to cover herself 'with a decent dress'. Now in earnest she takes poison a second time because she truly feels herself to be stark naked.

When all that Pirandello had to say to us about art and life, the individual soul and the world outside it, has been turned over in discussion, his central problem of communication in the theatre remains one of the most interesting sides of his work. He attempts communication at once by presenting character on the stage in all its instability and by compelling his audience to undergo a corresponding sense of instability. Leone Gala in *The Rules of the Game* (*Il gioco delle parti*) is both the protagonist of the action and its chorus. Through him we too are encouraged to play a dual role, understanding his mind with compassion while simultaneously commenting on the triangular action: his relation to his pretty wife Silia and her lover Guido. As in *Henry IV*, the theatrical task is to marry the external action of the play precisely with our direct response to the suffering of Leone's soul in order to bring us to a fully realized emotional and intellectual sense of the play's meaning. When the character on the stage is stripped of its mask simultaneously with the stripping of the spectator, Pirandello achieves a first objective of great drama. If in this way Pirandello, like Kafka, can lower our defences, the nightmare can run its course.

Leone is meticulous in his habits and scrupulous in his morality. He now lives apart from his wife, devoted to cookery on the one hand and books on the other, all he needs for physical and spiritual nourishment. He visits his wife for precisely one half-hour each evening. It is evident that Silia is haunted by this man, drawn to him, yet she cannot abide him: his eyes are 'sharp as needles and vacant at the same time'. Significantly the comedy of his character is established in this way well before he enters: we are prepared for some kind of ludicrous monster. In fact he is seen to be quiet and unassuming, and within a few minutes we are playing our dual role.

For we quickly discover the tragedy of his life. His apparent nonchalance is a most careful pose: he has consciously drained himself of feeling and lives the life of a rational automaton in the face of the cruel and uncertain world of other people, and particularly of his wife, who is all perverse irrational instinct. The pessimist Leone treats life merely as a 'game', the only way he knows to survive its vicissitudes. Silia for her part finds this intolerable and determines to seek a way to have him killed. She invites an insult from four drunken young men, one of them a noted duellist, and then demands that her honour be avenged. Leone accordingly arranges for the fiercest of duels to the death, knowing that he has no experience whatever with sword or pistol. When all is prepared, he calmly informs the lover Guido at the last moment that it is for him to defend his wife. In a melodramatic *dénouement* Guido is killed. His death is but one more move in the game: it is an ugly joke, one which in its terrible outcome shocks us into understanding the tragedy in the comedy of life.

This account hardly suggests the skilled counterpoint of the macabre and the farcical in Act III of the play, and the calculated modulations of the tempo which sound the ticking of the clock to the end. With thoughts of the ugly duel planted strongly in our minds, Pirandello opens the act with the slow, ponderous servant Philip, comically only half awake at the early hour set for the event, reluctantly opening the door to the doctor who is to be in attendance. Philip lays out the breakfast table as Dr Spiga lays out his instruments: 'Scalpels... bone saw...forceps...dissectors...compressors....' Now the pace accelerates as the agitated seconds Guido and Barelli enter and make a stiff and formal greeting, only to find that Leone is, astonishingly, still asleep. He finally enters and stands sleepily in his pyjamas and slippers. At this point comes a complete change of tone and tempo, from that of near-farce to the terrible tension of Leone's revelation that he will not fight, but that the strictly honourable Guido must replace him. At the end, the fatal result of the duel is communicated to the distraught Silia, and to us, in a frightening mixture of acute sensations by the dishevelled Dr Spiga, who 'dashes in with grotesque discomposure: flings himself at his surgical instruments laid out on the table: rolls them up in the cloth, and rushes out without saying a word'.

Like his successor Anouilh, Pirandello is often at a loss to know what more there is to be done once his audience is naked, and like Anouilh, he must repeat himself somewhat negatively from play to play. Often at such points of no return he will weaken his effect by argument, telling us what we have already felt through the agency of his play; at other times he will wisely drop the curtain with the spit and the laugh we conceded to Shakespeare's Pandarus. At the curtain, the announcement of Leone's breakfast, the laughter of Laudisi of *Right You Are*, or of the Stepdaughter of *Six Characters*, pack us off with a flea in the ear, as do Undershaft in Shaw's *Major Barbara*, Jacques in Anouilh's *Dinner with the Family* and M. Henri in his *Point of Departure*, Barbette in Giraudoux's *Duel of Angels*, and Irma in Jean Genet's *The Balcony*.

Although Pirandello calls *Henry IV* 'a tragedy', lets it run to the limits of its sardonic conclusion, and takes the laughter to the point of vomit, it seems to me no different in kind from the 'comedy' of his other plays. Since nowhere has Pirandello more successfully employed his 'humourism' than in this play, it is used in the next few pages to demonstrate briefly his exquisite sense of theatre.

'Henry IV', Act III

ANALYSIS: 'HENRY IV', ACT III

Preparation for torture

The story of *Henry IV* is ingeniously worked out, though only the barest framework is supplied to hold the play together and to tease the audience. We gather that, at the age of twenty-six, Henry had played the part of the eleventh-century German emperor Henry IV in a pageant A fall from his horse had rendered him insane, and his insanity had taken paranoiac form: he continued to think himself the Emperor. For twenty years he has kept his household as counterfeit as himself: his servants dress in eleventh-century costume, and pay court to him as if he were a despotic monarch. But for about the last eight years it is 'suggested' that he has in fact been sane, though he now so hates his fellows that he prefers to remain playing the part he has grown used to, somewhat like Gaston, the soldier suffering from loss of memory in Anouilh's *Traveller without Luggage*, a man who so hates himself that he prefers his anonymity. Henry is 'a poor devil already out of the world, out of time, out of life.[1] Now his friends—Matilda, his former lover, and Belcredi, his former rival—have brought a doctor to try to cure him. With them are Matilda's daughter, Frida, and her fiancé, Charles di Nolli. The Doctor has devised a dangerous cure: Frida is to dress as her mother was twenty years before, and so shake into life 'the stopped watch' of Henry's brain.

The structure of the play is devilishly planned to give the audience two split focal points for their sympathies and interest, and these are dramatically in opposition. First, Henry's own mental suffering must invite our compassion, and his pain is in the end to be our pain. Second, our other, perhaps better, selves are represented by all those who pay

---

[1] Trans. by E. Storer from *Three Plays by Luigi Pirandello* (London, 1923).

II   161   SDC

court to him, the apparently sane; in effect, the second centre of interest is in the auditorium, and our sympathy is to be checked by our sense of the cowardice of a sick man trying to stop the movement of time and make the transitory permanent. Yet, for all that the horror of this inhibits intimacy, some intimate and subjective feeling for Henry's plight is to war with our objective understanding of his insanity, for the more we enter into his mind and make his standards our standards, the more do we make his insanity temporarily our sanity, and the more we make the other characters' sanity our insanity. Here is a revolving see-saw of a play devised to send us home dizzy and startled, for an audience must lose its free-will in any tussle with Pirandello's stage.

The first two acts of the play set a tone not far removed from farcical, and it is important to notice this attempt to put us off our guard. The servants mix their modern speech and behaviour, their cigarettes and their modern nicknames most incongruously with the medieval costume and décor. The hero and his problem are introduced to us only through the uncommitted eyes of such servants and with their kind of levity. The visitors in their modern dress again strike the ludicrous note when they enter the medieval scene. Henry himself, with his badly dyed hair, the 'two small doll-like dabs of colour' on his pallid cheeks, there to mark fantastically the grotesque tragedy of a man trying to defy the onset of age, in fact make him seem clown and puppet at the same time. When Matilda, Belcredi and the Doctor are received by the Emperor, Henry's diatribe tests their powers of masquerade and reveals their embarrassment, and this is the funnier since we are not at this point sympathetically attached to either party.

This tone continues to colour our impressions well into Act II. The Doctor's plan is proposed and prepared with not a little mockery; and the Doctor himself is painted as a figure of fun, with the pomposity of his 'analogical elasticity', his 'symptomatized delirium', his 'considerable cerebral activity' and so on. Unexpectedly Henry seems to let his mask of madness slip for a moment, suggesting that he knows the truth. We, like the servants and the visitors who thought him mad, begin to wonder too late whether we have been trapped.

Productions of the play have sometimes destroyed its important central irony by demonstrating to the spectator that Henry *is* sane, but Pirandello is very careful not to have him confess in so many words that he has been merely playing the madman. He speaks in an ingenious series of ambiguities which suit equally the enraged Emperor and the fiendish impostor: 'Don't you see, idiot, how I treat them, how I play the fool with them, make them appear before me just as I wish?...' Then he seems to tell us the truth—by the astonished reactions of the servants we are encouraged to believe him—until we begin to ask ourselves desperate questions. If a sane man says he's mad, he may well be sane. If a madman says he's mad, he too may well be sane. But if a madman says he's sane, must he be sane? We arrive at the centre of the puzzle of 'all statements in this square are false'. So we return to his behaviour for guidance, only to hear him giving his imperious orders in a terrible voice once more, bringing them all to their knees. Yet further teasing is to follow. In a flash his thunder turns to crazy laughter as he mocks them—and us:

HENRY. ...Let's have a jolly good laugh!...
   (*Laughs*): Ah!...Ah!...Ah!...
LANDOLPH–HAROLD–ORDULPH (*looking at each other half happy and half dismayed*). Then he's cured!...he's all right!...
HENRY. Silence! Silence!

Pirandello has his hero voice a thought as it chases across our mind: 'it's a terrible thing if you don't hold on to that which seems true to you today'. We look at this man as we look at ourselves.

Towards Tragic Inversion

The moonlit darkness gathers in the room, and in our ripe imagination. We are as uncertain of the truth as ever, but the scene has been set for the horror of Act III, the shaking of the watch.

The biter bit

On either side of the throne, the two life-size portraits of a young man and woman dressed in the carnival costumes of the Emperor Henry and the Marchioness Matilda of Tuscany have, since the start of the play, dominated the room. They have been the reminder of present misery accentuated by the knowledge of a happy past and careless youth, though we have by now taken their presence for granted. At the rise of the curtain they have imperceptibly changed, and they stand on a darkened stage. Within the frames, dressed for their new parts, Charles di Nolli and Frida have become the portraits. We had not been told directly what the Doctor's trick was to be: it was hinted that this exchange would take place, but the details were whispered only to Charles and Frida. We are ourselves to be sufficiently startled by the discovery of the impersonations, that we may begin emotionally to understand something of the shock Henry will suffer. This is essentially an effect of theatre, and is not to be reproduced on the printed page. We must sense Henry's horror from within, and, when Henry enters with his lamp, what he sees shall be what we see.

Now a tired man, he walks slowly across the stage—until he is stopped by one word, the first of Frida's prepared speech: 'Henry...' It is enough. Immediately the play leaps alive again. We see him stop, we see his terror-stricken face, grotesque with the red spots on its cheeks, we see his arm raised in fear. We do not halt the careering of the image to ask why he is afraid, for we have caught his fear. One word has destroyed his composure and ours. We must ask again whether he is sane; for him, his command of the game he was playing is challenged. Terrible doubt lingers through the act. As the biter is bit, so the comedy is transformed in tone: it is a hint of what is to come. Henry has been so long confident of his acting, secure in his knowledge of his part, that one jolt to his control, one detail of performance which goes awry, must make him doubt his free agency. It flashes across his mind that there is a control outside himself that he is defying: this is the hint of the essence of the tragic conflict. Perhaps he is the puppet and not the puppet-master? We feel his deflation of spirits, just as we are amused by marionettes until make-believe becomes reality.

We are not into tragedy yet. Frida's fear remains an object of curious interest. Upon Henry's 'dreadful cry', she continues to scream his name 'like a mad woman'. She fulfils a double dramatic function as innocent victim, hysterical-mad herself, and as chorus cognizant of madness in others. She passes on her fear to us as the stillness of the stage is broken by her movement from the picture-frame and by the rapid entrance of the rest to comfort her, all talking together. They crowd in the upper part of the stage, which is now lit: they remain the reasonably clear world of sanity. They look towards us and towards Henry who stands stock still, a silhouette in the darkness downstage, symbolizing the uncomfortable recesses of our mind.

Like each new revelation of 'the truth' in *Right You Are*, which sharpens the point of the play but serves only to confuse us more, the problem here has been accentuated by this moment of terror, but neither character nor audience know any the better whether Henry is mad or sane: if mad, we should weep; if sane, we should laugh. We do neither. We sit transfixed.

Towards Tragic Inversion

The tables turned again

We sit transfixed, and Pirandello takes his pleasure in confounding our brains. He uses the formula of the age-old riddle of the man who looked at his son's portrait and declared, 'Brothers and sisters have I none, but this man's father is my father's son'. In a revenge of sheer dialectical brilliancy, the madman is to make each doubt his own sanity.

Agnes, the mother of di Nolli and the sister of Henry, had died a month before, firmly convinced that her brother would regain his sanity; but for all her care of him, Henry had refused to comfort her on her death-bed by disclosing his recovery to her—if he had any such recovery to disclose. Now di Nolli accuses him of deceiving her 'right up to the time of her death', and Henry retorts, 'It isn't *your* sister only that is dead!' Pirandello's italics make it clear that Henry must be looking upon his new rival, di Nolli, as someone pretending to be his twentieth-century self, since di Nolli has no sister. The two emperors stand facing each other dressed exactly alike, and, venomously, Henry sees the younger man both as a character playing the part of the Emperor and as the actor behind the character, that is, as Henry's double. Or, of course, perhaps Henry too is pretending.

The confusion increases when di Nolli asks in bewilderment, 'My sister? Yours, I say, whom you compelled up to the last moment to present herself here as your mother Agnes!' Agnes was also the name of the mother of the eleventh-century Emperor, and Agnes, Henry's sister, had been play-acting for the sake of flattering Henry's delusion: for twenty years of 'insanity' the sister had been accepted as the mother. We are to assume therefore that Henry sees her as di Nolli's mother in his part as Henry the Emperor; thus he can say, 'And was she not *your* mother?' Agnes was di Nolli's mother in real life, and di Nolli quickly assumes that this is what Henry means: 'My mother? Certainly my mother!' But it is evident that Henry does not mean it so, since he retorts, 'But your mother is dead for me, *old and far away*!' Here 'your mother' can only mean the mother of the Emperor who died in the eleventh century, and his statement suggests that he now has a twentieth-century sanity upon him, seeing di Nolli as his old self, the insane play-actor.

Henry has contrived to spin the wheel full circle. For di Nolli, a flesh-and-blood mother has become a figment of another man's imagination remote in the past, and to prove Henry sane, di Nolli must almost prove himself insane. Or so perhaps Pirandello would have us see it, since the dramatizing of the argument has to a degree failed in the realization. Nevertheless, the author kept his effect even incomplete as it is, and he was quite justified in retaining it. The spectator is confused and left gasping at the vicious brilliance of the man supposedly mad. It is no wonder that Matilda looks with dismay at the others.

This is Henry taking his revenge indeed. Do you wish to guess whether I am mad or sane? he seems to be asking. What impertinence for you fools to imagine that one can recognize sanity, identify mask or face, in others! First tease your brains and decide, if you can, whether you are sane yourselves, whether it is not you who are wearing the mask.

Henry pursues his victims, Belcredi and the others, and, through their agency, us. He turns on Frida and addresses her as if she really is the Marchioness of Tuscany, asking her whether Agnes was not the Emperor's mother, prepared to cross-examine her savagely as he did di Nolli. Frida, the Doctor and Belcredi respond in the three separate ways in which we are at that instant responding ourselves, with fear, with belief, with doubt:

FRIDA (*still frightened, draws closer to di Nolli*). No, no, I don't know. Not I!

Towards Tragic Inversion

DOCTOR. It's the madness returning...Quiet now, everybody!
BELCREDI (*indignant*). Madness indeed, Doctor! He's acting again!...

Henry has his friends in an impasse; and thus Pirandello has us. Yet can we avoid sharing some of the joy of his triumph over those who tried to test him so cruelly? We trust and mistrust our judgments, and love and hate ourselves.

The touch of a flower on the neck

There follows an extraordinary sequence of confusions, both the characters' and ours. This sequence is in fact a clever equivalent of the dramatic pause which permits an audience to weigh a new impression and adjust the shifting pattern of the play's meaning to a point of temporary equilibrium. The pause that is traditional allows us to review the situation, as when Robert de Baudricourt is left winded by his encounter with the Maid: we sum up the situation and estimate her power, anticipate the opposition to her and guess at the probable extent of her success. When the Steward runs in and cries that the hens are laying, our judgment is confirmed.

The crux in *Henry IV* differs from the traditional pause in that the author knows we are unlikely to reach a point of equilibrium, although he also knows we must try for it. He has so devised it that with one utterance we pronounce Henry sane, and with the next condemn him to insanity. We do this in order to maintain the rational order of things; we must try to the end to measure Henry from the standpoint of what we take to be normality. The truth is, we are undergoing, and we are to feel, the self-delusion of every man who attempts to pass judgment on his fellow.

Thus in this 'pause', the action is in no way furthered, but in it Pirandello leaves us rope enough to hang ourselves. On the stage we hear only a futile contest of words: from Belcredi and Donna Matilda who think him cured; from the Doctor and the servant Landolph who thought him cured,

but who are now none too sure; while Henry himself passionately declares that he is cured, though his every remark casts
further doubt on the truth of this. He talks of his recovery,
yet because of his burning anger, his sudden turns, his
trembling, his sharp changes of mind in the full course of
passionate speech, we remain unconvinced. Is he still deluded?
He speaks of the triumph of the Marchioness at the carnival,
addressing his remark to Donna Matilda, yet pointing to
Frida, who is of course still dressed as Matilda was then. He
alludes to the servants' betrayal of his 'recovery' as if they
had denounced him merely to make fun of him; but since
the visitors now laugh 'shamefacedly' at this, perhaps they
are still in doubt whether the servants did not tell them a lie
to have a further joke at their expense.

This sequence might well be tinged with farce, were it not
for two comments from Henry, directed, as it were, straight
at us. These relate the contorted action going forward on the
stage to conventional life as we know it. They provide sheet-
anchors for the play, extending and deepening its image.

Our consciousness of time and of its power, which will not
let us rest, which gives us no comfort, which defeats our
efforts to control ourselves and our environment, which at the
last sets at nought the emotions and impulses of human
nature, as at the last it does with Henry, this sense of time has
been one of the strongest threads running through the first
two acts. Now the keynote of this theme is sounded when
Henry refers to his lost years:

HENRY. Look at my hair!
BELCREDI. But mine is grey too!
HENRY. Yes, with this difference: that mine went grey here, as Henry IV,
   do you understand? And I never knew it! I perceived it all of a sudden,
   one day, when I opened my eyes....

Pirandello first provides the link with everyday experience:
we recognize those appalling moments of realization when we

sense the speeding passage of the years. Such an experience is one to savour gently, and to grow used to slowly, that ageing may be gracious. Here the way that Henry discovers his age is sudden and terrifying; we hear the horror in his voice. Thus Pirandello presses on us the full statement he wants to make, the sense of irretrievable loss, the worse because youth did not exist: '...and I was terrified because I understood at once that not only had my hair gone grey, but that I was all grey, inside; that everything had fallen to pieces, that everything was finished; and I was going to arrive, hungry as a wolf, at a banquet which had already been cleared away....' The meaning of this fearful statement Pirandello has still to recreate in us. His malicious effort to disrupt our moral security is to become explicit at the crisis.

Our false trust that we have the knowledge and power to lift or replace our mask at will is the second thread woven into the play, one that is indeed tightly interwoven with the theme of our powerlessness against time and its mysteries. The force that controls our dying also holds the tyrannous mirror which will not allow us to know whether we see our real selves or not.

Henry declares that we are the involuntary puppets of a continuous, everlasting masquerade, just as madness had caricatured the life of the Emperor Henry. For who, other than the astute artist, can tell what is true and what is caricature in our behaviour? Certainly not ourselves. Henry gesticulates in the tragic manner: 'You know, it is quite easy to get accustomed to it. One walks about as a tragic character, just as if it were nothing....' To stress the point, he tells the story of an Irish priest, asleep and dreaming in the sun in a public garden:

One may be sure that in that moment he did not know any more that he was a priest, or even where he was. He was dreaming....A little boy passed with a flower in his hand. He touched the priest with it here on the neck. I saw him open his laughing eyes, while all his mouth smiled with

the beauty of his dream. He was forgetful of everything....But all at
once, he pulled himself together, and stretched out his priest's cassock;
and there came back to his eyes the same seriousness which you have seen
in mine....

That touch of innocence is something we may never re-
experience. We may continue forever to play our part, be it
that of priest or emperor or humble man, and never know the
repose of reality and integrity. If we did awake, it might be
only to realize the terror of our loss, not in lowering and
losing a mask, which in itself matters nothing at all compared
with finding alien the genuine life we might have led: we
should be 'all grey inside'.

Henry felt the touch of the flower on his neck when Frida
called to him, and his horror was absolute. Pirandello has set
himself to make us feel that touch as well. Is the task proving
greater than his playwright's art? Else why should he stop to
tell the stories of his grey hair and the Irish priest? They re-
emphasize Henry's realization of his central problem, but will
they persuade us to the realization of it too?

Fiction becomes fact

The play's argument on the relativity of madness has risked
being too conceptual, each event providing only for the further
development of the argument. We have reached, in this
manner, a final paradox. Henry is sane because he knows he
is mad; he is cured because, as he says, he can act the madman
to perfection. The author cannot resist a fling at us, pursuing
the natural corollary: 'I do it very quietly, I'm only sorry for
you that have to live your madness so agitatedly, without
knowing it or seeing it.' Pirandello has used the others on the
stage to demonstrate our immediate state of mind, as he has
used the play to demonstrate our general state of ignorance.
In this pursuit of truth, Henry has remained the omnipotent
figure, the author-figure, the pupper-master using his puppets

for a cynical revenge. Now with a masochistic joy, Pirandello twists his comedy to a tragic *dénouement* and turns cerebral excogitation to vividly realized sensation in the auditorium. He has Henry take his triumph one step further, and one step too far. It is *hubris* indeed, for in allowing Henry to believe he has removed his last mask, and that the sanity he had discovered in himself is the absolute one, the author, as it were, acknowledges his limitations in writing the play at all.

Henry's gross error, and the annihilating stroke, is his attempt to mix fiction with fact. He returns to his role of emperor, and tries with make-believe to govern events that lie outside the make-believe world, as is our frequent habit in ordinary life. Of course, as he declares, di Nolli is not the Emperor, because Henry wishes to be; but Matilda is not the Marchioness because after twenty years she has become a woman he can no longer recognize. The Marchioness he *can* recognize is the young girl dressed in the carnival costume— Frida! Frida, young, pretty, innocent of the world, stands there in fear as the masquerade makes its claims on reality: 'The dream alive in you! More than alive in you! It was an image that wavered there and they've made you come to life! Oh, mine! You're mine, mine, mine, in my own right!' As he holds her in his arms, 'laughing like a madman', we suddenly sense a reality above the masquerade: we see an ageing lunatic claiming a terrified girl twenty years his junior, the mad and the sane intermingled preposterously. Pirandello has dramatized his paradox; we are revolted, and the true cutting edge of this kind of comedy makes its incision felt.

When Henry lays claim to Frida, innocence is trapped by experience and polluted by life. Frida has played her part unknowingly and fallen victim to society's jest. In life, suggests the author, we unwittingly enter a masquerade which is devitalizing, which will kill our souls. Frida must now play the mad game of society in earnest.

On the other hand, Belcredi was never innocent. He has seen Henry's tragedy growing to its crisis and he has laughed. He was Henry's rival and his mind's assassin. Fortune now decrees that it shall be Belcredi who moves to stop Henry's assault on the girl: 'Leave her alone! Leave her alone! You're no madman!' In a flash Henry takes a maniacal and physical revenge on his enemy: he draws a sword and drives it into Belcredi. The line that marks the climax is superb in its complex simplicity: 'I'm not mad, eh! Take that, you!....' It is a line which brings together the several strands of the play's paradox in one astonishing contradiction, and even if we have by now guessed that Henry could not consciously control reality with the same success as his attempt to live in history, this single gesture in a waste of words, like the shot fired in *Uncle Vanya*, like that in *Six Characters in Search of an Author*, and that in Anouilh's *Ardèle*, like the vicious slap on his Colombe's face after Julien's laughter, is calculated to leave us dazed and wholly unsure of ourselves.

In the confusion that follows—again our horror echoes the actors'—Pirandello stresses the absolute and inseparable mixture of appearance and reality we have been faced with since Frida assumed her character as the Marchioness. Still Henry refuses to say directly whether he is mad or sane, and still we are left to deduce what we can for ourselves. If Henry is taking a just revenge on his rival, it is the action of a sane man perhaps momentarily crazed by his fury, but nevertheless that of a man with his mask removed, not acting a part. On the other hand, the strange assassination by sword thrust strongly suggests that Henry is more than using the licence of his 'authority' as Emperor, more than acting a part, but may be so obsessed by his role that he has followed his absolute prerogative as despot. Any man may in part assume a mask, but at any time a less conscious part of him may erupt to shatter it. The excitement of the debate within our minds is thus completely dramatized, and Henry's anger against the limitation of life is translated into an energy at once keenly critical and highly emotional.

Belcredi is carried off crying with his last breath that Henry is not mad—which might mean that Belcredi feels his enemy was justified in striking him and that he had been responsible for the accident twenty years before, or that in spite Belcredi wishes to ensure that Henry will pay the penalty even though he is mad. We remain desperately uncertain. Nor even can we be sure that the thrust of the sword, an action incongruous amid so much logistic argument, was not itself another symptom of make-believe.

Then follows the ace the playwright has been waiting to play. The stage is at last suddenly silent. Henry, standing between the stupefied servants, enacts a gigantic pause, which is broken by a piercing cry from Donna Matilda—Belcredi is dead! Henry has committed murder...as a man, not as an emperor.

HENRY (...*with his eyes almost starting out of his head, terrified by the life of his own masquerade which has driven him to crime*). Ah now...yes now...inevitably (*calls his valets around him as if to protect him*) here together...here together...for ever...for ever. (*Curtain*)

Henry for his *hubris* is caught in the toils that bind us all. The man who thought to rise above his human limitations by disentangling fact from fiction has so intermingled them that he has unwittingly condemned himself to continue, like the rest of mankind, in the life of masquerade he was so anxious to discredit. His parable is tragic in the extent to which his struggle towards the superhuman has brought him down hard to the lowest level...'inevitably'. A power greater than he has condemned him to his madness.

Comic and tragic

But this is no tragedy, although Pirandello calls it one. The world against which the hero has been struggling is that of petty humanity as well as his own. It is a comic world, depicted in strong critical colours. For us to realize that our man has been pushed down among those we despise, for us to realize that Henry is another Belcredi, holds no exultation, only bitter debasement. The social comedy which had provided the excuse in its fantasy and had given weight to Henry's struggles of evasion must leave us in that characteristic discomfort of dark comedy. The play grew away from its author's hands.

If this discomfort is Pirandello's 'tragic' note, it echoes that shrill familiar Pirandellian laugh which torments the theatre at the end of *Six Characters*. Nobody, neither villain nor hero, audience nor author, leaves the play with peace or honour. Whatever efforts Henry made to be master of himself, whatever efforts the author made towards an analysis of personality, life reasserted itself. In defeating Henry, life defeats his creator, and Pirandello in the magnificent gesture of his curtain lines is acknowledging his own limitations: we withdraw a mask only to discover another beneath it, and life will compel us to act another part to the end whether we know we are acting or not. Again, our puny impotence is ludicrous—and to do anything else but laugh at this 'tragedy' is to court a terrible humiliation.

Yet it is a play, like many of Pirandello's, which takes its greatest effect after the final curtain. The play's technique is geared to the task of outwitting its audience, shaking our faith in order that we may look twice at ourselves and the world around us. In the issue, drama and life perform a mutual service. It is because of this that the tragic impulse of the play, although presented within a comic framework, has its unusual repercussions.

The play's special note of terror is intensified because of a remarkable dramatization of a sense of time and its tyranny. Its examination of the mind and its powerlessness to govern itself would have less meaning were it not for what the Doctor in a lucid moment calls 'the sensation of the distance of time'. The Doctor's intention, of course, is to have Henry realize that he is living in the twentieth century and not in the eleventh, a very limited objective after all. It is Pirandello's intention to have us realize how relative time is: to the individual, that eight hundred years of history matter far less than the precious twenty of personal experience. For the Doctor, the 'stopped watch' is a very general problem of mental delusion. For Pirandello, Henry, and us, it is the immediate horror of being 'out of the world, out of time, out of life'. Henry had comforted himself with the knowledge that he was 'already in history', with 'everything determined, everything settled'; he was not like the men of the twentieth century 'torturing themselves in ceaseless anxiety to know how their fates and fortunes will work out'. But Henry also tasted the misery of living an existence in which every event took place 'precisely and coherently in each minute particular', while life passed him by. Our sympathy for Henry is in his intensely personal experience.

Thus from this position, *Henry IV* is certainly not only a play of social criticism, no mere comedy of manners, but a deep exploration of mind and soul, of a psychological and spiritual problem. It offers a statement about the way we live in terms of comedy, and proves it in an experience of tragedy. A deep acquaintance with time, and the knowledge that we have no control over its passage, is the driving power in the play. Its determinism gives it the complexion of classical tragedy, but its ultimately hysterical, even farcical, pessimism is characteristic of Pirandello's touch and another sign of the spirit of the age. As the mind is a maze, in which to seem to

176

find an exit is only to re-enter the maze, so *Henry IV* offers us, in the end, spiritual anarchy.

Pirandello's definition of his theatre, which Professor Tilgher has called *teatro dello specchio*, 'the mirror theatre', is particularly appropriate to this play:

> When a man lives, he lives and does not see himself. Well, put a mirror before him and make him see himself in the act of living, under the sway of his passions: either he remains astonished and dumbfounded at his own appearance, or else he turns away his eyes so as not to see himself, or else in disgust he spits at his image, or again clenches his fist to break it; and if he had been weeping, he can weep no more; if he had been laughing, he can laugh no more, and so on. In a word, there arises a crisis and that crisis is my theatre.[1]

He is here helping to define dark comedy.

Pirandello's influence on modern drama is ambiguous and difficult to assess. His tone is pervasive through the century, but it is possible to see explicit correspondences in the particular treatment of plot and character especially in plays by Anouilh (from *Traveller without Luggage* to *Colombe*) and Tennessee Williams (from the illusions of the mother in *The Glass Menagerie* to the self-deceivers of *Camino Real*). Yet the approach also seems to be applicable to subjects and content as diverse as those of Priestley's *They Came to a City* and Robert Bolt's *Flowering Cherry*. It seems that the Pirandellian stance, once caught, is firmly held. It is sometimes melodramatic and sometimes paradoxical in a forced and narrow way, but the achievement for which he is unlikely to be forgotten is his astonishing ability, at his best, to play the disturbing dramatic game of cat and mouse with the spectator. He wrote a new Socratic drama whose only parallel is that of Bernard Shaw.

[1] Quoted by W. Starkie, *Luigi Pirandello* (London, 1926), from A. Tilgher, *Voci del Tempo* (Rome, 1923).

4

COUNTERPOINT AND HYSTERIA

> NELL. One mustn't laugh at these things, Nagg.
> Why must you always laugh at them?
> NAGG. Not so loud!
> NELL. Nothing is funnier than unhappiness, I
> grant you that. But—   SAMUEL BECKETT, *Endgame*

ELIOT'S 'DOUBLENESS'

In spite of his early censures in his essay on 'Four Elizabethan Dramatists' against mixing realistic and abstract conventions, T. S. Eliot made the following arresting statement at the conclusion of his book *The Use of Poetry and the Use of Criticism*:

I once designed, and drafted a couple of scenes, of a verse play. My intention was to have one character whose sensibility and intelligence should be on the plane of the most sensitive and intelligent members of the audience; his speeches should be addressed to them as much as to the other personages in the play—or rather, should be addressed to the latter, who were to be material, literal-minded and visionless, with the consciousness of being overheard by the former. There was to be an understanding between this protagonist and a small number of the audience, while the rest of the audience would share the responses of the other characters in the play.[1]

---

[1] T. S. Eliot, *The Use of Poetry and the Use of Criticism* (London, 1933), p. 153. An interesting and relevant discussion of 'pure and impure drama' is to be found in chapter 2 of D. Krause, *Sean O'Casey, the Man and his Work* (London, 1960), which came to hand after the completion of this book. Krause anticipates our theme when he writes, 'Playwrights like Shakespeare, Chekhov, Shaw, Synge, O'Casey, Pirandello, Giraudoux, Anouilh, Sartre, Wilder, Beckett and Ionesco have freely used "music-hall devices in the service of the highest dramatic aims" (a phrase from S. L. Bethell, *Shakespeare and the Popular Dramatic Tradition*, London, 1944, p. 29). All of these playwrights, and many others in our time, write what is essentially impure drama. One might even say that the bastard *genre* of tragicomedy has been one of the dominant forms of twentieth century drama' (pp. 51–2).

Eliot's 'Doubleness'

This implied division of characters and spectators into the two groups of the sensitive and the insensitive has run through much of Eliot's drama, and has often lent an ironic and satirical force to his playwriting which is characteristic of the modern theatre. Leaving aside the obvious point that a divided audience of the kind he envisages can never ensure an embracing artistic success for such drama, since only a presumed minority of the spectators could receive the ironies central to its structure, we should nevertheless look briefly at some of the creative results of this policy.

The statement in *The Use of Poetry* has, of course, direct application to his experiment in *Sweeney Agonistes*, two fragments of a verse play demonstrating a life of dull parties and empty living in which the girls Dusty and Doris entertain a variety of men in their flat. Two or three times a menacing note is introduced, through the sinister background figure of Pereira who 'pays the rent' but who is never seen, through hints of dark evil in an interlude of fortune-telling, and through the melancholy Sweeney who eclipses the gaiety of the second scene by suggesting that existence for these girls is bound by the repetitive facts of life:

> SWEENEY. Birth, and copulation, and death.
>   That's all, that's all, that's all, that's all,
>   Birth, and copulation, and death.
> DORIS. I'd be bored.
> SWEENEY.   You'd be bored.

Sweeney then embarks on a smoke-room story of a horror hidden behind the vacuous normality of daily living:

> I knew a man once did a girl in
> Any man might do a girl in
> Any man has to, needs to, wants to
> Once in a lifetime, do a girl in.
> Well he kept her there in a bath
> With a gallon of lysol in a bath.

179   12-2

Counterpoint and Hysteria

Behind this flat toneless voice is the grim tinsel life of *The Waste Land*, of Madame Sosostris, of the neurotic sophisticate who sits in Cleopatra's chair, creatures who are foils for the makeshift existence of Lil in the pub and the typist seduced in her bed-sitter, peopling the limbo of the half-alive. Voices and attitudes set one against another and the underlying threat of the unknown introduces a sly dramatic element in these early non-theatrical attempts at communication.

Perhaps the most successful of such semi-dramatic gambits is the earlier and lesser poem *Portrait of a Lady*, in which the predicament of society, its disillusion and its nightmare of inarticulate feeling, is given expression through the silent young man caught in the web of an over-civilized but ultimately insensitive lady whose boredom with life feeds upon his vulnerability.

In his essay on John Marston, which appeared just before *Murder in the Cathedral*, Eliot wrote, 'It is possible that what distinguishes poetic drama from prosaic drama is a kind of doubleness in the action, as if it took place on two planes at once'.[1] This 'doubleness', or, as he calls it later in the essay, this 'sense of something behind', this 'pattern behind the pattern', Eliot attempted to exploit as a method in his own plays. The ironic address of the Knights in *Murder in the Cathedral* springs immediately to mind. Naturally, most of the characters in this play are apprehending their situation on a plane lower than that of the hero Thomas à Becket, whether the Tempters, the Priests or the Women of Canterbury. The Knights not only think and feel with all the limitations of their calling, but offer the only instance in the play where the difference of levels is *realized* for the audience in the theatre or the congregation in the church. When after the killing of Thomas they step out of the play with all the force of an aside in Molière and a *Verfremdungseffekt* of Bertolt Brecht

[1] T. S. Eliot, *Selected Essays* (London, 1932), p. 229.

rolled into one, they cease suddenly to be symbolic figures in an abstract design, and become recognizably representative men from modern political life. This abrupt shaking of the audience's confidence in the image they have been creating is sufficient to jolt it into reassessing the play's meaning in modern terms. The untrammelled direct address to the audience has become more and more familiar in the contemporary theatre, and even in television and the cinema.[1] It is proving a refreshing means of shattering the image of an audience largely lulled into anticipating a complete naturalism. This device of the Knights is a fully legitimate shock tactic.

For instances of Eliot's comprehensive exploiting of the theatre for his own ends we must return to *The Family Reunion*. In this play the experiments with verse forms and the adroit sliding between prosaic conversation and the more 'poetic' inner thoughts of the characters are most happily married to the two or three levels of sensibility in the characters and the two or three levels of action on the stage. The Ibsen-like story of Harry and his family and the attempt to link the Greek curse of an ancient house with a Freudian domestic trouble at Wishwood are neither of them so successful as the moments of fully theatrical irony when Harry's theme of self-discovery and the audience's image of a dead society are given stage life.

Lord Monchensey, in love with his wife's sister Agatha, had many years before planned the murder of his wife Amy, who was at that time pregnant with the unborn Harry. Because Agatha felt that the child was in part her own, she prevented the crime; but the sin of the wish to kill was not so readily suppressed. When the father died, Harry grew up in the care of the sisters. When Harry chose to marry, his mother

---

[1] Cf. the effect of Olivier's first soliloquy in his film of *Richard III*, seemingly the first time that a soliloquy in a film of Shakespeare has been used as originally intended.

had other plans and her possessiveness compelled Harry and his wife to leave the house. They led an itinerant life abroad until, one 'cloudless night in the mid-Atlantic', the girl was drowned. Whether Harry drowned her or only desired to drown her, we never know; but the sin of the father had been visited upon the son. In the course of the play, Harry learns finally from Agatha that the cause of his suffering is hereditary and not personal. His mind is so illuminated and so relieved that, although he knows his action will kill his mother with grief, he leaves Wishwood and the play happily able to expiate the family's curse.

The play is a construction of contrasting attitudes, of Harry living a life of fierce intensity set against the four uncles and aunts of the Chorus who 'do not understand'; of Amy, slave to a dead and helplessly chronological past, set against Agatha who wisely recognizes the 'loop in time' and understands that the 'curse is like a child'. Very soon after the rise of the curtain we begin to place the characters by the way they think and speak and respond to Harry's predicament. We place them on a scale which corresponds to the intensity of the verse, and as soon as this scale is meaningfully established, the larger jumps between its two extremes become immediately noticeable. As the drama proceeds, we become more sensitive to slighter jumps. We respond more and more in the way in which we respond to thoughtful comedy with its calculated contrasts of values.

To select a short instance of this effect in operation we need turn only to the opening scene of the play in which most of the family have gathered to celebrate Amy's birthday and Harry's homecoming. Ivy is a type of impoverished snob who freezes in Bayswater 'by a gas-fire counting shillings'; Violet is a snob of a more inverted species, harder and more malicious, but equally a 'type'; Charles is a soft country-bred clubman who enjoys 'a glass of dry sherry or two before dinner';

Gerald is a vapid Indian Army soldier who misses his native servants. It is these ludicrous, cardboard people who prepare us for Harry's entrance by irritating us with generalities about the younger generation and their lack of stamina and responsibility. Amy, only slightly less hollow a person than these, because she is now an old woman afraid of death, speaks of the past as something to be firmly reclaimed for her son's future, and she is angered by Agatha's suggestion that 'everything is irrevocable' and 'the past is irremediable'. For Agatha too has affectionate thoughts of Harry's future, although she knows that 'he will find a new Wishwood' to which he will not easily be able to adapt himself. In this way the family plans to make Harry 'feel at home', most senseless of clichés, and Amy with finality issues these words of advice:

> Do not discuss his absence. Please behave only
> As if nothing had happened in the past eight years.

Although we had in some degree been forewarned of what now happens, by Agatha's stronger verse, by her position on the stage apart from the family group, by the innuendoes of her tones, nevertheless the verbal tautness of her next speech so destroys the illusion of naturalism that the action of the play stops in its tracks and our image flutters madly till we readjust it:

> Thus with most careful devotion
> Thus with precise attention
> To detail, interfering preparation
> Of that which is already prepared
> Men tighten the knot of confusion
> Into perfect misunderstanding...

This is another alienation-effect. The faint hint of rhyme, the formality of the rhythms and the incantatory weight of the Latinisms after the looser, lighter colloquial manner of what preceded, take us out of this play into another. It is as if the 'exposition' is complete and the actors are fixed in time, and Agatha speaking in soliloquy—for she is addressing none other than the audience—gives us direct instructions for the interpretation of the narrow views we have heard. To the rhythm of the lines we see her move for the first time from her place apart, walking like a visitation round the statuesque group of the Chorus, gently and sadly accusing them on our behalf.

Then Agatha halts to address us with the emotive imagery by which the Women of Canterbury guided our feeling in *Murder in the Cathedral.* She accuses us of

> Neglecting all the admonitions
> From the world around the corner
> The wind's talk in the dry holly-tree
> The inclination of the moon
> The attraction of the dark passage
> The paw under the door.

Suddenly the flat abstractions have sprung alive to suggest sensuously the mysteries and the terror of living in time. Speaking together with expressionless faces and expressionless tones, the Chorus now voice the nightmare of their failure to understand:

Why do we feel embarrassed, impatient, fretful, ill at ease,
Assembled like amateur actors who have not been assigned their parts?...

This is a daring attempt by the author, risking indeed the 'titter in the dress circle', to mark out firmly the plane of the lesser mortals of the play, to make articulate their inarticulateness. It is designed to promote the irony of the contrast between those whose 'ordinary day isn't much more than breathing', like brother John's, and those who are 'living on several planes at once', like Harry. The Chorus has the traditional task of speaking the unspoken, saying what we might wish to say ourselves; they do not explain the past or anticipate the future or excite us emotionally at all; and they are different from most choruses in that they remain actors in the play who negatively enhance our sense of Harry's solitude and suffering, offer a social context for his martyrdom, and identify Wishwood as a place without a soul. As much as Harry, the family group of Ivy, Violet, Charles and Gerald are the subject of the play, since with every step towards illumination that Harry takes, the Chorus is cast into greater darkness. To the end their presence contributes to the play's meaning, and such tricks as this switch in the play's angle of vision intermittently reinforce the doubleness of the action throughout.

Eliot in his post-war plays is less anxious to break the continuity of his drama for the sake of securing the positive awareness of his audience; he encourages a more even and sometimes more convincing, certainly more naturalistic, performance. *The Family Reunion* suffered from a theatricalism which often distracted the spectator from the issues of the play; and Eliot could not in any case have repeated this play's kind of chorus. Yet his vision of a split between two worlds of sensibility continued to exercise his mind, and he continued in spite of himself to introduce ironies of interpretation. Unhappily, he could never make his prosaic people strong enough to withstand the imaginative assault of his more spiritual heroes and heroines; he seemed unable to grant them a philosophically justifiable and theatrically demonstrable value in their own right. In *The Cocktail Party*, a play which traces the translation of sinners into saints of greater or lesser degree, Celia Coplestone, Peter Quilpe and Edward and Lavinia Chamberlayne all begin the race together, each contributing equally to the inanity of the social whirl. Before long Celia has outstripped the rest of the field, and even in the last scene when she is dead, her unseen presence dwarfs the merely banal plodders. Like the action of *The Family Reunion*, that of *The Cocktail Party* 'ceases' with striking effect as Alex and Julia perform their ritual before Reilly their priest, suddenly showing us the roles of guardian they are playing, suggesting with a sudden, if not quite convincing, clarity that such people are moving among us as potential directors of our fate. But the play in its unbalance loses the ironies present in *The Family Reunion* since the Chamberlaynes are not granted the unnatural power of a chorus to accentuate their part.

The Confidential Clerk has the form of a superficial farce of recognitions in which a number of foundlings discover both their parentage and their true vocations, their past and their future. The farce provides a good deal of the repartee which might well belong to such drama. However, the play manages to evoke some serious overtones: most of the characters have two parts to play, one at the surface and one more thematically significant. Thus Lady Elizabeth, trivial follower of society cults, suggests also that she has a prophetic insight; her husband Sir Claude, the successful financier, when not making money seeks the inner satisfaction of making pottery; kind old Eggerton, the confidential clerk, when not on duty has also the ways of a guardian, showing Colby his spiritual vocation; Lucasta is the spoilt child, but she is also disillusioned with her empty world. Colby wanders among these people trying to find his destiny. But while in this play there is now almost no gap between the levels at which the characters play, since each embraces his doubleness within one personality, the quick tempo and improbable pattern of farce sorts ill with the sober themes of freedom and destiny, faith and understanding, and as a whole the play hardly avoids fragmentation. The two levels fail to govern the spectator's fleeting centrifugal impressions.

Like Coleridge's, Eliot's range of work is notably of a kind. Therefore it may be appropriate to call upon evidence of his thinking from a different context. In his seminal book *Notes*

Eliot's 'Doubleness'

Towards a Definition of Culture we may read this: 'Neither a classless society, nor a society of strict and impenetrable social barriers is good; each class should have constant additions and defections; the classes, while remaining distinct, should be able to mix freely; and they should all have a community of culture with each other which will give them something in common'.[1] The people of Eliot's drama have in a sense been moving towards another community of culture, one which seems to have thrown over the very additions and defections which he declared were essential to a vital society. Acknowledged distinctions between tones and attitudes were a source of real dramatic vigour in his earlier writing, which was then dramatically capable of bringing both tragic and comic life to his stage. Now the ironic pincer of contrasting planes of sensibility has relaxed its grip, and his tragicomic interest has finally slipped away. As we watch his latest play, *The Elder Statesman*, we are distinctly not involved. We sit like a smug audience of psychiatrists listening as their patient, Lord Claverton, strips himself of his illusions for purely clinical purposes.

BRECHT'S 'ALIENATION'

Modern morality plays from Brieux to Brecht must inevitably suffer from some of the pains of propaganda. Whether by devices of emotional persuasion on the one hand or of disguise by exaggeration or other comic method on the other, we are given a necessarily limited view which, however sane, can be unpalatable. When the preacher moves into the theatre, his play risks the gripes of sentimental over-persuasion, or the cynical over-exaggeration of the subject. An attack of moral righteousness brings out the characters in rashes of naked black or white, and otherwise healthy people are thrust into pro-

---

[1] T. S. Eliot, *op. cit.* (London, 1948), p. 50.

crustean sick-beds. However, it must be said that most good dramatists are preachers at heart, reinforcing their work by some preconceived moral pattern, though only the best know how to sink themselves and their lessons in living characters in a living play.

The play by which to date we shall remember the naturalistic but moralistic Arnold Wesker is one which survives the death-kiss of theatrical lecturing by an astonishingly virtuoso piece of dramatic trickery. *Roots* is a play in which the audience is alienated by villain and victims alike. It presents a raw, real and therefore largely unsympathetic family of simple country people whom Beatie, a daughter down from the metropolis, tries to educate into more liberal ways of thought. Through Beatie, of course, Wesker is intent upon educating the audience too. But, delightfully, it is made clear that all she has to say is really the second-hand, even ill-digested, tub-thumping of an unseen boy-friend Ronnie, who indeed deserts her before the lesson is done. Thus in pitying our teacher Beatie, despising the family who might otherwise have stood as pupils alongside us, the author has us drop all our defences.[1]

Bertolt Brecht's indefatigable pursuit of an effect of estrangement or alienation both in his playwriting and his producing was a calculated cover for his teaching, although it could be argued as a lifelong attempt at avoiding the responsibility of the greatest drama, which uses the theatrical medium to explore reality in humble communion with its audience. As a playwright he has been somewhat overrated, because his impulse to treat the sentimentality of his subjects with the

---

[1] Since this was written, J. Mander has published an interesting essay on *Roots* in *The Writer and Commitment* (London, 1961), in which he draws attention to this alienation-effect in the dialectic of the play. 'The play is swarming with ideas; but they are Ronnie's ideas, and the spectator is meant to take them with a large pinch of salt... by the end of the play we know for certain what we had suspected all along: Ronnie is a phoney. No playwright could do more to revitalize his own ideas, and to alienate the autobiographical element by the use of critical irony.... What is more, he can afford to let his audience laugh into the bargain, as Mr Osborne in *Look Back in Anger* cannot' (pp. 198–200).

comic eye of the estranger produced a series of plays having the rough edge which must increasingly appeal to a cynical generation. Brecht started writing in the atmosphere of a theatre purveying the early abstract expressionism of Georg Kaiser and Ernst Toller in the chaotic Germany of the 'twenties, an enthusiastic, revolutionary drama now almost forgotten. He ended by seeking every means of shaking off the crudities of its naïve sermonizing while still holding fast to an equally premeditated moral purpose.

The advance of the 'epic' theatre over the romantic expressionist theatre appeared first in its particularity: he put characters on the stage with recognizably firm physical and sometimes psychological individuality. He tried to give his subjects the concrete reality of ordinary life, in the rough justice of the underworld in *The Threepenny Opera*, the suffering of the oppressed in *The Private Life of the Master Race*, the detailed business of keeping body and soul together in *Mother Courage and her Children*, the broad hypocrisy of people in *The Good Woman of Setzuan*, the simple compassion of a woman for a child in *The Caucasian Chalk Circle*. Enough drama, one might say, for any playwright. But in spite of their subjects' naturalistic elements, all these plays display in the strongest terms the symbolic fight of the individual in an alien society, sometimes protesting, sometimes acquiescing, but always dramatically purposeful. In spite of their refreshing particularity, the plays are too simple in conception to conceal their Marxist tendency towards didacticism.

What must chiefly interest us here are the forms his dialectics took. They were not the give-and-take of contrasting attitudes with which Shaw efficiently cloaked his preaching. Nevertheless, as Brecht, like Shaw, repeated at length, his drama was designed to unsettle the composure of an audience. Didacticism under a mask of alienation was part of his idea of the theatre's purpose, and the implied paradox in this contradiction is the puzzle of Brechtian theatre. Arguments which surround a play like *Mother Courage* are a natural consequence of the mixture. Mother Courage is a tough but pathetic old woman who lives through the havoc of the Thirty Years War. The conduct of her life is relevant to the practice of war generally: she steals, lies, makes a profit out of scarcity, is indeed carried along on the tide of the misery of others. At the best, one would think, she could be a grotesque character of comedy; at the worst, a painful object lesson in vice. She is something of both, but this is only the beginning of her complexity. Brecht's intention is to show us war through the frame provided by one individual life; yet the audience's desire to see both its terror and its pity in the end defeats all attempts by the actress wholly to alienate the part and have us judge for ourselves.

In Eric Bentley's account of an alienated production of this play by Brecht in Berlin, this reliable witness and confessed admirer of the author's talent demonstrates that 'alienation is an instance of the principle: *reculer pour mieux sauter*',[1] and in *Mother Courage* he suggests that it actually adds to the emotional content of the drama. Thus while Mother Courage's poor dumb daughter Katrin privately dresses herself up in a camp-follower's gaudy clothes, thereby expressing a pathetic wish to live in greater luxury than her spare existence will ever allow, the Dutch cook sings lustily, 'A mighty fortress is our God', and what starts as a joke 'gradually reinforces the pathos it begins by checking'. Ronald Gray adds further testimony to this: 'do what Brecht might, he could not rewrite the tragic scene, in which [Mother Courage] loses her son Swisscheese, in such a way as to destroy all sympathy for her in her grief'.[2] She leaves the play with the song which she

[1] E. R. Bentley, *In Search of Theater* (London, 1954), p. 154.
[2] R. Gray, *Brecht* (London, 1961), p. 100.

sang when she made her first entrance; but to avoid the sentimentality of such an ending, harsh military music is simultaneously brought in to drown the singing and neutralize the pathos. Yet, as Bentley says, 'Brecht also succeeds in enriching the drama of the scene. It becomes more moving.' A parallel effect is to be found at the end of O'Casey's *Juno and the Paycock*, where Juno's poetic prayer is coldly contradicted by the coarse drunken singing of Joxer and Boyle. The misunderstandings about dark comedy are the likely consequence of such counterpoint in performance.

Brecht was anxious that the techniques of the epic theatre should suppress the natural wish of the audience to identify itself with a serious character, without the need for comic distortion. Identification will prevent the audience from thinking. The suffering of the character is to move the spectator, but he is to remain free to laugh about those who weep on the stage, and weep about those who laugh.[1] But his theory bore little relation to his practice, for Brecht was fighting a losing battle against the irrepressible impulse towards shared feeling. The social situations he chose and the characters he placed in them were frequently equivocal enough to lend themselves to the tragicomic response. The contrapuntal structure of the drama encouraged both affection for Macheath the philanderer defying the law and repugnance for Macheath the thief and parody of capitalism; it encouraged both repugnance for Galileo the social coward and affection for Galileo the man. Alienation as a production method, like the comic 'relief' in Shakespearian tragedy, served to intensify rather than to weaken any incipient emotionality in such equivocations and it increased such ironic tensions as the plays possessed. As well as being an object lesson, Mother Courage can be a comedy or a tragedy queen; she is all these. Martin Esslin, a recent critical

[1] See Brecht, 'Vergnügungstheater oder Lehrtheater' (1936), *Schriften zum Theater*, p. 64, quoted in M. Esslin, *Brecht: a Choice of Evils* (London, 1959), p. 115.

biographer of Brecht, sums up the position in these words: 'He sought to spread the cold light of logical clarity—and produced a rich texture of poetic ambiguity.'[1]

The truth is that whatever tricks of an anti-illusory nature were employed by the Berliner Ensemble in the performance of Brecht's plays, illusion rapidly reasserts itself. The bare white stage set only with the paraphernalia of skeleton backstage properties, and with film projections and lantern slides and so forth, is quickly forgotten. The actors in merely 'pretending to be' rather than actually 'being' their characters may even wear masks, as some of his caricatures did, but the convention is soon assimilated, as it was in the days of Aristophanes and of the *commedia dell'arte*. Direct address to the audience with interpolations of song and narrative will startle at first, but the audience will quickly adjust itself to each break in continuity until it can be surprised no longer. In spite of everything, the flexibility of a willing spectator's imagination in conditions of theatre resists the naked exposure of actuality. The dream world of illusory theatre develops and proceeds as before, and pathetic overtones inevitably arise wherever there is a hint of sentiment. Even though the narrative drama is not troubled by the need to create suspense, Brecht supplies enough thrills and tension in one play to satisfy any average melodramatist of the last century. The real novelty, if it is novelty, of Brechtian theatre lies elsewhere—in its episodic structure.

If a pattern of alienation effects in the structure of his later plays did not produce the results he intended—later characters like little Shen Te, the good-hearted prostitute in *The Good Woman of Setzuan* (for all that her benevolence is denied by her other self in the person of Shui Ta), and like Grusche, the selfless servant-girl in *The Caucasian Chalk Circle*, could hardly fail to gain the sympathy of their audiences, and even

---

[1] M. Esslin, *ibid.* p. 236.

equivocal characters like Galileo and the rogue Azdak strongly invited it—we can recognize in these plays the kind of counterpoint and ambiguity which grows familiar as the drama of the century develops. The openwork episodic shaping of epic drama permitted rare logistic juxtapositions and sharp comic contradictions. The pretty philanthropist Shen Te is dependent on her ruthless racketeer and profiteer double Shui Ta. The Gods who praise Shen Te for her good deeds desert her in her poverty and despair, and comically take their leave for heaven. Grusche's painful journey over the mountains is related in a cold voice and in the past tense by the Story Teller, and this is followed by the cruel farce of her reception by the peasants, as we saw. For the sake of the pathetic fatherless child, pathetic Grusche is comically wedded to a man she thinks moribund ('The son of that peasant woman is just going to die. Isn't it wonderful?'), but he is quick to rise from his deathbed when he hears the war is over. This hilarious scene is cut short in turn by her unhappy realization that she is now irrevocably married to a man she does not love and that her true lover is on his way to her.

Thus farce and melodrama succeed each other unpredictably. The epic construction offers a place for mime and a place for argument, lends itself to bursts of feeling and to the irreverences of comedy and a parody which 'mocks and imitates at one and the same moment'.[1] If the didacticism has not troubled us too much, the dialectical mixture of impressions can be immensely stimulating.

ANOUILH

Jean Anouilh is well in the running to be the natural successor to Pirandello. He touches here and there on the grim game of mask and face—we remember Général St Pé in *The Waltz of the Toreadors*, the Mother and her lover Vincent in *Point of*

[1] M. Esslin, *ibid*. p. 222.

Departure[1] and many others—do not all his old roués wear their masks uncertainly, if rakishly? He reverts to questioning our need to accept reality—Anouilh's *Traveller without Luggage* prefers not to regain his memory, and Gaston's situation derives directly from plays like Pirandello's *Henry IV* and *As You Desire Me*. The dream world of the Prince in *Time Remembered* and of Georges in *Dinner with the Family* (Act I in this is all Pirandello) is set in direct opposition to the humbler, if not seedy, truth. By the superimposition of *marivaudage* on the dialogue of *The Rehearsal* and in the last act of *Colombe* which takes us 'behind the scenes', Anouilh even seems to adopt a little of Pirandello's theatrical trickery from *Each in His Own Way* and *Six Characters* to suggest the relative fiction of human behaviour.

Having said this, one must acknowledge that Pirandello brings more weight to bear on his plays and pursues his arguments to remorseless conclusions, though Anouilh's lighter touch and apparent cynicism often tend to conceal an equally committed interest in problems of truth and reality. This kind of dramatic echoing is fairly common in these days of international theatre, and the differences between the Italian and the Frenchman are of more importance than their likenesses.

Pirandello repeatedly contrives an inversion of the mental image we derive from the play, deliberately disrupting its stability. Anouilh selects a contraposition from which we are to view his subject, necessarily upsetting our mood. Pirandello has us pirouette dizzily, where Anouilh has us leap acrobatically from one position to the next. Again and again his *pièces noires*, his *pièces brillantes* and his *pièces grinçantes* (respectively 'black', 'sparkling' and 'grating' plays) are just saved from melodrama by his throwing a harsh ironic light

---

[1] The titles of Anouilh's English versions have been used where they are likely to be more familiar to the reader.

on to an unsophisticated pathos. In *Point of Departure* he demonstrated how an over-simple love story between two young people could be made unstable by calculated counter-point, not like the simplicity of the love of Othello and Desdemona subverted by conscious evil in the person of Iago, but by introducing the callous insensibility and the corrupt but comic attitudes of Eurydice's mother and her lover, by the outrageous memories of the hotel waiter under whose eye the lovers spend a night in Marseilles, by the pressure of the past on the future. In *Ardèle*, the characters revolve in cynical circles round a woman whose spirit is by implication pure; a paradoxical edge is lent to the drama whenever we are re-minded that her body is twisted as their minds are twisted. Colombe the dove is caught in the net of unfeeling society, but her tragedy, like that of Général St Pé in *The Waltz of the Toreadors*, is presented to us in terms of the rudest farce. We may suspect at times that the farcical interpolations are intro-duced a little easily, and this is especially true of the uproarious troubles of the Général with his mistress and the grotesque intrusions of his wife in the last-named play.

In his progress from the 1930's to the 1950's, Anouilh has, by trial and error, transmuted his private anger to the public elements we now expect to find in his particular theatrical concoction. He has done this often with more of a nimble insight into what the theatre can carry, and how an audience can be manipulated, than his predecessor. His 'sense of theatre' may keep him on the boards when Pirandello is read only in books. This is a dangerous criterion in itself, of course, and Anouilh's constant risk is that his own developed technique will become 'well-made' in the service of the *boulevard* theatre.

Like Pirandello, he usually found it necessary to invent a 'fairy-tale' world of make-believe in order to win our consent to his ideas, and to lend him freedom to arrange them in a way that would make nonsense of them in a naturalistic convention.

Counterpoint and Hysteria

His frequent choice of the twilight 1910's for his style and setting, even his occasionally facile resort to Greek myth, may lie in his wish to 'play with his characters, with their passions and their actions'. As he explains, 'to "play" with a subject is to create a new world of conventions and surround it with spells and a magic all your own...',[1] and he does this with more obvious theatricality than Pirandello. His early *pièces roses* ('pink' plays) are unmistakably of the genre of artificial comedy. *Thieves' Carnival* is launched with this kind of bold, if somewhat cheap and easy, flourish:

HECTOR (*passionately*). I want to inhale the perfume of your hand! (*He bends over Eva's hand, and surreptitiously draws a jeweller's eyeglass from his pocket to take a closer look at her rings...*)

EVA. Till tonight. (*She goes.*)

HECTOR (*weak at the knees*). My beloved...(*He follows her out of sight, then comes downstage again, putting away his eyeglass, and mutters with icy self-possession.*) A good two hundred thousand. And not a flaw in the lot.

There can be no mistaking the nature of the play that is to follow, any more than we can miss the opening note of *Twelfth Night*,

> If music be the food of love, play on....

or of Wycherley's *The Gentleman Dancing Master*:

> To confine a woman just in her rambling age!

Anouilh will refer again and again to this flighty, frivolous manner, but usually when he is about to make a particularly poisonous statement or compel his audience to undergo a particularly gruesome experience. It may appear as a comic character with a sinister charge, like Général St Pé's harridan of a wife, or Robinet, Desfournettes and du Bartas in *Colombe*; as an acrid comment on the scene, like the presence of Toto and Marie-Christine in *Ardèle*; or as an hilarious situation,

[1] Quoted in E. O. Marsh, *Jean Anouilh, Poet of Pierrot and Pantaloon* (London, 1953), p. 189.

like the midnight meanderings in the same play, or the tearing of the money in *Ring Round the Moon*.

Remarkably, Anouilh saw a profit in keeping the same light touch for certain moments in his *pièces noires*. Notably in *Point of Departure*, he employs an admixture of farce as a glittering foil for his pathos. The same ironic edge will not be missed where the gentility of Florent's way of life is balanced with a revolting and ridiculous father for Thérèse in his earlier play *Restless Heart*; nor in the lazy drifter of a father and the mocking brother Lucien granted to Julia in his later *Fading Mansions*. In these back-handed Cinderella stories Anouilh is feeling towards the peculiarly mettlesome mixture of his post-war plays. There is to be more sugar-coating on the pill and more iron at the centre, so that, once in the mouth, the flavour is to taste all the more putrid. The contrasts between single characters or groups are not gentle like Chekhov's but more obvious and acute.

A brief example at the tail-end of *Point of Departure* will indicate the singular tone the comic element produces in these earlier plays. Heavily charged emotionally—we should say 'over-charged' if it were not for the refining action of the irony—the final scene shows its hero Orpheus as youth in deep despair: his Eurydice has been killed in an accident. He is being goaded by M. Henri, the death figure, to the suicide which will reunite them. The weight of the play is behind this scene, and the mood of the audience is wholly sober. With a striking ingenuity, Orpheus's feelings are explored and exposed by their contradiction, and their meaning communicated in the main by Orpheus's father. The father, speaking now selfishly, now sensually, now rhetorically, his words empty of any understanding of his son's condition, is given the part of counsellor for life's defence. He is all clown:

FATHER. ...the man who is talking to you has suffered. Drunk life to the very lees. He often kept silent, bit his lips till the blood flowed, to stifle his moans. His companions of the festive board little dreamed the torture he sometimes bore....Betrayal, scorn, injustice....You sometimes wonder why my back is bent and my hair prematurely white. If you but knew how heavily life lies on a man's shoulders.

(*He pulls at the cigar without success, looks vexed and flings it away with a sigh. M. Henri goes up to him and holds out his cigar-case.*)

M. HENRI. Another cigar?

FATHER. Thank you....

The clichés he uses mark him down as hollow and fit only for derisory laughter. His lachrymose self-portrait as white-haired age stooped by the troubles of an unjust world cannot be taken seriously, since we see him thoroughly enjoying himself smoking someone else's cigars and revelling in the opportunity to make a confessional speech. His hypocrisy makes us laugh, but also throws us angrily into sympathy with the silent Orpheus, and when, rightly or wrongly, the latter accepts death's proposal, we feel we know more precisely his state of mind. When we talk of Anouilh's sense of theatre, we partly have in mind that he knows the exact quantity of salt to rub in the wound.

The *pièces brillantes* and *grinçantes* he has offered us since the War hold within them the ideas of his earlier plays, and exploit the techniques of *rose* and *noir* in unique conjunction. In *Ardèle, Colombe, The Waltz of the Toreadors* and *L'Hurluberlu* in particular, he calls on the artificial world of his lighter comedies to give himself the greater freedom for irreverence; the angry protest against the cruelty of existence of his 'tragedies' remains to provide his dramatic impetus. The farcical and the pathetic are counterpointed in perfect balance, a balance so pleasing that one suspects that Anouilh has reached the limit this form will allow him.

The blackness of the black plays, whose passionate, idealistic attack on man's animalism and hypocrisy inclined too easily to sentimentality and melodrama and often to the simple romantic and irresponsible negation of life, has been relieved. Anouilh now makes his apologists of idealism blatant hypocrites like Orpheus's father and the grotesque Mme Alexandra of *Colombe*:

MME ALEXANDRA. It's very profound! But don't you think it's a little hard, dear poet?

ROBINET. It's hard, but it's the truth, dear lady. And it's our duty to be hard. We mustn't hide the truth, never....

MME ALEXANDRA. Dear poet, that's blasphemy!...I believe only in the ideal! I want to sound a great clarion call. I want to show them my faith in self-denial, in youth, in all that is fine and beautiful in love!

The cold douche of farce is offered as a prophylactic against the inadequately objective view, and claims our more active and intelligent participation. The violence of the farce combined with the sensationalism of its subjects may not leave us with the warm, smouldering glow we experience with Chekhovian comedy, but it leaves us burning and crackling merrily.

ANALYSIS: TRAGICOMIC COUNTERPOINT IN 'ARDÈLE' AND 'COLOMBE'

'Ardèle': interactions

Ardèle and *Colombe* are chosen in order to investigate the effect of the later Anouilh on his audience. The first, once likened by Roy Walker to a 'grotesque quadrille of amatory partners', is at pains to establish its fantasy in a variety of ways. The excessive number of its lovers, with the jigsaw plotting that must result if the play is not to collapse, should lower our naturalistic defences. Its element of social high comedy, found in the persons of the Countess, her husband and her lover, suit admirably with its mellowed period, '1912 or thereabouts'. Its free sprinkling of typed characters with their raw language and wild situations of a lower tradition, in the old Général with his scarecrow hag of a wife Emily and his

Counterpoint and Hysteria

'ripe, juicy peach' of a chamber-maid, in the Count's relationship with his 'monkey darling', his 'little dove', his 'lambkin' of a little sempstress, are disarming. The increasingly funny echo of the Général's Christian name Léon by the cry of the peacock in the garden, with its strident sound adding at the same time an overtone of horror, and the mounting incongruity of the two imps Toto and Marie-Christine, children who eavesdrop at the inappropriate times and shockingly ape the adults, are at first in the lightest vein. In this jumble of theatrical conventions, we may not be surprised that, as the pivot of the play, Anouilh has supplied *two* hunchbacks as true lovers: this is just beyond the bounds of credibility, and we are to be forgiven if we realize too late that we should not have laughed. But there are yet another pair, Nicholas and his elder brother's wife Nathalie, to convey to us the sense of guilt: they, like Ardèle and her lover, play in the manner of the realistic *drame*.

Clearly this is a play that at every performance is in danger of fragmentation, and it represents Anouilh's most daring experiment in testing the possibilities of the stage and juggling with our responses. Its success rests upon the extent to which the variety of characters, the ill-assorted styles of making love, and the mixture of realistic and farcical manners of writing are related. The statement of the play is to emerge by the contrasts between the characters, the interactions of its parts, and the revolutions of feeling we sustain. As in all of Anouilh's plays, at its core is a bare simplicity—that those we think of as tainted may in fact be pure—but the author turns all his energy towards shocking us into a full recognition of his platitude. Amid the ludicrous decorums of the Countess, the clowning of the Count and 'fishlike' Villardieu, the bedroom titters and the groping in the dark, Nicholas and Ardèle are struggling tragically for a dignity among the undignified. Nicholas may have failed, but Ardèle may well have succeeded, for she, the unseen player, measures them all: 'Aunt Ardèle is Love.'[1]

Before the amazing transitions of feeling of the last act, we make a series of comparisons between one character and another, and between one set of standards and another.

Age is judged by youth, and experience by innocence. The Général is fighting a losing battle against senility and sterility, and he knows it; he declares he is like an old tree: '...I blossom every spring. It's a fine show, but the trunk, alas, is hollow.' He fears the unspoken comment of Nathalie his daughter-in-law, a girl of twenty:

NATHALIE. It is not for me to judge you.
GENERAL. And yet I feel you are in some way my appointed judge. The Lord knows why.

Yet Nathalie, the accuser, is not innocent herself, and later she tells her lover that she is afraid that someone will suddenly call her name as Emily calls her peacock husband. They have a lesson for each other. Even Toto his youngest son, aged ten, criticizes him by echoing in his squeaky voice his blandishments to the maid. When Ardèle, an elder sister and a hunchback to boot, sends him a message by the Count that he revolts her, the Général cannot understand it: 'Ha, that's good! That's very good! She is in love with a hunchback, and it's me she finds revolting!' Though he cannot understand, we can. In the chain of relative values Anouilh is constructing, the old man, for all our laughter and all our sympathy, is at the earthy end of it.

The Countess philanders with her lover while at the same time she is madly jealous of her husband's attentions to his mock-suicidal mistress down in the village. In her turn she comes under fire when she rashly offers Ardèle her advice from her familiarity with the world's ways: '...I am younger than you are, but I know so much more about life. Will you

[1] Trans. L. Hill (London, 1951).

let me give you some advice? (*She listens a moment at Ardèle's door, then straightens, tight-lipped with fury*). Ardèle, how dare you!' And the Countess utters the remark which Anouilh has been working to have us ask and answer ourselves: 'What can she possibly know of love?'

Nicholas and Nathalie, the adulterers, are the last to be weighed in these treacherous scales. Unlike Ardèle's other critics, Nicholas allies himself with her, and sees in her defiance of social convention the enactment of his own extremity: 'Aunt Ardèle! It's Nicholas. Stand firm! Laugh at the world! Laugh at what they are pleased to call scandal! Love whom you want to love, and don't listen to them! If they didn't tell you you were deformed and too old, they'd say you were too young...' He is pleading his own cause, but ironically he is incapable of seeing that his position is not Ardèle's, for the kind and quality of his love is inferior, as in the issue it will appear.

These dramatic logistics are, like Pirandello's, expertly organized, but they are insufficient in themselves to urge upon us a strong and committed passion. This is to be done by the shifts in convention and style, in tone and feeling, that he brings about at the crisis.

'*Ardèle*': modulations

If we are right in supposing that in this play Anouilh has perfected his device of counterpointing pathos and comedy, then in his last act it is we who are to be probed and tested by our see-saw reactions to his effects. In this act he shows his instinct to be essentially Pirandellian. We may trace briefly its sequence of dramatic styles and its transitions of feeling.

The act opens with a mimetic summary of most of the relationships expounded in the previous two acts, with Toto, the precocious child, as apparent puppet-master. His appearance on the gallery which serves the bedrooms causes

Nicholas, seeking a midnight rendezvous with Nathalie, to hide. Toto makes sure that the Général is safely in bed, then tiptoes back to his room 'laden with hats, walking-sticks, furs and coats', all the paraphernalia of dressing up, tokens of the adult world. The Count, soaked through in spite of his rain-coat, his straw boater and his umbrella, enters stealthily from the garden and prepares to escape to his room, but in the light of the bronze Cupid, which stands symbolically at the foot of the stairs, his wife sees him. All the elements of this furtive activity in the night are those of horse opera. Comic characters in a ridiculous situation make themselves more ridiculous, and we respond at the lowest level of appreciation.

The short exchange between the Countess and the Count which follows raises this level by a fraction only. The Countess veers between sarcasm and a false sympathy in order to discover what her husband has been doing. When this fails, she strikes another pose, and addresses him with the coy and winning tone that has in the past presumably subdued Villardieu: 'Gaston, had you noticed that we had virtually stopped speaking to each other? I have felt for so long the need of a quiet talk with you.' As she smoothes out the phrases and proposes a clandestine meeting in a teashop or the station, we are, as earlier, reminded how ludicrous it is that a wife should need to speak like this to her husband, and that the remote conventions of the artificial *ménage à trois* call for the derisory laughter of the comedy of manners:

COUNT. ...Think of Marie-Christine. You have no right to risk a scandal....

The Countess's coquetry, the Count's scandalized strictures, their exaggerated guilt, the absurd earnestness of their argu-ment, are all in the strongest tradition of the Molière of farce, rather than of Marivaux and de Musset. Then an angry Villardieu appears, and the Countess with a startled cry runs into her room. When this is capped by the appearance of Ada

the maid in her nightgown on her way upstairs to the
Général's study where the old man immediately follows her,
we are truly back to the tone of bedroom farce of the scene's
opening.

Only for a brief interval. A very sober Nathalie now descends to Nicholas the romantic idealist, and with her first
words the mood has changed:

NICHOLAS (*in a whisper*). . . .You are here—at last.
NATHALIE. Yes, my darling.

At first we may be inclined to respond to this as we do to the
Count and Countess, or to the Général and Ada, but we are
quickly corrected. Nicholas's dark comment: 'You are my
brother's wife!' is spoken in a tone which must modify our
attitude. A deep pathos, passionate and bitter, rapidly
discolours their interview.

In contrast to what has gone before, the latest manner is
wholly realistic. This is suggested by the solemn tones, the
limping tempo, and the new note of uncompromising criticism:
'They are ugly, all of them.' Nathalie's confession of her
reasons for marrying Nicholas's brother Maxim is sincere and
earnest, and this love duet, unlike the others, is forlorn,
humiliating and hopeless: fate has laid none too light a hand
on this relationship. The dry ironies grow stronger as the pace
increases and as Nathalie feels their love to be as 'ugly and
horrible' as Ardèle's: she confesses to having abandoned
herself to Maxim in spite of her hate for him. The change in
her reflects our own response when we see Ardèle's lover
('the hesitant figure of a man, misshapen, wrapped in a big
hooded cloak') seek and enter her room. The farce is submerged in disgust, and we are once more 'guilty creatures
sitting at a play'. To clinch the effect, the terrifying figure of
Emily the Général's wife emerges shrieking his name. She and
Nathalie might be the same woman, having the same distaste for physical sex, at different stages of its obsession. A

moment of sheer sensation brings to its crisis this sequence of incongruities.

The seriousness of the scene between Nicholas and Nathalie is soon modified. All the contrasts are embodied as the whole company from the ludicrous Général to his grotesque wife fills the stage. Even the peacock joins in. We are whirled back to the fantasy in which the scene was conceived, and we are near to laughter again. Only Aunt Ardèle and her lover are absent.

Two shots interrupt Emily's extended hysterical accusations against her husband. In a second, the whole fantastic fretwork has been collapsed by this simple symbol of tragic reality: Ardèle and her lover have shot themselves. In this highly contrived context, these shots wake us as after a dream: a realistic death is shocking in fantasy, and here we are brutally assaulted: but only to be asked to laugh again by the crazy efforts of the Count, the Général and Villardieu to break down Ardèle's door: 'this must almost be a clown act'. In fact, we cannot laugh. Yet their stupidity, their lack of human compassion, is firmly transmitted by having the reality condemn their behaviour as a mockery.

Nathalie and Nicholas are alone again, now our spokesmen: 'You see, we don't even have to kill ourselves now. These two who were made for the world's laughter, they have done it for us.' The former prisoners, the hunchback lovers, have become the arbiters in this trial of sexual relationships. Incongruously they set the only standard of perfection, and we have been forced to accept it. We, the former judges, have been convicted in our own court. Having thus confounded us, Anouilh brings down his curtain in a mood of absolute mockery. 'Two grotesque little dwarfs', Toto and Marie-Christine dressed in adult clothes, mimic the game of sex we have been analysing emotionally. They telescope the love–hate quarrels of their elders, and the inherent pathos of the subject is finally shown as a monstrous burlesque. Anouilh ends his play with the Pirandellian mixture of the spit and the guffaw that brings the curtain down on *Right You Are If You Think So*.

This play has added interest for us because of its introduction of symbolism into an already crowded image, and this symbolism turns on the invisible presence of Ardèle. She is the only positive character in the play, but she is never produced for examination and she is defined only by the negation of the characters we do see. In this the play worries us rather like a sermon: for it is easier and stronger for a dramatist to speak a negative 'don't be like this' than a positive 'do be like that'. Anouilh knows that sinners are more exciting than saints. By hiding Ardèle away he deftly avoids the danger of making his symbol unreal and uninteresting or of having to make her too real and therefore unsymbolic. He avoids putting pure virtue on the stage, because he knows that goodness tends to be seen as priggishness, and this is a risk to his theme too great to run. Perhaps he guessed that her spiritual beauty might be marred by showing her deformity. He knows his audience well enough to lock the lovers in the room, hint at the romance of an elopement and then, as a romantic if not symbolic reinforcement, shoot them in adversity.

'Colombe': preparation as hoax

A short exegesis of *Colombe* will demonstrate the outrageous extent to which Anouilh will go to find a symbolic pattern for his view of life. For *The Rehearsal*, the play which followed *Ardèle*, he hit upon the formula of presenting his subject as if it were set in the tinsel world of Marivaux: its characters rehearse their parts for *La Double inconstance* at the opening of the play, and their situation is deliberately confused with the plotting of the play-within-the-play. Anouilh made an essay at this kind of device in *Dinner with the Family*, where a hired actor and actress play-act the parts of Georges's idealized mother and father to mark the difference between wish and actuality. In *Point of Departure* four years later, Lucienne and Vincent are again provincial actors, and when they find themselves automatically speaking about their love in lines from de Musset's *On ne badine pas avec l'amour*, it is strikingly suggested that their attitude is a second-hand rhetorical gesture. In all these plays, the theatrical climate is illusory and bogus.

The young girl Colombe is absorbed by the sham *fin de siècle* magic of the theatre: its atmosphere of extravagant melodrama, inducing the amoral behaviour of romantic fiction, at once corrupts her, embarrasses us with laughter, and provides an extreme contrast to unromantic reality. In the person of the doyenne Mme Alexandra we see the gay, tyrannical hypocrisy of middle age and the degradation of worldly success to which Colombe may descend: Mme Alexandra is the Colombe who will be. In the settings, back-stage and on-stage, we see where the two realms of fact and fiction overlap: in the last act Colombe's story is even played out in crude terms by her counterpart Mme Alexandra. At the same time the fantasy of theatrical life gives the author that margin of licence to paint certain of his characters with his former glaring colours of grotesquerie.

The characters of the lovers in *Colombe* are thin and, by comparison with that of *Ardèle*, the plot is thin too. A stern and idealistic young man, Julien, marries Colombe, a pretty flower-girl. When he goes into the army, she is left with his actress mother, and Colombe in her turn goes on the stage. When Julien returns, he discovers to his horror that his Colombe is no longer the sad Cinderella, the little dove, he left behind. That is all. But from what we know already of Anouilh, his plot is the merest peg on which to hang a multi-coloured coat, and the exposition and tracing of the theme, the mixing of the audience's feelings, and the form of their development, give the play its values. The trite becomes novel because the process is novel.

The theme is simply stated early in the play:

JULIEN. The world's a much harder place than you believe.
COLOMBE. I know.
JULIEN. I want you to...to try to grow up a little, and take life more seriously.
COLOMBE. Yes.
JULIEN. If you don't, you'll become one of Mother's kind of people: never happy without pleasures.
COLOMBE. I know. You've explained it before.
JULIEN. It's the world of pleasures you'll see now. It'll all seem so new, so dazzling—
COLOMBE. Yes.
JULIEN. But it's all false, my darling—you must realize that.
COLOMBE. Yes, I'm sure.[1]

So she counters his warnings of evil with a giggle, '*à un petit rire*'. This contest between respectable principle and primitive simplicity is enacted through the play. Interestingly, even here the author is misleading us: we must rethink the moral position from the start. Julien sounds priggish and prudish in our ears, and we react against the Puritan and in sympathy with the natural girl. Yet it is this girl who, in tormenting Julien, is to torment us when we try to fix her in the kaleidoscopic pattern.

Mme Alexandra, who 'can never attend to family matters unless she's playing a mother at night', initiates the device for the restatement of the theme. She is presented as a brilliant planet round whom all others are satellites. At her first entrance she flashes across the stage followed by a little host of attendants, and after one curt remark is gone again. We greet her with the laughter which dissociates us from her

---

[1] This is not from a translation, but from a 'version' of the original, done by Denis Cannan (London, 1952). There are no substantial differences of intention in the excerpts quoted.

florid attitude to life and does not allow us to take her seriously. We listen to her artistic pretences as she makes suitable noises for the approval of Robinet's new play, but it is transparent that she is all *poseuse* and utterly self-centred:

ROBINET. I will begin: 'O moon so wan, my heart's chill friend in death—'
MME ALEXANDRA. Superb! Beautiful beyond belief. 'My heart's chill friend in death.' I know exactly how I shall say it. (*She has never stopped looking at herself in the mirror. Suddenly she shouts.*) Lucien!
HAIRDRESSER. Madame?
MME ALEXANDRA. Look at this! You've made me look like a poodle....

This little episode visually confirms the earlier suggestion of the theme, but the line of our response remains uncertain as we struggle to assess the woman. Her flamboyance is disarming, but although we are as innocent in the theatre as Colombe herself, we no longer accept it uncritically as wide-eyed Colombe is doing. When Colombe appears at the end of Act I beautifully dressed by the personal care and attention of Julien's brother Paul (Armand in the original), 'bejewelled, transformed' and 'forgetting everything in her ecstasy at the glory of her reflection', our identity with Cinderella is not so strong, and our sympathy for the husband, helpless before her innocent enthusiasm, is growing:

COLOMBE. Oh, Julien—is it me? Is it me?
JULIEN. Is it my wife? Colombe, I don't know any more....

'*Colombe*': counterpoint and violence

Anouilh can mount his hobby-horse from either side. Having slyly misdirected our judgment, he has us pursue the tragicomedy of life by tossing us freely between Julien and Colombe, the rivals for our affection. Julien is the deserving poor, but such an unpleasant young man. Colombe holds the glittering riches, but we are never sure that her apparently naïve cruelty is not calculated. The evidence is not presented forensically as pro and con, but sensationally as ruthless pathos mingled with beguiling farce. The comic balance is ours to assert, if we can.

In the second act, the kaleidoscope begins to revolve. The farcical note is struck resoundingly by the ludicrous flirting of Lagarde, an actor (du Bartas in the original). With a 'wide-brimmed hat, an elegant cane, a flower in his button-hole', he is as affected as Mme Alexandra. The ridiculous is drained to the dregs by the stylized repetition of Lagarde's formula for the seduction of Colombe, 'a drop of port, nibble a biscuit' after rehearsal—which is echoed by Desfournettes the manager and Robinet the '*poète*'. Colombe accepts these approaches so lightly that we can only place her in fairyland and refuse to admit evil of her. We are reminded of Lamb's comment on the comedy of the Restoration: he

could never connect those sports of a witty fancy in any shape with any result to be drawn from them to imitation in real life. They are a world of themselves almost as much as fairyland....They seem engaged in their proper element. They break through no laws, or conscientious restraints. They know of none....It is altogether a speculative scene of things, which has no reference whatever to the world that is.[1]

This scene concludes with an exchange with Paul, during which Colombe shows herself to be an accomplished actress:

PAUL. ...when we come to rehearse the scene of farewell, will you really feel unhappy?

COLOMBE. Not really. But the tears will come into my eyes just as if it were life.

We are sober again, wondering indeed whether it is not Colombe who is seducing Paul. We are ready to apply our normal standards of judgment when Paul offers us his estimate of her at the curtain: 'You devil. You dirty little devil....'

The procedure has been first to set her at a distance, deceiving us with all the patter of the conjuror, then gently to

[1] Lamb, 'On the Artificial Comedy of the Last Century' (1823).

bring her nearer for closer inspection. Now on guard, we see Colombe through the passionate eyes of her husband who has returned. The switches in style alternate more rapidly, now that by the use of Julien our eye is hard on the object. With Julien predisposed to jealousy, the third scene[1] at its beginning quickly evokes pathos, and the reunion between Julien and Colombe is presented sentimentally. Out of context, this episode would be cloying, since Anouilh goes as far as he dares in lubricating our tender emotions; in context, Colombe remains on trial, and we, like Julien, are torn between submission and revolt.

It is a stroke of pure theatre when Anouilh follows this uncertain mawkishness with a repetition of the bizarre farce that characterized the previous scene. Lagarde, Desfournettes and Robinet appear once more in succession, each with a new excess of seductive prattle: 'Are you there, my little puss-puss?'...'Are you there, my little mousey?'...'Are you there, my little wolfie?' They are cut short only by the presence of the husband. Their comic appearance in a situation of traditional farce makes laughter again irresistible, and even Julien's justifiable anger must to a degree become risible, since he has automatically fallen into place in the pattern of the conventional triangle. He is the traditional cuckold, fit only for further scorn as his temper grows warmer. This farcical mood is increased by the particular stage arrangement devised for the scene: the stage is divided between Colombe's dressing-room and the back-stage passage, so that while Colombe is being interrogated, a silent, gesticulating group of buffoons eavesdrop outside her door.

In the issue, one cannot be sure that this effect comes off. For Julien is still at times the cold, realistic centre of the action that develops, and as he and we attempt to ascertain whether or not Colombe is a little cheat, his new tone of

---

[1] Act II, sc. ii in Cannan; Act III in the original.

disgust, a tone wholly inappropriate to farcical comedy, spreads through the theatre. Our attempt to reconcile this with the unassimilated pantomime in the back-stage passage demands an effort which is untenable. Anouilh resolves the position with a device which reproduces the effect of the pistol shots in *Ardèle*:

> JULIEN (*striking her suddenly across the face*). You whore! You grubby little whore like all the rest!...

That blow and that word, shockingly of the real world, bring to an abrupt end the buffoonery on the stage, and smother the free, garish colouring of the first three scenes. This is the first of two crises of feeling we sustain in this scene. We begin violently to reorientate our image of the play in order to entertain the ugly sequence between Julien and Paul which follows immediately.

Elements of farce at the end of this act cannot reassert themselves, and perhaps are not intended to: the unnaturally rapid recovery of Colombe at Surette's call for the actors to be on stage, her quick concern for her appearance before the mirror, must seem as unsympathetic to us as Julien finds them himself. We undoubtedly veer towards Julien's point of view, and we are sure that Colombe is the whore he thinks she is. The moment at the end of the act when Julien forces his mouth against Paul's to discover insanely what Paul has to offer his wife, is a moment of acute sensation and the second crisis, as effective in its place as Eddie Carbone's insulting embrace of Rodolpho in Miller's *A View from the Bridge*; its bitterness reflects our feelings.

We are a long way from the play which 'tells a story', the play with a strictly narrative line. We have been taken through an emotional attack and counter-attack which is better compared with music than with narrative, and yet which is peculiar to any dramatic medium. The two women, Mme Alexandra and Colombe, have embodied experience and inexperience (we dare not talk of Colombe's *innocence* now), while the fun and games back-stage, the surface gaiety and its sinister undercurrents, have forced us to respond with both feeling and intellect. A simple tale of pretty Columbine and clumsy Pierrot has become a sharply satirical, violent experience for an audience.

'Colombe': the play's form emerges

The play's story is over; there is no more to tell. Colombe is corrupt and the marriage is ruined. No event, however extraordinary, can reverse our verdict. Yet, surprisingly, Anouilh's curtain rises again. We may not be able to reverse the verdict, nor may the story be extended; but it is characteristic that he should devote his whole last act to making the significance of that verdict more precise by juggling exclusively with the play's formal patterning. That the author adopts two disparate methods to illuminate his intentions and have us review our feelings, suggests not so much padding as that he is straining to give his play an added complexity. He resorts first to the artifice of the ironic play-within-the-play, and concludes with a 'flashback', suggestive of the play-that-might-have-been.

The English version by Denis Cannan appeared a few months after the French. It presumably had the blessing of the author and perhaps at the opening of its final act enjoyed the 'elfish' inspiration of its producer Peter Brook.[1] It is this version which uses a clever, noticeably Pirandellian, trick in the presentation of the play-within-the-play. We find ourselves looking at the stage of Mme Alexandra's theatre from where the back wall would be, while Mme Alexandra, Lagarde Colombe and Surette, their backs to us, act *La Maréchale d'amour* to an imaginary audience we cannot see. We are given the odd impression that we are looking towards ourselves, the audience that had been looking at this same stage

[1] Cf. H. Hobson, *The French Theatre of Today* (London, 1953), p. 29.

during the second act. At once we are aware that conclusions we reached earlier were those of a fiction deriving from a fiction, and that we too were playing a part. It compels us to suspend our judgment by separating us from the play of Julien and Colombe by several removes: what was pathetic then must become like the sad event of years ago that today we smile over—perhaps wistfully, perhaps more wisely, perhaps with unconcern. This effect of chill distancing is enhanced by our seeing all the dead apparatus of back-stage: the reverse sides of the flats and ground-rows, the wire that supports a cardboard moon, the stage-hands in the wings, the waiting actor who reads a newspaper. If this were not enough, the scene is spoken in stilted verse in complete contrast with the earlier dialogue.

Under conditions which must incur our criticism of the scene to be played, we are offered a burlesqued résumé of Julien and Colombe's story. Mme Alexandra plays the wife surprised with her lover by her husband. She is a Colombe who, through the prismatic lens of the romantic theatre, has been awakened to passion by a true love:

> Is't me? I only know
> A girl stood here before, so long ago
> And yet, an instant hence; now woman stands,
> Possessed of new-found wisdom....

War intervenes, and the lover and the husband depart with a heroic flourish, prepared to forget that 'in the clash of war ... wives scarce wed may play the whore'. The lady and her confidante are left wondering whether they should remain faithful to lover or to husband:

> Shall we thus mourn, and let our beauty fade
> In loveless chastity?

Abruptly they depart in a gondola for 'mirth and pleasures gay'.

Once more we have been forced to mock Julien's little tragedy. We reject the imaginary audience now applauding the false romanticism and gay abandon of the scene: in doing so, we reject a little of ourselves. Nor are we alone: immediately the play is finished, Lagarde confirms that our view is his: 'Phew! What a damn silly lot of swine out there tonight!' Which is, of course, a venomous remark addressed indirectly at us. Yet, because of the convention of the play-within-the-play, we cannot be insulted, but remain receptive to the second and final irony which Anouilh has yet to inflict.

Before this arrives, and the more to disconcert us, he presents us with yet another Colombe, perhaps the only real one, disarmingly unaffected, but emphasizing the character of Julien's jealousy. She explains that she was happier in his absence:

> ...I cleaned the rooms as if it were a game, and I put a basin of water in the sunshine and stood in it naked, to wash myself—and what did it matter if the old man opposite was getting a treat through his binoculars? It was a natural joy to both of us, a present from God as much as the sun on the trees.

Their duologue has the effect of modifying the 'before-and-after' shape of the play. The *naïveté* of the inexperienced Colombe we first knew had become, it seemed, a cunning and sophisticated laxity; the sympathy we had felt for her charm had hardened to a colder, dispassionate assessment of her weaknesses. Now her naturalness returns and with it our understanding. As she says, her head has been so stuffed with his 'sacred opinions of right and wrong' that her childlike heart had dried up. Thus, just when Anouilh is ready to play his last card, we are again hung in the balance between sympathy for Julien and understanding of Colombe. Surette confirms Julien's disgust at the female principle, while Mme Alexandra confirms Colombe's distrust of the male.

The flashback that concludes the play is introduced solely as a new measure for audience participation. By an easy transition of music ('*on entend un piano lointain, fanto-*

matique...') and lighting ('*la lumière baisse jusqu'au noir*'), with some preparatory suggestion in the dialogue, we rehearse the first meeting of Julien and Colombe. This scene has been criticized as unadulterated sentiment offered as a sop to a jaded audience. It is true that Anouilh writes the sequence in an understated language which is deliberately sickly. Its simplicity may be illustrated by the closing lines:

JULIEN. Now our story begins. I'll never forget what you've given up for my sake.

COLOMBE. Oh, it's been too quick—I'm sure it's been too quick. It can't be the real thing, can it?

JULIEN. I think it is. And I think it will last. (*He kisses her. She leans tightly against him*).

COLOMBE (*a whisper*). My darling!...Now I am sure of it...for always.

JULIEN. For always....Not a second less.

(*They kiss, and*)

The curtain falls

This certainly is an idealized demonstration of love at first sight; but the words, the embraces, are only different in degree from the burlesque tone and manner in which Mme Alexandra and Lagarde had opened the act: this curtain with this kiss is a convention of the type of theatre Anouilh travestied. Because of the play-within-the-play, we are doubly the sceptical audience we were: we simply do not respond sentimentally to the sentiment with which the words are spoken. To believe that the author intended us to, would contradict the total meaning of the play, not to mention his others.

This last device is used to cap the climax of bewilderment in which we find ourselves: weighed against the indecisions that troubled us before, set against our knowledge of the two years of marriage that are now fact, and the parting of Julien and Colombe that resulted, this tailpiece can be only ironic. In itself, a simple enough reversal: in context, irony is a term rather too narrow to convey the complexity of its effect. The wink between the author and his audience is certainly implicit here, but into these last exchanges Anouilh has also squeezed his statement of value, disagreeable as it may be. We are still not to apply standards of moral right and wrong to our hero and our heroine; but in the corners of our minds we hear whispered an anguished and a passionate plea for human understanding in a world where nothing remains sacred.

Is this a *statement* of values? The effect of this curtain, as of other devices, on the play is to press its feeling upon us as if we had lived the experience ourselves: we are forced to participate beyond our natural will. It is achieved by Anouilh's ingenious tragicomic counterpointing, by the ironic discomfort in which we find ourselves when we attempt to assume comedy's attitude of omniscience.

TENNESSEE WILLIAMS

Tennessee Williams has always written freely about his life, his feelings and his way of making plays. We can sense some of the spirit behind his drama when he writes biographically in a programme note,

In St Louis we suddenly discovered there were two kinds of people, the rich and the poor, and that we belonged more to the latter. If we walked far enough west we came into a region of fine residences set in beautiful lawns. But where we lived, to which we must always return, were ugly rows of apartment buildings the colour of dried blood and mustard. If I had been born to this situation I might not have resented it deeply. But it was forced upon my consciousness at the most sensitive age of childhood. It produced a shock and a rebellion that has grown into an inherent part of my work.

Williams calls it a 'bitter education', and his work reflects strikingly the American condition, found generally throughout serious American drama: in a world of prosperity and of unlimited opportunity for prosperity there remains the great immovable doubt that the central values are not as yet discovered. As O'Neill said in 1946, 'the United States, instead of being the most successful country in the world is the greatest failure...because it was given everything more than any other country. Through moving as rapidly as it has, it hasn't acquired any real roots. Its main idea is that ever-lasting game of trying to possess your own soul by the posses-sion of something outside it too....'[1] Galbraith's affluent society has a moral 'imbalance' as well as an economic one.

Equally important to recognize for an understanding of the nature of Williams's peculiar sensationalism is the background of influences on a young man embarking on the career of a playwright at the end of the 'thirties. The American indige-nous theatre is at the most only fifty years old. It missed the Ibsenite vogue of inquisitive realism, and until recently it lacked a broad tradition of playing and playgoing. Serious drama on Broadway had for years been losing the fight against the evils of commercialism, the star system and the prohibitive costs of production. The song–and–dance routine of the musicals, plays of 'homey' sentiment about the Ameri-can way of life, the bedroom farces and the cheap thrillers had their content inevitably dictated by the taste of the majority. Williams had to enter the jungle of big business, and he has never quite ceased to play it at its own game.

Nevertheless, he would have been well aware in the 'thirties of the watery trickle of serious drama off Broadway, from such as Eugene O'Neill with the Provincetown Players and Clifford Odets with the Theater Guild. The plays of these writers and others were essentially social in character and content, aiming at a frank realism of dialogue and subject, grinding out plays about sex and prostitution, about misce-genation and the Negro problem, about morals and divorce, about social issues and strikes. There was always a certain romance in the realism of this pre-war theatre, and especially in the drama of O'Neill, the greatest single influence of the

[1] Quoted in E. R. Bentley, *In Search of Theater* (London, 1954), pp. 233–4.

time. O'Neill used local colour and dialect, but with a fury suggesting that an honest representation was not his first concern. His settings achieved novelty in aiming at originality, and, as in *Desire under the Elms*, realistic drama soon slid into melodrama. His special interest in psychopathology, as in *Strange Interlude*, in 'the duality of human character', as in *The Great God Brown*, and in the subtleties of self-delusion, as in the pipe-dreamers of *The Iceman Cometh*, became an obsession. These comments on O'Neill's romantic realism could as well have been written about Williams.

At the same time the American theatre must be grateful to O'Neill for furthering in practical terms the American concept of the 'art' theatre. He did much to promote the limited successes of a presentational drama deriving from Gordon Craig, Max Reinhardt and others in Europe: he made repeated excursions into dramatic symbolism, and his technical curiosity about the use of mask and monologue, expressionistic character and chorus, myth and mood play, was insatiable. At the other end of the scale, his more naturalistic plays of neuroticism gave new opportunities to the 'Method' actors of Lee Strasberg's Group Theater. Again, in this, Williams's own symbolic and naturalistic mixture can find useful precedent.

Unlike O'Neill's, however, Williams's plays have been all of a piece, and his earlier plays were trials for his later ones. The frightened Matilda of *You Touched Me*, a girl unwilling to face realities, provided a pattern for Laura of *The Glass Menagerie*: Matilda 'has the delicate, almost transparent quality of glass' just as Laura 'is like a piece of her own glass collection, too exquisitely fragile to move from the shelf'. Mrs Hardwicke-Moore, who is *The Lady of Larkspur Lotion*, a prostitute with grand illusions about a Brazilian rubber plantation, about men-friends and a coat of arms on the wall, is a prototype for Blanche of *A Streetcar Named Desire*, as is

Counterpoint and Hysteria

Miss Lucretia Collins of *Portrait of a Madonna*, her hair 'arranged in curls that would become a young girl'. Miss Collins is, like Blanche, removed to an asylum. *Baby Doll* is made up of two one-act plays from *27 Wagons Full of Cotton*. *Orpheus Descending* is a revision of *The Battle of Angels* of seventeen years earlier. Williams in his revisions and self-parodies is rather like a man gnawing at his own vitals.

He speaks through his overheated settings, usually inspired by New Orleans and the South. In *A Streetcar Named Desire* 'the houses are mostly white frame, weathered grey, with rickety outside stairs and galleries and quaintly orna-mented gables.... The sky that shows around the dim white building is a peculiarly tender blue, almost a turquoise, which invests the scene with a kind of lyricism and gracefully attenuates the atmosphere of decay.' The old house in *Baby Doll* is appropriately dilapidated and in its attic we see 'dusty late afternoon beams of light through tiny peaked windows in gables and a jumble of discarded things that have the poetry of things once lived with by the no-longer living'. The accent is on the decaying and the seedy, always with a strong hint of ironic symbolism. The Wingfield apartment in *The Glass Menagerie* 'is in the rear of the building, one of those vast hive-like conglomerations of cellular living-units that flower like warty growths.... The apartment faces an alley and is entered by a fire-escape, a structure whose name is a touch of accidental poetic truth, for all of these huge buildings are always burning with the slow and implacable fires of human desperation.' The yellow stains on the walls behind torn wallpaper, the hot porches on which sweaty people sit drinking cans of beer in the late evening, such images are for him the recurrent metaphors of his dramatic vision.

Music of all kinds, from old gramophone records of the 'twenties, from the juke-box and the Mardi Gras, to the 'hot trumpet' and the 'blue piano', almost any noise can, as in the cinema, subserve his characters' states of mind, sometimes with ironic accentuation, sometimes adding a simple dimension of memory. As Tom of *The Glass Menagerie* says, 'In memory everything seems to happen to music'. When the sounds are harsh they suggest external realities; when they are soft they identify a thought or gently echo an idea identified before, binding the play together.

To apply still more pressure, Williams treats stage-lighting in a highly conventional fashion. He selects a character for special attention by the use of spotlights, like the silent Laura in her pool of light in the supper scene, or he sharpens the image of a character like Blanche who goes mad to the accompaniment of 'lurid reflections' on the walls, 'grotesque and menacing'. Colour tones make an insistent contribution, like the sky in *Summer and Smoke*, 'a pure and intense blue like the sky of Italy as it is so faithfully represented in the religious paintings of the Renaissance', or in *Cat on a Hot Tin Roof* where 'the set should be roofed by the sky; stars and moon suggested by traces of milky pallor, as if they were observed through a telescope lens out of focus'.

Symbolic characters and properties assert themselves, some garishly, like the blind Mexican woman in *A Streetcar Named Desire* chanting 'Flores para los muertos', 'flowers for the dead', or like the poker players dressed in their primary colours who watch Blanche taken away, like the stuffed canary in a cage in *Lord Byron's Love Letter*, the goat in *The Rose Tattoo* and the statue of Eternity in *Summer and Smoke*; some more subtly, like the boisterous family of lusty infants or like Brick's crutch in *Cat on a Hot Tin Roof*, like the rose silk shirt in *The Rose Tattoo*, like the fancy lampshade which Mitch strips from the naked bulb in *A Streetcar Named Desire*, like Laura's boot and her glass menagerie. The ramifications of meaning that Williams devises by such means seem inexhaustible. Nor does he hesitate to call up a surfeit of theatrical pathetic fallacy, the weather of nineteenth-century melodrama: heat, wind, thunder, all the rage of heaven or of the diseased minds of his characters.

These effects add up to an impressive hot-house theatre to accommodate those who people his world: mostly neurotic and lonely women, immoderately romantic, leaning hard on a Southern gentility which can no longer support them, caught in the toils of a society which will not easily admit weaklings. There is a great compassion behind the conception of such people as Laura the cripple and Amanda her mother, Serafina the widow and Maggie the cat, Baby Doll Meighan and Blanche Dubois. They are not held up for ridicule, nor to satisfy our salacious curiosity about those who live on the fringes of life. They are exposed because, in the words of Peter Hall, 'they are symptoms of the stresses and strains of modern living'.[1]

Williams's career to date is that of a man concerned to say one very big thing only, to say it over and over again, and to say it with all the strength of the agencies of the modern theatre working together: that life is never what it seems, but that it must be faced. The failed writer who sympathizes with the unhappy prostitute 'of larkspur lotion' is asked his name at the end of the play, and he speaks in what seems to be a tone of gentle irony: 'Chekhov! Anton Pavlovitch Chekhov!' With Ibsen too, Williams saw that irreverent society, if not life itself, could shatter the individual's romantic image of reality. With Strindberg he saw people torturing each other and themselves in their impulse 'to avoid fluidity and differentiation and to exist and function as one interfused mass of automatism', as he says with usual aplomb in *The Glass Menagerie*. And he wrote the following remark in his preface to *Cat on a Hot Tin Roof*: 'We're all of us sentenced to solitary

---

[1] P. Hall, 'Tennessee Williams: Notes on the Moralist', *Encore*, no. 10 (London, Sept.–Oct. 1957), no pagination.

confinement inside our own skins.' In this he speaks with the voice of Pirandello. Williams, it seems, attempts to sum up for his compatriots much that has been expressed before in the best of modern theatre.

To make his points in the theatre Williams ultimately relies on an accumulation of many little ironies, but these are superimposed upon one powerful and sustained tension which arises from the roots of his conception of life. If Laura's long sought-after 'gentleman caller' in *The Glass Menagerie* had not been already engaged to be married, we might have known that her disappointment had to come in some other way. In a situation where her mother will not see her own illusions for what they are, any breath of normality would have swept that glass menagerie from its table. Yet, amazingly, we are pleased to find Amanda a devoted mother for all her insensitivity to her daughter's sufferings: she is both comically clumsy and pitifully anxious for Laura's happiness.

The suffocating atmosphere of the Wingfield home is reproduced in *Summer and Smoke*, in which Alma, all soul, is the inhibited virgin daughter of a minister of religion, fighting against her natural affection for a wicked charmer, the son of a doctor, all body. Again we might have known that, by the time when finally she can restrain her desire for him no longer, he too has become inhibited. As Alma says at the crisis, 'You've come around to my old way of thinking and I to yours like two people exchanging a call on each other at the same time, and each one finding the other one gone out, the door locked against him and no one to answer the bell!...The air in here smells of ether....' Sexual ideals are rubbed against hard reality; there is no final communication between people: and a clear conflict is depicted which allows of no compromise.

From *Camino Real* and *Cat on a Hot Tin Roof* onwards, all the apparatus of his theatre strains under the weight of an increasingly metallic and mechanical contrast of attitudes.

Counterpoint and Hysteria

With the exception of *Baby Doll*, which introduces a new frivolity in the child-play between Baby Doll and Silva Vacarro, the Sicilian with a strong sense of humour, Williams never recaptures the simplicity of *The Glass Menagerie* or the subtlety of *A Streetcar Named Desire*. *Cat on a Hot Tin Roof* overreaches itself to play off a trio of self-delusions against one another: in Big Daddy the rich merchant, strong in everything except the courage to accept the fact that his cancer is more than 'a little spastic condition'; Brick his homosexual son crippled with drink and with shame, living out an impossible marriage, challenged by a virile brother with a teeming family; and Maggie his oversexed wife who can find no way to breach her husband's defences. The play soon becomes a riot of sensational exchanges in which his paralysed characters taunt and accuse and torture each other into a condition of mental stalemate.

By contrast, scenes in *A Streetcar Named Desire* yield little gems of a somewhat less hysterical irony. While we may admit that Stella's simplicity and single-minded sexual acceptance of Stanley Kowalski is of questionable psychology, and that Stanley's unsubtle and ape-like approach to life is crudely painted to provide a glaring foil to Blanche, nevertheless Blanche herself probably remains Williams's most notable creation. It is because she is such an amalgam of contradictions and because all the barbs are directed at us through her alone that the comic-pathetic note is sounded so frequently through the play. She is a woman of refinement of attitude as well as of manners, while she is also a sensualist tippling in private and teasing the other sex. She lies and evades, and yet in her effort to bring a touch of magic into her life, she speaks for us too. She is too sensitive to be able to reject her fantasies in the midst of the ugliness she finds around her, and in this we understand her and want to shelter her, while we also criticize her and want to change her.

224

Tennessee Williams

The chiaroscuro of Williams's action is as well sampled in Scene vii of the play as anywhere. It is the scene of preparation for her birthday supper and to it she has invited Mitch, the man she hopes to marry to escape from it all. The birthday cake and the flowers stand on the table, and Blanche is in her bath singing happily,

> It's only a paper moon, Sailing over a cardboard sea,
> But it wouldn't be make-believe If you believed in me.

On stage Stanley is telling Stella of the lies Blanche has been telling Mitch about her life at the Hotel Flamingo. As his voice grows more insistent and Stella is stunned into silence, so Blanche's song swells to the point where ' In the bathroom the water goes on loud; little breathless cries and peals of laughter are heard as if a child were frolicking in the tub'. Then Stanley tells Stella that he has informed Mitch of the whole story of Blanche's background, and that he is not now to be expected at the party. Blanche grows more and more jocular through the bathroom door, until she is answered with angry sarcasms from Stanley:

STANLEY. Blanche! Oh, Blanche! Can I please get in my bathroom?
(*There is a pause.*)
BLANCHE. Yes, indeed, sir! Can you wait one second while I dry?

Stanley then caps his performance by announcing to Stella that he has bought her a bus ticket to take her away from New Orleans. At this moment Blanche bursts from the bathroom with a gay laugh:

A hot bath and a long, cold drink always gives me a brand new outlook on life! (*She looks through the portières at Stella,* standing between them, *and slowly stops brushing.*) Something has happened!—What is it? (...*The distant piano goes into a hectic breakdown.*)

The counterpoint in the song, the bathing and the happy comments, with the presence of the cake on the table, heightens the horror of Stanley's revelations. The double world in which Blanche is living is epitomized. The ingredients exert a perfect tension on the scene, a tension maybe of the villain preying on his victim, deriving from the simplest of melodramatic formulae; and yet while we weep for Blanche, she has, we know, earned her deserts. We know that we share with her the instinct to live in some sort of consonance with circumstances. A quality of inevitability lifts our response from that of a merely sordid pleasure in the cruelty of the scene.

Notwithstanding Tennessee Williams's command of the theatre, doubts about the quality of his work are not unfounded. His drama gravitates to sensationalism and melodrama because he does not trust his audience to accept his ironies without their being overstated. He paints in primary colours and avoids the shades between wherein we mostly lurk ourselves. He risks sacrificing that quality of universality which belongs to the restraint and innuendo of real suffering. He too often mistakes the theatrical for the dramatic and again and again overloads his vehicle. He feels he has to stress the pain of reality on the one hand and the hopelessness of the aspiration to overcome it on the other, until his stresses grow destructive, and, sensing insincerity in the drama, we sit there like a professional audience witnessing a conjurer with a ragbag of tricks.

BECKETT, IONESCO AND OTHERS

The comic *danse macabre* is today at its height in Western Europe. The work of the Irishman Samuel Beckett and the Rumanian Eugène Ionesco for the French theatre lies in direct line from that of Pirandello and Anouilh. They are of the same breed in method, if not in feeling. Their plays go to the limits, and take all the risks, in their dramatic tactics of stimulus and response. They are of their time, not so much in their eager pursuit of grisly symbols across the stage, which after all derive from the dream fantasies of Strindberg written in the early years of this century, but in their search for a new language, a new *poésie de théâtre*, which will speak the striking ambivalences of feeling of the post-war years.

The arguments that have surrounded Beckett's *Waiting for Godot*, to choose the outstanding example of current dramatic nightmare, have arisen partly because in it the author has refused to make a defined statement. He has instead used the medium to the full in order to depict a common attitude, whether we care to acknowledge its universality or not. He will have us ask questions, but will not supply the answers; we commit ourselves without the author's committing himself. To some extent this accounts for the state of high excitement in which we find ourselves as we watch the play: imaginatively, we are driven at a rate of acceleration which is exhilarating, and the clashing colours of existence speed past us. We find the destination approaching too fast, without having observed the signposts. Yet paradoxically this effect is achieved through creatures suffering a slow, slow death by waiting.

A second source of excitement in the play lies in the operation of its parable. An extended metaphor, it makes itself felt at several levels. It compels us to complete an equation and find the *tertium aliquid* which the play evolves. We are shown a universal setting, the drab muck-heap to be found on the fringes of any town in the world. The characters answer to names of strange international currency, and their speech is as lively and as apparently inconsequential as most trivial conversation. Its hang-dog pauses occur and recur illogically, though with the odd power of giving alarming emphasis to the most commonplace word or the most colloquial phrase. For the duration of the play we live and assess and blench at the life of vague anticipation that excludes suspense, the life we may generally expect at home but not in the theatre: we are to be entertained by watching others pass time that hangs heavy in the way that most people most of the time pass it themselves. And, like most people, the characters are waiting for something to turn up, knowing, like most people in their hearts, that nothing very helpful will. When something or someone does turn up, it is difficult to recognize or beyond their power to control. So they turn again to their feeble jokes and their petty quarrels, and limit their interest to matters that press most nearly, matters which are intimately personal but which can at least be understood, matters which chiefly concern their animal bodies. The very idea of waiting is burlesqued, like the idea of living in Beckett's bald mime *Act without Words*.

The allegory of the play thus carries the interest of an imaginative detective story, but one in which the clues are found in ourselves and the discoveries are about ourselves. 'Whodunit?' We did: Didi and Gogo, Pozzo and Lucky are each part of ourselves. There is a thrill to be had in recognizing that a grossly fantastic morality play may be telling the truth; there is another thrill in finding where we differ from our representatives on the stage, where we conceal within ourselves a greater or lesser share of Didi or Gogo or Pozzo or Lucky. The play stimulates in its negation of our illusions and in its affirmation of our confident denials. As in the play, so in ourselves, there is Christ and anti-Christ, and its near-blasphemy tends to act as a homeopathic purge. It does not diminish itself with nihilistic propaganda: it is too ambiguous.

The special feature of *Waiting for Godot* that must especially interest us in this study is its manner of presentation. 'The saddest play and yet the funniest', declared the English press. Beckett chose to paint his urgent portrait of life-in-godlessness in the lowest terms for which he had a precedent. He wrote an overdrawn music-hall or vaudeville sketch, with its comics and a cross-talk dialogue of cohesive and suggestive rhythms, with its mimicry and fooling. When his clowns think, they press their foreheads; they say goodbye, but they do not move; they peer into their bowlers and exchange them; and so on.

Gestures such as these articulate many of our common attitudes in life as they have always done since Chaplin and before: we dare not commit suicide because of the indignity of having our trousers fall down, so to speak, and, of course, we lose our self-assurance when we lose our hat. What is absolutely right in this ingenious way of speaking, is the general ridicule it also calls down upon characters who behave in this way—we must laugh at their antics before we weep at them. It combines the surreptitious attack on the spectator with the redoubling of its satirical implications: an economy of means to secure an outrageous end. It is worth remarking that elements of vaudeville generate a prickly irony in other recent plays, like John Osborne's *The Entertainer*, Brendan Behan's *The Hostage* and Félicien Marceau's *The Egg.*

All That Fall was a more gentle extension of this manner; *Endgame* was an astringent retreat. The former presents the story of a rheumatic and grotesquely fat old Irishwoman, Maddy Rooney. It enacts her painful walk to meet her blind, sour husband at the station, the strain of waiting for a train that has been delayed, and the misery of the struggle back home in bad weather with the blind man on her arm. The sense of anticlimax is dramatized here as in *Godot*, but it retains the excitement of the human allegory in its trancelike, condensed journey through life with its unanswered questions. Again 'unaccommodated man' is shown living his bizarre existence: it is 'one great squawk and then peace', like the hen killed on the road. Presented for radio with the quaint, non-naturalistic sounds of farm animals, of the weather, a bicycle, a car and the train; its events curiously ridiculous; its language just missing the normality of conversation but allowing an Irish fluency ('sometimes I feel you are struggling with a dead language'), *All That Fall* creates its mood with the *Godot* mixture of laughter and tears rather more carefully stirred, its suggestions pointing more decisively to the compassionate struggle of a crazy existence. As a result it lays claim to be the most accomplished play Beckett has written to date.

Endgame would seem to be a recession. Maddy Rooney conveyed a singular kind of majesty; Hamm the tyrant waiting for his end is all degradation. The mutual dependence of Hamm and Clov, all but lacking the music hall give-and-take of Didi and Gogo, suggests only misery, a life made up of a series of empty moments, where the most hopeful event is to ask for the pain-killer. In Nagg and Nell, Hamm's parents imprisoned without legs in two dustbins, we see Hamm's own future—like an animal, living in sawdust, fed upon biscuits. The allegory has grown so remote as to be almost meaningless; the humour so desiccated that all comic balance is lost; the audience so numb that there is no participation.

Many attempts have been made in recent years to establish a timeless reference through the traditional use of myth, whether Greek or biblical. It is outside character and more in structure that the past and future are recognizable in the present particularity, just as in *The Waste Land* it is in the verbal structure, the superimposition of ideas upon one another, that London Bridge is located in Dante's *Inferno*, that Stetson, contemporary man, is remembered from the Battle of Mylae, that mythical Cleopatra descends to be the familiar neurotic sophisticate, and so on.[1] Such plays as Giraudoux's *Tiger at the Gates*, Anouilh's *Antigone* and Fry's *A Sleep of Prisoners* operate in this way, and we are familiar with the excitement of discovering how closely the ancient formula may match contemporary experience. Used in this way, myth becomes a means of compressing a large statement into a tiny space, stressing 'timelessness' with extraordinary weight.[2] If one does not resort to myth, one must resort to

[1] See G. Melchiori, *The Tightrope Walkers* (London, 1956), p. 76.
[2] Cf. F. Fergusson, 'Poetry in the Theater and Poetry of the Theater' in *English Institute Essays*, ed. A. S. Downes (New York, 1950), p. 69.

some other means of suggestion. Chayefsky wrote of his *Bachelor Party*, 'I wanted to show the emptiness of an evening about town, and emptiness is one of the most difficult of all qualities to dramatize';[1] we might add, especially if the play is tied to naturalism. Samuel Beckett on the other hand has invented a theatrical form where life can be as dull as a recurring decimal. 'The point lies in the pointlessness.' Built up through an indefinite but recognizably drab setting, played by characters with no particular individuality (though the feelings that pass between them are familiar enough), Didi and Gogo, like Hamm and Clov, pass their time passing their time, and this we understand intimately. We watch the events of a universal limbo. These are the means by which time is dramatized: telescoped to frighten us, extended to make us lose our bearings, the very absence of time makes us crave it. Didi can say, 'We met yesterday. (*Silence.*) Do you not remember?' Pozzo can respond, 'I don't remember having met anyone yesterday. But tomorrow I won't remember having met anyone today. So don't count on me to enlighten you.' The Boy we have just seen can declare he wasn't there, until the pin-point of temporal life is lost in a dramatic eternity. We 'give birth astride of a grave, the light gleams an instant, then it's night once more'. Shall we go? We do not move.

As did the hero of Pirandello's *Henry IV*, we recognize that there is drama in knowing life can be like a 'stopped watch'. Paradoxically, we watched life recur timelessly through the single day depicted in *Under Milk Wood*. Now, we sourly declare with Dan Rooney of *All That Fall*: 'If I could go deaf and dumb I think I might pant on to be a hundred. Or have I done so? (*Pause.*) Was I a hundred today? (*Pause.*) Am I a hundred, Maddy? (*Silence.*)' In that silence, do we laugh or cry?

[1] P. Chayefsky, *Television Plays* (New York, 1955), p. 263.

Ionesco, writing in the same genre, is less restrained, and therefore more prone to the huge failure of a disintegrated audience. How much ridicule can you pour over your characters and their situation without destroying that measurable link with the audience's reality? If an audience can perceive no relationship between the stage and themselves, or if an audience laughs so much that *belief* remains suspended, the play lapses into extended knock-about charade. To call upon the extremity of absurdity to make one's point is to risk all in a monstrous gamble. Ionesco shows us the familiar and slowly disrupts it. He has a talent for presenting his characters as imbecile clichés in the context of a serious dissertation, as immobile puppets in a world that is alive and constantly threatening. *Grand Guignol* violence surrounds the unconscious victims, and the walls rock ironically round their doomed heads. It is the method of classical comedy grown cruel and cold, and its satire grown hysterical.

The Chairs offers a quick illustration of the method. His theme is serious in the extreme, one recurring in Ionesco: that, stifled by banalities, we ache to express ourselves, to forge a link with another person, to discover the artist within ourselves, to lower the mask and speak our minds. Unhappily, many of us can never do this, lacking the power, the opportunity and the language. How does Ionesco present this idea? Not by a realistic picture of someone struggling to find himself, perhaps like Solness in Ibsen's *The Master Builder*, or Konstantin in Chekhov's *The Seagull*. He shows us two old people, but absurdly old—they are each ninety years of age—so that their very wish to articulate is eccentric and their message derided. Significantly they live on an island in a river, isolated from their fellows, thrown upon each other.

Crazy characters are established in a crazy world, and their situation is developed. In this development there can be no subtleties that are not subtleties of visual and verbal rhetoric and magniloquence: there can be only the one given position for the concept and one deployment of its parts—hence Ionesco's fondness for the one-act play form. All else is anticlimax. He must prepare the joke and then crack it, holding his face and his breath until our laughter follows. It is remarkable that he can sustain the jest to the extent he does. In *The Chairs* the two old people have invited guests to hear the statement to the world the old man wishes to make before he dies. They begin to arrive, but we do not see them. They are figments of imagination, products of a wish. With each new arrival a bell rings, a door swings, conventional noises of greeting are made and a chair is placed. More and more guests arrive, until at the climax the room is full with chairs packed together, the host and hostess ludicrously running hither and thither. As with the furniture which the Gentleman in *The New Tenant* admits into his apartment, or with the fantastically extended conversation of Mr and Mrs Smith in *The Bald Prima Donna*, the author stretches his absurdity to breaking point.

At this stage in the structure of his drama, Ionesco seems uncertain how to turn easy laughter towards the dark mood in which his subjects are conceived. As in *The Lesson*, he holds his top note for too long. He may introduce sex to add heat and bite to this theme. He is least happy when he has to bring his curtain down, since he can never be sure he has made his effect complete—his audience may no longer be riding with him. In *The Chairs*, a professional orator is finally brought in to address the 'gathering', but when the old man and his wife have jumped to their deaths through the windows, he discloses that he is a deaf mute. Nothing can cap the climax of the chairs themselves. No one can say whether these last details of the suicide or the disclosure can sober us and leave the force of the irony which is clearly intended. Unlike the violent shocks of reality which conclude *Henry IV*, *Six*

Counterpoint and Hysteria

Characters and *Ardèle*, effectively prepared by some touch-stone of realism in the plays, in Ionesco caution of this kind is thrown to the winds, our image of the drama rocks groggily, and it may never achieve stability.

With an immense and unequalled verve, Ionesco has gone on to write the ghastly social comedies of *The Killer* (*Tueur sans gages*) and *Rhinoceros*. In both of these, his Kafka-like sense of the nightmare of fear that lies hidden among a community of people has grown stronger, and its horror has been brought more into the open. Yet the more urgent his statement, the more hilarious his manner. *The Killer* depicts Bérenger, Ionesco's little man ('his behaviour should seem sincere and grotesque at the same time, both pathetic and absurd'),[1] who tries to save his society from the hatred at its heart, but whose own bookish ethics and arguments become meaningless. At the end he stands indifferent to evil in spite of himself. Tragedy is presented as comedy again in *Rhinoceros*, which takes up and continues the earlier theme. The play begins with a startling incident by which a human being is strangely translated into a rhinoceros. This fantastic peculiarity rapidly becomes the dreadful normality as more and more people are caught up in the epidemic. With the physical transmutation comes a more frightful change: the human mind, at first full of platitude rationalities and excuses about moving with the times and peacefully coexisting with the rhinoceroses, is caught up by the herd instinct and becomes animal. Ionesco's plays have the power to make sense, if at a loosely political, certainly at a sharply personal level: he is writing of the death of the soul. When they touch us on a raw spot as they frequently do, they are cautionary tales indeed.

In Beckett's and Ionesco's progress towards this frontier of comedy we may get very little farther. In England at any rate, comic ironists like John Arden, David Campton, N. F. Simp-

---

[1] Eugène Ionesco, *Plays*, vol. III, trans. D. Watson (London, 1960), p. 99.

son and, especially, Harold Pinter are now digging over the territory newly claimed. These dramatists practise a new illogicality, yet one pregnant with the logic of feeling that belongs to a subconscious world of tragicomedy. As in the novels of Franz Kafka and William Golding, the normal world of ordinary human relationships can suddenly become quick and sinister and even violent. As the playwright moves into another dimension of drama, so the audience is drawn into another dimension of life.

N. F. Simpson pursues a wild verbal extravaganza to the point of monotony. He offers a lighter, more milky view of his fellow man than does his master Ionesco, and echoes from the nonsense writings of Edward Lear, Lewis Carroll and the B.B.C.'s Goon Show seem to have drowned Ionesco's important element of tragedy. *A Resounding Tinkle* presents a very humdrum, sober and suburban English couple who accept any outrageous notion without turning a hair, whether it is an invitation to 'form a government' or a report that there is an elephant in the front garden. The point is presumably that an announcement that the H-bomb was on its way would leave them equally unruffled. There might have been real impact in *One Way Pendulum* had the tragic touch been admitted: Mrs Groomkirby is a supremely patient wife whose husband is an insurance agent so interested in law for the layman that he must build a do-it-yourself Old Bailey in the sitting-room, and whose son is engrossed in training speak-your-weight machines to sing the Hallelujah Chorus. The manner is that of the straight face of traditional farce, but Simpson has yet to forge any really purposeful link with reality. Perhaps the dramatist must learn how to write with the cumulative force of the well-made drama before he can write with any effect in terms of anti-drama.

Pinter, by contrast, is a light-heavyweight Beckett with a firmer sense of theatre. His audience is made to feel, through an exquisite friction of nightmare and normality, the earthy human need for security, recognition and acceptance. But society, by forcing us to conform, can destroy the very security we seek from it. His key play, *The Birthday Party*, is a comedy of menace which in its turn tends to sacrifice vital comedy to the horrors of the subconscious hell. Here in a squalid seaside boarding-house a very proletarian Everyman called Stanley has buried himself from the world, without work, without hope and without washing himself. Unexpectedly a Jewish business-man named Goldberg and a unfrocked Irish priest named McCann, agents of our imperious society, come to claim him. In the sinister scene of Stanley's so-called birthday party, in which a terrifying game of blind-man's-buff is played with an obsessive intensity, Goldberg and McCann reduce their victim to speechlessness. Next day they dress him in 'striped trousers, black jacket and white collar', and he is marched off in his bowler-hat, completely without identity.

We are never fully told the motives of a character in a play by Pinter, but, as in life, we can have powerful presentiments about those with whom we are half-acquainted. In a programme note for a production of *The Dumb Waiter* and *The Room*, the author wrote,

A character on the stage who can present no convincing argument or information as to his past experience, his present behaviour or his aspirations, nor give a comprehensive analysis of his motives, is as legitimate and as worthy of attention as one who, alarmingly, can do all these things.

As in life again, one's fortunes can change without warning and God's purpose be hidden: seen by an outsider, this will be hilarious, until he reflects that it may happen to anyone. *The Dumb Waiter* tells the tale of two nervous gangsters, Ben and Gus, who await orders in an hotel basement. The dumb waiter in the wall suddenly clatters into motion, and Gus takes from the serving-hatch a piece of paper:

BEN. What is it?
GUS. You have a look at it.
BEN. Read it.
GUS (*reading*). Two braised steak and chips. Two sago puddings. Two teas without sugar.
BEN. Let me see that. (*He takes the paper.*)
GUS (*to himself*). Two teas without sugar.

They try pathetically to fulfil this and other requests in order to avoid discovery, until the dumb waiter becomes an unfeeling monster of urgent commands. When Ben is unexpectedly ordered to kill Gus, the play ends abruptly.

Part of Pinter's comic effect arises from the idiom of his characters' speech, which is so utterly casual and naturalistic as to be laughable. But the inflexions of his repetitive colloquialisms are able to carry far more than at first appears: not only do they precisely control the actor who speaks them, but they manage to guide the audience too. An inconsequential phrase in *The Caretaker* can have repercussions that put the spectator into a full state of theatrical activity. When Eliot in *The Family Reunion* wishes us to understand how an old lady lives a limited life dominated by time, he devises an emotive rhythm and imagery thus:

O Sun, that was once so warm, O Light that was taken for granted
When I was young and strong, and sun and light unsought for
And the night unfeared and the day expected
And clocks could be trusted, tomorrow assured
And time would not stop in the dark!

Amy's clock is the deceitful clock we know as we grow older. No less, probably more, do we know the tramp Davies's clock:

See, what I need is a clock! I need a clock to tell the time! How can I tell the time without a clock? I can't do it! I said to him I said, look here, what about getting in a clock, so's I can tell what time it is? I mean, if you can't tell what time you're at, you don't know where you are, you understand my meaning? See, what I got to do now, if I'm walking about outside, I got to get my eye on a clock, and keep the time in my head for when I come in. But that's no good, I mean I'm not in here five minutes

237

and I forgotten it. I forgotten what time it was! (*Davies walks up and down the room.*) Look at it this way. If I don't feel well I have a bit of a lay down, then, when I wake up, I don't know what time it is to go and have a cup of tea! You see, it's not so bad when I'm coming in. I can see the clock on the corner, the moment I'm stepping into the house I know what the time is, but when I'm *in*! It's when I'm *in*...that I haven't the foggiest idea what time it is! (*Pause.*) No, what I need is a clock in here in this room, and then I stand a bit of a chance.

This too is emotive language of controlled rhythm and imagery, and through it we find that we talk Pinter language as M. Jourdain discovered that he was talking prose. Davies's clock is re-experienced ludicrously, frighteningly as part of the world we live in and a very condition of existence. Leaving your papers in Sidcup or living a life without a clock can plumb a true tragicomic despair.

The correspondence between the fabulous province of Franz Kafka's mind and the nightmares of Beckett and Pinter grow more striking. Modern man falls helplessly before the inscrutable power of *The Castle*, or of Godot or Goldberg. Time stands still as he becomes obsessed with his own soul, as in *The Trial*, and feels the ridiculous paralysis of living in infinity and eternity, like Joseph K. or Maddy, Didi or Gogo. In the teeth of coincidence and the unknown, the laws of nature crumble and distort, while a hostile and obscene universe arbitrarily transmogrifies him into louse like Gregor Samsa in *Metamorphosis*, or puppet like Lucky or Davies, or into the despicable or pathetic animal of Hamm or Stanley.

From Chekhov to Pinter fifty or sixty years later, we might guess that a highly original phase in the history of comedy has been completed. In the 'sixties the comic dramatist leaves us alone and giddy in a spinning world: it is very funny and very terrifying. And he has proved Dr Johnson's contention that there can be no certain limit to the modes of composition open to the dramatist.

5

THE DARK COMEDY

'...Such, then, is the love of the heavenly Aphrodite, heavenly in himself and precious alike to cities and to men....And this, Phaedrus, is all I have to say, extempore, on the subject of love.'

The next speaker...should have been Aristophanes; only as it happened, whether he'd been overeating I don't know, but he had got the hiccups so badly that he really wasn't fit to make a speech.

PLATO: *Symposium*

INVOLVING THE AUDIENCE

To understand modern tragicomedy, we must first understand afresh the role of an audience in the theatre. The suggestion that drama is a structure of shifting relationships between character and spectator in the course of performance asks for closer definition. It means rather more than that the interplay between the actor and his audience brings the play to life.

Every human being is an actor *manqué*: nor do we need the psychologists to tell us this. Besides the faculty of laughter and the faculty of thought, he has also the faculty of taking the part of others.[1] He reproduces within his imagination situations and circumstances which are not his own in order to comprehend the life about him. From the early years he learns to enter into the thoughts and feelings of those he sees outside himself, and in this way he civilizes himself, and his mind and spirit grow. This is perhaps the supreme faculty he brings with him into the theatre. The spectator's willingness to identify himself with characters on the stage, or to have feeling for conditions that are not his own—temporarily

[1] The idea that 'man is a role-taking animal' is helpfully discussed by Ian Watt, *The Rise of the Novel* (London, 1957), pp. 201–2.

239

to understand them, perhaps later to reject them—is the dramatist's greatest asset, his means of reaching out to an audience to win it or repel it. A word coined by the psychologists has been borrowed by dramatic criticism to express these qualities in the spectator: 'empathy'—and in the most conventional of theatres from Aeschylus to Bertolt Brecht a degree of empathy has been the starting-point, and provided the norm of theatrical experience, in the construction of a dramatic pattern of feelings. We must first understand *by sharing* the mind and situation of Agamemnon in order to feel any significant pathos afterwards; in the same way, we must understand Macbeth in order to feel any significant repulsion afterwards. These are fundamental elements of theatre which still persist in the changed conditions of twentieth-century drama. Even Brecht was working from such assumptions for his iconoclastic drama when he asked us to think of

a sister lamenting that her brother is off to the war; and it is the peasant war: he is a peasant, off to join the peasants. Are we to lose ourselves in her agony? Or not at all? We must be able to lose ourselves in her agony and at the same time not to. Our actual emotion will come from recognizing and feeling the double process.[1]

The spectator may be immersed in the thoughts and feelings of the character on the stage, becoming more and more at the mercy of the puppet-master as his own personality is sunk in that of the puppet; but at this point the other-world of the character, the world of his environment, may be brought into focus. Then the character's responsibility towards others, his place in a family, his relationship to a social group, moves into the field of the spectator's consciousness. Out of this handling of the innocent spectator some of the true tensions of drama arise. So the case of Shakespeare's Henry V is made our own,

---

[1] Brecht, 'Gespräch über die Nötigung zur Einfühlung' in *Die Dialektik auf dem Theater, Versuche 15*, p. 104, quoted from J. Willett, *The Theatre of Bertolt Brecht* (London, 1959), p. 186.

and we are as keen as he to make the Dauphin 'blush', before we are made to see through the eyes of Williams, the common soldier: 'But if the cause be not good, the King himself hath a heavy reckoning to make, when all those legs, and arms, and heads, chopped off in battle, shall join together at the latter day, and cry all, We died at such a place....' So Hjalmar Ekdal of *The Wild Duck* obsesses our consciousness until the details and events leading to the death of Hedvig compel us to cut him down to size as a well-meaning but impossibly selfish man.

Or else a social situation is presented as something living for the spectator to observe objectively—until from this impersonal yet identified world emerges the personality of one or other of its victims. This is the pattern of *Romeo and Juliet*. Even in the introspective *Hamlet* the particular sufferings of mind of the protagonist do not make their mark on us until our general sense of mischief and evil in Denmark has been vividly suggested by the presence of the Ghost and by the bland forensic manner of Claudius on his throne. Only after this do we hear Hamlet say

> It is not, nor it cannot come to good,
> But break my heart, for I must hold my tongue,

and a new, vastly more urgent because more personal, issue grips our attention. So Ibsen shows us the world of Nora of *A Doll's House* before the woman herself. So Shaw indicates the madnesses of *Heartbreak House* before Ellie, our curiosity and our mouthpiece, emerges.

Sometimes situation and character are one and the same, and we spend out time in fearful activity fighting within ourselves for the supremacy of the subjective or the objective view. In this way we meet and know Antony and Cleopatra, or Coriolanus, or Alceste, or Solness the Master Builder, or Saint Joan. To examine in any detail the varieties of dramatic structure is to write the history of the theatre: this general mixing of our impulse to identify ourselves with a character, with our impulse to withdraw the better to see him in perspective, provides the common ambivalence of all drama except extreme kinds of impersonal farce, like that of the *commedia dell'arte*.

Encouraging this worthy ambivalence, the theatre is, we remind ourselves, similar to life with its contradictory pressures. Without feeling and compassion we should be ugly mechanical beings; but without reasonable circumspection we should be the fanatics of too many ill-considered enthusiasms. Having both, we see the world warmly, yet in proportion. Not that the drama wishes us necessarily to sustain this sane balance: it will require its moments of uncontrolled enthusiasm, and there will be other times for weighing and considering. But it is properly the strength of theatre that it can make us behave like over-energized creatures living a life-span of human activity within the two hours' traffic of the stage. The play is in its way a microcosm of natural life. For its mysterious purposes it can isolate and separate particular kinds of response, of a thinking or an emotional kind, or it can mix and join them. Some of the greatest plays of Shakespeare's maturity or of Molière's best period, as we have seen, are great because of this very mixture. They torment the spectator with the perplexing reality of laughter and tears that he is not unfamiliar with. It is not surprising that in an age like ours, an age we believe to be of greater generosity in moral understanding and finer clarity in psychological insight, we find that out best plays are given to experimenting with this sublunary mixture of attitudes in the minds of men and women.

So the spectator arrives in the theatre today with less prejudice of the kind that restricts the drama's breadth of characterization and situation. In a modern play he will not be so disconcerted if the comedy becomes cloudy with feeling or the tragedy suddenly illuminated by witty breaks of sunshine. But he does expect to be in some agreement with his fellow spectators when he laughs or when he suffers; and if the degree of laughter or feeling, being lessened and adulterated, is not strong enough to overwhelm the individual spectator completely, can the dramatist be sure that his audience, jostled this way and that, will remain united?

It is a generally accepted premise that the playwright must attempt to unite his audience in pursuit of the thoughts or emotions of his play. In tragedy and melodrama this is perfectly possible where our hates and sympathies are turned upon one character or group of characters; in high comedy and in low farce it is comparatively simple to choose the object for ridicule shrewdly, making a character sufficiently gross for an audience to know how it is to respond. A straightforward identification of spectator with character, or withdrawal from character, and a refusal by the author to distract the spectator's attention from this, coupled with the spectator's willingness to bow to his wishes, is the pattern of an easy success. Today, when a play enjoys a long run, it is likely to be a play prepared to embrace an audience strongly and to follow such rules as these.

The case is very different where an audience is not allowed a facile agreement with itself, or, to put this another way, where the mind of the spectator, busy in the attempt to build a firm emotional or rational image of the play, is divided in its loyalties. Panic and rejection may ensue. A writer may hold such an independent point of view that he will not let his play slip into the ready-made formula of preconceived opinion, nor into the convention of established tradition. Eric Bentley rightly suggests, discussing Meredith's convenient proposition that comedy 'is an interpretation of the general mind', that 'comedy might also be the individual's protest against the general mind'.[1] Bentley instances the

[1] E. R. Bentley, *The Modern Theatre* (London, 1948), p. 133.

outstanding example of Shavian comedy which does not speak for the audience at all, but for the audience as Shaw would have it. In this case as in others, the rebel may wish to lead his fellows, but, short of howling to himself in the wilderness, to satisfy his wish he must adopt a measure of theatrical 'deception'. If the issues are truly controversial— and this is not to speak necessarily of political, religious or moral ideas, but rather of ambiguous feeling, such as that prompted by such plays as Strindberg's *The Ghost Sonata*, Jean Genet's *The Balcony* or the drama of Samuel Beckett, for example—the deception may take the form of tricks of stylization or the use of myth and symbolism to make an unwelcome point obliquely. Whatever conventions are used, it is important that the spectator who might be prepared to scoff must remain to pray.

Thus the unpalatable hypothesis of *The Ghost Sonata* is, as we saw, that we can live happily in self-delusion, and yet suffer from the terrible fear of having our illusions smashed and our self-corruption exposed. Genet in *The Balcony* portrays with immense wit and abandon the Napoleonic complex in human character and society. He places on the stage a sample of men who have resorted to a fantastic brothel where they may assume in greater reality the grandiose masquerade of their most private wishes, and we see the frightening picture of what monsters of a bishop, a judge and a general might emerge were human desire given enough licence. To coax the spectator to accept these particularly unpleasant views, it may be necessary to divide him against himself. It may even be necessary to divide a whole audience against itself.

In our own time, many attempts have been made to make the spectators feel, in Diderot's words, 'like those who in the presence of an earthquake see the walls of their homes rock, and feel the earth yawn before them'. Violent ends demand violent means. On the one hand the audience may be righteously shocked and baffled, as they were with Anouilh's *Ardèle* and Beckett's *Endgame*, plays which in the execution seem to lose touch with the spectator. On the other hand, the explosive response to John Osborne's symbolism in *The Entertainer* was a calculated effect, as it was in somewhat less degree in his *Look Back in Anger*. Using the last ugly stages of the senility of the English music-hall as a devastating symbol for England in the 1950's, Osborne's Archie Rice and his bawdy clichés compel us to resent our own laughter, and even each other, as we laugh. One correspondent to *The New Statesman* at the time of the first performance reported on her reaction as a member of the audience as follows:

I am still not sure how we were induced to play the part written for us—to emit that deadly sound of luke-warm laughter, willing but uncertain, which gave the cue for Archie's ironic impromptu about bringing the roof down and gave point to the venom behind his surface heartiness. Pretty flat it would all have fallen if we *had* been bringing the roof down, wouldn't it?...Maybe John Osborne knew just how much corn and bawdy he could include and be sure that the guffaws of the randy and the distaste of the squeamish would both be tempered and confused by reverence for the leading player.[1]

The leading player in question was Sir Laurence Olivier.

The kind of play we are growing more accustomed to ✔ prohibits easy solutions of the problems of 'involving' the audience. In order to recreate the effects of ambivalent life, in order to make us more aware of our minds working through our feelings, the good modern dramatist will insist, by refreshingly questioning illusion and convention in the theatre, that we remain aloof although implicated. There can be no comforting sense of 'belonging to a side' in the experience of his theatre. There can be no relaxation in a play that acquits us by laughter at one moment and then convicts us the next. To place us in this unhappy limbo, the playwright will be busy

---

[1] E. Morgan, letter in *The New Statesman* (London, 11 May 1957).

measuring, expanding and contracting that vital gap between the world of his actors and the world of his audience, between art and life. The characters stand there on the stage—how are we to regard them? As next of kin or as distant poor relations? What if we are unsure? That is the uncomfortable state of mind the writer of dark comedy aims to create. He must control our infinite little decisions of heart and head. We are ready poised to cast our vote, but repeatedly we hesitate. The detachment of comedy is not allowed us, nor the sympathy of tragedy. All the instinctive psychology of the man of the theatre is needed to achieve this particular tension: he must mix sufficient reality to hold our belief, with sufficient unreality to have us accept the pain of others. At the point of balance, we are in pain ourselves, and the play is meaningful.

A case of some interest in recent years has been Osborne's brash dramatic adventure in *Look Back in Anger*. Whatever the ultimate judgment passed on this play, diverse reports suggest that in performance it captured its audience. Whether enmeshed by love or by hate, no spectator could escape it. The play caught fire because Osborne diabolically promoted amongst the audience a clash of generations and a clash of classes: it was at once a play hitting out at the older generation and a story of a socially mixed marriage. Stressing the divisions in our society, it criticized its failures. This 'success' was not due to any substantial degree of sympathy conjured for its hero, nor yet did he leave us detached. Jimmy Porter, the young working-class graduate who loves and hates his middle-class wife as he loves and hates the human race, demanded much of our sympathy as an isolated, over-sensitive idealist 'raging against the evils of man', in the words of A. E. Dyson,[1] but he loses it as soon as we see him also as 'a cruel and even morbid misfit in a group of reasonably normal and well-disposed people'.

[1] A. E. Dyson, 'Look Back in Anger', *The Critical Quarterly*, I, iv (Hull, 1959), p. 318.

Involving the Audience

Jimmy's character, central to the play and primarily directing our responses, is intended throughout to remain an enigma to us. What he says and does, together with the way other characters regard him, so complicates our image of him that we can quickly cease to trust our own judgment. As Dyson has usefully illustrated, Osborne is from the beginning offering us a bold and theatrically daring ambiguity for a character. The stage directions read:

> He is a disconcerting mixture of sincerity and cheerful malice, of tenderness and free-booting cruelty; restless, importunate, full of pride, a combination which alienates the sensitive and insensitive alike. Blistering honesty, or apparent honesty, like his, makes few friends. To many he may seem sensitive to the point of vulgarity. To others, he is simply a loudmouth. To be as vehement as he is is to be almost non-committal.

His stage behaviour swerves violently between the honest indignation of a warm-hearted man and the attitudes of a moral egotist. His worst action is to blaspheme against life in hoping that his wife 'will have a baby, and that it will die'; but Alison his wife does have a baby, and it does die; and so he is punished. It is impossible to admire his ugly, self-defensive manner, but perfectly possible to love the man for his genuine misery, as do Alison and her friend Helena, in spite of everything. Simply to retreat from the paradox of Jimmy Porter is to ignore the persistent existence of human ambiguity with which Osborne vitalizes his stage.

This essay has tried to explore a little of the great variety of such capricious and contrary drama which has arisen now that the dramatist has felt the new freedom of the dark comedy. We mock the absurdities of the clowns Didi and Gogo in Beckett's *Waiting for Godot*, who pass their time on the stage fruitlessly 'passing their time', abortively contemplating their future, half-heartedly telling themselves a dirty story and half-heartedly questioning the meaning of Christ's Crucifixion. We laugh at their antics of mind and body, but under the growing realization that what they are doing is only a modest parody of what we do ourselves; we know before the piece is done that they are ourselves.

Anouilh's hunchback Aunt Ardèle is determined to hold fast to her belief in herself and the purity and disinterestedness of her love for the other hunchback, and she does so in the face of every opposition from her family and society at large, who romantically consider that physical sex can only be beautiful where the body is beautiful too. She deserves, and perhaps gets, all our sympathy for remaining steadfast to her ideals in a world of corruption, since it becomes increasingly apparent that every one of her critics is corrupt in his or her own way; yet we are irked, as the pretty adulterers Nathalie and Nicholas are, by the knowledge that the physically repulsive should thus represent our finest feelings.

Giraudoux's gentle warrior Hector of *Tiger at the Gates* is a man who has tasted the horrors of war. Just before the impending conflict with the Greeks over the rape of Helen, he finds himself a man inclining to pacifism against his own nature, looking in his wisdom for every avenue of escape from the miseries he foresees. He is a full symbol of the modern circumspect mind. But having had his mortal way for the whole of the play, at the very end his careful control of the situation slips through his hands. In the first flash of anger he has shown, Hector kills his compatriot Demokos; Demokos in revenge declares with his dying breath that it was the Greek envoy Ajax who killed him; the crowd falls on the Greek, and war is unleashed like the tiger of the play's symbol. It is troubling to realize that, like ourselves in more contemporary circumstances, it is Hector himself who must in the end bring war about his head.

Pirandello's mock emperor Henry IV is the man who teases other people apparently by feigning madness, making his friends and his enemies play parts in a game of his own invention, delighted to see how readily they now abase themselves for him. He plays his own part with a light *élan* until he too succumbs to a moment of anger and kills his rival Belcredi. With this momentary act after years of calculated restraint, he sentences himself to play his part of the madman not only for this performance but for ever. Indeed, was he ever sane? His make-believe, like ours, condemns him utterly to a life of self-torment.

The paradox of the excitement of this kind of play-writing, which ought logically to leave us unaffected, but which can enthrall us mercilessly, is not easily resolved. Perhaps it may be explained by reference to I. A. Richards's general theory of art, and in particular to his theory of an aesthetic equilibrium within the mind:

> We cease to be orientated in one definite direction; more facets of the mind are exposed and, what is the same thing, more aspects of things are able to affect us....At the same time since more of our personality is engaged the independence and individuality of other things becomes greater. We seem to see 'all round' them, to see them as they really are; we see them apart from any one particular interest which they may have for us....To say that we are *impersonal* is merely a curious way of saying that our personality is more *completely* involved.[1]

In making his audience respond by ironies and contradictions, playing off the reason against the emotions and the emotions against the reason, the writer makes us earn our experience the harder way. 'More of our personality is engaged.'

The achievement of such dramatists as we have discussed and especially of Chekhov, Pirandello or Anouilh, each in his own sphere, is to make his audience suffer without the relief of tears and to make it mock without a true relief of laughter. The audience remains at a distance, yet within immediate call; impersonal, yet strangely involved. However, the attempt at a descriptive account of such effects upon an audience was

[1] I. A. Richards, *Principles of Literary Criticism*, 2nd ed. (London, 1926), pp. 251–2.

A: G!: G: B~RO~

immediately an encounter with the great variety of individual methods and private subtleties employed. In particular we felt that extraordinary theatrical quality of *irony* which is the chief controlling agent of an audience undergoing a play.

IRONY AS A CONTROLLING AGENT

To discuss the mutual support and peculiar inclusiveness and unity of incongruous ingredients is to discuss the methods of mixing them. To recast an image in our minds, to secure a calculated reaction, to achieve a precise control over the feelings running in the auditorium, and to know how much rope we need to hang ourselves—this is the difficult technique of the new comedy.

An audience goes willingly into the theatre, its imagination open to receive without undue question a great variety of impressions. On his part, the dramatist tries to start, sustain and elaborate the pattern of interest that constitutes his play, and his power to develop that interest is the measure of his skill. The alert playgoer will exercise his image-making faculty by his accurate scrutiny of idea and feeling, his eyes and ears finely attuned to the actors' suggestions. The play develops as the stage action shifts the kaleidoscope; suggestion follows and anticipates suggestion as the dramatist refocuses the picture for us.[1] For this the audience's active contribution is essential.

An emotional sequence once begun under these conditions is not easily restrained: it makes its own momentum. There is every danger that an audience will take the play in charge: thus Shylock can grow to be a tragic hero, and Willie Loman can come too close to our hearts for us to criticize the system he symbolizes. To require an audience suddenly to turn from

[1] See the author's *The Elements of Drama* (Cambridge, 1960), ch. 4. In one sense, all that the spectator sees on the stage is seen ironically, since he is always on the outside looking in. This has been suggested, too, by G. G. Sedgewick, *Of Irony, especially in Drama* (Toronto, 1934).

such emotional anarchy and become more detached may call for an uncommon juxtaposition of impressions. On the other hand, to build and then break our comic attitude, as happens in plays as varied as *Pygmalion*, *The Playboy of the Western World*, Pirandello's *Henry IV* and Tennessee Williams's *The Rose Tattoo*, is to intoxicate and then sober an audience which is also reluctant. Both processes demand an equally delicate flexing of the play's fabric to manipulate its audience and induce its embarrassment.

A reorientation of attention in the audience may be decided by a subtle turn of mood or tone, even at a verbal level simply, as in conversation when a stray remark from a stranger arrests us, or when a new note in a familiar voice makes us start and look. Or it may call for a complete revolution of convention, wholly altering the drift of the play, with intent to give us some theatrically traumatic shock. Both methods may be equally exciting. The superimposition of a comic tone upon a tragic one was not uncommon in Elizabethan drama, nor in Molière, as we saw; but the exploitation of 'convention', though not wholly unknown in plays like *Troilus and Cressida*, is rather a characteristic of more modern times when the dramatist sets about his task quite conscious of the variety of conventions available to him. This has been Anouilh's particular opportunity and occasional triumph; it has been the persistent object of Brecht's stagecraft. But in some degree 'alienation' by breaking the continuity of mood or style or both is found in the very great variety of plays that have been mentioned.

Dark comedy is drama which impels the spectator forward by stimulus to mind or heart, then distracts him, muddles him, so that time and time again he must review his own activity in watching the play. In these submissive, humiliating spasms, the drama redoubles its energy, the play's image takes on other facets, the mind other aspects, and the spectator 'collects the

The Dark Comedy

force which again carries him onward'.[1] But now progression is more cautious, and he is on guard. He is charged with a tension as a result of which he is a more alert and therefore responsive participant. This tension is one of dramatic irony.

Such tension can be a reinforcement, not a weakening, of the structure. Wilson Knight in his brilliant essay on *King Lear* is certain that the tragedy is incomplete without its explosive ingredient: 'This is of all the most agonizing of tragedies to endure: and if we are to feel more than a fraction of this agony, we must have sense of this quality of grimmest humour.' He insists that 'the pathos has not been minimized: it is redoubled'.[2] It is redoubled because Lear's suffering is so painful it has a final authority over our response to the play and ensures that the element of comedy is unquestionably of the 'double-faced' kind, and is received as such.

This kind of renewal is particularly noticeable at the climax of a sequence of disruptive sensations, though often the process is operating throughout the play. The real climax of dark comedy may be, not the place in the play where the hero is pressed to a decision, the villain unmasked, the situation brought to a crux, but the place where the tensions are so unbearable that we crave relief from our embarrassment. At the end of *Juno and the Paycock*, we move with relief towards Juno's prayer, are reconciled by her loss, and comforted by tears; then, cruelly, O'Casey scourges us with the drunken platitudes of Boyle and Joxer. We hear their words while Juno's grief echoes round our brains, till we hear only the mechanism of our own thinking, and the curtain disburdens us.

It is enlightening to find Bronislau Kaper, the musical director of John Huston's film of Stephen Crane's novel *The*

[1] Coleridge, *Biographia Literaria*, ed. Shawcross (London, 1907), vol. 2, p. 11.
[2] G. W. Knight, 'King Lear and the Comedy of the Grotesque' in *The Wheel of Fire* (London, 1954), p. 175.

Irony as a Controlling Agent

Red Badge of Courage, asserting that the continuity of the film would be strengthened, and the audience's view of the major characters defined, by ironies. He was of course thinking of musical ironies: 'After the Youth's regiment wins the first battle, the soldiers act happy.... But I come along, and I tell the audience, with sad music, what is so good about this? I make a little ridiculous the whole idea of one American killing another American.' The visually gay is counterpointed with the aurally cheerless. In the scene in which the Youth writes his letter home, Huston insists that his fear on the eve of battle is not to be treated tragically, and he hits upon the sound of the banjo to touch in the ridiculous: 'We have a funny sound coming from outside while the Youth sits in his tent and writes. A funny sound to a sad situation.'[1] We saw how Serafina of *The Rose Tattoo* felt her heart break to the music of the graduation-day band. The playgoer will not have missed the likeness to the effect of the military march with which Chekhov's three sisters are bade farewell, nor of the waltz which heralds the news of the sale of the cherry orchard. We remember that Hedda Gabler played her wild dance tune just before her suicide. The villagers danced on Midsummer's Eve while Jean and Julie were alone in Jean's room in *Miss Julie*. Similarly, O'Casey's *The Silver Tassie* welcomes the wounded with a foxtrot and a waltz. Tennessee Williams's Blanche has her unhappy story told while she sings 'blithely' in her bath, and she loses her mind to the music of the 'Varsouviana', in a polka rhythm, the blue piano and the muted trumpet. The bright jazzy musical interpolations into the sordid themes of Shelagh Delaney's *A Taste of Honey* and Brendan Behan's *The Hostage* tend to echo these effects. Such means in the film or play can be devised to catch the right tone of the dramatic theme, and start the appropriate degree of tension.

[1] L. Ross, *Picture* (London, 1952), pp. 136–7.

The Dark Comedy

Like the fit of laughter we suppress in church, tragicomic tensions can be mortifying. They can be induced as well by an incongruity of the solemn and the ridiculous, as by the sudden quirk of mind that recognizes the ugly beside the beautiful. So at Cleopatra's death, she can regally, and indeed like a Roman matron, demand her 'best attires', prepare to robe herself for death in words as well as clothes; but this inspired pomp is raised upon the earthy mockery of the clown with his 'worm': 'those that do die of it do seldom or never recover'. The senses are twisted sharply in prelude to the experience to follow. Flights of sentiment undermined by prosaic detail were of course a feature of Shakespearian tragedy at its moments of crisis: the raucous comedy of Capulet and the County Paris on the eve of catastrophe, Hamlet's mockery of himself, the irreverence of the Porter in *Macbeth* and the mad trial in *King Lear*, the simplicity of Lear at the death of Cordelia. The parody of the serious by the 'low life' in *Henry IV*, as identified by William Empson,[1] and the parallelism between the conduct of war and the conduct of love in *Troilus and Cressida*, is equally to be found in modern drama, even where the grey of naturalism is the dominant colour.

If Chekhov allows us to feel some spark of elation in the last act of *The Cherry Orchard* by showing us with what pride and vigour the new generation, in Anya and Trofimov, leave the ineffectual house, we are not allowed to forget that the older generation of Mme Ranevsky and Gaev are departing in sorrow, spending their feelings only on the useless past, while the oldest generation, represented by Firs, is sunk in oblivion before the curtain has finally fallen. This firm juxtaposition of the generations throughout the play is there to mark the polarity of our response. So, too, in John Osborne's *The Entertainer* and in Anouilh's *Point of Departure*, the divergence of parent and child in their attitudes towards the dramatic

---

[1] W. Empson, *Some Versions of Pastoral* (London, 1950), pp. 29 ff.

issue is devised to force us to reorientate *our* attitudes: the device forestalls the too simple verdict, even prompts an ironic anguish.

In another sphere, we are pivoted upon the sane norm of Aunt Ardèle in Anouilh's play or of Sir Henry Harcourt Reilly in *The Cocktail Party*; in this position we are engaged first by those we may only despise, then by those who elicit sympathy, until the two responses fuse. The behaviour of the General, the Count, the Countess and Villardieu in *Ardèle*, weighed against that of Ardèle herself, is fit only for satirical comedy, because we see them only through our imaginary ideal in Ardèle, just as we tend more and more to see the light inanity of the guests at Eliot's cocktail party through Reilly's objective eyes. But before these plays are over, the rope has grown shorter. We are implicated by the insistent presence of those we were once free to shrug off: Ardèle, in conjunction with a passionate Nathalie and Nicholas, becomes a mine with which to blast the dandlers and flirts; the slight problems of Edward, Lavinia and Celia are made weighty when Reilly, our mouthpiece, decides to aggravate them.

The dark drama is exciting because one pattern of feeling, dramatized perhaps by one character or group of characters, is countered by a contrary pattern from an opposite character or group, or by the same character or group seen in another light. Obliquely the dramatist approaches his goal. By contradiction, Pirandello edges nearer to the 'truth' in *Right You Are If You Think So*: Signor Ponza declares that his mother-in-law, Signora Frola, is mad in thinking that his wife is her daughter; she is in fact his second wife, for his first, her true daughter, actually died in an earthquake, an unhappy event the mother has never been able to accept. This seems convincing until we hear from Signora Frola that Ponza is the insane one, since he actually believes that his wife has died in an earthquake; and they have had to let him remarry the same woman, her daughter, convinced that she is another. Both stories tally, and we are never told the answer.

We want the truth? The truth is that *both* Ponza and Frola are right—for that is the nature of truth. Dark comedy is built with impressions which modify and contradict what has gone before. By the unseen presence of the martyr Celia Coplestone in Act III of *The Cocktail Party*, we are enabled to measure the quality of life in Edward and Lavinia Chamberlayne. This kind of treatment is ironic parallelism with a difference: the final decision is ours, and we are permitted to be responsible adults. In suffering this change of interest from irresponsibility to responsibility, we are leaving behind the kind of comedy in which the spectator wields the satirical weapon with a glee equal to the author's. We unhappily find ourselves sharing the punishment with the victim. The irony is the more incisive and painful because we have felt the peculiar misery of changing sides.[1] We are brought low from the indifferent heights of the spectator to be tumbled on the rack ourselves.

In the two-toned twilight drama we are discussing there can be nothing that might properly be called comic *relief*. The sensation derived from the moment of farce in high comedy, or the element of clowning in romantic comedy, is very different: one effect is but an extension of the other, and relief is found in a sudden sense of irresponsibility. But any sensation of real discord in the *tone* of a play is a felt lack of equilibrium, and is no relief, but only strain. This tension is only to be relaxed by an effort of consent and adaptation from the spectator himself.

I. A. Richards in one place discusses at once the 'catharsis' of tragedy and the irony of Rabelais and Flaubert in such terms as these: 'Besides the experiences which result from the building up of connected attitudes, there are those pro-

[1] Cf. A. R. Thompson, *The Dry Mock* (California, 1948), p. 19.

duced by the breaking down of some attitude which is a clog and bar to other activities.'[1] By this argument he may also be explaining the motive behind Macbeth's Porter and Hamlet's Gravedigger, Cleopatra's Clown and Juliet's Nurse, as well as Ibsen's Molvik, Chekhov's Epihodov, O'Casey's Fluther, and many subsidiary 'comic' characters in Brecht and Anouilh. As the playwright's plotting is clearer, the danger arises of having the spectator's image flow too easily into pre-conceived patterns of his own making. Thus one way of restraining and yet refreshing his energy is to introduce a dis-cordant note, which, though out of key, will also contribute to the total music of the play.

The traditional reasons given for comic relief seem to have been two: first, and even today the most common, it has been a 'shot of spirits'. So Dryden: 'A continued gravity keeps the spirit too much bent; we must refresh it sometimes, as we bait in a journey that we may go on with greater ease.'[2] It is certainly true that if an audience is taxed too hard, if the play is too demanding of the emotions, and especially if its mood is too grim, the audience itself will supply the relief without hesitation, laughing mercilessly at any detail, however irrelevant, that it can use as an excuse. This has been proved many times with new plays which have made no provision for the natural impulse to reassert the sane balance. But far from proven is the implied corollary that from the retrogres-sive movement the spectator collects the force which again carries him onward.

The second is the theory of the 'gypsy laughter in the bushes', where the comedy acts as a foil to the pathos, a nineteenth-century view. In David Daiches's words, the comic scenes provide 'an oblique commentary—illuminating by the sudden difference of its point of view from that exhibited in the tragic

---

[1] I. A. Richards, *Principles of Literary Criticism*, 2nd ed. (London, 1926), p. 209.
[2] Dryden, *An Essay of Dramatic Poesy*, ed. Arnold (Oxford, 1889), p. 56.

scenes—on the same kind of human world in which the tragic action takes place. True comic relief completes the picture of the tragic world.'[1] By this interpretation we are certainly able to comprehend the content of what is spoken by, for example, the Porter and the Gravediggers. But it is difficult to believe that that is the only reason for the intrusion of these characters into emotional sequences so carefully built up. Nor does it explain moments of pure farce in O'Casey's tragedy of Juno or Anouilh's tragedy of Ardèle, where the farce would seem completely to undermine the spectator's emotional attitude and the play's created image.

We must now assume a third explanation which shall include the earlier and the modern drama alike. An explanation in terms of 'from Philip drunk to Philip sober' falls logically into place in this essay. The comic scenes in many of Shakespeare's tragedies serve to enrich the pathos both by measuring the wealth of our feeling on the objective and precise scale of our more normal resilience to emotional experience, and by complicating the significance of the drama with a new and exciting ambivalence of attitude. For how many of Shakespeare's tragic heroes have a divinity we are to accept without question? We are to know their corporeality as we know our own, and we work hard to know it. The comic moments are not happy after-thoughts: as with *King Lear*, a degree of comedy is at the root of the play in its conception. The comedy is there to discolour the bright image in our minds—for at calculated moments we are compelled to give *equal weight* to Lear sane and Lear mad, and to the Porter and to Macbeth, as we are to Serafina the tragedienne and to Serafina the clown, and to Joxer and to Juno. The play may suffer a momentary paralysis, but it leaps forward again because the spectator is alive to more of the drama.

It is worth remembering that A. P. Rossiter, in a brief dis-

---

[1] D. Daiches, *Critical Approaches to Literature* (London, 1956), p. 236.

cussion of that supremely mongrel play *Measure for Measure*, argued that Shakespeare adopted a medieval ambivalence because his experience did not let him rest untroubled: 'The play is a searching analysis, an *empirical* moral investigation— not an application of ready-made Christian *a priori* moral schemes where all the answers are known. Shakespeare does not know the answers. He pokes and probes around, a duke of dark corners.'[1] We might add that many a good dramatist will see it as his task to pass on his empirical but enigmatic knowledge of experience as well as to meet it 'within himself'; to do so may be more a release than a relief of feeling.

THE COMIC-PATHETIC HERO

It is probably helpful in this general conclusion to notice the odd residue of 'characterization' left after the distillation of tragicomedy has taken place.

Traditionally one character has provided the keystone of the structure of the play, whether tragedy or comedy. This commanding position of a towering central character has, and still can, determine where the audience's interest is to be, loving or deriding it. Falstaff or Tartuffe, Hamlet or Harpagon must shine his light bright enough to take the eye and lead it on. But where the audience's affections towards the character are equivocal, as they might be if the action that surrounds him brightens and then dims the spotlight on him, or shows him in this and then that colouring, then the character, our human link with the make-believe, begins to work upon us to other purposes. His centrality may still epitomize the world in which he lives, as Peer Gynt suggests the forces at work in modern Norway, or as Willie Loman stands for the self-deceptions of modern America in *Death of a Salesman*; but the spectator is participating in the performance in a different way,

[1] A. P. Rossiter, *English Drama from Early Times to the Elizabethans* (London, 1950), pp. 146–7 (Rossiter's italics).

still concerned and yet vastly more critical. Character is aiding and abetting the disruptive intentions of the playwright-anarchist, while the audience grows creative and constructive in its turn.

Bergson, evidently following such strong hints as those thrown out in Strindberg's preface to *Miss Julie*, declared firmly that 'every comic character is a type',[1] presented with one side only towards the spectator, whereas tragic heroes tend to be many-sided individuals. Tragic heroes may well have many-sided, individual characteristics, but of course in the last resort an Oedipus or a Hamlet must be simple enough to 'embrace half the world' if the tragedy is to take on universal qualities. In dark comedy, the comic-pathetic hero, a creature who at the crisis is so human as to remember and hope rather than heed and act, often tends to assume universal qualities through the very individual and contradictory details that go to make him up. In Walter Starkie's phrase of 1926,[2] this character is an 'anti-hero'. He is a character capable of suggesting complexity because he has implicitly two or more sides towards the spectator. More than this, he calls for two or more *responses*, positive and negative and all the shades between. A Peer Gynt or a Willie Loman will absorb and quicken us with pleasure and pain in the theatre as we are absorbed and quickened by the mortal of flesh and blood we meet in life.

The argument suggests that, as the structure of tragicomic action grows complex and ambivalent, so must the structure of character: our reaction to the tapestry of varied impressions will ensure it. We remember the thrust and recoil of curbed emotion in contemplating the sad mordancy of Lear's Fool, the pitiful cuckolding of Molière's Georges Dandin, the early portraits of Charlie Chaplin the pathetic simpleton, and the

[1] Bergson, *Laughter*, trans. Brereton and Rothwell (London, 1911), p. 148.
[2] W. Starkie, *Luigi Pirandello* (London, 1926), p. 247.

anguished repartee of Archie Rice of Osborne's *The Entertainer* in his seedy palace of varieties, though these instances
would at first sight seem incongruously placed together. This
kind of double response arises when our initial recognition of
the clown in his traditional role of wit and joker is denied and
contradicted, when he is shown as capable of suffering the
pains of mundane life, pains which would not have mattered
to him or to us in his artificial character. The clown can be
an Everyman, whether hero centre-stage or merely onlooker.
As with Mr Polly's, his pose cannot be sustained if reality comes
too close; as with Falstaff, death is the leveller. If we cannot
play the hero, we can play the fool, even as Hamlet descends to
play the clown to Polonius, Fortinbras, even Laertes.[1] It is
the special force of dark comedy to show us that a clown can
also be a hero: we see him playing both parts.

We are not discussing those parts inserted to provide such
horse-play as we find in *Doctor Faustus*, which has rightly been
found suspect, nor those written to provide the music-hall
buffoonery of Gobbo-Launce tradition, through to the comic
policemen of today. There is a whole category of mixed
attitudes which is probably inexhaustible. It must include
Edgar, simulating madness with earnest sanity, 'the most
complex of all Shakespearian parts'; Jaques, who is 'halfway
to revolt against the world and wants to be a fool';[2] it must
include dear old Gaev of *The Cherry Orchard*, a clown because
he still retains a faith in himself, and Captain Shotover of
Heartbreak House, a clown because he has lost such faith in
himself as he had; Pirandello's Emperor Henry, who has
clowned himself to destruction; Synge's Playboy, clown to his
audience but not to himself or Pegeen, and Azdak of Brecht's
The Caucasian Chalk Circle, clown to himself but not to his

---

[1] Cf. F. Fergusson, *The Idea of a Theater* (New York, 1954), p. 116.
[2] These comments on Edgar and Jaques are taken from J. Isaacs's excellent remarks
on the Shakespearian fool in 'Shakespeare as Man of the Theatre' in *Shakespeare and the
Theatre* (The Shakespeare Association, 1927).

audience; Anouilh's Général St Pé and Osborne's Archie Rice, so full of doubts that they act the clown to reassure themselves; and the Jimmy Porter of the post-war years, so certain that the rest of the world is a clown that unwittingly he becomes one, down to Didi and Gogo who wait for Godot, fashioned in the shape of clowns the better to symbolize and to satirize every speech and gesture we make ourselves.

The quintessential clown and anti-hero of today's conception even appears stripped of almost all particularity now in Samuel Beckett's plays, and never more concisely than in the pathetic, ludicrous figure who is flung on to the stage for *Act without Words*, a mime for one player set to music. On a bright, dazzling stage, a 'desert' of a stage, a single actor is 'Man', alone and open to inspection. A whistle is heard from the right, and he reflects and goes out right, only to be flung back again. 'He falls, gets up immediately, dusts himself, turns aside, reflects.' The teasing whistle is heard next from the left, and the same frustrating performance is enacted again, until he responds no more. This is man being conditioned as Köhler conditioned his apes. But his role as Tantalus son of Zeus has only begun. A little tree descends from the flies to offer a circle of shade, and he is offered scissors with which, perhaps, to cut himself a hat, but he uselessly trims his nails instead and the shadow disappears. A tiny carafe, bearing a large label inscribed 'WATER', is hung just out of reach, together with three cubes on which to stand to reach it, the insatiable whistle still blasting its directions. No sooner has he so arranged the cubes to reach the water, than the carafe is pulled just out of reach again. So the torment goes on, his own efforts unavailing, until our protagonist lies there on the stage, the carafe dangling and playing about his face, the whistle imperiously inviting his attention. But 'he does not move'.

The meaning of this little piece is clear enough: man is

always to be at the mercy of unremitting, impersonal, unseen forces, despite his own efforts. For all the actor has no words, he assumes the zany character the action lends him. Since he is so mocked, we must laugh at his antics as he tumbles about the stage. Yet when he lies there finally, looking at his hands, wondering at his own impotence, the pathos of his situation is unmistakable.

This and the other dramatic 'clowns' are most serviceable agencies for the playwright to enable us to see in immense variety the mixture of the comic and the pathetic in man. For the audience, the quasi-clown either stands outside the scene as commentator, or else moves towards the middle stage until his state of mind is recognizably our own. Thus Gaev is on the fringe; Uncle Vanya is central. The Général in *Ardèle* is an oblique commentary from without, but in *The Waltz of the Toreadors* he is measured instead of measuring others. Hamlet at times is the clown who stands at dead centre of the action in a world that cannot admit clowns.

Perhaps the clown's function is to be seen as an echo, even an extension, of the parody in the traditional sub-plot, A. P. Rossiter's 'shadow-shows', Falstaff in his burlesque of Hotspur, Polonius unconsciously underscoring the father's role of King Hamlet, Thersites debunking the Grecian heroes, and so on. Where these sub-plots mock the serious issues of their plays, the clown mocks himself. The irony of the sub-plot grows bitter; the clown grows melancholy. As we feel and comprehend the relevance of the sub-plot to the main plot, so we understand the schizophrenia of the clown.

Today the force of the sub-plot has been largely replaced by ironies within character. The illumination of an issue from more than one angle is often apparent from the structure of the individual character and the incongruity of the details with which he is built. Characters like Mme Ranevsky are complex because warm-hearted foolishness is complex. She

has it in her to be both tragic heroine and fool. That she holds
a precarious balance between the two is evident from the ease
with which actresses tip her towards one or the other. It is
true there is a sub-plotted, reduplicating structure for ironic
ends in, for example, Eliot's *The Cocktail Party* and *The
Confidential Clerk*, and in *Point of Departure* and the *Ardèle* of
Anouilh. These writers, like Chekhov, are nevertheless using
several clowns on the stage at a time. Their achievement is to
rub two or more together to make them the more comic and
the more pathetic. The contemporary hero may be the clown,
the broken-hearted clown, wearing the mask-like paint of
Pirandello's Henry IV, 'two small, doll-like dabs of colour' on
a pallid base, heightened features hiding the grey within.

The broken-hearted clown is a grey hero. How tiresome that
Aristotle should have chosen to write,

The objects the imitator represents are actions, with agents who are
necessarily either good men or bad—the diversities of human character
being nearly always derivative from this primary distinction, since the line
between virtue and vice is one dividing the whole of mankind. It follows,
therefore, that the agents represented must be either above our own level
of goodness, or beneath it, or just such as we are.... This difference it is
that distinguishes Tragedy and Comedy also; the one would make its
personages worse, and the other better, than the men of the present day.[1]

It does not matter whether Aristotle meant good and bad, or
high and low, or serious and trivial; the contestable words are
'this primary distinction'. They state a palpable untruth
which has misled us when making judgments on dramatic
characters from Oedipus and Macbeth to Miss Julie, Halvard
Solness, Blanche Dubois and Jimmy Porter.

For us to interpret such complex characters as these on
grounds of vice or virtue or other moral status is not only to
diminish their size, but to misconceive the drama in them.
The impulse behind the greater play is rarely a preconceived

[1] Aristotle, *On the Art of Poetry*, trans. Bywater (Oxford, 1920), pp. 25–6.

moral system; rather, the good dramatist starts, proceeds and finishes by an intuitive and honest assessment of experience, if the characters are to convince and come to life, and if the resulting play is to reflect an experience of any value to an audience. The villainous and the virtuous characters spring from what Walter Kerr has recently defined as 'the thesis play'. He asserts rightly that 'it is better to make a man than to make a point'.[1]

'People don't have their virtues and vices in sets! they have them all anyhow', declares Hesione Hushabye of *Heartbreak House*, discussing the mixture in her husband Hector. Dark comedies, grey comedies, encourage subtle and living characters, quite apart from any close psychological portrayal which may also be present, because the pure white or the plain black soul is specifically excluded. The force of *The Wild Duck* lies not in the melodramatic pathos of a little girl's suicide, but in the failure of its hero Hjalmar Ekdal. He is the small man who responds as a small man when he is torn between truth and pretence; he is the normal man who corrupts what he touches when he finds himself caught between his wife's guilt and his daughter's innocence. The force of *The Cherry Orchard* lies not in the melodrama of having your dear old home sold out, but in understanding how a small woman, Mme Ranevsky, may well let such a thing happen. She may loom larger when she suggests that she knows the meaning of love where Trofimov does not, but her capacity to comprehend the world about her and its pressing issues is frighteningly limited. The power behind *Death of a Salesman* is not in the self-evident disease of the society depicted, but in the small man, Willie Loman, who displays his tragedy through a comic obsession. Yet we are not asked to hate these people: if we are not to love them, we are to live with them. 'May you be ordinary', writes Philip Larkin: for we respond to such charac-

[1] W. Kerr, *How Not to Write a Play* (London, 1956), p. 58.

ters with the understanding and feeling with which we read his ironically named poem, 'Born Yesterday':

> In fact, may you be dull—
> If that is what a skilled,
> Vigilant, flexible,
> Unemphasized, enthralled
> Catching of happiness is called.

'Let us not take it for granted that life exists more fully in what is commonly thought big than in what is commonly thought small', urged Virginia Woolf.[1] The modern movement has been to admit triviality into human stage behaviour, and to make drama of it. The hero of twentieth-century dark comedy is the character who makes the grand speech, but who has to clear his throat and scratch his nose. The dark comic dramatist tends to make special use of the duller elements of human personality in order to extend the content of drama: stupidity, boredom, carelessness, doubt, disappointment, caprice, reluctance, vacillation, bungling, mediocrity—everything that seems paltry in us. All the virtues and all the vices have their commonplace aspects: courage can be accidental, pride can be humiliating, love can be animal, revenge can be spiteful, just as cowardice can be understood, avarice can be pathetic, and selfishness and petty vanity can be amusing. The dark comic dramatist suggests it is a mistake, whether moral or aesthetic, for us to see the trivia of life, the gewgaws and baubles that bedeck the human spirit in public and in private, as unimportant.

However, a real problem remains for the dramatist if he is to show on the stage how important little people and petty behaviour are. The technical difficulty is to dramatize boredom without boring the audience, to demonstrate bungling without bungling the play. This task faced the authors of *Peer Gynt*, *Uncle Vanya*, *Heartbreak House*, *Right You Are*, *The Plough*

---

[1] V. Woolf, 'Modern Fiction' in *The Common Reader*, 1st series (London, 1925).

and the Stars and *Waiting for Godot.* A full account of their success, or partial success, would need to call upon the testimony of many spectators over many years and would be a study on its own; but it would be a study of the great theatrical experiment of our age.

Where is the value in the unpretentious? It is not enough to argue that audiences do not go to the theatre to see mediocrity: do we cease to eat because we have eaten before? The best of these plays are nourished by the actuality of our experience, as the best plays have always been.

There will be little glory in the unheroic hero. Just as every reader asked himself whether he felt sympathetic towards, or critical of, Emma Bovary when she first made her appearance, in much the same way, everyone who saw *Look Back in Anger* questioned his personal response towards Jimmy Porter. We respond with sympathy *and* criticism, both. In detail after detail, Osborne, like Flaubert, ensures that each surge of warm feeling is undermined by a cold current of reality. Osborne moves us to compassion for Jimmy's personal past, 'For twelve months I watched my father dying—when I was ten years old...', then impulsively turns his hero face-about to address his wife in an affected tone of self-mortification: 'I want to stand up in your tears, and splash about in them, and sing. I want to be there when you grovel. I want to see your face rubbed in the mud—that's all I can hope for.'

While Emma and Jimmy have their heads in the air, we remain with our feet on the ground. They are victims of themselves and of society—that is their tragedy, and we feel for them; they are also members of that society—that is Flaubert's and Osborne's comedy, and we criticize them.

The romantic centre of the modern novel and drama, the hero, is replaced by a pattern of feeling, which the central character, if there is one, may not be able to recognize because

267

it is part of him.[1] Only we, the observers, may see the whole pattern. The beetle has a narrow view of the garden; the gardener can observe all his stupid motions, can admire his efforts, laugh at his failures, help him to safety, or crush him with a touch of his toe.

In a letter to Suvorin in 1888, Chekhov wrote:

...Dividing people into successful and unsuccessful means looking at human nature from a narrow and prejudiced point of view. Are you successful or aren't you? What about me? What about Napoleon? One would need to be a god to distinguish successful from unsuccessful people without making mistakes. I'm going to a dance.[2]

That is the dark comic attitude. From the troubled and unsuccessful Ivanov to the confused Mme Ranevsky, whose modest aim for success was a happy love-affair, Chekhov dispenses with a hero. He invites us to look beyond the figure we see standing there, and, especially in *The Three Sisters* and *The Cherry Orchard*, he does it by placing others with him at the centre. Our eye cannot rest on any one replica of him, but must float between several, resting on none. Thus we find ourselves giving a rarer attention to the distances between them, to the relationships between them as they move in private and public. We watch with psychiatric eye how they affect others in the play. We do not pin any one of them down for anatomical examination: we gladly let them pursue their course. We make use of each in order to estimate the particular climate in which each lives, and measure one against another in order to eliminate divergencies of eccentricity. We may arrive at a just conclusion about the general source of each particular little dream, each show of temper, burst of laughter or silent grief. So the pattern emerges; indeed, the more clearly we see it, the clearer grows the corporeality of the characters who make it up.

[1] Cf. S. O'Faoláin's concept of the 'anti-Hero' in *The Vanishing Hero* (London, 1956).
[2] Chekhov to Suvorin, quoted by R. Hingley, *Chekhov* (London, 1950), p. 211.

The Comic-Pathetic Hero

Forty years after Chekhov, Brecht returned to the observation of people and their behaviour, in order to arm himself with theories for drama in a very different convention, and with lessons for a very different way of acting. He wrote a poem of 'Everyday Theatre',[1] which, like dark comedy, shall be 'serious and gay', yet 'full of dignity', and he addresses it to his actors. 'Artists', it begins,

> Artists, you who make Theatre
> in great houses, beneath artificial suns of light,
> in front of the silent crowd—go and seek now and then
> the Theatre of everyday,—thousandfold and without fame
> yet so very full of life; Theatre of the earth; Theatre
> fed by the living together
> of people; Theatre played in the streets.

Here a woman imitates her landlord, he goes on: the man there at the street corner 'demonstrates how the accident happened'; but he remains only 'a signpost that points', and he himself is not involved. Brecht will put no heroes on his stage, and if he must have a central character, the actor must leave us emotionally free to watch him with detachment. Such, at least, were his intentions. The actor, the character and the spectator were to be on equal terms:

> ...what we do is something universal and human
> which hourly occurs in the busy throng of the streets,
> nearly as dear as eating and breathing is to man.

THE DARK TONE

The Elizabethan audience's ability 'to shift rapidly its modes of attention', as S. L. Bethell has put it,[2] is not essentially an Elizabethan gift, nor is it to be found only in a non-naturalistic drama like Shakespeare's. An assumption by the playwright of some such psychological mechanism is evidently pervasive

---

[1] Brecht, 'Über alltägliches Theater', trans. W. M. Marckwald (unpublished), from 'Der Messingkauf', *Theaterarbeit*, ed. Brecht, etc. (Dresden, 1952), p. 398.

[2] S. L. Bethell, *Shakespeare and the Popular Dramatic Tradition* (London, 1944), p. 108.

through much modern drama. There are to be found in audiences only degrees of alertness; the spectator is either awakened or he is not, and the shift between comedy and pathos, and their delicate balance, is one way of startling him into wakefulness.

In the same way, the shift between happiness and misery, or more usually between a little buoyancy and a little melancholy in a variety of degrees, is common to most people's wakeful moments. Some unconscious apprehension of life's vagaries may impel us to weep at moments of great happiness and laugh at times of great anguish. Perhaps in the concentrated and freely responsive atmosphere of the theatre, we are not too different from the child who displays that extraordinary facility for switching his mood from tears to smiles and back again within a moment.

We are so made that we can respond by such extremes if we will, and the nature of existence itself, by which, to echo Dr Johnson, in one home there may be joy while in the next suffering, by which the morning may be shining and the evening overcast, makes this oscillation necessary. From his observation, the reader will be able to multiply examples of this dark, jaundiced comedy of living. It may arise when we see the social ritual which surrounds the dead, while we also contemplate death itself. It may colour international politics, where we see the fencing and weaving of the diplomats as we reflect on the momentous issues that concern them. In the theatre many dramatists have recognized the usefulness of this ambivalence. In drama as in life, nevertheless, the impulse to laughter and the impulse to tears sit uneasily together. It is tantalizing, first, that artificial forms like those of tragedy and comedy should admit their opposites, and, second, that a dramatist, knowing the discomfort of juxtaposing two discordant responses, should deliberately exploit the tensions they set up when put together.

The Dark Tone

Plato, at the tail of his *Symposium*, dropped the explosive hint that has been irking us since, that the tragic poet might also be a comedian: 'Socrates was forcing them to admit that the same man might be capable of writing both comedy and tragedy.'[1] In 1950 Christopher Fry confessed that his idea for a comedy presented itself to him first as tragedy: 'If the characters were not qualified for tragedy, there would be no comedy, and to some extent I have to cross the one before I can light on the other.'[2] This was certainly true of the 'October' comedy, *Venus Observed*, which he had just completed when he wrote this. This presents a man in middle age, the Duke of Altair, who has reached a point in life where he has to make a prodigious decision: not whom he should choose as wife, but rather whether he should allow his remaining years to drift into sentiment for the past, which is the tragedy of age, or to grasp his future and marry Rosabel, 'sharing two solitudes'. He chooses Rosabel, but this is no conventionally happy ending, rather an admission that age and the resignation of age may be viewed as comedy. The whole play analyses the Duke's decision, and the experience of the play is to share the comic-tragic embarrassment of life to which the Duke testifies.

Life is still the reference point. Shakespeare would on occasion measure the scale of his tragedy against ordinary life and the simpler human feelings, but until nearly the twentieth century the ideal of naturalistic representation in the theatre had not complicated the forms that drama might take. The playwrights to discover, through an inimitable observation of people, that powerful meanings could be created in the theatre without resort to the exaggerations, and sometimes distortions, of classical tragedy and comedy, were Ibsen and

---

[1] Plato, *Symposium*, trans. M. Joyce, in *Five Dialogues* (London, 1938), p. 81.
[2] C. Fry, 'Comedy' in *The Adelphi*, vol. 27, 1 (November 1950, p. 28), quoted by G. Melchiori, *The Tightrope Walkers* (London, 1956), p. 168.

Chekhov, but especially the latter. Chekhov saw that every-day life holds its own incongruities. There he found sufficient to create the comic attitude in the audience, and sufficient to sound the echoes of tragedy at the same time. In seeking a satisfactory form for his new drama, he hit upon what Wilson Knight has called 'a new sublime incongruity' that is neither comedy nor tragedy.[1] This study has tried to show how this form reached perfection in *The Cherry Orchard*, but today the special colouring of this method tinges all manner of drama. Thus in *Look Back in Anger*, when Cliff is bandaging the burn on Alison's arm, the touch is typical, not to say hackneyed:

> CLIFF. ...What is it, lovely?
> ALISON. Nothing.
> CLIFF. I said; what is it?
> ALISON. You see—(*Hesitates*). I'm pregnant.
> CLIFF (*after a few moments*). I'll need some scissors.

But Chekhov's Alison would have called it indigestion, and Chekhov's Cliff would have lost the scissors.

In one way Chekhov and his successors were safely disciplined while ordinary life applied a steady brake to the play. Less assured is the mixture of farce with tragedy, or sentiment with comedy, acted out at some remove from naturalism.

There are moments in Ibsen's largely naturalistic play *The Wild Duck* when the behaviour of Hjalmar and Old Ekdal comes so close to farce as to risk upsetting the balance of feeling in the play. Indeed, the whole business of the ridiculous attic is one of the most daring strokes in this author's repertoire: intended to provoke a degree of laughter at the outset, the significance of the attic grows as the theme of the play emerges. Our first response is turned against us, as the attic symbolizes a whole way of life we recognize to be one we often cherish ourselves. While Eric Bentley says, as we saw, that 'in this play the farce takes its life from the pathos, the

---

[1] G. W. Knight, *The Wheel of Fire* (London, 1954), p. 160.

pathos from the farce, the whole practical problem being one of controlling the subtle interactions of the two contrary modes',[1] such a problem is capable of a smooth resolution in a convention close to naturalism.

Of a different order is the violent mingling of farce with pathos in the work of Anouilh, Samuel Beckett and Eugène Ionesco. The risk here is that, even if the producer and his actors do hit upon the precise level of playing to keep the balance of the play, there can be no guarantee that they can hold all the audience all the time. Audiences pricked too hard will kick.

Of sentiment in comedy, one can only echo the remarks of critics[2] who have found the sentimental comedy of the eighteenth century an undramatic cheat and a bore. But where in Molière's *The Misanthrope* or in Shaw's *Heartbreak House* and *Saint Joan* the comedy is just as deliberately, but more subtly and dramatically, displaced by motions of sympathy towards the hero or heroine, something more fundamental is happening. Both Molière and Shaw in these plays almost miscalculate the pressure of their situations upon their audiences' feelings. Perhaps they intended to try us with tears and shudders, interested in the peculiar flavour of the resulting mixture. The honesty of Alceste, in love with his coquette, turns a mannered comedy into something closer to melodrama; the comedy of authority in its various guises challenged by Joan the individualist cannot be sustained— the sober dealings of history take charge; the farcical education of Ellie Dunn of its own momentum is driven to a point where it becomes an implied baptism in the terrible. Yet both Molière and Shaw felt the need at particular moments to retrieve their balance and tone—with the comic Du Bois,

[1] E. R. Bentley, *In Search of Theater* (London, 1954), p. 45.
[2] See L. J. Potts, *Comedy* (London, 1948), pp. 144 ff., and A. Sherbo, *English Sentimental Drama* (London, 1958).

with Joan's Epilogue, with the explosion over Heartbreak House. In wrenching us back into an objective frame of mind, they gave their comedy that extra touch of ice missing from Farquhar, Steele, Cumberland and others of the sentimental English drama, and from the *comédie larmoyante* in France.

To the fact that this sentimental tradition is not dead, London's West End and New York's Broadway perennially bear witness. Promising comedies are still maimed in the tearful way, as was John Whiting's early play *A Penny for a Song*. Otherwise an excellent satire on crazy English attitudes towards war, the pathetic love of Dorcas Bellboys for blinded Edward Sterne quarrels incessantly with the dry mockery of the rest of the play. It is not an extension of Whiting's argument that their love should flourish and be doomed, but an interpolation from another play, happily unwritten.

Clashing tears and laughter are uncomfortable companions, but, where in life their reconciliation is necessary if we are to make peace with ourselves, in drama their conflict is serviceable if that peace is to be disturbed. David Daiches argues that 'tragic relief' in comedy would destroy the 'magic circle' in which comedy moves.[1] But reference to modern drama, where this kind of conflict is part of the dramatic philosophy of the serious comedian, will again and again show the dramatist stretching the fabric of his comedy in order to trouble an audience whose expectations have become callous and settled. The new craft of dark comedy, which eventually sours the laughter and redoubles the emotion, is likely to be drama at its most cheerless and uncompromising.

The dramatist who can swing between the extremes of tragedy and farce within the same framework is today the man to sting us. Nevertheless, if he is not to drive his audience to distraction by offering a drama too inharmonious to be

[1] D. Daiches, *Critical Approaches to Literature* (London, 1956), p. 237.

acceptable, he must of course have a sense of the unity of his piece.

It is easy to see why critics, whether standing by the ancients or their experience, have thought that a play should leave a single, unalloyed impression, and that this was a virtue in itself. Dryden's Lisideius is to be excused for arguing that mirth and compassion are 'things incompatible' and that 'the poet must of necessity destroy the former by intermingling the latter',[1] because this can happen. The opinions of Diderot, Manzoni, Voltaire and many others who thought that opposites destroy unity must command some respect: in plays from *The Changeling* of Middleton and Rowley to *The Cocktail Party* of T. S. Eliot precisely this happens.

It need not do so. The unity of a play is not to be conceived narrowly as a matter of forms, as unity of 'action', but as a final tone and climate, a 'fourth' unity in which opposites may flourish together in the audience's mind. Indeed, Aristotle himself seemed to be arguing towards this position when he qualified his 'one action' with the gloss, 'a complete whole, with its several incidents so closely connected that the transposal or withdrawal of any one of them will disjoin and dislocate the whole'.[2] The implication that the parts must mutually support each other is Coleridgean. Augustus William Schlegel further insisted that the separate parts must be 'comprehended by the understanding': 'they are all subservient to one common aim, namely, to produce a joint impression on the mind...the Unity lies in a higher sphere, in the feeling or in the reference to ideas'.[3] The fourth unity is possible even where the ingredients are mixed, provided that the author burns with his thesis, has made an accurate assessment of his audience, and can keep it strictly enslaved.

---

[1] Dryden, *An Essay of Dramatic Poesy*, ed. Arnold (Oxford, 1889), p. 43.

[2] Aristotle, *On the Art of Poetry*, trans. Bywater (Oxford, 1920), p. 42.

[3] See A. W. Schlegel, *Lectures on Dramatic Art and Literature*, trans. Black (London, 1846), pp. 243 ff.

It may often depend on a flair for hitting the appropriate note for the time, as with Shakespeare and Chekhov; perhaps, as with O'Casey and Fry, conjuring a unifying mood to subdue us.

Schlegel's is an appeal to the end, an appeal for the serviceableness of the parts, which was Johnson's appeal in his celebrated defence of tragicomedy. As Schlegel saw the unity of tragedy, so we might see a unity in dark comedy. 'We must not suppose', he wrote,

> that the order of sequences in a tragedy resembles a slender thread, of which we are every moment in anxious dread lest it should snap. This simile is by no means applicable, for it is admitted that a plurality of subordinate actions and interests is inevitable; but rather let us suppose it a mighty stream, which in its impetuous course overcomes many obstructions, and loses itself at last in the repose of the ocean. It springs perhaps from different sources, and certainly receives into itself other rivers, which hasten towards it from opposite regions. Why should not the poet be allowed to carry on several, and, for a while, independent streams of human passions and endeavours, down to the moment of their raging junction, if only he can place the spectator on an eminence from whence he may overlook the whole of their course? And if this great and swollen body of waters again divide into several branches, and pour itself into the sea by several mouths, is it still not one and the same stream?[1]

It seems an essential task for the contemporary critic to observe the manner in which a play's contradictory ingredients, while seeming to destroy each other, can be contrived for mutual support. He is today challenged to investigate whatever new unity any particular mixture of opposites may create. He will certainly find himself looking for the common roots of the tangle confronting him. If the elements of a play as kaleidoscopic as *Troilus and Cressida* or *Peer Gynt* do not disintegrate in performance, it is because its pattern was determined by natural pressures and organic processes, reflected in the vitality of the play.

William Empson suggests that 'the drama in England has

[1] A. W. Schlegel, *Lectures on Dramatic Art and Literature*, p. 245.

always at its best had a certain looseness of structure'.[1] Complexity in plotting, contradictions in tone, seem again and again to be reproducing the sensations of life with its complexities and contradictions (in recent times, not only in England). We get the feeling that, in Empson's words, 'the play deals with life as a whole'. From the spontaneous eruption of tomfoolery within the sacred framework of the medieval mystery plays, to the contrivances of O'Casey to show his subject from opposed points of view in, say, *The Plough and the Stars*, we are reminded again that the point of reference is life; but if this is true, the looseness is merely apparent and not real.

After the magnificent Shakespearian rhetoric of Henry's 'Once more unto the breach...', which ends, we remember, with an injunction to 'follow your spirit', what better way of having us keep our wits and hear a ring of truth than by dragging on Nym, Bardolph and Pistol immediately?

> BARDOLPH. On, on, on, on, on, to the breach, to the breach.
> NYM. Pray thee Corporal stay, the knocks are too hot...

Is not the 'looseness' of this bathos perfectly justified in the structure of *Henry V*?

There is a primary urge within us to make sense and to make a whole of the plurality and variegations of life, and to do so without procuring an abortion of the truth by excluding what may not fit. In a play which arises from such motives as these, there may be a conviction of feeling which has nothing to do with consistency of character, the external unity and progression of plot, or of the maintenance of the conventions within the play. The dark comedian echoes Goethe: 'it is at bottom better to make a confused piece than a cold one.'

Dark comedy may initially anatomize, but it does it to free us of stereotyped but arbitrary attitudes. It makes elastic

[1] W. Empson, *Some Versions of Pastoral* (London, 1950), p. 27. See especially ch. 2, 'Double Plots'.

those thoughts and feelings grown rigid, in order to offer us a dramatic experience before the parts of that experience are drawn together again. The farcical and the pathetic will flow by imperceptible motions into one another, as they do when life is seen at a distance, as when age reflects on youth; or they will be violently thrown together, as when we stand close at the centre of it. Yet life is still of a piece, and so the play can be.

Affairs in dark comedy rarely conclude: they persist, and their repercussions may be felt to be unlimited. This drama does not make decisions for us, but at the most suggests likelihoods, depicts chanciness and stresses both sides. It stimulates us by implications, and it does not pass judgments—only the spectator may do that, if he feels he has the courage: but, as in life, he may never dare to commit himself so far. In dark comedy we are specifically asked not to be fanatics.

I. A. Richards argued that the structure of some poems and plays include contrasting elements in order to widen experience, the content of the writing deriving from relations between 'the opposite, the complementary impulses', thereby promoting 'a stability and order' possible only when the natural inclusiveness of the mind is satisfied.[1] It is natural, in our better moments, to balance our loves and hates, and sympathize with the villain and laugh at misfortune and forgive the sinner. Such antitheses may shape clumsily in the mind as a grotesque patchwork, or resolve a muddle into an uncommon mood. That such antitheses are valuable for literature is suggested by Empson's fourth type of ambiguity: 'when two or more meanings of a statement do not agree among themselves, but combine to make clear a more complicated state of mind in the author'.[2]

Jean Paul Richter confessed that 'In my consciousness, it is always as if I were doubled: as if I were two I's in me. Within

[1] See I. A. Richards, *Principles of Literary Criticism*, 2nd ed. (London, 1926), pp. 247 ff.
[2] W. Empson, *Seven Types of Ambiguity*, 2nd ed. (London, 1947), ch. 4.

The Dark Tone

I hear myself talking.'[1] The split mind of a writer has always lent him a force and a great appeal, once his reader has been persuaded to identify himself with him. This is easier for a novelist than for a dramatist, who cannot too simply call up a character's thoughts. It accounts for the modernity of a story like Conrad's *The Secret Sharer*, in which the position is explored where a man can be a stranger to himself. It accounts for the complex sense of truth in the novels of Dostoevsky, where minor characters enact the minds of the major, as Raskolnikov understands himself in Sonia and Svidrigaylov, and Ivan Karamazov in Smerdyakov; or where several contradictory characters complement each other in a pattern which exposes the complete mind of the author, like the brothers in *The Brothers Karamazov*. For this is the writer using his 'third voice',[2] essentially the dramatizing approach to artistic expression. Such dualism permits a fullness of statement: it is inclusive, as the mind is inclusive, of the passionate with the bawdy, the sacred with the profane, the sublime with the ridiculous.

These things we perceive simultaneously; in art it has often been taken as duty to separate one from the other, to clarify the issues, even to simplify for the lay mind. It is comforting to be told that any issue is black or white, and that we have only to know which is black and which is white. But it may take a fine degree of moral courage to admit a grey into our thinking. It is especially daring to send an audience home in a dark mood, and then to try to draw it back into the theatre for similar medicine. Yet to do so is to urge a truth about the nature of people and things. It is no work for the playwright-preacher or playwright-politician: it excludes the overt propagandist. The didactic drama of Georg Kaiser (*Gas*), Ernst

---

[1] Quoted by A. R. Thompson, *The Dry Mock* (California, 1948), p. 66, from Walden, *Jean Paul and Swift*, p. 53.
[2] See T. S. Eliot, *The Three Voices of Poetry* (London, 1953).

The Dark Comedy

Toller (*Masses and Man*), and J. B. Priestley and Graham Greene more recently, does not easily admit the irony of dark comedy.

Like Rickie Elliot in E. M. Forster's *The Longest Journey*, the new playwright suffers from 'the Primal Curse, which is not—as the Authorized Version suggests—the knowledge of good and evil, but the knowledge of good-and-evil'. For this reason he is taking a risk: he may produce a dark entertainment, a cold pudding mixed of antithetical moral ingredients which will not blend but which lie leaden on the stomach. Yet the success of the best plays of Chekhov and Pirandello, for example, tells the story of writers who have explored their medium to its particular limits in order to overcome an intrinsic ugliness in their subjects. Their synthesis of contradictory impressions is managed by a careful anticipation of their interactions. The new playwright must solve Coleridge's gigantic conundrum of the creative imagination and explore the mystery of 'the balance or reconciliation of opposite or discordant qualities'[1]—if, in the theatre, the audience is to find it possible to steady the pendulum.

UNHOLY JOY: ATTITUDES OF DRAMATIST AND AUDIENCE

A casual prophecy by Hazlitt in 1817, that 'the progress of manners and knowledge has an influence on the stage, and will in time perhaps destroy both tragedy and comedy',[2] has been largely fulfilled in our time. The reasons for this are as difficult to assess as 'manners and knowledge' are to measure, and the temper of the twentieth century is particularly volatile. Yet no art form is so directly related to the thoughts and feelings of its audience, so sounds its pulse, as drama. Especially

[1] Coleridge, *Biographia Literaria*, ed. Shawcross (London, 1907), vol. 2, p. 12.
[2] Hazlitt, *Lectures on the Literature of the Age of Elizabeth and Characters of Shakespeare's Plays* (London, 1884), p. 22.

does dark comedy, the drama of the split mind, with its seemingly sceptical motives, reflect the mood of the times. In the delightful burlesque of an 'anti-drama' which Anouilh introduces into his *L'Hurluberlu*, the dramatist gives himself away in the mocking stance he adopts:

MENDIGALES. ...The modern theatre has made a great stride forward. The idea that it should offer simple amusement, or relaxation, is out.
GENERAL (*good humouredly, as he sits down*). Heavens, why? Mustn't we laugh any more?
MENDIGALES. Temporary inhabitants of a planet threatened by atomic destruction, we have no time for amusement. Now it is a question of working to grip the consciousness of man, by man, for man,—and in humanity. Which does not in the least exclude, you will see, metaphysical anguish and a kind of humour of despair.
GENERAL. That promises us a happy evening!...[1]

There follows an account of 'Whizz! Bang!' or 'Julian the Apostate' and the frivolous tone scarcely conceals Anouilh's own instinct for the 'humour of despair' with which he reproaches Samuel Beckett. Troubled himself, the modern dramatist is intent on troubling the spectator, and his handiest device has been to thrust remorselessly together the laughter and tears.

It is a kind of blasphemy that, when Gogo in *Waiting for Godot* prepares to hang himself with the cord that holds up his trousers, we should be compelled to laugh at the abject man whose trousers have fallen about his ankles. Should we not be sobered by the thought of suicide, even supply a degree of admiration? But Beckett wishes us to mock, and so doing touches a willing spring within us. Our impulse to shout aloud in a solemn gathering, to laugh in church, is a human response to restraint. We are restrained in society only by the conventions of society. In art, the artist will dare to do what in life may be impossible if he feels his audience can respond as he

---

[1] Trans. Miss D. J. Hardy, unpublished.

wants it to. We saw how the Mystery Cycles could jest about what awes man most: life, death and the hope of salvation.

The drama that we have examined is drama that is self-analytical and self-conscious. Through a more finely spun texture it is harder to see the blasphemy against life. Bawdy will show itself if fashion permits; but the motives for domesticating the sublime, and for exalting the trivial, may be hidden.

There may be a simple skirmish between the reason which rejects and the sympathies which are loth to be denied: so Chekhov pricks at his three sisters separately, but adores them together; so Dylan Thomas ridicules the villagers of *Under Milk Wood*, and yet loves the village. It may be the wish of the author to keep tangible and recognizable what is feared as a mystery, to make a chance of destiny, to make a man of God and an animal of man, so that, in Philip Leon's words, 'his blasphemy makes the divine more present than the most solemn of hymns':[1] this is the faith of Shakespeare in the raging of Lear, and perhaps also of Pirandello[2] and Beckett. Or, in reverse, 'hot baths of sentiment' may be followed by 'cold douches of irony', and Irving Babbitt's account of romantic irony aptly fits Anouilh's peculiar taste of tears: 'When disillusion overtakes the uncritical enthusiast, when he finds that he has taken some cloud bank for *terra firma*, he continues to cling to his dream, but at the same time wishes to show that he is no longer the dupe of it';[3] the writer may introduce the tensions of self-mockery as a safeguard *against* mockery, 'a kind of homeopathic treatment'.[4] In each case we see a mask of mockery hiding the passion behind it.

In the twentieth-century drama we have glanced at there arises another factor. It is the writer's anxiety to counter the

[1] P. Leon, 'Holy Nonsense', *The Listener* (London, 29 November 1956), p. 879.
[2] See F. May, 'Drama of Reality', *Drama* (London, Winter 1954), p. 22.
[3] I. Babbitt, *Rousseau and Romanticism* (Boston and New York, 1919), p. 264.
[4] Cf. D. Daiches, *Critical Approaches to Literature* (London, 1956), p. 161.

glibness of the fixed idea, and to block a too easy response. At its worst, this may appear as a novelty for the sake of shocking us, an attempt to cover a deficiency by taking the audience off guard; at its best, it is a shaking of the bottle before the dose is administered, a skilfully controlled dramatic irony.

It is possible to identify loosely some of the attitudes implied in the playwrights we have discussed. Their drama is that of a culture in which man, rightly or wrongly, has placed himself at the hub of the world. He has no sure God to leap to, or else he will not leap without first arguing the point. It is a drama of human vanity in which 'hell has no vastness'. It is a drama which must exclude tragedy while there is no apparent virtue in rising above the sordidness of the human condition or in trying to reach a decisive conclusion about its problems. As Shaw wrote in his preface to *Three Plays by Brieux* in 1911, you do not leave a modern play with the feeling that the affair is finished or the problem solved for you by the dramatist: 'the curtain no longer comes down on a hero slain or married: it comes down when the audience has seen enough of the life presented to it to draw the moral, and must either leave the theatre or miss its last train.'[1] If on his way home the spectator is not still talking, he feels that the characters are.

For ours is also a disputatious drama, making an argument of itself, taking nothing on trust. Bertolt Brecht adopted the term 'dialectical' to describe his theatre;[2] nor was he borrowing the word from Marxism. He was drawn to the Hegelian dialectic, as was Shaw to the Socratic, and he understood Hegel's contradictions of thesis and antithesis in order to apprehend the nature of the real world. Brecht wrote that Hegel

had such a sense of humour that, for example, he could not even conceive of, say, order without disorder....He denied that one equals one, not

---

[1] Shaw, *op. cit.* p. xvii.
[2] See Brecht, *Die Dialektik auf dem Theater* (1957).

only because everything that exists is continually turning into something else, namely its opposite, but because generally nothing is identical with itself.[1]

This very neatly reflects the tragicomic sense with its dramatic ambivalence; it reflects the friction and contrariety of Pirandello's *Umorismo*.

Dialectical writing stands less chance of suffering from disease by decadence: it may indicate disillusion and pessimism behind the façade of laughter, but in remaining relativist it is not passive and it does not drift. Pirandello was much taken with Machiavelli's confession: 'If at times I laugh and sing, I do it because this is the only way I have to provide an outlet for my painful tears.'[2] To feel about experience in this way suggests at least an activity of spirit alive to the variety of life, and perhaps not far removed from Keats's poetical character:

it enjoys light and shade; it lives in gusto, be it foul or fair, high or low, rich or poor, mean or elevated—It has as much delight in conceiving an Iago as an Imogen. What shocks the virtuous philosopher delights the camelion [*sic*] Poet.[3]

Yet the spectator may shuffle his feet at all this. The electrifying incongruities made possible by the non-naturalistic methods of the later dramatists repeatedly risk the accusation of writing in 'bad taste'; but when our barriers are down and the vitality of the conception compels a synthesis in the mind, we are left in a glow of new experience. This drama is the modern tragicomedy finding its way and coming to maturity. It offers the shock-tactics Shaw noticed in Tolstoy's *The Fruits of Enlightenment*, his 'terrible but essentially comedic method'[4] applied with more deliberation and a wider sense of

[1] Brecht, 'Flüchtlingsgespräche', *Aufbau* (E. Berlin, February 1958), pp. 181–2, quoted in M. Esslin, *Brecht: a Choice of Evils* (London, 1959), p. 129.
[2] Quoted in D. Vittorini, *The Drama of Luigi Pirandello* (New York, 1935), p. 89.
[3] Keats, *Letters*, ed. M. B. Forman (1935), p. 245.
[4] Shaw, *London Mercury* (May 1921), reprinted in his preface to *Tolstoy, Plays*, trans. Maude (London, 1923).

stage convention. Bad taste is of the essence of every rebellion, and rebellion is of the essence of artistic vitality.

It is understandable that critical estimates of the dark comedy are so much at odds: audience ratings can never apply to such plays. The critical assumptions of the audience are challenged and their critical passions laid bare. Says one, 'Don't we go to the theatre for pleasure, not to be improved? Discomfort is not entertainment.' 'Pleasure', 'entertainment' —these are the shovel-words of a vexed spectator. Says another and rarer bird, 'Isn't each new play properly an experiment in the uses of the imagination? We go to the theatre to feel afresh and to think again.' The B.B.C.'s Audience Research Department reported that Beckett's radio play *All That Fall* had an appreciation index of 58, a below-average figure, the result of an amusingly wide distribution of ratings: A+ 17%, A 34%, B 22%, C 17% and C− 10%. The Head of Audience Research commented, 'Fascination, revulsion, cynicism, boredom—and even abuse—were all evident in the comments of listeners'.[1] In gaining complexity and integrity, dark comedy must inevitably lose the popular market. If, as perhaps in the cases of Brecht, Anouilh and Tennessee Williams, the dark comedian strains to win gratuitous affection, a peculiar sensationalism may disturb the balance of feeling, and, as we have seen, contradictory impressions within the mind of the spectator may fail to blend.

What of dramatic criticism? In spite of Dr Johnson's defence of tragicomedy there has always been some critical unease in the presence of, for example, the parodying of heroics in drama by Falstaff and Parolles and their kind. We can understand Dryden's anxiety for the spectator who may be 'confounded' by the mixture of the ingredients of comedy and tragedy. It was a similar distrust, in this case justifiably, that

[1] B.B.C. Audience Research Department News Letter no. 205 (March 1957).

set the more astute dramatists and commentators against that special brand of tearful comedy of the eighteenth century, and equally, a distrust of the sentimentality that made short-lived the comedy of Wilde (except in *The Importance of Being Earnest*) and Barrie and Bridie. But academic criticism often tends to be anxious for a fallacious purity of tone and a clarity of purpose in drama: it wants to separate the masque from the anti-masque, the tragedy from the comedy, the tears from the laughter. As Mary Lascelles said of *Measure for Measure*, 'any hasty interpretation..., or any which hardens into a formula, is likely to approach misconstruction'.[1] The best dialectical montage of scenes must always defy verbal exegesis in the end: the paradox of the spectator who is implicated in his own detachment can never be resolved in the study. Today we have moved closer to another of the frontiers of drama: this is the originality of the modern movement.

DIDACTICISM AND DESPAIR

It is apparent that the drama we are discussing is often unashamedly didactic. The simple disguises of satire, the imaginary worlds of Lilliput and Brobdingnag, of Evelyn Waugh's *The Loved One* and Aldous Huxley's *Ape and Essence*, devised temporarily to deceive while we coolly pass judgment on ourselves—these are mission-school parables compared with the hoaxes and snares of Chekhov and Pirandello and their disciples. With these dramatists we torture ourselves with the agonies we witness on the stage, because the methods of dark comedy invite our warm immersion in the experience of the creatures of the play, where literary satire must keep us cool and critical. Hence the danger is always present in the new comic theatre that we accept melodrama, sentimentality and easy cynicism in disguise. Satire dare not

[1] M. Lascelles, *Shakespeare's Measure for Measure* (London, 1953), p. 164.

make us suffer until after the event, lest we revolt too soon; dark comedy will drag us passionate through the mud.

It is a modern morality drama. The simple medieval play-form was of life as a journey on a narrow path between the forces of good and evil, with its stage a simple symbol of the World set between Heaven and Hell,[1] though a certain delightful raciness broke in from time to time. Its abstract characterization was on the whole fixed and dull and incapable of development. In an age of faith, a simple hero binds the medieval play, a justifiable symbol for a universal view, but still an Everyman without individuality.

Since those times, the journey has grown more complicated, the symbols less definite. The freedom that expressed itself before in racy characterization, in humour and the pursuit of side-issues, has more and more taken charge of the drama. We have seen thin little Everyman grow dramatically robust in his passage to Faustus and Hamlet, and on to Peer Gynt and even Jimmy Porter. This is of course not necessarily a mark of artistic 'progress', but in an age of doubt simplicity is hardly admissible; there may be no blatant preaching, and the sermon must be muffled. The sophisticated of the twentieth century, like the judicious of the seventeenth, resent it if they are over-persuaded by the sentiment of melodrama, or find the satire cynically over-exaggerating its object of contempt. The early Anouilh (of *L'Hermine* and *Jézabel*) makes his forces of good and his forces of evil too blunt and artless. Beckett's *Endgame* is so negative that only those in the audience who admit no positives will look on with more than clinical interest. Brecht, too, can underestimate his audience when in *The Caucasian Chalk Circle* his Grusche is just another girl with a baby pushed out into the snow, and his drunken monk is there to make parasites of the whole church. We are right to resent sentimentality and cynicism in drama, since both must

[1] See R. Williams, *Drama in Performance* (London, 1954), ch. 2.

287

simplify what is complex. Bad drama cuts off the loose ends; good drama ties them up.

Nevertheless, the drama remains a metaphor, the good dramatist a whole man with an involuntary attitude and therefore willy-nilly a man with a 'message'. No apology is needed for a suspect term, for today the disguises for didacticism are many. First, there is the drama that looks like life, but is not: the coterie of *The Cocktail Party* stripped to reveal tentative religious implications, the elaborately rigged choice between religion and 'psychology' in Graham Greene's *The Living Room*. Secondly, there is the generalizing of human experience willingly conceded behind a screen of myth, in plays like Giraudoux's *Tiger at the Gates*, Christopher Fry's *The Firstborn* and Anouilh's *The Lark*. As in Greek tragedy, the repetition of a known plot distracts attention from the credibility of the story and places a convenient emphasis on its values; and where the disguised naturalist stands in danger of making his character a puppet, the downright allegorist can devote his whole attention to making his puppet human. Thirdly, there is the vast field of deliberate fantasy, from the dream plays of Strindberg, Maeterlinck and Pirandello to wilder extravaganzas like *Under Milk Wood*, *Waiting for Godot* and *The Chairs*. In this genre, we may resent the unbalanced simplifications of Priestley's *They Came to a City*, but be duped into accepting the partiality of Beckett. The didactic level of the play may lie shallow or lie deep; or we may be blinded by technique.

The play most likely to succeed in any of these disguises is the play which works through our experience. *Waiting for Godot* perhaps needs to pull few punches because there is enough of recognizable life in Didi and Gogo; even more in their cheerless Micawber situation—who dare answer No to the query, 'Aren't you waiting for something to turn up?' Nevertheless, complete honesty must be the quality that makes the symbolism in these plays viable, and in a questioning age like ours it is understandable that dramatists should take up an apparently safe position and join with Chekhov in saying, 'You would have me, when I describe horse-thieves, say, "it is wrong to steal horses". But that has been known for ages without my saying so. Let the jury judge them; it is my job simply to show what sort of people they are.'[1] Yet only the pedagogue would choose to describe a horse-thief.

The drama of the modern theatre is an earnest and didactic drama because it is a drama of dismay and sometimes of despair. Like the Elizabethans, our writers all express the fascination of horror, and the blend of laughter and tears this essay has been examining is expressly the kind of ambivalent gesture made towards what is deeply repulsive. Nevertheless the mixture of grief and embarrassment and pity and derision, if spicy and rarely dull, is in the end melancholy and dispiriting. It demonstrates disillusion; it rarely incites to action. It can therefore fairly easily become comfortable, self-pitying and morbid.

This is not to say that dark comedy need leave us complacent; but the time has passed when we can respond to the sick despair of the post-1945 theatre with the moving account Shaw wrote after seeing *The Wild Duck* in 1897:

To sit there getting deeper and deeper into that Ekdal home, and getting deeper and deeper into your own life all the time, until you forget that you are in a theatre; to look on with horror and pity at a profound tragedy, shaking with laughter all the time at an irresistible comedy; to go out, not from a diversion, but from an experience deeper than real life ever brings to most men, or often brings to any man: that is what *The Wild Duck* was like last Monday at the Globe.[2]

This fairly describes our response to the naturalistic techniques of Ibsen and Chekhov—we are moved to feel a unique

---

[1] Chekhov to Suvorin, quoted by W. H. Bruford, *Chekhov and his Russia* (London,)48), p. 18.

[2] Shaw, *Our Theatres in the Nineties*, vol. 3 (London, 1932), p. 138.

dismay, even disgust, but never despair. We remain in partly insulated detachment which leaves us free to understand a passionate experience. We do not laugh as sceptics, but as participants who share an insight.

Today, there is no forgetting we are in a very much more strongly demonstrative theatre: we are more frequently bludgeoned, not wooed, into an attitude of cynicism, sometimes of nihilism. In post-war plays like *Endgame*, *The Entertainer*, *Cat on a Hot Tin Roof* and *The Birthday Party* dismay has sunk into despair; the characters are sick where Chekhov's ineffectual drifters were only ailing.

It is the sickness of Hamm whose hope for life ranges between the inaccessible window, love for a broken toy dog and the security of a dustbin with the comfort of a dog-biscuit to suck. It is the sickness of Archie Rice, who has ceased to fight. Or of Jimmy Porter racked with emotional doubts, shrieking at society and religion in the person of his wife, a man for whom life is dirty and moreover not worth cleaning up: 'There aren't any good, brave causes left.' It is also the mortal sickness of Big Daddy's 'little spastic condition' he deceives himself into accepting, and of the moribund hypochondria of Dan Rooney's reply in *All That Fall* when Maddy asks whether he is 'not well':

Well! Did you ever know me to be well? The day you met me I should have been in bed. The day you proposed to me the doctors gave me up. You knew that, did you not? The night you married me they came for me with an ambulance. You have not forgotten that, I suppose? (*Pause.*) No, I cannot be said to be well. But I am no worse. Indeed I am better than I was. The loss of my sight was a great fillip. If I could go deaf and dumb I think I might pant on to be a hundred.

It is the self-tormenting sickness of a Nathalie in Anouilh's *Ardèle* who moans with delight on the discovery of sex, and next morning wishes to kill herself from disgust. Or the sickness of blind credulity in Willie Loman, riding for a fall on a shoe-shine and a smile.

Didacticism and Despair

'A neutral tone is nowadays preferred', writes the poet of the 'fifties with grim understatement.[1] And we have called ours the comedy of despair. But at least these dramatists are aware of the ambiguities and uglinesses of life, and are not afraid to speak. They are not blind, and the contemporary theatre insists upon offering more than a diversion and an escape.

In a troubled century, writing a play which can daringly hold a balance between the emotions of melodrama and the detachment of comedy may be described as artistic tightrope-walking. Indeed, 'funambulism' has been used as a vivid term by Giorgio Melchiori to describe a characteristic of our time:

> I think it is as good a term as any to express the sense of danger—or should we say with Auden, anxiety—and precariousness so vividly reflected both in the form and in the content of the artistic and literary works of the first half of this century. And since a work of art cannot be such if (even expressing uncertainty and doubt) it does not achieve a temporary balance, funambulism seems indeed to convey also that: the achievement of the true artist in our age, who, like the successful acrobat, succeeds in keeping step by step, moment by moment, his balance, while being aware of the void or turmoil around him.[2]

The satisfaction of dark comedy, when it arises, lies in watching the playwright keep this balance; the significance of it lies in his finding it important to do so.

There would be a cowardice in remaining on ground level, drabbling in self-pity. This is not the appropriate time for desertion into outmoded forms of comedy: one could argue that the criticism of the earlier comedy is ineffectual, its detachment an escape, its field of social observation a limitation. A renaissance today of the comedy of Congreve and his contemporaries or the confident comedy of Goldsmith,

---

[1] D. Davie, 'Remembering the 'Thirties' in *New Lines*, ed. Conquest (London, 1956), p. 70.

[2] G. Melchiori, *The Tightrope Walkers* (London, 1956), p. 8.

19-2

The Dark Comedy

Sheridan and Oscar Wilde would be an affront to the dignity of the atomic-age audience. *The Cherry Orchard*, Pirandello's *Henry IV*, the *pièces brillantes* and *grinçantes* of Anouilh invite anguished experience; their ironies can sicken; their flavour can be acrid and nauseous—but they may be the only dish we could find savoury. Far more appropriate is the pain of Pirandello's *umorismo*, where 'every feeling, every thought, every impulse which rises in the humorist unfolds itself suddenly in its opposite'.[1]

Today it can be a mature drama, and it can be a positive experience, which accepts the pain and yet keeps the balance. To walk the tightrope is probably to evolve by hard practice a relevant philosophy of tolerance, one which does not strike poses or make rhetorical gestures, but which deals in the honest problems of *l'homme moyen sensuel*.

We should not therefore be too inclined to think that this drama is unhealthy. Although it is implicitly didactic, it is encouraging that there is sometimes a reluctance on the part of its authors to deliver explicitly their implicit sermon: at its best it is merely humble before the facts. At its best it does not approve, yet it will not readily place blame or condemn wholesale: it will not draw hard and fast lines. It flinches when it feels the urge to preach, or it is careful to flirt with us. Thus Chekhov puts his words of positive hope, 'Humanity is advancing towards the highest truth, the greatest happiness that it is possible to achieve on earth, and I am in the van!' in the mouth of Trofimov, the immature, the eternal student. It is his self-confessed failure Vershinin who prophesies that 'in two or three hundred years life on this old earth of ours will have become marvellously beautiful'. We are left guessing. Pirandello offers us a romantic finale in *Henry IV* and the hero kills the villain, but only to find that he has

---

[1] Pirandello, *L'Umorismo*, 2nd ed. (Florence, 1920), p. 196. The original reads, 'Ogni sentimento, ogni pensiero, ogni moto che sorga nell'umorista si sdoppia subito nel suo contrario'.

condemned himself to absolute imprisonment within his own masquerade. At the end of *The Waltz of the Toreadors*, Général St Pé is advised by his doctor that 'Life should be led like a cavalry charge', and in this way he prepares himself to lead it with a 'Take aim! Steady! Fire!' only to be surprised into his habitual inconsequence by the curtain entrance of pretty little Pamela, the new maid. 'The writer must be as objective as a chemist', declared Chekhov.[1]

If we are lucky, we read between the lines of a life as it should be lived; yet it is a drab morality that is being advocated and demonstrated. Yet whether wistful or passionate in complexion, it remains rather uncertain, with all the irony of a lucky Jim.

It can be healthy, too, in being scrupulous and self-aware, as Shakespeare's Lear is self-aware when he discovers his humility, or as Dostoevsky's Mitya Karamazov is aware as he leaps between his divine vision and his animal lust, discovering the angel and the insect inseparable within himself. 'Yes, man is too broad, too broad, indeed. I'd have him narrower.' His effort is to understand why beauty is so terrible; to admit that God sets us nothing but riddles, and that all contradictions exist side by side; to know that in the little dark back-alleys behind the main road—there one finds precious metal in the dirt.

The laceration of making such discoveries is felt implicitly in the best of the drama we have discussed. When Fry declared he must look for tragedy before he can find his comedy and to some extent cross the one before he could light on the other, he added, 'In a century less flayed and quivering we might reach it more directly; but not now unless every word we wrote is going to mock us'.[2] The pure and tragic impulse may have been a symptom of a rocklike civilization, and shown

[1] Quoted by W. H. Bruford, *Chekhov* (London, 1957), p. 24.

[2] C. Fry, 'Comedy' in *The Adelphi*, vol. 27, 1 (November 1950), p. 28, quoted by G. Melchiori, *The Tightrope Walkers* (London, 1956), p. 168.

man's wish to see his place among the angels. The shifting sands of this century enjoin each man to build alone. Through each new play he writes, the dark comedian is saying, with William Blake, 'I must create a system or be enslaved by another man's.'

READING LIST

Babbitt, I., *Rousseau and Romanticism* (New York, 1919).

Bentley, E. R., *Bernard Shaw* (London, 1950).

—— *In Search of Theater* (London, 1954).

—— *The Modern Theatre: A Study of Dramatists and the Drama* (London, 1948), earlier *The Playwright as Thinker: a Study of Drama in Modern Times* (New York, 1946).

Bergson, H., *Laughter: An Essay on the Meaning of the Comic* (London, 1921).

Bethell, S. L., *Shakespeare and the Popular Dramatic Tradition* (London, 1944).

—— *The Winter's Tale: a Study* (London, 1944).

Boas, F. S., *Christopher Marlowe: A Biographical and Critical Study* (London, 1940).

Bruford, W. H., *Chekhov* (London, 1957).

—— *Chekhov and his Russia: A Sociological Study* (London, 1948).

Chayefsky, P., *Television Plays* (New York, 1955).

Chekhov, A. P., *The Selected Letters of Anton Chekhov*, ed. L. Hellman (London, 1955).

Chiari, J., *The Contemporary French Theatre* (London, 1958).

Clark, B. H., *European Theories of the Drama* (Cincinnati, 1918).

Clinton-Baddeley, V. C., *The Burlesque Tradition in the English Theatre after 1660* (London, 1952).

Coe, R. N., *Ionesco* (London, 1961).

Daiches, D., *Critical Approaches to Literature* (London, 1956).

Daniels, M., *The French Drama of the Unspoken* (Edinburgh, 1953).

Donoghue, D., *The Third Voice: Modern British and American Verse Drama* (Princeton, 1959).

Downs, B. W., *Ibsen: The Intellectual Background* (Cambridge, 1946).

—— *A Study of Six Plays by Ibsen* (Cambridge, 1950).

Dryden, J., *An Essay of Dramatic Poesy*, ed. T. Arnold (Oxford, 1889).

Eliot, T. S., *On Poetry and Poets* (London, 1957).

—— *Poetry and Drama* (London, 1951).

—— *Selected Essays* (London, 1932).

—— *The Use of Poetry and the Use of Criticism* (London, 1933).

Ellis-Fermor, U. M., *The Frontiers of Drama* (London, 1945).

—— *The Irish Dramatic Movement* (London, 1939).

—— *The Jacobean Drama* (London, 1936).

Reading List

Empson, W., *Seven Types of Ambiguity*, 2nd ed. (London, 1947).
—— *Some Versions of Pastoral* (London, 1950).
Esslin, M., *Brecht: A Choice of Evils* (London, 1959).
Fergusson, F., *The Idea of a Theater* (Princeton, 1949).
Findlater, R., *The Unholy Trade* (London, 1952).
Freud, S., *Wit and its Relation to the Unconscious* (London, 1906).
Gardner, H., *The Art of T. S. Eliot* (London, 1949).
Garten, H. F., *Modern German Drama* (London, 1959).
Gassner, J., *Form and Idea in the Modern Theater* (NewYork, 1956).
Gerhardi, W., *Anton Chehov: A Critical Study* (London, 1923).
Gray, R., *Brecht* (London, 1961).
Grossvogel, D. I., *The Self-conscious Stage in Modern French Drama* (Columbia, 1958).
Hazlitt, W., *Dramatic Essays* (London, 1895).
Henn, T. R., *The Harvest of Tragedy* (London, 1956).
Hingley, R., *Chekhov* (London, 1950).
Hobson, H., *The French Theatre of Today* (London, 1953).
Inskip, D., *Jean Giraudoux: The Making of a Dramatist* (London, 1958).
Johnson, S., *Johnson on Shakespeare*, ed. W. Raleigh (London, 1908).
Jones, D. E., *The Plays of T. S. Eliot* (London, 1960).
Kerr, W., *How Not to Write a Play* (London, 1956).
Kitchen, L., *Mid-Century Drama* (London, 1960).
Kitto, H. D. F., *Greek Tragedy: A Literary Study*, 3rd ed. (London, 1961).
Knight, G. W., *The Wheel of Fire: Interpretations of Shakespearian Tragedy* (London, 1949).
Krause, D., *Sean O'Casey: The Man and his Work* (London, 1960).
Krutch, J. W., *American Drama since 1918*, 2nd ed. (London, 1957).
Lamm, M., *Modern Drama* (Oxford, 1952).
Lascelles, M., *Shakespeare's Measure for Measure* (London, 1953).
Lavrin, J., *Aspects of Modernism from Wilde to Pirandello* (London, 1935).
—— *Ibsen: An Approach* (London, 1950).
Lawrence, W. W., *Shakespeare's Problem Comedies* (London, 1931).
Lewis, D. B. W., *Molière: The Comic Mask* (London, 1959).
Lucas, F. L., *Tragedy in Relation to Aristotle's Poetics* (London, 1928).
Lumley, F., *Trends in Twentieth Century Drama: A Survey since Ibsen and Shaw* (London, 1956).
MacCarthy, D., *Shaw* (London, 1951).
Magarshack, D., *Chekhov the Dramatist* (London, 1952).
Mander, J., *The Writer and Commitment* (London, 1961).
Marsh, E. O., *Jean Anouilh: The Poet of Pierrot and Pantaloon* (London, 1953).

Reading List

Matthiessen, F. O., *The Achievement of T. S. Eliot*, revised ed. C. L. Barber (London, 1958).

Melchiori, G., *The Tightrope Walkers: Studies of Mannerism in Modern English Literature* (London, 1956).

Meredith, G., *On the Idea of Comedy and the Uses of the Comic Spirit* (London, 1903).

Moore, W. G., *Molière: A New Criticism* (London, 1949).

Morgan, M. M., *A Drama of Political Man: A Study in the Plays of Harley Granville Barker* (London, 1961).

Mortensen, B. M. E. and Downs, B. W., *Strindberg: An Introduction to his Life and Work* (Cambridge, 1949).

Murray, G., *Euripides and his Age* (London, 1913).

Nicoll, A., *The Theory of Drama* (London, 1931).

Norman, C., *The Muses' Darling: The Life of Christopher Marlowe* (London, 1947).

Northam, J. R., *Ibsen's Dramatic Method: A Study of the Prose Dramas* (London, 1953).

O'Faoláin, S., *The Vanishing Hero: Studies in Novelists of the Twenties* (London, 1956).

Palmer, J., *Comedy* (London, 1948).

Peacock, R., *The Art of Drama* (London, 1957).

—— *The Poet in the Theatre* (London, 1946).

Phelps, G., *The Russian Novel in English Fiction* (London, 1956).

Pirandello, L., *L'Umorismo*, 2nd ed. (Firenze, 1920).

Poirier, M., *Christopher Marlowe* (London, 1951).

Potts, L. J., *Comedy* (London, 1948).

Praz, M., *The Hero in Eclipse in Victorian Fiction* (London, 1956).

Price, A., *Synge and Anglo-Irish Drama* (London, 1961).

Priestley, J. B., *English Humour* (London, 1929).

Richards, I. A., *Principles of Literary Criticism*, 2nd ed. (London, 1926).

Robinson, L., *Ireland's Abbey Theatre: A History, 1899–1951* (London, 1951).

Rossiter, A. P., *English Drama from Early Times to the Elizabethans* (London, 1950).

Schlegel, A. W., *Lectures on Dramatic Art and Literature* (London, 1846).

Sedgewick, G. G., *Of Irony, Especially in Drama* (Toronto, 1934).

Sherbo, A., *English Sentimental Drama* (London, 1958).

Sprigge, E., *The Strange Life of August Strindberg* (London, 1949).

Stanford, D., *Christopher Fry: An Appreciation* (London, 1951).

Starkie, W., *Luigi Pirandello* (London, 1926).

Steiner, G., *The Death of Tragedy* (London, 1961).

Reading List

Styan, J. L., *The Elements of Drama* (Cambridge, 1960).

Tennant, P. F. D., *Ibsen's Dramatic Technique* (Cambridge, 1948).

Thompson, A. R., *The Dry Mock: A Study of Irony in Drama* (California, 1948).

Thomson, J. A. K., *Irony: An Historical Introduction* (London, 1926).

Tillyard, E. M. W., *Shakespeare's Problem Plays* (London, 1950).

Toumanova, N. A., *Anton Chekhov* (London, 1937).

Tynan, K., *Curtains* (London, 1961).

Van Druten, J., *The Playwright at Work* (New York, 1953).

Verrall, A. W., *Euripides the Rationalist* (Cambridge, 1895).

Vittorini, D., *The Drama of Luigi Pirandello* (New York, 1935).

Watt, I., *The Rise of the Novel* (London, 1957).

Welland, D., *Arthur Miller* (London, 1961).

Wellek, R., *A History of Modern Criticism, 1750–1950*, 2 vols. (London, 1956).

Willett, J., *The Theatre of Bertolt Brecht* (London, 1959).

Williams, R., *Drama from Ibsen to Eliot* (London, 1952).

Wimsatt, W. K. (ed.), *English Stage Comedy* (Columbia, 1955).

Worcester, D., *The Art of Satire* (Cambridge, Mass., 1940).

INDEX

Index

Index

Index